The exhibition has been organized
by Olivetti's Cultural Relations Department,
the Procuratoria of San Marco,
the Réunion des musées nationaux in Paris,
and The Metropolitan Museum of Art in New York

Photography
Mario Carrieri

Catalogue design
Egidio Bonfante

Catalogue translation
Jane Clarey, Aileen Dawson,
Paul Hetherington and Margaret Lyttelton

Edited by David Buckton with the help
of Christopher Entwistle and Rowena Prior

© 1984 Olivetti, Milan
Published by Olivetti
Printed and bound in Italy

The Metropolitan Museum of Art

The Treasury of San Marco
Venice

olivetti

Grants were received from The Robert Wood Johnson, Jr. Charitable Trust and the National Endowment for the Arts.
Indemnification from the Federal Council on the Arts and Humanities.

Under the Special Patronage of
President Sandro Pertini
of the Republic of Italy
and
President Ronald Reagan
of the United States of America

Contents

Prefaces

The treasury of San Marco

Catalogue

Classical and Early Medieval

Byzantine

Islamic

Western

Prefaces

The places in Venice which hold an intense, almost disturbing, fascination for those who venture into them are numerous. But there is perhaps nowhere one feels this more than in the narrow vaulted halls, flanking the patriarchal basilica, which house the treasures of Saint Mark. Here the fragile and precious symbols of empires now vanished have found their last resting place beside the trophies from the Alexandria of the Ptolemies, the Rome of the Low Empire, and Byzantine and Frankish Constantinople, all put into the service of the Most Serene Republic of Venice which had conquered, enriched and conserved them. It is therefore by the greatest of favours that the treasures of Saint Mark have, for the first time, been able to leave their Venetian sanctuary and be exhibited outside Italy.

The principal purpose of these treasures is certainly religious: these gems, set in gold and silver-gilt, are liturgical vases and the pieces in all shapes were made, used or even diverted from their original function, to encase the innumerable relics which, as much as the jealously-guarded secret of the channels of her lagunes and the power of her navy, protected Venice from her enemies. The contemporary visitor may be astonished by this accumulation of holy relics, and may even be irritated at what might seem to him an inversion of values such as the reliquary holds, in his eyes, over the relic. To understand such a collection one must take into account its fundamentally religious character.

However, it is undoubtedly true that love of beautiful objects also guided the Venetians' choice, eager to adorn their Basilica with the richest and most precious items that the Mediterranean world could offer. It was not by chance that, at the time of the Sack of Constantinople, Venice managed to acquire in its share of the spoils, the rarest gems, the finest enamels and the most exceptional pieces. No less significant is the presence among the treasures of the reliquary-cross of Henry of Flanders, Latin emperor of Constantinople, since it is one of the most beautiful of the Western objects known from that period; and what can one say of the "Grotto of the Virgin" where a silver-gilt statuette, fashioned in the Venetian style, has come to give its own significance and name to an ancient temple in imperfect rock-crystal and to reduce a Byzantine *basileus* crown to an inferior role?

The piece which best reflects Venice's attitude towards its Byzantine works, gained after intense battle, is perhaps the *Pala d'Oro*. Its size and fragility prohibit its displacement, but the same complexity and contradictions can be seen in many of the pieces presented; the Byzantine enamels set in mountings where the Venetian filigree plays its subtle games, become the main adornment of new objects. Amongst so much richness and splendour should one recall the importance of perhaps a more severe work?

"Saint Mark's Throne", the origin of which and certain aspects of its function remain a mystery, fittingly recalls, in this exhibition, the role played by the legend of Mark in the history of Venice. The miraculous patronage of the Evangelist, companion of Saint Peter and martyred in Alexandria, entrusted the Republic of Saint Mark with a divine mission which justified all her audacity, gave comfort in her Eastern calling and guaranteed eternal life to the town which was built on the site of the divine vision.

Hubert Landais
Director of the Museums of France

Philippe de Montebello
Director of The Metropolitan Museum of Art

In the fundamental work on the Treasury of San Marco that Hans Hahnloser directed about twenty years ago to crown a long, uninterrupted period of study we are reminded that, amongst the masterpieces of jewellery, enamelwork and stone carvings of which the Treasury is made up, the first Western works in silver come from the North, from the regions of the Rhine and the Meuse: there is a rock-crystal cross, another cross of pure gold signed by Master Gerard, and the silver plaque of the Christ Pantocrator which the author says was probably the work of the same workshop at Tournai that produced the shrine of St Eleutherius. Hahnloser puts forward the theory that, after the fire of 1231 which destroyed the original nucleus of the Venetian Treasury, the craftsmen of the Northern workshops sent their works to Venice, or even carried out their work there on the spot. A few years after that fire, in fact, Venetian goldsmiths copied the Mosan decorations and became so skilled in working the gilded silver filigree of the North, which was previously unknown in Venice, that examples were still to be found around 1350, when this type of craftsmanship, which was even called *opus venetum ad filum*, had already vanished a hundred years previously. And Steingräber, in his studies on fifteenth century Venetian jewellery, draws attention to the typical Venetian use of colour in polychrome enamelwork on silver decorations, suggesting a link with the French and Dutch Gothic schools, and also quoting Zuanne Lion of Cologne as one example of those artists who, coming from the North, exercised a recognizable influence on this kind of art.

In the Treasury of San Marco, therefore, alongside the imposing ranks of Byzantine or Islamic works and a few examples of oriental art, we can clearly trace, in the group of Western works of art, the existence of a thread that links Venice and its art with a vast area of European cultural exchanges, influences and contributions that constitute one of the most fascinating and most studied aspects of medieval art, and which show us that if, in a past age that, remote as it is, has still something to tell us, Europe, from North to South, was already a cultural entity – even when, with the dissolution of the Roman Empire, its political cohesion was lost – we have perhaps to return to all this and draw inspiration from it to find once again subjects and ideas as a basis on which to resume the common way forward. For this reason also, which is certainly not the only one, it seems to us that this exhibition comes just at the right time, facing us again, as it does, with the question of the influence that the intersecting currents of art have in a world that, in other directions, is deeply divided, and the character which the work of art, through the mysterious paths by which it penetrates and spreads, overcoming all difficulties and obstacles, never fails in the end to impress on an epoch and a civilization; and it seems to us that it, too, can remind us of our common and ancient heritage.

It is certainly no coincidence that an initiative such as this one, that does credit to the countries that are respectively its promoter and its host, should have been sought, taken on and organized with so much enthusiasm by an Italian concern which, not for the first time today, has demonstrated its international vocation, and has to its credit an examplary list of initiatives in the field of culture that have taken place in recent years in the largest countries in the world.

Not least for this reason, as well as for the highly, scientific approach and great ability of all those who have worked on the exhibition, to which this catalogue testifies, and above all for the intrinsic, exceptional importance and beauty of the works exhibited, the ministry that I have the honour to be in charge of has done more than simply express its agreement, it has made the exhibition in some way its own, adopting it as an act of national cultural policy; and it is as such that I am happy to present it to the public in the United States of America. I extend the warmest thanks to the Patriarch of Venice, Cardinal Marco Cè, and the Procuratoria di San Marco, for having authorized the loan of such precious works; and to the American institutions for the warm welcome they have given to this initiative.

Antonino Gullotti
Minister for the Environment and Cultural Heritage

This book and the exhibition which it describes and catalogues mark the fulfilment of a project that was already taking shape in Olivetti's dreams at the same time as work was going on preparing the Horses of San Marco exhibition, which was held in the Spring of 1980 at the Metropolitan Museum in New York, where it marked an important stage of a grand tour that took it to six major cities in two continents. In fact it could be said that the two exhibitions draw their inspiration from the same source, and have a common subject; and that they are mutually complementary even though their time span differs in many details. Both exhibitions have their origins in an event that exerted a profound influence on the history of Europe – the conquest of Constantinople by the Venetians during the Fourth Crusade, with all the consequences that that had on the development of art and culture, and on the history and civilization of Europe in general. They have as a focal point a unique edifice, the Basilica of San Marco in Venice that is a centre both of religious and civic life; a sublime fount of spiritual inspiration, and a monument to human genius.

Both exhibitions are devoted to a specific theme. In the case of the first it was the origins of the mysterious Byzantine quadriga, which eventually found its way to San Marco and was displayed on the façade of the basilica by the Venetians, to form the dominant decorative motif. In the case of the present exhibition the theme is a "treasury" which is probably a richer one, despite the ravages, fires and mutilations that accompanied the vicissitudes of the last years of the Venetian Republic (historians have written of the 537 kilograms of gold and silver obtained in 1797 by melting down religious objects, not to mention the precious stones and pearls taken to pay the running costs of Bonaparte's army). This treasury is also, perhaps, unequalled for the rarity (and in certain cases, the absolute uniqueness) of the objects which it contains. Both exhibitions embrace a varied spectrum of figurative cultures, civilizations, and eras.

The Horses of San Marco exhibition was concerned with Greek and Roman art and its influence on the moderns, from the Renaissance to neo-classicism (Pisanello to Leonardo da Vinci, Dürer up to Canova). The present covers Byzantine, Islamic, Oriental and Medieval Western art, its different schools and aspects, taking in a period which, with a few more distant ramifications, starts around the third and fourth centuries and extends to the period of the Renaissance and political supremacy of Venice. Beyond that point no further analogy or comparison is possible. I think that this exhibition provides telling proof that every human artefact is essentially unique, even in the uninterrupted, constantly renewed succession of needs, attitudes, formal standards, ritual requirements, and the desire for self expression, coupled with that irreducible determination to survive which marks man's progress from prehistoric times down to the present day.

This collection of objects, originally created as ornaments or intended for religious use, which we have been able to bring together here, is a collection of inestimable value, selected in accordance with the strictest possible standards from what still remains of the ancient treasury of San Marco (bearing in mind their state of preservation and the difficulties connected with their transportation). It constitutes in fact one chapter of a story that is totally inseparable from the story of Venice – the initiative, developments, influences, contributions, cultural currents, and the expression and manifestation of power – that has made the Basilica of San Marco what it is. But, first and foremost, this collection of objects must be seen and studied for itself, and for what each work of art which it contains represents – its origin, its special history, significance and symbolism, its unchanging quality and its expressive value. That is what this exhibition sets out to do, designed as it is to isolate and display the individuality of each object by allowing it to be seen from close to and from all sides, and which, in its general layout and the way the available space is organized, brings out the unique significance and history of this collection of works of art that are separated from one another by great intervals of time, have such widely different origins, and are crafted so differently, using such diverse techniques.

It is easy to imagine the difficulties with which the realization of such an exceptional event was surrounded. But in spite of the problems that had to be faced and solved, we have never been lacking in courage and determination. In the first place, it was easy to justify the temporary absence of these works from the Treasury Museum in Venice, in view of the restoration work and refurbishment that was necessary inside the museum, and which would in any case have caused the removal of these works of art from their customary place for a certain length of time. This provided a unique opportunity but we must also add that, circumstances having made it possible, our proposal for a major exhibition presenting the masterpieces of the treasury of San Marco met with consistently warm – though nonetheless vigilant – acceptance from the Italian institutions concerned who were, I think, well aware of the very high cultural standards that mark our initiatives in the field of art.

Our proposal was accepted in the first place by those in charge of this precious heritage – the Patriarch of Venice, Cardinal Marco Cè, and the Procuratoria di San Marco, together with its First Procurator Alberto Cosulich. Then by the different bodies that come under the Ministero per i Beni Culturali – the ministry responsible for the cultural heritage – starting with the Soprintendenza ai Beni Artistici e Storici of Venice and its Superintendent, Francesco Valcanover, who had the initial responsibility for deciding whether this enterprise was feasible, and subsequently for defining and supervising the transport procedure; by the Comitato consultivo per i Beni Storici at the Ministero per i Beni Culturali, and its chairman Decio Gioseffi; by the Direttore Generale per le Antichità e Belle Arti at the Ministero per i Beni Culturali, Guglielmo Triches, by the Direttore Generale per le Biblioteche, of the same Ministry, Francesco Sisinni; and finally by the Direttore Generale dell'Istituto Centrale del Restauro, Umberto Baldini. The Ministers who held office at the Ministero per i Beni Culturali during the preparatory and implementation stages – Vincenzo Scotti, Nicola Vernola and Antonino Gullotti – were kept in constant touch with the progress of the different operations – namely the identification and restoration of the objects, the question of whether they could be transported, the way the exhibition was taking shape as the objects were chosen one after another, and the negotiations that took place for the loan of the objects, within a framework of reciprocal exchange. To all of these are due not only our warmest thanks but also the expression of our admiration for the truly exemplary sense of responsibility and strictness with which each proposition was assessed, for the competence and dedication shown at all times in the service of the national heritage, and for the full final agreement that enabled the exhibition to take on the shape that we see today – a truly impressive collection of representative works from all of the cultures and eras included in the treasury, of which not one of the most important or rarest master-pieces is lacking, with the exception – for obvious reasons – of the Pala d'Oro, which could not possibly be moved, but which is documented in detail both in the exhibition and catalogue which includes an important essay on it by Sergio Bettini. In the meantime, both in France and the United States, work was progressing, with the preparation of the catalogue and the organization of the exhibition, in collaboration with the institutions which were, with us, its co-promoters. Mr. Hubert Landais, Director of the French Museums, and Mr. Philippe de Montebello, Director of the New York Metropolitan Museum of Art appointed Mrs. Danielle Gaborit-Chopin, Conservator at the Département des Objets d'Art of the Louvre Museum, and Mr. William D. Wixom, President of the Department of Medieval Art and the Cloisters, of the Metropolitan Museum of Art, to be Commissioners for the exhibition, and an international team of specialists was set up to prepare the catalogue.

These details make it easier to understand how this exhibition was made possible not only by international collaboration between scholars but also by both public and private institutions, civil and religious organizations from different countries, officials and technical experts with different fields of responsibility, and an industrial firm that for many years has been conceiving and implementing cultural programmes that have attracted the attention and gained the approval of both connoisseurs and the general public. As examples I might mention, in recent years alone, Olivetti's participation in the arrangements for the restoration of Leonardo da Vinci's "Last Supper" in the refectory of Santa Maria delle Grazie in Milan and, more recently, the restoration work at the Brancacci Chapel in the church of Santa Maria del Carmine at Florence, containing frescoes by Masaccio, Masolino and Filippino Lippi. Again, in the field of major international exhibitions, following the "Horses of San Marco" exhibition (1979-1982) and that of the restored Crucifix by Cimabue (1982-1983) – which was exhibited at the Metropolitan Museum in September, 1982 – there is the exhibition of Leonardo da Vinci's drawings for the "Last Supper" from the Royal collection at Windsor, graciously lent by Her Majesty the Queen. After being exhibited in Milan, the drawings were on display at the Washington National Gallery in December, 1983. And finally we come to this exhibition of the "Treasury of San Marco" which – if it is permissible to attribute a scale of values where art is concerned – is from many points of view the most important of the various cultural initiatives promoted by Olivetti.

After its stay in Paris (Grand Palais), London (British Museum) and Cologne (Römish-Germanisches Museum), the exhibition now comes to the American continent, where Olivetti has been present for many years and where the company interests are so extensive. However, on this occasion, we wish only to celebrate this event and, through San Marco and this exhibition, remind ourselves once again of the glory and universal genius of Venice, and immerse ourselves in a past which, as the splendour of these objects proves, is still vividly alive.

Carlo De Benedetti
Chairman of Olivetti

The treasury of San Marco

Venice and the treasury of San Marco

Guido Perocco

The treasury of San Marco, which contains the most precious objects belonging to the basilica, was a great source of pride to the Venetian Republic over the centuries. The objects were essentially for religious use, in the services celebrated in the basilica, but it is above all their value as witnesses to the vicissitudes of history which gives them their exceptional character.

To see them properly, one has to try and look at them with the eyes of Venetians and foreigners of the past, who knew how to discover in these works of art, despite their modest size, the expression of an ancient beauty long treasured in Venice: the *Pala d'Oro*, sculptures, icons, chalices, enamels, vessels and reliquaries are all invitations to dream.

The basilica of San Marco (fig. I), with the treasury which is its heart, became a permanent mirage for the city of Venice – a point of reference for its future and a reason for aspiring to greatness and for feeling sure of its destiny. The basilica is intact, but the treasures which have withstood the adversities of time and history are but a fraction of what the treasury once held. They nevertheless form a document, regarded with the greatest respect over the centuries, not only because of its precious nature, but also because it accurately reflects the taste of the city as it became great and acquired the unique character it retained from the Middle Ages to the present day.

One should read the accounts of visits to the treasury of San Marco, for example in the diaries of Marino Sanudo, the most important Venetian historian of the first half of the sixteenth century, who – in fifty-eight substantial volumes – chronicled daily the public and private life of the Serenissima between 1496 and 1533. One should savour, as he did, the beautiful colours, the precious stones, the gold, the enamels, the filigree; one should appraise the fabrics – the damasks, the velvets and the silks – in the processions on the Piazza San Marco (fig. II), all through a detailed and penetrating chronicle sensitive to the pleasure of beautiful colours, golden reflections and the splendour of precious works of art, vessels, candlesticks, reliquaries, luxury caskets and silver plate, in a continuous exaltation of the imagination which made each precious object even more marvellous. The city constantly presented this spectacle as it prepared itself for feast-days. In another passage Marino Sanudo relates how, on 3 August 1502, the queen of Hungary came to San Marco to visit the basilica and view the "jewels" of the treasury. When her ladies-in-waiting approached to tell her it was getting late, the queen responded: "Who would not go without eating in order to see such precious things?" (Sanudo, *Diari*, IV, col. 95).

One could go on quoting indefinitely from the mass of accounts, facts and impressions. Beyond the vivid sensation we experience in front of a precious jewel, we should try to re-create the model which the work of art evoked, so that we can see it with the eyes of the Venetian artists who looked at it in former times: painters, sculptors, architects, craftsmen of genius, who, with a heritage of patience, came close to perfection. On this point we cannot do better than quote an even earlier Venetian chronicler, Martino da Canale, who wrote (in French) *Les Estoires de Venise*, in a hundred and ninety-six chapters, at the time when Marco Polo was beginning his fabled travels to the Orient in the second half of the thirteenth century.[1] Martino da Canale was a proud and enthusiastic citizen of Venice, who participated as a frank and vivid chronicler in the festivals on the piazza and in the church of San Marco, "which is the most beautiful in the world, and if anyone doubts it, let him come and see". He tells us, among other things, of the old mosaic on the façade of the basilica, which illustrated the translation of the body of St Mark to the cathedral (fig. III). In the accounts of the tournaments there are descriptions of the costumes worn by knights; in his account of the festivities which greeted the election of the doge Lorenzo Tiepolo in 1268, there is a particularly vivid and colourful description of the precious works of art, the fabrics, silks, jewels, robes, furs, glass, gold, precious stones and everything that represented the essence of Venetian life at that period.

The procession of the craftsmen as they go to salute the new doge and celebrate with him is incredibly vivid; they are all there and, as if in a ballet, await their turn to greet the doge and his consort: the locksmiths, the furriers (divided into three categories), the weavers, the tailors, those who made coats of wool or of cotton or of gold brocade, the master cobblers, the haberdashers, and other guilds, among which were the barbers, dressed as knights errant, and those we are interested in here – the master glass-makers, with their banner at their head, and "*les honorés maistres orfievres*" (the honourable master goldsmiths). "The goldsmiths are clothed in precious robes, their heads and backs decorated with gold and silver beads and rich and precious stones: sapphires, emeralds, diamonds, topazes, hyacinths, amethysts, rubies, jaspers and carbuncles; and they dress their apprentices very richly." These stones remind us of the jewels which still glitter today on the *Pala d'Oro* and in the treasury of San Marco.

In pride of place is the *Pala d'Oro*, the most important single work in San Marco. A sumptuous display of gold, enamels and jewels, it stands above the altar of St Mark, attracting the eyes of the faithful to the high altar by its physical presence as a masterpiece and by the spiritual meaning it seeks to express.

The *Pala d'Oro* bears the names of four doges who assembled the Byzantine enamels with which it is decorated, and who then gave it its final form – a rich but austere frame of gold and jewels. It was the doge Pietro Orseolo I (976), at the dawn of Venetian history, who had a first *Pala d'Oro* made in Constantinople; the doge Ordelafo Falier (1105) enriched it with new enamels, among which is his portrait, next to that of the Byzantine empress Irene. The doge Pietro Ziani (1209) assembled the most precious of the enamels and goldwork, immediately after the Fourth Crusade; finally, the doge Andrea Dandolo (1345) gave the *Pala d'Oro* its present form.

During this period a large part of the treasure had been assembled, when Venice, as an independent maritime republic, began to establish political and commercial relations with the principal powers of the eastern Mediterranean and collected in San Marco the most precious works of art of its long history.

But, like the *Pala d'Oro* above the altar of St Mark, the works of art in the treasury have the power to reach beyond their aesthetic worth and assume with time a significance transcending their physical character: these are the symbols both of the city and of its spiritual unity throughout the centuries. The basilica of San Marco (fig. IV) has collected and preserved through so many vicissitudes not just the

1. Martino da Canale, *Les Estoires de Venise*, ed. A. Limentani, Florence 1973.

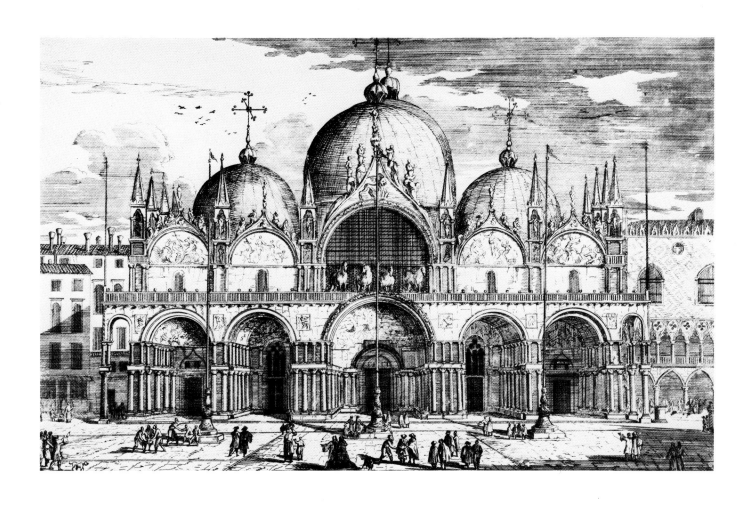

I. The basilica of San Marco, after Luca Carlevarijs, *Fabbriche e Vedute di Venezia*, 1703.

Pala d'Oro but the Virgin *Nicopeia* and the objects in the treasury, as well as titles of greatness which over many centuries attended the arms of the ancient Republic of Venice. The basilica of San Marco is the cathedral of Venice, but it is also the depository of the symbols from which the old Venice drew part of its strength and its faith in some of the fundamental concepts on which the Venetian State was established.

The throne of St Mark, which is shown among the earliest works in the exhibition (no. 7), bears the sign of the power transmitted to Venice by the divine grace of St Mark the Evangelist. Over and above historical and philological concerns, it is of the greatest interest to examine the spiritual values which were attributed to this object and others in the treasury in line with the principles of religious politics pursued by the doges and the Venetian government from the dawn of the history of the Serenissima: St Mark was destined by divine will to be the protector of the Venetian State and the guarantor of its greatness (fig. v). Everything had to contribute towards this end: history, legend, myth and relics, according to principles which were expressed in Venice with a warm enthusiasm animated by a love of country, in a wonderful interdependence of earth and heaven, and which were to shape certain profound and constant concepts.

Venetian historiography exemplifies this persistence of thought: even at the end of the Middle Ages and even when myths were going into the crucible of a new age, it held to a constant course, which knew no deviation, until the end of the Republic. For historians, the throne of St Mark is a symbolic throne, a throne-reliquary of alabaster, probably given at the beginning of the seventh century by the Byzantine emperor Heraclius to the patriarch of Grado, Primigenius, and of Egyptian manufacture. According to Bettini, the throne, originally without decoration, was re-modelled, transformed into a reliquary and decorated at the beginning of the ninth century, at the moment when Venice took over the religious heritage of Grado, the seat of the patriarchate, in conflict with its neighbour Aquileia, the oldest Christian city of the Veneto.

The presence of this throne in the exhibition reminds us of the Synod of Mantua of 828, and of the secular rivalry between Grado, protected by Byzantium and Venice, and Aquileia, protected by the emperor of the Germanic empire of the West, and then the seat of the patriarchate. Venice resolved the dispute between Aquileia and Grado in its own way: the arrival of the relics of St Mark the Evangelist in Venice in 828 gave extraordinary power to the young republic so close to the patriarchate. Venice would have to wait for centuries – until 1451 in fact – before the seat of the patriarchate was established in its lagoons, but the symbol of this power had by then been in Venice for centuries, for St Mark and his throne were in the basilica: the throne was placed behind the *Pala d'Oro*, in the centre of the apse, remaining there until the construction of a new altar in 1534; it was then placed in the baptistry.

It is thus that the precious character of the completely Byzantine architectural space and its decorative unity is explained. It is a space which also contains the myths of the birth of Venice and of the heavenly predestination of St Mark to be the protector of the city and its maritime empire. The legends of the life of St Mark provide the subjects of the mosaics of the façade, the atrium and the presbytery of the basilica as well as inspiring some of the enamels on the *Pala d'Oro*; they became in time the history of the country.

Legend tells how St Mark was invited to Aquileia by St Peter to preach the gospel, but that, overtaken by a great storm at sea, he was forced to take refuge among the islands in the lagoon. In a dream an angel addressed to him the words which are engraved on the book held by the winged lion (fig. VI): "Peace be with you, Mark,

8

II. Gentile Bellini, *Procession of the relic of the True Cross* (detail), 1496. Venice, Gallerie dell'Accademia.

III. San Marco, mosaic in the portal of Sant'Alipio: the translation of the relics of St Mark.

10

IV. San Marco, interior.

V. San Marco, statue above the façade of the basilica (detail): St Mark.

my evangelist" (*Pax tibi Marce evangelista meus*). The legend is entwined with the story of his martyrdom at Alexandria, in Egypt, and with the account of the translation of his body from Alexandria to Venice in 828, in the time of the doge Participazio.

The treasury of San Marco is immersed in this crucible, and our aesthetic vision cannot totally ignore the typically medieval aura of myth which has formed round it. It could almost be said that the government of the Republic of Venice had forged a crown for itself, ever more impressive and august, as the Serenissima felt the urgent and compelling need to exalt its origins and to find in St Mark the apostolic confirmation of its destiny as heir to the Roman empire.

It is this same idea which can be found at the root of the Carolingian empire and, later, in a ruler close to Venice, the emperor Frederick II. The genesis of the basilica of San Marco was fed by these ambitions, even to the awe-inspiring architectural structure, which goes beyond tradition. Frederick II Hohenstaufen (1220-1250) could never be regarded by Venice as anything but a rival.

Demus quite rightly recalls this fundamental concept in his history of the basilica of San Marco. Who could in fact regard themselves as the legitimate heir to the Roman empire? One of the proudest and most frequent claims in the history of the Venetian Republic was that Venice had its origin actually in the Roman empire, and that an almost direct bond with the grandeur of Rome fully justified the pride which the city felt in its own power.[2] The most immediate inspiration for this came from the medieval idea that there had never been a complete break between Classical Rome and the Holy Roman Empire, and that this extraordinary relationship had been formed particularly at Venice, in a Romano-Christian city; that is, it was born the antithesis of the barbarians who wished to destroy every vestige of Rome. According to a rather partial interpretation of this ancient Venetian tradition, there had never been a hiatus between Rome and the birth of Venice, a city built with Roman stones and Roman thought, and protected by St Mark, an apostle. It is absolutely clear why Venice insisted on this direct relationship with a world which, from the start, was remote in time and which had been totally changed by events. But Venice was not alone in seeing things this way: the aura of the glory of Rome was such that it had never been forgotten by the great powers. It was from Rome that the broad principles of the law of the Holy Empire derived, as well as the moderating force which it assumed, as much at the summit of the temporal hierarchy, with the church at its side, as at the pinnacle of religious authority; Venice, with its patriarchate in direct descent from St Mark, with Aquileia as intermediary, prided itself on being the faithful guardian of these laws, both civil and religious.

Thus when Frederick II came to Venice in 1232, as Demus points out, he was received with cold politeness, for he claimed the same prerogatives as the Serenissima, as heir to the Roman empire. When a Venetian goldsmith was instructed to make him a gold crown, the commission was discussed by the Grand Council in case Venetian interests might be injured by the transaction, at a time when even Constantinople was under Venetian domination.[3] As for the heritage of Byzantine power, it went back to Justinian himself, to the first Byzantine golden age, because Venice had grown up after the destruction of Ravenna and was built from stones from Aquileia and Ravenna. The presence of monuments from Ravenna certainly provided an ambitious precedent, a secret strength which, without the slightest doubt, manifested itself in the first Venice. The most

2. G. Perocco and A. Salvadori, *Civiltà di Venezia*, 3 vols, Venice 1973-6.
3. O. Demus, *The Church of San Marco in Venice, History, Architecture, Sculpture (Dumbarton Oaks Studies)*, Washington, D.C., 1960.

VI. The lion of St Mark, wood (polychrome), 15th century. Venice, Museo Marciano.

VII. Constantinople (Istanbul), after the Chronicle of Nuremberg, 1493.

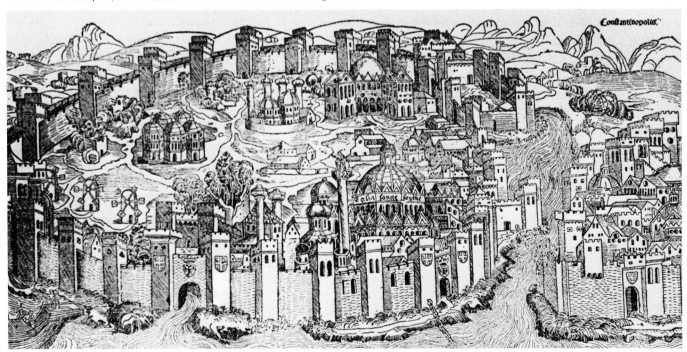

immediate impression of the city at its beginnings can be obtained above all at Torcello, where the cathedral is a perfect example of the type determined in the exarchate of Ravenna.

Venice immediately showed, above all, a pronounced predilection for mosaic, which appeared for the first time at Torcello, as in other Adriatic cities. By the end of Late Antiquity the colour which could be obtained in mosaic was already imparting a character more abstract than naturalistic: a vibrancy created by the chromatic intensity of the compact matter and the luminosity of the gold grounds and by the different zones of colour which themselves take on a symbolic value. So eventually, the absolute ideal was achieved: a Byzantine art, but with the typically Venetian accents of a Byzantine artistic province always attracted to the centre from which this art radiated, Constantinople (figs VII-VIII). In the art of mosaic, and in the luxury arts, the link between Venice and Byzantium is at its most direct: the architectural influence is vaguer, diffused, one might say, in the atmosphere of Venice. But many of the palaces on the Grand Canal, in their airy elegance above the water, have a certain affinity with the buildings of Ravenna, like the Palace of Theodoric, with its harmonic composition, or the cadence and rhythms of Sant'Apollinare in Classe and other buildings of that city. But for Bettini, the parallel can only be taken so far, "for in Byzantine art, decoration, whether for example sculpted or painted, forms a whole: to separate one from the other as if they were different arts is to a large extent wrong, for they are indirectly related and make up a unified and coherent whole".[4]

In Venice the cathedral of St Mark was not formed solely, in the Middle Ages, from the fruits of the earth and the artistic creations of Ravenna, or of the Carolingians or Lombards or those native to the Paduan plain on the shores of the Adriatic: among the civilizations which grew up on the shores of the Mediterranean, the Serenissima was privileged in that it appeared the best adapted to its own ideals – it made its own certain qualities which had come from afar, from a remote corner between Europe and Asia, Byzantium.

Venice made a very special contribution to an artistic civilization which profoundly fascinated her, that of Byzantium. She grew in strength from this fascination, taking it on, making it her own and consecrating it in the style of the basilica of San Marco, its architecture, its art and in the outward appearance of its processions, its festivals and its historic celebrations, which had, as in Byzantium, a ritual significance. The most important works in the treasury of San Marco are Byzantine, but with additions that are always sensitive to Western styles, Romanesque or Gothic. The official model came from the East Roman Empire, which survived legitimately in Byzantium until the fall of its capital to the Turks in 1453.

The Italian Renaissance fatally severed Venice from Byzantium in the very years when, through the invasion of the Turks, the ancient empire was collapsing. There followed a methodical conquest by Renaissance forms of certain details in the basilica, but this did not breach its fundamentally Byzantine stylistic unity. This came about in the *quattrocento*, a marvellous harmony of composition: it is only necessary to see how the Byzantine, Gothic and Renaissance styles have been transformed, in painting, at the hands of Giovanni Bellini. But in its most intimate and authentic structure Venice conserved her medieval heritage, the fundamental substratum, Byzantine, Romanesque and Gothic, which would never wear away, whatever the changes in style over the centuries, like the interior of a great convent built on the water, in the tangle of embankments and canals,

4. S. Bettini, *Venezia, nascita di una città*, Milan 1978.

VIII. St Sophia, Constantinople (Istanbul), interior.

16

IX. Vittore Carpaccio, *Miracle of the relic of the True Cross* (detail). Venice, Gallerie dell'Accademia.

such as the city appears in the plan of Jacopo de Barbari, made at the end of the *quattrocento*.

Venice therefore assimilated, even in its costumes, some of the characteristics of a Christian Europe dominated by Byzantium, which stretched from the shores of the Adriatic to the Black Sea, to Kiev and Novgorod in Russia. The city even founded itself on these ties, growing up at the very height of this civilization, between the ninth and the twelfth century, at the same time ally and rebel. With the freedom of a maritime republic, she sought models outside her own territory, in works of art, the style they introduced and the archetypes they constituted, in particular for enamels, textiles, silks, damasks, mosaics, icons, miniatures and all kinds of precious metalwork.

Today we see Venice despoiled by time, but the objects of the treasury rightly make us think of all the pomp which necessarily accompanied private life as well as the most splendid moments of the old Republic, a city of merchants desirous of objects from the Near East, a people fascinated by the brilliant and intense colours of the enamels, the rare and costly fabrics, the purple silks, and the marbles from distant places. Because of this varied and many-faceted symbolism, of colours, precious works of art and even architecture, "enlightened foreigners", driven to a kind of exaltation, thought of Venice as a part of the Orient, more a creation of the imagination than of reality.

The painting of Paolo Veneziano, in the middle of the fourteenth century, was born of this chromatic background, this passion for colour, an essential prelude to his greatest achievements. Certain pictures of Gentile Bellini and of Vittore Carpaccio have as their subject the city on feast days: in them can be seen objects from the treasury, which figured in the ceremonies, the pomp, and the festivals. Let us choose from among all these pictures the celebrated *Procession* by Gentile Bellini (fig. II) and the *Miracle of the Relic of the Holy Cross* by Vittore Carpaccio (fig. IX), belonging to the cycle of works produced during the last years of the *quattrocento*, to illustrate the two miracles which occurred during the solemn translation of the relic of the Holy Cross to San Marco and to San Giovanni Evangelista. Important relics were to be found not only in the treasury of San Marco, but also in private palaces and in the possession of the guilds: that given by the Grand Chancellor of the kingdom of Cyprus in 1369, for instance, and solemnly installed in the *Scuola di San Giovanni Evangelista*. Equally famous is the reliquary of Cardinal Bessarion (fig. X), presented to the *Scuola della Carità* in 1463, on the day of the enrolment of the cardinal in the *Scuola* (it is now kept in a room in the galleries of the Accademia, which also comprise those of the *Scuola*). The reliquary (470 x 320 mm) consists of a painting of the Crucifixion, which serves as a lid; inside, the relic – a fragment of the True Cross – is contained within a filigree crucifix.

This was the last official gift to Venice from Byzantium, lodged first at San Marco and then transferred to the *Scuola della Carità*. The only great *Scuola* which kept its treasury intact after the fall of the Republic is that of San Rocco, which contains remarkable precious metalwork of the fifteenth to eighteenth centuries. Venice prided herself, under the doge Pietro Orseolo (991-1008), on having been proclaimed "the privileged daughter of Byzantium". The doge Domenico Contarini (1043-71) founded the present church of San Marco on the model of the church of the Holy Apostles in Constantinople. The doge Domenico Selvo (1071-84) even married a Byzantine princess, sister of the emperor Michael VII Doukas and daughter of Constantine X; her elegance provoked admiration and astonishment in the city.

Some doges obtained privileges in the best markets of the Mediterranean; others

18

X. Reliquary of Cardinal Bessarion.

XI. The bronze horses of San Marco, before their transfer to the Museo Marciano in the basilica.

brought Byzantine artists to Venice, and the whole city covered itself with a wealth of decoration ranging from metalwork to architecture, like that which appears on the façade of the Doges' Palace. A breeze of fantasy passed over the city, totally Venetian, but deriving its inspiration from Byzantium; this remained true of its style until the fall of the republic in 1797, even though the Byzantine empire had by then not been heard of for over three centuries, since 1453, in fact, the date Constantinople fell to the Turks. The Serenissima absorbed certain Byzantine characteristics into its medieval customs and preserved them intact until the end of the eighteenth century. The Byzantine emperors, for their part, had often had Venice on their side in their struggles against the Saracens, the Normans and Frederick II; some provinces in Italy constituted, for Byzantium, part of its empire.

The Serenissima was bound to Byzantium by economic ties of fundamental importance. It was a city of merchants, and therefore every war, every undertaking, however heroic and idealistic it might be, had an economic dimension in the varied and many-sided fabric of political reality. It was this that took Venice to the seas of the Orient, in a constant direction dictated by her mercantile instinct. It was the business of the merchants to assess the value of the rarest and most precious works of art, moreover; there developed a medieval merchant class attracted to the acquisition of knowledge, both particular and universal, exemplified by Marco Polo.

One of the concrete advantages of the close contacts between Venice and Byzantium was the *Bolla d'oro*. This was an agreement signed with the emperor Basil in 992, and subsequently renewed, guaranteeing an open road to commerce with Constantinople; it was obtained by the doge Orseolo II in recognition of his help against the Saracens. From a purely physical point of view it was the sea which united East and West and could forge strong bonds between populations widely separated geographically but bound together by constant ideals which exist in the glitter and swell of the sea, the favoured channel of communication. Using the same ports builds up an understanding between men of the sea, a kind of accord, and this was particularly widespread in the Mediterranean basin; it was an accord, however, which could be very difficult, even impossible in many cases, and when Constantinople became the capital of the enemy, the capital of the Turkish empire, the memory of the Byzantium of old, despite the violent conflicts, always remained alive in Venice.

Ravenna during the early Middle Ages, from the fifth to the eighth century, and Palermo in the twelfth and thirteenth centuries, not to mention numerous areas of southern Italy, were for some time Byzantine provinces and graced themselves with some magnificent monuments. But in Venice Byzantine style was the result of a deliberate choice made in the tenth, eleventh and twelfth centuries, which has left indelible traces on the city.

The most precious of the treasures of San Marco are Byzantine. The basis of the predilection of Venice for Byzantium is a series of bonds which even bitter and sometimes bloody conflicts could not break. The most spectacular of these conflicts was the consequence of a violent love-hate relationship between the two cities: the most coveted works of art in the treasury of San Marco are the spoils of war, the booty of the Venetians and the crusaders of the Fourth Crusade of 1204, who, instead of going to liberate the Holy Sepulchre in Jerusalem, conquered Constantinople and the whole of the Byzantine empire which, from 1204 until 1261, became the "Latin Empire of Constantinople".

Here history took a dramatic turn, casting shadows between Venice and Byzantium which time could not dispel. After a long siege, the Venetians and the

XII. San Marco, at the corner of the *Piazzetta*, near the *Pietra del Bando*.

XIII. San Marco, door to the treasury.

crusaders found at their feet the city which was the richest in works of art in the whole world, and which had remained intact over the centuries thanks to defences, in part provided by nature, which had seemed impregnable.

The doge Enrico Dandolo and the crusaders in this way made the most brilliant of their conquests, the symbol of which the doge (who was buried in Constantinople) shipped to Venice: the four bronze horses, which were placed on the façade of the basilica (fig. XI).

In the course of the long history of Venetian art this event remains the most important. The Serenissima was literally fascinated by the works of art which the victory, quite unthinkable a few years earlier, had placed in its hands with extraordinary liberality.

Constantinople, its palaces, its monasteries, its churches, its artists, all the goods from the caravans which came out of Asia, and all the experiences and perspectives of a new world passed in large measure through the hands of the Venetians for over fifty years; the patriarch of the city was a Venetian patrician. Fragment after fragment, capital after capital, columns, marbles, mosaics, pavements, sculptures, cornices, and works of art now in the treasury of San Marco should be examined, one after the other, in the light of this exceptional event, which was decisive for the *duecento*, the century which opened with the personality of Enrico Dandolo and closed with that of Marco Polo.

The doge was the statesman, who could appear brutal in his political realism; Marco Polo was the merchant, who carried within him an unquenchable thirst for knowledge in the most diverse fields of learning, hidden behind the modest appearance of his occupation. Both of them nevertheless responded in their own way to the aspirations of the medieval era, although they were already typical men of the Renaissance with a strong, lucid and serious enquiring spirit.

The conquest of Constantinople gave rise to a renewal, a "*renovatio*", of all Venetian art – painting, sculpture, architecture, the applied arts – a kind of renaissance before the Renaissance, which continued even after the political adventure in Byzantium ended in 1261, when the Palaeologan dynasty mounted the throne for the last two centuries of the existence of Byzantium. The *renovatio* was immediately manifested in the basilica of San Marco, the church of the Venetian State and the centre where the most precious works of art from all the Venetian dominion were gathered. In the case of the capitals of the basilica, for example, it is often difficult, as Deichmann has shown us in his fundamental study,[5] to be sure which are pieces looted from Constantinople and which were made by Venetian artists (fig. XII).

At this period Venice became the centre of the Mediterranean, a cosmopolitan centre to which foreigners would come from the East as well as from the West. By their presence on the Rialto they contributed new knowledge which the government of the Republic could channel and control, thanks to the strength of its structures and a decisive concept of the State, particularly since the Venetian territory had expanded, with outposts as distant as the Black Sea and Syria. Art harmoniously reflects this game of alliance, economy, dominion and even religious politics, in which San Marco in Venice acted as the pivot by its contacts with St Sophia in Constantinople. There was an upsurge of new life, born of a transplanting in Venice after the expedition to the Levant: the grafts found fertile ground and blossomed unexpectedly in the unforeseen breath of spring. For Venice the *duecento* is the great century, two centuries before the advent of the Tuscan Renaissance.

---

5. F.W. Deichmann, *Corpus der Kapitelle der Kirche von San Marco zu Venedig*, Wiesbaden 1981.

XIV. San Marco, the "Pillars of St John of Acre" in front of the basilica

The works in San Marco, especially those in the treasury, were valuable models for the entire city, archetypes for new creations inspired by their perfection. They came to a large extent from Constantinople, the centre of all Byzantine art, but in the course of the *duecento*, the artistic interest turned more and more towards central Europe. Indeed, the two fundamental literary works of *duecento* Venice, *Les Estoires de Venise* by Martino da Canale, and the *travels* of Marco Polo, are in French.

The city opened itself to wider artistic exchange, with Italian provinces such as Lombardy, Emilia and Tuscany, as well as older ones like Apulia and Sicily. But the exchange extended even farther, into France, as far as Champagne, to Germany, to the Rhine, and to Austria. The Serenissima became ever more active in commerce, establishing itself as the link between East and West through a market deeply attracted by the beauty and the prestige of works of art, wherever they may have come from.

Twenty-one precious objects in the treasury of San Marco are of Islamic origin (nos 29-32, 37), the glass and the rock-crystal items making up the most important and earliest group dating from the ninth to eleventh centuries.[6] Where do they come from? Were they gifts, or purchases, or spoils of war? They are in any case important evidence of the "sympathy", to adopt the term used by John Ruskin, felt by the Venetians for the art of the peoples of the East – in a word, Islam, a fierce enemy, certainly, but a source of great inspiration to the Venetians from the beginning. Alexandria, in Egypt, was the second most important port for Venice, despite prohibitions on dealings with enemies; it was second only to Constantinople, which after 1453 became the Muslim Istanbul. Alexandria was the great Arab market, of tremendous importance before the destruction of the city, which began in the second half of the fourteenth century.

The basilica of San Marco itself has many features of Islamic art, side by side with elements of Byzantine architecture. Sometimes they are unmistakable, like the arch of the "Door of Flowers"; sometimes the Islamic and Byzantine elements harmonize so perfectly that it is difficult to distinguish the one from the other. The colours, sometimes intense and sometimes delicate, spread over the marbles with the aristocratic refinement of the oldest mosques of Cairo (fig. XIII).

The same phenomenon is perfectly reflected in the precious metalwork and the decorative arts, of which only a few items survive, of gems and metal, out of all the textiles and precious fabrics destroyed by time. The old chronicles tell of the great care with which luxury works of art from the Arab world were looked after by families.

The Venetian *duecento* artist's spirit of assimilation was that of someone eager to learn from, and if possible to surpass, the master; he was, above all, universal and receptive to anything to do with precious metalwork, since wealth was always increasing in Europe.

Venetian goldsmiths certainly did not have to hide their impatience when they contemplated the new acquisitions in the treasury of San Marco, particularly as quantities of jewels such as had never before been seen were coming to Venice by way of trade. The treasury's acquisitions were often gifts from the richest and most important families, patricians who had in their palaces their relics, usually brought from the Holy Land or Constantinople, and their jewels. They would usually assemble them in a small "cabinet of curiosities", in which would be a great variety of works of art, among them, without doubt, an icon of the Virgin on a gold background, which no Venetian patrician household would be without.

6. *Il Tesoro di San Marco* (K. Erdmann), 1971, 101.

26

XV. Antonio Canaletto, the *Campo San Giacometo*, where the *Scuola degli Orefici* was situated; to the left, the shops of the goldsmiths, with their signs.

XVI. San Marco, centre portal: detail of *voussoirs* showing the occupations of smithing and fishing.

XVII. San Marco, marble tabernacle of the Dalle Masegne family, 1387-8.

Numerous works of art in the treasury have been adapted to a new use by Venetian artists, who, above all, fashioned the mounts of ewers, chalices and vases (e.g. nos 32, 35, 37, 42, 43). This adaptation of works of art to new uses is an ancient tradition in a city like Venice which had even had to bring from afar the stone of which it was built. The works of the treasury did not escape this tradition. The Venetian historian Francesco Sansovino, son of the great Jacopo, states that many ships from the East had to bring their contribution to San Marco: marbles, columns, capitals – all were then incorporated in a new architectural whole.

One is always wondering at San Marco where a column, decoration or sculpture came from, how it got to Venice, and what modifications it might have undergone (fig. XIV). But we often overlook the fine chromatic relationship, the beauty and the harmony of the colours produced in the new creation by the Venetian artist, which has, in the final analysis, the subtle and indefinable charm of old Venetian precious metalwork. The mounting is always of great value.

In the treasury, a work from Byzantium, Egypt or Iran often has a mount made by thirteenth-century Venetian artists. This step represented an emancipation vis-à-vis the models and a new departure, not only in Venetian policy but also in heaping more and more prestige on the master craftsman. Filigree, for example, was known in the Middle Ages as "Venetian work", *opus venetum ad filum*. This Venetian filigree, which became almost a monopoly of the Serenissima from the thirteenth to the fifteenth century, as Hahnloser has rightly pointed out, was modified and perfected by Venetian craftsmen, but it is basically a perfect imitation of Rheno-Mosan work, examples of which are preserved in the treasury of San Marco itself (cf. nos 35-37).

Even the art of carving rock-crystal, so important at the end of the *duecento* and in the *trecento* (nos 38-39, 45), derives from an industry known from 1250 in the regions of the Rhine and the Maas, subsequently developed in Venice.[7]

Side by side with the guild of goldsmiths (fig. XV), the statutes of which are known to go back to 1233, there was a guild for craftsmen specializing in rock-crystal, an exquisite form of quartz as transparent as glass and cut like precious stone. The most important collection of Islamic rock-crystal objects is that in the treasury of San Marco, dating from the tenth century onwards (nos 30-32, 37). Venice first sought inspiration from the ancient models and then looked for new masters of the art among Venetian craftsmen. The art of working in glass, in which the city was already supreme in the *duecento*, had regulations jealous of the prerogatives of the craftsmen, particularly where the distinction between glass and rock-crystal was concerned. The very first statutes of the workers in rock-crystal, drawn up in 1284, issued a warning against imitating rock-crystal in glass: "*vitrum contrafactum ad cristallum*". The first lenses for reading were of rock-crystal, but later their manufacture in glass was allowed, and a little later, in 1317, spectacles appeared in Venice. The regulations of the workers in crystal,[8] initially strictly opposed to glass, eventually had to admit defeat, in 1301, in the face of an ever increasing demand for "glass for reading".

It is important for us to know the obligations of a category of Venetians who had their own legal system, officially recognized by the Republic. The crystal workers have left evidence of their high artistic standards in certain works in the treasury of San Marco (e.g. nos 38-39), produced after a study of earlier Byzantine, Islamic or Rhenish models.

As is the case, particularly with sculpture and with other aspects of the precious

7. *Il Tesoro di San Marco* (H.R. Hahnloser), 1971.
8. A. Gasparetto, *Mille anni del vetro a Venezia*, Venice 1982.

XVIII. Paolo Veneziano, *Pala feriale*, 1345: *Miracle of St Mark* (detail). Venice, Museo Marciano.

arts, Venice in the *duecento* was attracted by the West. The Fourth Crusade, undertaken after a long period of preparation, first at Venice, then at Zara and at Constantinople, threw together Venetians and crusaders, offering new possibilities of knowledge. Master Gerard, a disciple of Nicolas of Verdun, was certainly in Constantinople in 1206, where he made a reliquary of the True Cross for the emperor Henry of Flanders, soon to find its way to San Marco (no. 34). The presence in Constantinople of Gerard, one of the most famous artists of the Mosan school, means a certain meeting of Frankish and Venetian artists, which is an invaluable starting-point for new study. If the art of mosaic remained tied to Byzantium in a give-and-take relationship which was to last for the whole of the *trecento*, sculpture and the luxury arts, above all precious metalwork, were enlivened with new currents from Romanesque art, and their interests were directed into a much wider European space, without restraint: the city responded to its role as a capital which could choose its provisions from a vast department-store. The two churches of SS Giovanni e Paolo, of the Dominican order, and of the "Frari", of the Franciscans, established at the end of the *duecento* in the centre of Venice, provide impressive affirmation of the thought and religious ideas as well as of the rules of St Dominic and St Francis. There is a frank overstepping of Gothic proportions and architectural dimensions in these two churches, which impose themselves on the connecting tissue of the city by their relation to the earlier Ravennate, Byzantine and Romanesque pattern, so precious and discreet in its volumes, in the proportion of its decoration and in the relation of its different architectural spaces articulated by the autonomous plastic forms, which do not allow dissonances or the cadences of different rhythms.

The contrast between the Byzantine basilica of San Marco and the completely Western Dominican and Franciscan churches of SS Giovanni e Paolo and the "Frari" almost immediately inspired, in 1340, the totally Venetian solution of the Doges' Palace, a masterpiece of Gothic architecture but also of the Byzantine tradition born in Venice.

From this point on, the objects destined for the treasury of San Marco were no longer chosen in another city – Constantinople, for example – but created in Venice itself. The conquest of Constantinople and the Latin domination of the city for over fifty years changed the relationship between Venice and Byzantium. Certain characteristics, appropriate to a state religion, lived on under the precious cloak of the doge in the ceremonial of San Marco, but in its aesthetic taste the Serenissima now turned more and more to the West.

In the aesthetic domain, San Marco was a lighthouse: nothing new was introduced which did not immediately thrive in the basilica. By the middle of the *duecento*, for example, the fundamental influence of Romanesque sculpture had forced its way through on to the entrance arches of the portal of the church, which have the clear stamp of authority of the great art of Emilia and Lombardy (fig. XVI). In these sculptures can be seen a new inspiration which also clearly appears in the objects of the treasury, though in other ways: it was an artistic language common to all of Europe, of already ancient Early Christian origin, revived by Franciscan and Dominican religious ideas as much in Italy as in Germany and France. Thus, as Roberto Longhi says, on the altar by Wolvinius in Sant'Ambrogio in Milan, or at Regensburg, Metz, Vienna or Aachen, "can be seen the same vigour as in the eyes fo the penitent angels of Cimabue...; it is pointless to make Reichenau rival Corbie, or St Gall rival Rheims".[9]

9. R. Longhi, "Arte italiana ed arte tedesca", *Da Cimabue a Morandi*, Milan 1973, 6.

If the *Pala d'Oro* above the altar is a witness to the devotion of Venice to the highest expression of Byzantine art, the front of the altar in San Marco, an embossed work of around 1300, installed at the base of the same altar, is also manifestly a witness to the Romanesque and Gothic influences which characterize Venetian sculpture of the *duecento* and *trecento* (no. 40).

The richest works, and those most readily revealing the taste of each period, succeeded one another in the basilica. The high altar of San Marco was closed off by a screen, the *iconostasis*, which was twice re-made before the end of the fourteenth century. The first version responded to a Ravennate Byzantine orientation appropriate to the first centuries of the history of San Marco; the second was a Venetian work in which new accents were inspired more by miniatures and mosaics than by examples of Byzantine sculpture. Thus we come to the third *iconostasis* of San Marco, which we can admire today (fig. IV), a masterpiece of Pier Paolo and Jacobello Dalle Masegne, completed in 1394 at the high point of the flowering of the Gothic style, as also is their large marble tabernacle of a little earlier (fig. XVII).

The *iconostasis* harmonizes oddly with the Byzantine style of the whole church by the richness of its coloured marbles, the precision of its installation, the precious character of the jewels of precious metalwork which accentuate it from the lowest elements to the sculptures above, which crown the whole screen.

The raised high altar, in the choir of the church, stands under a *ciborium* of precious green marble; its lower part was at one time decorated by the altar-frontal in the exhibition, while above there is the *Pala d'Oro*. Taken as a whole the work is a witness to the fundamental characteristics of Venetian art, which, against its Byzantine background, was open to new dimensions, which are explored in detail by the precious metalwork in the treasury.

In the middle of the *trecento*, after the baptistry and the chapel of St Isidore at San Marco had been decorated in mosaic, this particular art entered a long crisis. The government of the Republic sought to solve this, but times had changed. They would have to wait for the *quattrocento* and the new mastery of the Tuscan school: in this way the end of the Middle Ages and the advent of the Renaissance were signalled in Venice; in the course of the new era Venice would free herself for ever from Byzantium.

But it is important to point out that the first significant paintings of the Venetian school, those of Paolo Veneziano, reveal their Byzantine inspiration, though with characteristics of Western Gothic painting; they also therefore achieved the unique synthesis peculiar to Venetian art.

The procurators of San Marco turned to Paolo Veneziano (fig. XVIII) to create a figurative work worthy of covering the *Pala d'Oro*, in 1345, the same year that the master goldsmith Paolo Bonensegna fashioned for it the austere frame, at the wish of the doge Andrea Dandolo.

So we have a meeting that was fundamental to the history of Venetian art: the large panel, divided into compartments, with the legend of St Mark, dated and signed by the sons of Paolo Veneziano, Luca and Giovanni, the first important masterpiece of Venetian painting on wood, has found its fulfilment in the same universe as the treasury of San Marco.

Venice, the *Pala d'Oro*, and Constantinople

Sergio Bettini

Venice, as we shall see, was always so constantly present in the Levant and in Constantinople that the influx of objects from the East into the Venetian lagoon at the time of the Crusades constitutes quite a different problem from that of their arrival in various other places in Europe, even in other parts of Italy. It therefore seems advisable to restrict this discussion to the spoils of war (*exuviae*) which could have been of value as models to the artistic culture of Venice. Even here, moreover, we shall further restrict our inquiry to a single class of object of particular significance, enamels, which, with other imports, led the Venetians to the remarkable idea both of *opus ad filum* and of the *scole cristellariorum*.

It would be out of place here to review and to classify stylistically and chronologically all the enamels in the treasury of San Marco which have survived despite notorious disasters. It is perhaps enough to point out that in the second half of the thirteenth century, when *opus Veneciarum* apparently first appeared, Byzantine examples of objects decorated with enamels must have been not only more numerous in Venice than they are today, but also of greater variety. For we must not forget the objects which have disappeared because they were particularly susceptible to fire, by which I mean textiles and fabrics. For craftsmen did not, in fact, confine themselves to decorating icons, portable altars, crosses, reliquaries, chalices, patens, bookcovers and so on with simulated enamels, but also worked them into fabrics, particularly for ceremonial robes, whether for secular or religious occasions (for example the Traù mitre). This followed Byzantine practice: at Constantinople it was the well established custom to attach enamels to clothes, weapons, parade-saddles and liturgical vestments. These precious and sparkling objects formed the main stock of objects on which emperors might draw when they had to present gifts to sovereigns and important foreigners. The Venetians imitated this custom. It is thus not improbable that Byzantine textiles decorated with enamels formed part of the booty taken from Byzantium, especially during the period of the Latin hegemony (1204-61). Indeed, it appears that the monastery of the Pantocrator, the most important and the richest in the Byzantine capital, was more or less totally despoiled by the Venetians.

In any case, from these models and perhaps from the Constantinopolitan craftsmen they had seen at work, the Venetians learnt to work their materials, to make filigree, to hammer gold and silver, and to set jewels. The theory that these techniques came to the fore in Venetian art as a legacy of Late Antiquity by way of Ravenna is not to be credited. By this route one comes to confer a Classical pedigree on Murano glass. Byzantium, however, was a powerful reality in the sphere of culture and technique, beyond her actual dominion. More concretely, it is possible to trace the cultural origin (technical as well as linguistic) of the artistic style of Venice in the use made of enamels and simulated enamels on objects, following the Byzantine custom (for example the profusion of pearls bordering haloes,

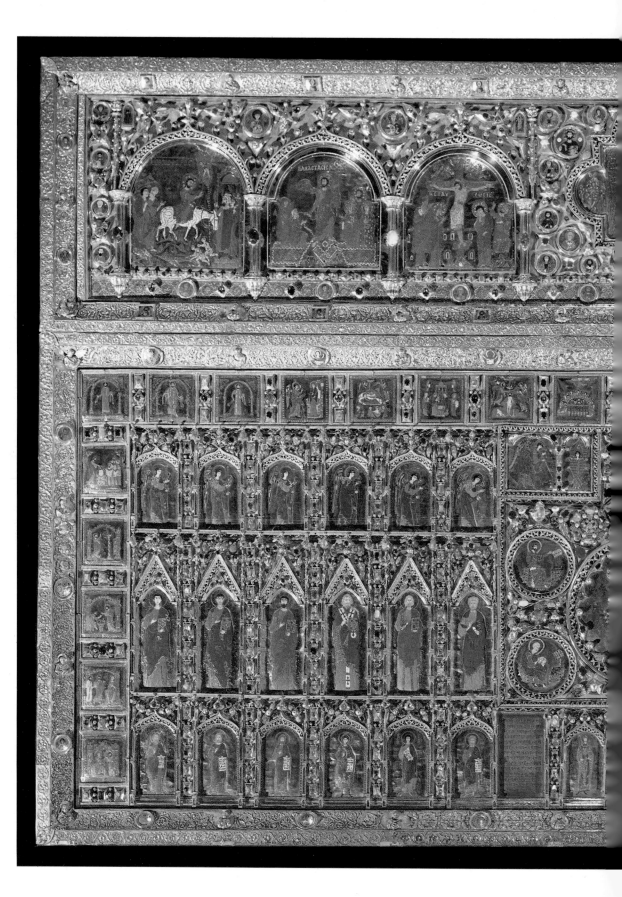

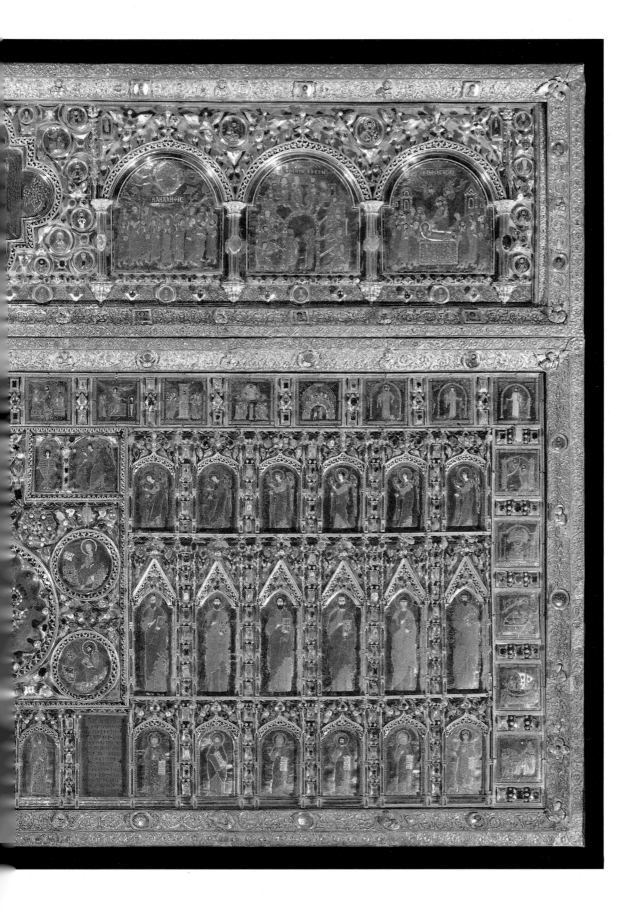

37

medallions, panels and arcs of enamel, and decorating the clothes of figures in rows, crosses or star-shapes, or framing a complete object and emphasizing its various components – all features which derived from the chalices, patens and crosses which came from Byzantium. On the other hand, certain details, for example the technique which consists of twisting together wires to increase the gauge of filigree – especially in "*ad filum*" work – and particularly the setting of jewels in claws instead of in collets, are not of Byzantine origin, but come from northern Europe. Here the results have the effect of distancing the image from the sophistication of Middle Byzantine art and reflecting much more the heavier and more "barbarian" taste of Mosan *cloisonné* and the like.

But it is patently from Constantinople that the Venetians took the technique of enamel, even if they were discernibly selective, as they were with mosaics. In Byzantium the technique of enamels (ἔργα χεμευτά, as Constantine Porphyro-genetos calls them)[1] attained the highest degree of refinement and of express-iveness in the period of the Comnenian dynasty (1057-1187), and it achieves its marvellous effects above all from the extreme slenderness of the *cloisons*, and from the extreme shallowness of the layer of glass (only half a millimetre in the best examples). The first produces, after the final polishing of the surface, a fine and slender design, a sort of spider's web in gold, which reflects on the colours of the enamels a warm and sparkling light, fragile but pulsating. The second gives these enamels – which are glass coloured by various metallic oxides – a transpar-ency which does not rob the gold underneath of any of its sparkle, but rather allows the gold to "fuse" with the usually clear and light colours of the glass, shad-ing them slightly with the greatest delicacy. It is enough to note (so as not to diverge from examples in the treasury of San Marco) the enamels on the onyx chalice (no. 11) on which is inscribed the name of the emperor Romanos, perhaps Romanos IV (1067-71), or on other related objects of the same period, such as the medallion of the Pantocrator, or those doubtless a little earlier, like the Christ at the centre of the large and splendid paten of alabaster (no. 18), or those at the base of the "Grotto of the Virgin" (no. 8), hollowed out of a block of rock-crystal, which are among the oldest in the treasury, contemporary with Leo VI the Wise (876-912), whose portrait, very like that in the lunette in the narthex of St Sophia, appears among the medallions on its base. There are those, too, which frame the two famous metal icons of the archangel Michael (nos 12, 19), and those, although later and looser in style, on the icon of the Crucifixion, and on the frame of the Virgin *Nicopeia*; finally, there are the large enamels of the Comne-nian period on the *Pala d'Oro*. We shall return to these enamels in order to compare them with their Venetian imitations (on the *Pala d'Oro* itself, for example, or the Linköping mitre) and to take note of the above characteristics in the Byzantine examples while comparing them with the Venetian imitations, with their obvious differences of technique, which produce a different artistic language: the *cloisons* of the Venetian enamels are thicker, less numerous, and

1. For the enamels: G. Stephens, *Queen Dagmar's Cross*, London 1863; J. Schulz, *Der byzantinische Zellenschmelz*, Frankfurt am Main 1890; N. Kondakov, *Histoire et monuments des émaux Byzantins*, Frankfurt am Main 1892; O.M. Dalton, "Byzantine enamels in Mr Pierpont Morgan's collection", *Burlington Magazine* 21(1912), 65ff.; M. Rosenberg, *Zellenschmelz*, 3 vols, Frankfurt am Main 1921-2; W. Burger, *Abendländische Schmelzarbeiten*, Berlin 1930; M. Barany-Oberschall, "The crown of the emperor Constantine Monomachus", *Archaeologia Hungarica* 22(1937); Y. Hackenbroch, *Italienisches Email des frühen Mittelalters*, Basle 1938; P. Kelleher, *The Crown of Hungary*, Papers and Monographs of the American Academy in Rome XIII, Rome 1951; K. Chytel, *The Byzantine enamels on the Zavis Cross at Vysse Brod*, Prague 1951; A. Grabar, "Un nouveau reliquaire de Saint Demetrios", *Dumbarton Oaks Papers* 8(1954); J. Rauch, "Die Limburger Staurothek", *Das Münster* 8(1955), 201-8; A. Bank, *Byzantine art in the Hermitage Museum*, Leningrad 1960; J. Beckwith, *The Art of Constantinople*, London 1961; C. Amiranachvili, *Emaux de Géorgie*, Paris 1962; D.T. Rice, *Art of the Byzantine era*, London 1963; Marvin C. Ross, introduction in the catalogue of the exhibition *Byzantine art an European art*, Athens 1964, 391-9.

their rhythm is weakened, if not extinguished. The glass, which is of stronger colours, is of considerable thickness, even to the point of losing its translucence.

As we have noted in earlier studies of mosaic (here it is perhaps still clearer), the perfect Middle Byzantine balance between colour and line changes and breaks down in Romanesque art, with its preference for the line, which itself becomes expressive, a *ductus* (particularly in the hands, hair, beard and nose in the enamels on the Linköping mitre) in which an earlier Western sense of movement, what might be called post-Ottonian "expressionism", is still present.

It is not surprising that the famous *Pala d'Oro*,[2] when taken as a whole, is a magnificent example of an amazing stylistic misunderstanding, even if it contains some of the most precious of all Byzantine enamels. It is not a homogeneous work, and its lack of coherence in part reflects the vicissitudes of its assembly. Originally it was an altar-frontal of smaller dimensions than the *Pala* of today. According to both texts and tradition, a first *antependium* of silver had been ordered from Constantinople by the doge Pietro Orseolo (976-8) – at his own expense (*de suis quidem facultatibus*) according to the Chronicles of John the Deacon. Although it was simply said that this was a marvellous work of art, without there being any particular mention of enamels,[3] one cannot, with all appropriate caution and despite the contrary opinion of Volbach, among others, rule out the hypothesis that a few of the small enamels which are set into the present altar-piece and which can be said to be close in style to late tenth-century Byzantine work, might have formed part of the altar-frontal of Pietro Orseolo. In 1105, however, Ordelafo Falier had the *antependium*[4] restored or, rather, had another altar-piece made, different from the first, entirely of gold embellished with precious stones and enamels. This work, and even the enamels on it, according to a note which commands little credence, were not executed in Constantinople, but in Venice "by a Greek craftsman",[5] which conjures up the later additions to the altar-piece by Venetian craftsmen. At the time of the doge Pietro Ziani (1205-29) and of the procurator Angelo Falier the altar-frontal was enlarged, actually in 1209, with, as all the evidence indicates, the *exuviae*, or spoils, amassed at the end of the conquest of Constantinople in 1204.[6] It is possible, although this view is not widely held among scholars, that only then were added all, or almost all, of the large enamels of the present altar-piece. As I have already observed, in agreement with others, the testimony of Sguropulos,[7] cited by

2. For the *Pala*: A. Pasini, *Il Tesoro di San Marco a Venezia*, Venice 1885-6, with a chapter on the *Pala d'Oro* by G. Veludo (141ff.); J. Ebersolt, *Les arts somptuaires de Byzance*, Paris 1923, 94; W. Bucher, *Die Zellenschmelze der Pala d'Oro zu San Marco in Venedig: eine Studie zur Geschichte dieses Kunstwerkes auf technischer Grundlage*, doctoral thesis, Breslau (Wroclow) 1933; S. Bettini, "La Pala d'Oro", *Illustrazione Vaticana* 8(1937), 1077 ff. (with bibliography); R. Pallucchini, *La pittura veneziana del trecento*, Venice & Rome 1964; O. Demus, *The Church of San Marco in Venice*, Dumbarton Oaks Studies 6(1960), 23, 27, 52, 74, 139 (cited on p. 23 is the doctoral thesis on the *Pala d'Oro* by J. Pomorisac-De Luigi); v. *Enciclopedia Universale dell'Arte*, "Bizantini smalti" (D.T. Rice), II, 1858, p. 707.
3. *Joannis Diaconi Chronicon venetum*, ed. G.H. Pertz (*Monumenta Germaniae Historiae, Scriptores*, VII), Hanover 1846, 26; *Danduli Andreae Chronica per extensum descripta*, ed. B. Cecchetti and F. Ongana, *Documenti per la storia dell'augusta basilica di San Marco in Venezia dal nono secolo fino alla fine del decimo ottavo dall'Archivio e dalla Biblioteca Marciana in Venezia*, Venice 1886, no. 39; for the chronicles of P. Cradengo and the *Cronaca Bemba*: *ibid.* (*Documenti...*), nos 38, 42.
4. *Ibid.* (*Documenti...*), nos 68-72, 812.
5. In Pasini, *op. cit.*; information not given by Andrea Dandolo, for whom the gold altar-piece was decorated with "*gemmis et perlis mirifice*" (the enamels, for Kondakov) and executed in Constantinople, as Marino Sanudo also believed.
6. *Documenti...*, op. cit., nos 88-9.
7. J.S. Sylvester, *Historia Concilii Florentini graeca scripta per Sylvestrum Sguropulum* (*Transtulit in sermonem latinum Robertus Creygton*), The Hague 1660, 87. The prelates of San Marco used to tell visitors that the enamels came from St Sophia; the patriarch Joseph, however, maintained that they originated in the Pantocrator. This uncertainty can be explained thus: after the conquest of 1204, the *Podestà* of Venice had his seat at the monastery of the Pantocrator; the Venetian patriarch (the first, Tommaso Morosini, was declared illegitimate by the pope Innocent III but reinstated on 13 May 1205) had his seat at St Sophia. Perhaps the Venetians could remember the enamels being

Veludo,[8] seems worthy of belief: in 1438 Joseph, the Patriarch of Constantinople, who had come to Venice with the emperor John Palaeologos, and his brother Demetrios, to take part in the Council of Florence, recognized these enamels as coming not from the great church of St Sophia, as was then thought in Venice, but from the monastery of the Pantocrator in the capital, which had been occupied by the Venetians in 1204.

But it was in the years 1342-5, and above all in 1343, when Andrea Dandolo was elected doge, that the altar-piece took on its definitive form. The work must have been started by Bonensegna, who signed it,[9] and carried on by his workshop (or by another workshop: the problem is not entirely resolved, but it is of little importance for our purposes, nor is the problem of the reliability of the facts reported by the contract, probably dictated by Andrea Dandolo himself). It was undoubtedly at this time that all the Gothic decoration was introduced; it is still in place today, despite numerous restorations. It was at this time too that the

sent to Venice by one of these two but were confused as to which. But how and when did these remnants of a great marble *templon* arrive in Venice? According to present-day historians, the Venetians, to whom the treaty with the crusaders had awarded three-quarters of the spoils from the sack of the capital, in their capacity as creditors to the expedition, took the lion's share. The patriarch Tommaso Morosini was later accused of having collected considerable plunder for himself, over and above the prescribed amount. In any case, while the crusaders pillaged and destroyed indiscriminately during the conquest, the Venetians – although doubtless also taking part in the pillage – far from causing destruction carried everything away with them, to the extent that the historian Kretschmayr gave them credit for having *saved* a large quantity of precious objects, even if they *stole* them. The attitude of the Venetians is hardly surprising, seeing that Venice itself was built on a succession of imported objects, like a magpie's nest, and that they were not only able, more than most, to appreciate these works but also considered themselves participants in Byzantine culture, of which they desired to see themselves in some way the legitimate heirs. For them Constantinople was not a foreign city but rather an "elder sister"; furthermore, the doge Enrico Dandolo went as far as proposing to the Senate that the capital of the Venetian Republic should be transferred from the lagoons to the Bosphorus. Nothing was done about this, but this single idea shows the way in which some of the Venetians looked upon Constantinople: one does not destroy the city one thinks might become one's capital. In order to judge the behaviour of the Venetians objectively it is necessary to discard the spiritual state in which historians evaluate such events. Up until the *trecento*, Venice was the capital of an empire of which nine-tenths stretched out towards the East and which, throughout the Middle Ages, turned away from Western Europe, despite the close connections. Finally it must be remembered that among the relics and their precious reliquaries (the most valuable part of the plunder, nearly four hundred objects according to the inventory published by Riant), the French share was much larger than that of the Venetians. Furthermore, neither Villehardouin nor Robert de Clari quote a single Venetian name amongst those guilty of theft or receiving, when, after several days of pillage, it was decided to gather together the plunder in three churches. There is also evidence to show that the Venetian patriarch did not damage the large church entrusted to him, and even strove, using every means, to preserve its inheritance. For his part the *Podestà* fought to keep in the Pantocrator its much venerated icon of the Virgin. In effect the pillage only took place at the moment when Constantinople was re-conquered by the Byzantines led by Michael Palaeologos on 15 August 1261. It was then, wrote Marino Sanudo, that "Baldwin..., carrying about him several jewels and some silver..., and the patriarch Pantaleon Justinian, who took with him a number of jewels and valuable objects, fled... to Negroponte"; among the precious objects taken away by Justinian were doubtless the furnishings of the church and the monastery of the Pantocrator, which went to swell the treasury of San Marco. Finally, even among the most important works which historians attribute to the plunder of the Venetians during the Latin hegemony of Constantinople, some have another origin. One case is sufficient example: the historiated columns of the *ciborium* of San Marco, nothing about which shows them to be Byzantine (the hypothesis has been advanced that they could have come from Dalmatia; the two columns could, in my opinion, have been taken from the basilica of Santa Maria di Canedo at Pola, which was founded by Maximiam and was almost in ruins by the year 1000); it is still, however, stated as a fact that they were part of the plunder of the Fourth Crusade.

Did the large enamels which came from the Pantocrator and which were re-used in the *Pala d'Oro* figure amongst the precious objects taken from this monastery by the patriarch Justinian in his flight from Constantinople in 1261? This would seem to be the most likely theory, or at least the only one supported by a text; if this were the case, however, the enamels were not included in the second or third altar-piece (of 1209) and were only added in 1342-5 at the time of Bonensegna's restoration. It is certainly possible, because nothing precise is known about the *Pala* prior to its present arrangement. It is, however, difficult to believe that, in his hasty flight, the patriarch would have found time to take all the enamels from a large marble *templon*: there were already more than enough portable objects. Perhaps this *templon* had been damaged in the early days of the Latin conquest of 1204, either during the sack of the city or at least before a return to normality and the installation of the Venetian *Podestà* at the Pantocrator. The *Podestà* would have collected up the enamels and sent them to his own country. On the other hand, the *templon* was not dismantled all at once and sent in its entirety to Venice (despite the example re-employed in the Baptistry at Pisa), for the Venetians would never have sacrificed half of the most important and precious enamels, the Feasts of the Church cycle.

8. G. Veludo in Pasini, *op. cit.*
9. *Documenti...*, *op. cit.*, nos 102-3, 812, 830 (inscription on the *Pala d'Oro*).

43

innumerable pearls and precious stones were introduced, as well as the enamels from earlier altar-pieces, probably changing the positions, as the arrangement of the figures is in harmony with the new Gothic frame. The new distribution follows an arrangement far removed from the canons of Byzantine art, corresponding closely instead with the iconographic canons of the West (as defined by the small altar in the cathedral of Cividale, for example). Finally, the whole was completed by the addition of Venetian enamels of the period. The *Pala d'Oro* has remained substantially thus ever since. Successive restorations have not modified its structure; they have cleaned it, reassembled it and given stability to the upper part, which used to fold over the lower part when, ordinarily, the whole was covered by the "*pala feriale*" (fig. XVIII, p. 31).[10] One must therefore take account of four periods in the chronology of the enamels of the *Pala d'Oro*: the end of the tenth century (Byzantine), the beginning of the twelfth century (Byzantine and Venetian Byzantine), the final decades of the twelfth century (Byzantine), and the fourteenth century (Venetian).[11] The upper part of the *Pala* (3.15 x 2.10 metres) has at its centre a quatrefoil with the image of the archangel Michael, surrounded by six scenes representing the great festivals of the Church, three on each side, all against a background studded with little enamels, thirty-eight in number. The lower part has at its centre a large panel with the enthroned Pantocrator surrounded by the four evangelists; above, the *Hetoimasia* is flanked by two cherubim associated with the tetramorph and in turn by two angels; below is the Virgin *orans* between the figures of the empress Irene and the doge Ordelafo Falier. On each side of the central panel are three tiers of enamels one above the other, with six in each row: at the top are archangels (forming part of a divine liturgy, or the Heavenly Host), in the middle tier are apostles and, at the bottom, prophets. The whole of the lower part of the *Pala* is surrounded on three sides by a series of small square panels (twenty-seven), in which are depicted Gospel scenes and episodes from the life of St Mark. The *Pala* as a whole is set within a frame which incorporates a large number of small medallions enamelled with various figures.

Certain Byzantine enamelled reliquaries or icons, the reliquary-crosses of Martvili in Georgia, for instance, or the large Khakhuli triptych (2 x 1.47 metres overall), although later than the enamels and provincial in execution (the triptych was made in Georgia in the second quarter of the thirteenth century: the enamels are of the second quarter of the eleventh), can give us some idea of the doge Orseolo's first altar-frontal: a *pala* entirely chased and set with precious stones, where the enamels were simply mounted, without the guiding principle of a pre-existing structural harmony. On the imponderable surface of the gold the

10. Successive repairs to the *Pala d'Oro* have been numerous: the addition of pearls and jewels under the procurators Michele Morosini and Pietro Cornaro in 1374; small repairs made after an attempt at theft in 1399; pearls added in 1522, 1575 and 1589; cleaning programmes of 1614, 1647, 1720, 1731 and 1780; an important and radical restoration between 1836 and 1847; the replacement of missing pearls; repairs to the frame and to ten silver saints; restoration of the enamels, etc. (There are also the two inscriptions: "*MCCCXLII Joha[ne]s Bone[n]segna me fecit. Orate p[ro] me*" and "*MCCCXLV a de 9 ag[ost]o Maistro Perin me fodare de legname*". The transcriptions present some discrepancies: in any case the only goldsmith mentioned is Bonensegna - not, as is sometimes written, Bonsegna - making it evident that the original signature was abbreviated; something the restorer omitted to reproduce or resolve.)
11. According to O. Demus (*op.cit.*, 24, no. 78): the tenth, the beginning of the twelfth, and the early thirteenth centuries (on the evidence of the inscription and the tradition of the chronicles). It is, however, difficult to share Demus's opinion that "the present lower part roughly represents the altar-piece of 1105; the upper part comprises additions taken from the plunder of Constantinople at the dawn of the thirteenth century, with the re-use of elements remaining from the *Pala* of Orseolo". Too many stylistic similarities exist between the Feasts on the upper *Pala* and the majority of the large enamels on the lower part (with the exception of the four *tondi* of the evangelists), which are evidently Gothic, dating from 1345; the whole arrangement of the images is Gothic, and it must therefore be supposed that there was a radical re-organization of the *Pala*, although one which more or less preserved the dimensions of the whole, framed by the earlier series of Venetian enamels.

enamelled figures were distributed with more freedom than in mosaics (which are always bound to the shape of the building and its architectural meaning) and with only a remote anthropomorphic relationship. More clearly than on mosaics, the contours and internal drawing of the *cloisons* – rather than emphasizing as in Western painting a certain spatial value – succeeded on the contrary in bringing out the boundaries of different qualities of pure colour which because they had been obtained from minerals were incorruptible, dehumanized, and without spatial meaning.

It is not easy to establish which of the enamels could originally have belonged to the first altar-frontal of Orseolo: some of the thirty-eight little medallions along the upper and lower borders (for example, a king on horseback with a falcon on his wrist, in the style of Sasanian horsemen; a symbolic tree, probably the *hazmà*, surmounted by a crowned female head, between peacocks; heraldic serpents; confronted griffins) perhaps belong to this first group. Their style must, in my opinion, be related to the time of Orseolo, on the grounds of the almost immaterial fragility of their lines, which, in the delicacy of the material, seem like scarcely visible veins in dense floral tissue, and above all of the Oriental elements which persist in their typology, vestiges of the Iconoclast storm which had only just been weathered. It is probable that they belong to the beginning of the chronological phase which culminated in the making of the enamels (important above all because they constitute a chronological landmark) on the crown presented by the emperor Constantine Monomachos (1042-54) to Andrew of Hungary (1046-61). Nine enamelled plaques of gold from this crown were found at Nyitra-Ivanka, and are now in the National Museum in Budapest. The enamels on the borders of the *Pala* could equally well have come from other objects forming part of the Venetian booty – chalices, patens, chests, the borders of icons, *polycandela*, *encolpia*, and so on. It is, however, clear that Bonensegna and his workshop must have made use of a considerable quantity of dismantled enamels, with which they filled their Gothic structure without paying too much attention to period, style or significance, aiming only at decorative magnificence. Some of them were only fragments (for example the fragment of a *Deesis*), while others, needed for balance, were without doubt executed in Venice so as not to leave any "gaps". By contrast, the medallions of the four evangelists could have been part of the second altar-piece, that of the reconstruction by Ordelafo Falier (1105). They can be counted among the first works in enamel made in Venetian workshops, and they are probably their greatest creation. Their basically Byzantine artistic language is in fact more mature than that of the former group, but it is clear that this is only the point of departure for a style of expression which can no longer be called Byzantine, and still less provincial: henceforth it is Venetian. In this group, linked at least in technique to the roundels with the evangelists, we can perhaps recognize the birth of the Venetian school of enamelling. It is not impossible that these craftsmen might have been pupils of that "Greek master" who came to Venice in the service of Ordelafo Falier (if indeed he came) and that, in short, they might have been "shaped" in his workshop. In any case we can easily discern in this group of enamels the technique and inflexion of artistic language of which we have been speaking: quite different from those of the Byzantine enamels, the *cloisons* are relatively thicker and coarser, and form a tentative, rather cursory design. One might say that the design cannot decide between the impeccable and highly skilled decorative spirit of the Byzantine models and a Western tendency towards realism which cannot forget that lines have in some way to define the parts of the body. The result is a language which is imprecise, bombastic, awkward and, in the last analysis, ambiguous.

It is to the embellishments carried out under the doge Ziani that the square panels with Gospel scenes and episodes from the life of St Mark now framing the lower part of the altar-piece must be attributed; also datable to this period are the solitary figures of saints beneath "arches of glorification", which are comparable with those seen on so many illuminated pages. There are certain iconographic connections with mosaics of same subject in the *naos* of the basilica of San Marco (e.g. the life of the Virgin cycle), which are a Venetian translation, though abridged and more basic, of the Late Comnenian pictorial style which asserted itself at Nerezi (1164) and spread, with the accentuation of mannerisms, throughout Macedonia (e.g. Kurbinovo, 1191). If, however, in dome-mosaics – above all in Ascensions – which are the product of much more skilled and informed artists the "Nerezi style" still seems strong and close to its models, then the scenes on the *Pala* show evidence of less advanced and sophisticated workshops. The linear intensity is diluted, perhaps because of the presence in these workshops of illuminated manuscripts related, for all that is known, to the Montecassino style. It was these, or similar manuscripts, by which the creators of the enamels, who were assuredly Venetian, were influenced. This is also suggested by a fineness of line, by a particular human shape (square-faced, especially in the cycle of St Mark), and by a certain fleeting, agitated and fragmented linear quality, which appears in both the cycles.

In these cycles, the linear style, defined by Gombosi, could indeed have been derived from miniature-painting, as Gombosi rightly suggests, rather than from recourse to the tradition of northern Italian mosaic pavements.

The problem of classifying the enamels seems to hinge on the origins of the two portraits which appear in the lower part of the *Pala*, on either side of the Virgin *orans* (and which are, in their turn, flanked by plaques with fourteenth-century inscriptions). We see here a portrait of the doge Ordelafo Falier on the left, and of the empress Irene on the right.

The enamel of Ordelafo seems to have been modified, even completely re-worked, and as it is possible to relate it to that of the *augusta* (even though the dimensions are not exactly the same); it has been concluded that it might originally have represented a Byzantine emperor who had a wife called Irene. But which? There are more than one. Even if the choice is limited, as surely it must be, to the Comnenian dynasty, a decision has still to be made between Alexios I (1081-1118), John II (1118-43), and Manuel I (1143-80). Some opinions favour John II,[12] some, on the other hand favour Alexios I.[13] The identification with John II, which I have supported elsewhere,[14] essentially depends on two facts. These are the acceptance of the patriarch Joseph's evidence that these enamels originally belonged to the monastery of the Pantocrator, and the historical fact that this monastery was founded (around 1124) by Irene, daughter of Ladislaus, the king of Hungary, with the support of her husband, the emperor John II. It would be natural to suppose that, if the enamels had come from the monastery, they might have included portraits of the founders.[15]

12. See E. Molinier, *L'Emaillerie*, Paris 1891, 42ff.
13. J. Ebersolt, *op.cit.*, 94; S. Lambros, *Catalogue illustré de la collection de portraits des empereurs de Byzance*, Athens 1911, 43; G. Veludo, in Pasini, *op.cit.*, 148; O. Demus, "Das älteste venezianische Gesellschaftsbild", *Jahrbuch der Österreichischen Byzantinischen Gesellschaft* 1(1951), 89ff.; C. Diehl, *Manuel d'art byzantin*, Paris 1925-6, 703: "a personage... none other than the emperor Alexios or the emperor John Comnenos, both of whom had wives named Irene".
14. S. Bettini, *La Pala d'Oro, op.cit.*
15. On the *typikon* (the act of foundation or endowment of a monastery) of the Pantocrator: A. Dimitrijevski, *Acts of the Academy of Kiev*, 1895, 537; for the architecture: J. Ebersolt, "Rapport sommaire sur une mission à Constantinople" (1910), *Missions Scientifiques*, n.s., pt 3, Paris 1911, 9; C. Gurlitt, *Die Baukunst Konstantinopels*, Berlin 1912, 33ff.; A. van Millingen and R. Traquair, *Byzantine churches in Constantinople*, London 1912, 219; J. Ebersolt and

48

The identification with the brilliant Alexios Comnenos – father of Kalojan and of the poetess Anna who honoured her father in the *Alexiad* – hinges more on historical probabilities. The *basilissa* would in this case be the beautiful, cold, green-eyed Irene Doukas, whom he took as his wife when she was very young. ΕΙΡΗΝΗ ΣΕΒΕΣΤΑΤΗ ΑΥΓΟΥΣΤΗ, can be read on the inscription accompanying the portrait, "Irene, empress full of piety". It is known that it was through the intervention of the patriarch Cosmas that Irene became *augusta* (for he in effect forced Alexios to crown her, even though the emperor was extremely hesitant, being very taken by the dowager empress Maria). Besides, it is well known that Alexios, much more so than John II, had developed friendly relations with Venice, closer perhaps than any other Byzantine ruler. The offensive of the Norman duke Robert Guiscard, whose ultimate objective was the Byzantine crown, could have been fatal for the emperor without the aid of the Venetian fleet and the defeat that it inflicted on the Normans at Dyrrachium; only with difficulty had Alexios avoided this outcome with only his own forces to back him. By the terms of the treaty of 1082, he granted the Venetians all they desired – possessions, titles, gifts, exemptions from salt-tax, and all sorts of privileges – so that, by this treaty, just as historians maintain, Venice in fact gained control of the Byzantine seas. Should it therefore seem strange in the circumstances that this *basileus* felt able, in 1105, thirteen years before his death, to offer to San Marco in Venice a gold altar-frontal strewn with enamels and graced with his own portrait and that of the *augusta*, his collaborator if not his inspiration in religious matters, particularly when he was known to be the very pious and gallant "defender of the faith", as for example in his fight against the Bogomil heresy and against Giovanni Italo, or in his protection of the monks of Athos and Patmos?

Recently Professor Pomorisac-De Luigi[16] has put forward a new hypothesis: the face of Ordelafo had never been the portrait of a Byzantine (the costume would militate against this), but from its conception that of a doge. Only the head would have been altered and the halo added later. The plaque showing the doge cannot, therefore, be associated with that of Irene, which is in any case slightly smaller. Professor Pomorisac-De Luigi, moreover, suggests that in 1105 there would have been not two but four figures of donors and rulers flanking the Virgin, those of the emperor Alexios I and the empress Irene in the centre, flanked by those of the doge and the co-emperor John II. When the altar-piece was re-made in 1209, relations between Venice and Byzantium had changed considerably and it was impossible, after the conquest of 1204, for the Venetians to tolerate the presence of likenesses of two Byzantine emperors, which were consequently disposed of. The portrait of Irene was spared because the *augusta* was related to Theodora Doukas, wife of the doge Domenico Selvo.[17]

This hypothesis, which is accepted by Otto Demus,[18] seems too complicated and not very convincing (cf. Marvin Ross). It is evident that the two portraits were placed in their present position during the refurbishments of the thirteenth century, without any reference to the arrangement of the enamels in the previous altar-pieces, on which these portraits might well have had no place. Even though there is a definite relationship between the dimensions of the lower part of the

A. Thiers, *Les églises de Constantinople*, Paris 1913, 185; G. Moravsik, *Pantokrator Monastor*, Budapest 1923; K. Wulzinger, *Byzantinische Baudenkmäler zu Konstantinopel*, Hanover 1925; J. Kollwitz, in *Römische Quartalschrift*, 42 (1934), 241; J. Arnott Hamilton, *Byzantine architecture and decoration*, London 1933, 94; A.M. Schneider, *Byzantinische Vorarbeiten zu Topographie und Archäologie der Stadt*, Berlin 1936, 68; R. Janin, *La géographie ecclésiastique de l'empire byzantin*, III, *Eglises et monastères*, Paris 1953, 529, 576.
16. Doctoral thesis quoted by O. Demus, *op.cit.*, 24.
17. O. Demus, *op.cit.*, 24-5.
18. O. Demus, *op.cit.*, 24, no. 80.

Pala and those of the small Venetian plaques with Gospel scenes and episodes from the life of St Mark which, we have suggested, go back to the very beginning of the *duecento* and which constitute the frame of the *Pala*, the fixing of these small plaques to the frame does not predetermine the internal divisions of the lower part of the altar-piece. What is more, the hypothesis of Professor Pomorisac-De Luigi does not explain the evident alteration, even if it is presumed to be partial, of the male figure. As a result, we must suppose that this came about on a subsequent occasion, that is to say during the third refurbishment, and therefore with a commemorative purpose in mind. It is not in fact necessary, assuming that it is a portrait of Ordelafo Falier, to believe that the likeness of the doge provides us with the precise date of its commission. Ordelafo was the originator of the gold altar-piece, and it is fitting that he is remembered in this way.

On the other hand, fundamental to these theories is the supposition that the presence of these enamels is due to the special links between Venice and Byzantium. This hypothesis losses all value, however, if one considers that, on the contrary, from the date of their original execution, without prejudging what is meant by that, these enamels could very well have been part of the plunder amassed during the Latin conquest of 1204. In this case, it will obviously be necessary to search in Constantinople itself for some explanation of the presence on a work of enamel portraits of an imperial couple including an emperor, still in need of a name, but in any case a Comnene (on the grounds already expounded: even if the style were insufficient evidence, there is the account of John Palaeologos and his companions recognizing the enamels in Venice, *en route* to the Council of Florence). If the object on which these likenesses appeared was an item of church plate or an altar, then the figures (to stay in the field of enamels, even though numerous comparisons can be found on coins or in miniatures) could well have been used like those of the emperor Michael VII Doukas and his wife Maria, who are crowned by Christ on the Khakhuli triptych mentioned above. There is no doubt that these are Byzantine, not Georgian, enamels, in spite of what has been suggested recently.[19] The figure of the imperial couple could also have had a totally different destination. I repeat once more, however, that I see no reason for discrediting the source according to which the large enamels of the *Pala* were to be traced back to the monastery of the Pantocrator in Constantinople.

The monastery of the Pantocrator had been officially founded by the empress Irene, wife of John II Comnenos, but it was only after her sudden death in 1124 that the construction was seriously undertaken (in 1136, to be precise). It is probable that the principal buildings date from the reign of John II (1118-43). Irene, in any case, was not buried there, and there is nothing to prove that her mortal remains were subsequently transferred there. John II died twenty years after his wife. It remains fairly difficult, therefore, to associate with the Pantocrator monastery the enamel figures of John II and Irene. The case of the funerary chapel, however, is different. After the construction of two central-plan churches (the larger and older southern one dedicated to the Pantocrator, the one to the north to the Theotokos *Eleousa*), the chapel was built between them and became the sumptuous mausoleum of Manuel I Comnenos (1143-80), who was buried there in a magnificent black marble sarcophagus beside his first wife Berthe of Sulzbach, who was sister-in-law of the Western emperor Conrad III and who had in Byzantium taken the name Irene. She had been buried there in 1161. If we allow ourselves to develop the hypothesis that the two portraits in Venice were originally those of Manuel and Irene, it would be possible to explain the very slight difference in

19. C. Amiranachvili, *op.cit.*, 99ff. (with bibliography).

53

size between the figure of Irene and that of Ordelafo Falier – the former Manuel Comnenos – in the *Pala d'Oro* by the chronological gap separating the figure of Irene, which would have been inserted in the *templon* of the mausoleum at her death in 1161, and that of Manuel, added when he in his turn was buried, nineteen years later. No accurate new measurements would have been obtained, for reasons which are easily understandable.

Be that as it may, the mausoleum of Irene and Manuel, made ready in life by the *augusti* and richly decorated as a shrine for their bodies and situated between the two main churches of the monastery of the Pantocrator, seems after all these considerations to be the least improbable original site of these important Byzantine enamels, which were subsequently imported by the Venetians and eventually arranged on the *Pala d'Oro*. It is a simple hypothesis, to be sure, but is it possible to refer, as people do, to the Pantocrator in general when it is, in fact, an immense monastery with at least three churches, each one having its *templon* along with numerous other parts?

Twenty years after the death of Manuel, the conquest of Constantinople in 1204 brought to Venice a considerable quantity of precious stones and enamel. As I have already said, all or nearly all of the large panels which are inserted in the present altar-piece belong to this period: the feasts of the Church and the archangel Michael with the *trisagion* in the centre of the upper part, the Pantocrator at the centre of the whole, and the row of superb angels which obviously belong to the "Nerezi style" and thus to the second half of the twelfth century. All these enamels together make up what is termed a "divine liturgy", as they advance in two lateral groups converging on the throne of the *Hetoimasia* in an arrangement with the rows of twelve apostles and twelve prophets one above the other and with several other minor plaques set apart. There is, however, some difference in quality, as well as in size, between the enamels in the most "precious" group, (that is to say the Pantocrator, the archangel and the Feasts) and that of the panels with standing figures to the sides, although not enough to suggest either a chronological or stylistic gap between them. This could however be due to the fact that they are the work of craftsmen of varying talent, though all working on the same project. The project could well have been the decoration of the *templon* of the funerary church of Irene and Manuel Comnenos, between the two main churches of the Pantocrator in Constantinople. In the *kosmitis* of this *templon*, which probably served to divide two domed chambers, it is easy to believe that there would have been a *Deesis*, the fragments of which, re-used in the gold altar-piece could well be the Pantocrator in the centre, St Michael (one of the two archangels most often found with him) and the large apostle figures which form a row. The other enamels would have been placed in the body of the *templon*; it would be rash, however, to want to locate them more precisely. We can at most try to put them into logical groups: the prophets, the angels of the liturgy, the Feasts, which should be twelve in number, in order that the traditional series be complete.[20] Only six of these arrived in Venice, or at least only six were used: the

---

20. For the *iconostasis*, the basic study still remains that of P. Kostantynowicz, *Ikonostas, Studien und Forschungen*, I, Lvov 1939; criticized by V. Lazarev ("La Scuola di Vladimir Susdal; due dipinti della pittura da cavalletto russa dal XII al XIII secolo per la storia dell'iconostasi", *Arte Veneta* 10(1956), 12, no. 1) for not "having evaluated all new discoveries in the fiels of ancient Russian painting made in recent years". See also, by the same author, *Feofan Grek*, Moscow 1961, 87 (in Russian); L. Bréhier, "Anciennes clôtures de chœur antérieures aux iconostases dans les monastères de l'Athos", *Studi bizantini e neo-ellenici* 6(1940), 48ff. (with bibliography); J. Collette, "De Ikonostase", *Het Gildeboek* 25(1942), 53ff.; S. Xydis, "The chancel barrier, solea and ambo of Haghia Sophia". *Gymnasium und Wissenschaft, Festschrift der Maximilian-Gymnasium in München*, 1939, 176ff.; A. Orlandos, Ἡ ξυλόστεγος παλαιοχριστιανσκὴ Βασιλική, II, Athens 1954, 509-35; W. Felicetti-Liebensfels, *Byzantinische Ikonenmalerei*, Lausanne 1956, 73ff.; G. and M. Sotiriou, *Icônes du Mont Sinaï*, I, Athens 1957; W. Felicetti-Liebensfels, "Ent-

54

DANIEL

CVM VENE RIT SCS SCOY

55

Entry into Jerusalem, the Descent into Limbo, the Crucifixion, the Ascension, Pentecost and the Dormition of the Virgin. But although incomplete, they form part of a cycle which is of great value to the study of Byzantine art and iconography and of their influence on the art of medieval Europe.

This whole group of enamels from the *Pala d'Oro* is stylistically akin to the most accomplished and typical Byzantine painting of the period of Manuel I Comnenos (1143-80). This was a reign which, as has been seen, was among the richest in terms of works in the history of Byzantine art, even if the great examples from the capital (the mosaics of St Sophia, of the Holy Apostles, of the monastery of the Pantocrator, of the Kataskepe, of the Komosotira, of the Chora and of the Forty Martyrs and those in the Great Palace and in the Blachernae residence, and so on) have been lost for ever and we are now forced to seek out the scanty remains of this marvellous blossoming in the little lost churches of the provinces, at Nerezi, for example, in the Macedonian mountains, or to catch glimpses of it in miniatures or in the mosaics closest to us, above all those in Macedonia, Dalmatia, the region of the northern Adriatic and in Venice itself. Staying, however, with enamels, and particularly with large enamels, I think the most immediate point of reference comprises the Feast icons from the Botkin collection, which were perhaps originally part of a Byzantine *templon*; they are today in the National Museum of Fine Arts at Tbilisi in Georgia, rightly attributed by their latest commentator Chalva Amiranachvili[21] to the end of the twelfth century. It should always be borne in mind, however, that these are works of lower artistic and technical quality than the enamels of the *Pala d'Oro*, which date from the end of the Comnenian period, but which undoubtedly share the same artistic language. Finally, I do not believe that any specialist in Byzantine painting would find difficulty in admitting that, even more than the Georgian Feasts, those of the *Pala d'Oro* belong to the last great flowering of Byzantine art (and certainly the strongest, not only in Venice but in Italy in general) before the Fourth Crusade, that of the Comnenian period, from which there remains but a single masterpiece, the frescoes created by the principal artist at St Pantaleimon at Nerezi.

Equally, the size of the panels make it improbable that the two series originally ornamented a small object, a *capsella*, portable altar or suchlike. It is therefore more probable that they came from a *templon*. This hypothesis is not unfounded. Apart from the information given by Sguropulos (concerning the *Pala d'Oro*), we know for certain that the *templa* of rich Byzantine churches were decorated with silver and gold reliefs: Italian specialists have only to recall the *templon* in silver that the abbot Desiderius commissioned in Constantinople for his church at Montecassino, consecrated in 1071. The detailed description in the chronicle of Leo of Ostia leaves few doubts about this and brings to mind a layout not dissimilar to the presumed arrangement of the *templon* of the Pantocrator. Other types of decoration were often also found, associated with marble structures, particularly sculptures but also mosaics and enamels. The great wooden *iconostasis* covered with painted icons is, as one knows, in a certain sense the answer to economic setbacks and to a provincial diffusion that Lazarev believed to have originated in Russia,[22] although not necessarily so. We have already seen a splendid example of

stehung und Bildprogramm des byzantinischen Templons im Mittelalter", *Festschrift W. Sas-Zaloziecky*, Graz 1956, 49ff.; S. Bettini, *Un libro su San Marco, op.cit.*, 274-5.

21. C. Amiranachvili, *op.cit.*, 60ff., the series incomplete originally (numbering only eleven and lacking the Annunciation).

22. See V. Lazarev, *op.cit.*, (*Arte Veneta*) and L. Bréhier, *op. cit.*, 53ff. The images on a *templon* must not be confused with the portable icons which were placed on *analoghia* (a sort of rostrum) for the veneration of the faithful, and which were therefore called "αι προσκυνήσεις". These icons were not normally found on a *templon* but on

a sculpted *kosmitis*, a masterpiece of Byzantine sculpture of the Comnenian period, indeed of all time, re-used to provide the architrave of the eastern door of the baptistry at Pisa.[23] We have a reminder of mosaic decoration in the description by the priest Theodore Padiasimos, published by Lambros, of the church of Serres, in Thessaly,[24] where the *templon* (ἡ στοὰ τοῦ βήματος) showed, in mosaic on a gold ground, the *Deesis* in the centre, surmounted by the Ascension and flanked by the images of the twelve apostles. As for enamelled *templa*, the well known one at St Sophia in Constantinople, dating from the time of Justinian, is sufficient example. Paul the Silentiary[25] specifies in his famous description that "the emperor had the twelve twin columns separating clergy from choristers covered in silver, in which a patient and skilled hand had chased medallions". It is permissible to think that these medallions were enamelled and represented Christ, the Virgin, the heavenly host of the angelic hierarchy, the prophets, the apostles – in fact the entire range that we find in the large enamels of the *Pala d'Oro* – and the monograms of the emperor and empress. On the *templon* of the Pantocrator, from where the enamels of the Venetian altar-piece came, there would have been, in place of the monograms, the effigies of the two rulers. The thousands of workshops in Constantinople which were producing enamels did not only work on the most sumptuous ecclesiastical or secular works of precious metal (decorated objects such as those in the sacred palace were very numerous: standing-lamps, tables, vessels, caskets, and so on, and portable objects intended to be displayed during solemn ceremonies, like votive crowns, bowls, bookcovers, vestments and shoes) but also on the decoration of architectural structures with the precious "pictures", which were inserted into the façades and inner walls of churches and palaces. This way of using enamels dates at least from the time of Basil I (867-86). Texts give accounts, for example, of an enamelled icon of the Saviour which was in the church of the prophet Elias. As for enamels inserted into screens, we know that the massive gold screen of the Nea Ecclesia, also from the time of Basil I, had at its centre a large enamel which represented Christ. No remnant of any of these is *in situ* today. We come across examples, however, where sculpture and painting are used together and which we can consider to be more ordinary and cheaper. These ἔργα χεύματα, as they are strictly termed, are a sort of inlay in marble, imitating enamel. The marble is chiselled out – except for the features, and pleats in the figures' robes – and the holes filled with

the *iconostasis*, originally simply a movable support for icons, not a barrier (the original sense of the term "εἰκονοστάσιον", or "εἰκονόστασις": Codinus, *De officiis*, C.VI – Christmas Eve – *Patrologie grecque*, ed. E. Migne, CLVII, 61; *v.* L. Bréhier, *op.cit.*, 52). The *templon* itself also eventually developed into an *iconostasis*, and in later periods became more complex (as in churches on the Ionian islands); all of which does not rule out the possibility that the *kosmitis* of the *templon*, in less elaborate examples, could have carried images painted on wood, or other small suspended icons.
23. *v.* S. Bettini, *Un libro su San Marco, op.cit.* Of the long Greek inscription in mosaic, in elegant characters of the Comnenian period, which runs right along the base of this architrave, only fragments remain at the beginning and the end (several isolated letters are still distinguishable in the middle register, but the rest has fallen down or, more probably, been taken off, like the gold mosaic which filled the haloes, and the stones which decorated the vestments and the books of the evangelists, etc.).
Without intensive study of the inscriptions, it would appear that, at the extreme left, we find the established formula of the *Deesis*: "ΔΕΗΣΙΣ (ΤΟΥ ΔΟΥΛΟΥ ΤΟΥ ΘΕΟΥ...)". For the significance of the *Deesis* in this part of a Byzantine church, reference can be made to the text of Simon of Thessaloniki: "Περὶ τοῦ ἁγίου νεοῦ"(C. 136, *Patrologie grecque*, ed. E. Migne, CVL, 345-7): the *templon* marks the division between the perceptible world and the intelligible world which contained the altar, "ἱερὸν βῆμα", the passage from one to the other is made possible through the intercession of the Virgin, St John the Baptist and other saints or archangels (*Deesis*). Through a coincidence of place and significance the *templon* is found right in the middle of the church between the "secular" space of the nave and the "divine" space of the *bema* where the liturgy unfolds itself.
24. S. Lambros, in "Νέος Ἑλληνομνήμον", XV, 171-4.
25. *v.* L. Bréhier, *op.cit.*, 51.

coloured molten glass or small pieces of hardstone, with precious stones or pearls inserted here and there.

An especially significant example of this technique is the *kosmitis* of a *templon* in the museum at Thebes in Beotia, shown at the exhibition of Byzantine Art in Athens in 1964.[26] On this *kosmitis* are engraved the busts of Christ, the Virgin and, in adjoining medallions, three apostles. The cut out figures would originally have been filled with coloured mastic or enamel. While the work is rather basic and provincial, it is important, because, possibly dating from the ninth century, it is perhaps the earliest surviving example of a historiated *templon* and, what is more, of one representing a *Deesis*. The well-known panel showing the apostles James, Philip and Luke in the Byzantine museum in Athens,[27] on which the technique, comparable with that of *cloisonné* enamel, is still clearer, would also originally have been part of the architrave of a *templon*-screen with a *Deesis* (without doubt that of the Vlattades monastery, Thessaloniki, where the panel came from); similarly, there are two panels in the Archaeological Museum in Istanbul, one representing St Eudoxia and the other a web-footed beast, which were found during the excavation of a chapel in the monastery of Lips (Fenari Isa Camii) in Constantinople.[28] They could date from the ninth or eleventh century, and, whether or not they were part of the architrave of a *templon*-screen, as André Grabar was the first to suggest,[29] they were in any case created in a technique close to that of *cloisonné* enamel. Another *templon* architrave which may exhibit a similar technique is that in the Archaeological Museum of Chios, dating from the ninth or tenth century,[30] originally, perhaps, in the church of St Isidore in Chios itself. This is a minor example of the technique, and is in any case too dubious to be given serious consideration.[31] Finally, it is probable that this technique was imitated in one way or another by the Venetians. In fact, in the Kunsthistorisches Museum in Vienna[32] – but originating from the palace of Cataio, which has important collections – is a panel representing a Pantaleimon which is, in my opinion, indisputably Venetian work of the twelfth century, executed in a manner very close to that of one of the sculptors who worked on certain reliefs at San Marco. The figure does not now seem to have ever had inlays of mastic or enamel, but it shows traces of gold and paint. This is perhaps an indication of, so to speak, a quicker and cheaper phase, comparable to what would later become, on a non-monumental scale, the work of the glass-engravers: the Venetians replaced the expensive luxury *cloisonné* technique while achieving a similar colour effect.

As to the vocabulary of iconographic motifs which we find in the enamels of the *Pala d'Oro* probably taken from the Pantocrator, and as to their original arrangement, the most significant clue, in my opinion, is that of the *iconostasis* of the church of St Catherine in Sinai[33] (which is known to have been an imperial foundation, imperially endowed). The work is of relatively late date – later, to my mind, than the twelfth century – and yet is important to the problem which concerns us, for it is possible to believe that it reflects and translates into more basic and economical terms the composition of *templa* in Constantinople during the

---

26. No. 17 in the exhibition catalogue *Byzantine art and European art*, Athens 1964.
27. Exh. cat. *Byzantine art an European art*, 1964, no. 23.
28. Exh. cat. *Byzantine art an European art*, 1964, nos 24-5.
29. A. Grabar, *Sculptures byzantines de Constantinople (IVe - Xe siècles)*, Paris 1963, 109, pls LV-LVI.
30. Exh. cat. *Byzantine art an European art*, 1964, no. 26.
31. e.g. the plaque showing David (in the Rotunda of St George at Thessaloniki), exh. cat. *Byzantine art an European art*, no. 22.
32. *Sammlung für Plastik und Kunstgewerbe*, no. 7385; exh. cat. *Byzantine art an European art*, no. 28.
33. Cf. G. Sotiriou, "Icônes byzantines du monastère du Sinaï", *Byzantion* 14(1939), 327, pl. V.

61

Comnenian period – in particular the example from the funerary chapel of Manuel I and Irene.

The *iconostasis* in Sinai was dismantled and over half of it turned into individual icons, which are today in the museum of the monastery. It is not difficult, however, to reconstruct the spirit of the object and to see, for example, that the complete series of the twelve Feasts, each within an arch as are the upper enamels of the *Pala d'Oro*, was situated beneath the architrave of the *templon*, which itself would have carried the *Deesis*. The earliest trace of a similar arrangement is found in the codex of the Keharitomenis monastery in Constantinople, which was built by the *augusta* Irene, wife of Alexios Comnenos (1081-1118),[34] and which reflects a doubtless earlier tradition. We can, at any rate, start from here, that is to say from the turn of the eleventh and twelfth centuries, in order to uncover possible hints of a similar "order". Bertaux and, after him, Bréhier have long drawn attention to Santa Maria in Valle Porclaneta, near Rosciolo (not far from Aquileia),[35] where, they maintain, there is an imitation of the silver *iconostasis* commissioned in Constantinople by the abbot Desiderius for Montecassino, and which is therefore an adaptation of a Byzantine *templon* from the end of the eleventh century (1071). Even if the example at Rosciolo is much later, it is in any case possible to extract from it evidence of the arrangement of a figural *templon*. It was inevitable that the original arrangement would be imitated innumerable times, either in abbreviated form or expanded to include new figures, not only on late examples of the *iconostasis* but also in the icons themselves (sometimes only the *Deesis* is preserved, occupying the upper space; sometimes other motifs have been inserted, and so on). To avoid having to search too far, I can add to the examples quoted by Lazarev the famous if neglected icon at San Giovanni in Bragora, Venice, which is certainly Byzantine, from the Palaeologan period, and shows St Nicholas and scenes from his life. The upper part shows a *Deesis* inspired by the *kosmitis* of a *templon*.

Not all the enamels on the *Pala d'Oro* that were part of the plunder of 1204 are considered to be intact. Some, probably damaged when they were being re-employed, were restored and finished by Venetian craftsmen, others had their inscriptions re-done (in Latin), and so on. These restorations, as well as some brackets which were also added, are easily recognizable. They are attributable to the renovation carried out in the thirteenth century and constitute the "fourth group" of insertions into the great altar-piece. It is pointless to dwell on them: compared with the rest they are few in number and only add to the history of the work in that they are evidence of the activities of Venetian craftsmen, who – although disciples of the Byzantines – had now achieved full maturity which was to last, in spite of their specialization in *opus cristellariorum*, then very advanced, right into the thirteenth century.

When faced, however, with the cycle of Gospel scenes and of the life of St Mark, the four evangelist medallions, the modification of the figure of Manuel-Ordelafo, the restoration of various plaques, and minor additions to the Pala d'Oro, we cannot add much to fill out the slender catalogue of Venetian enamel up to and including the whole of the *duecento*. The examples are few, but they do exist, and the group which, I feel, is the most consistent is that of the enamels added to the Linköping mitre under the bishop Kettil Karlsson Vasa (1459-65).[36] The enamel

34. Cf. E. Golubinsky, *History of the Russian Church*, I, 2, Moscow 1904, 210 (in Russian); V. Lazarev, *op.cit.*, *Arte Veneta*, 14.
35. L. Bréhier (*op.cit.*, 51) compares this screen in the choir of Rosciolo with that of San Pietro ad Albe (Abruzzi), and of Santa Maria in Cosmedin in Rome. The similarity lies only in the structure, however.
36. On the Linköping mitre: A. Branting and A. Lindblom, *Medeltida broderier i Sverige*, Stockholm 1928, 73-5;

medallions are, from all the evidence, two centuries older, and it is probable that they were taken from another similar mitre which had been damaged by wear and age. Parallel examples exist, and I particularly quote that of the mitre of Traù Cathedral in Dalmatia,[37] a Venetian work decorated with simulated enamels (miniatures on parchment, covered with crystal and bordered with pearls), attributable to the last years of the *duecento* or the early years of the *trecento*.

The thirty-five medallions of Linköping are, to my mind, undoubtedly Venetian work, to be related to the enamels on the *Pala d'Oro*, even if it is not possible to attribute them to the same workshop, taking into account the chronological gap created by the probable date of their execution. There is, however, a certain direct relationship with the plaques showing the life of St Mark, although it is clear that the craftsmen who made the enamels on the mitre (now in Sweden) were working at least a century later (I would even be inclined to date their activity later, in the thirteenth century). The suppleness and at the same time, the linear mannerism of the *cloisons*, the freedom of the arrangement and pose of the Christ figure, the angels and the evangelists, and even a certain physiognomic type all deny a date contemporary with the pictorial tradition of the mosaics in the north arm of the atrium of San Marco and the frescoes of San Zan Degolà. In any case, their Byzantine "point of departure" can only be found in works such as the enamel of the apostle Peter in the Museum of Fine Arts at Tbilisi, which is a product not of Georgia but of Constantinople, as Amiranachvili also believes,[38] rightly attributing it to the second half of the thirteenth century.

The enamels of the Linköping mitre are definitely not stylistically pure, which explains why experts have found it impossible to relate them to other works. I do not deny that the task is difficult. There is, however, at least one other small group of enamels – even if they carry inscriptions in Latin – which in terms of their pictorial manner come close enough to those of Linköping to make it easy to believe that they came out of the same Venetian workshop. These are four medallions from the Brummer Gallery, shown in 1947 at the exhibition of Early Christian and Byzantine art, organized by the Walters Art Gallery, Baltimore.[39] The notes, including those in the catalogue, state only that it is a work which seems possibly to have come from the Ferrara region. This could prove interesting for us, given the closeness of Ferrara to Venice and the improbability that enamel workshops existed in twelfth-century Ferrara. I draw the attention of Swedish colleagues concerned with this mitre to these four medallions, which have not yet been the subject of close study, for there seems to me no doubt that they are of the same origin. The Linköping and Brummer groups of enamels are in any case of great

C.R. Ugglas, Nationalmusei arsbrok, n.s., V, 1935, 7-19; Y. Hackenbroch, *Italienisches Email des frühen Mittelalters*, Basle 1938, 63; J. Deér, *Der Kaiserornat Friedrich II*, Berne 1952, 62, no. 40; catalogue of the exhibition *Konstens Venedig*, Statens Historiska Museum, Stockholm, 20 October 1962 – 10 February 1963 (here the mitre is dated by C. Nordenfalk, who rightly rejects a Sicilian origin, Venice? 1200?).

A Georgian origin could also still be considered possible if it is compared with the enamels on the frame of the icon of Khobi (C. Amiranachvili, *op.cit.*, 76).

37. See V.J. Djurič, *Vizantijske i italo-vivantijske starine u Dalmaciji*, I, Split 1960, 146ff. (with bibliography).

38. C. Amiranachvili, *op.cit.*, 91.

39. *v.* the exhibition *Early Christian and Byzantine Art*, Baltimore Museum of Art, 1947, 109, n. 529. I refer to the assertion of Urbani de Gheltof (*Les arts industriels à Venise au Moyen Age et à la Renaissance*, Venice 1885, 14) after the manuscript text of J. Grevembroch (*Varie Venete curiosità sacre e profane*, Venice, Biblioteca Museo Civico Correr, I, 1755, II, 1760, III, 1764): "We are still left with the memory of a pyx which was transported from Venice to Vicenza and there lost at the beginning of the century. It was a prodigious work in gilded copper, with the enamelled figures of saints and Latin inscriptions, which must be considered as one of the first Venetian attempts at enamelling."

The considerable series of precious enamels which ornament the two reliquaries of the head and arm of St Blaise in the Cathedral treasury of Ragusa (Dubrovnik) remains to be studied.

These are usually considered to be Byzantine but could, on the other hand, be products of a Venetian workshop, of which, if this is so, they would have been the masterpiece.

interest to historians of Venetian painting in this period. They provide evidence of a transition from Venetian true enamel to the work of the *cristellari* which supplanted it. The illuminators who worked with the *cristellari*, however, clearly belonged to the tradition of the miniature proper, that is to the illustration of manuscripts, but when they were employed to imitate enamels they had to take account of the particular inflections of the artistic language peculiar to that medium. Through lack of attention to this subject in the past, it will now be difficult to discover its history.

I am pleased to be able to conclude the examination of the *Pala d'Oro* for, as it exists today, it is ultimately a Venetian work, an adaptation and reduction of foreign works to suit a particular taste or *Kunstwollen*.

In its Gothic architectural structure the *Pala d'Oro* seems to anticipate the attempt at a formal solution which can be seen on the exterior of the basilica and which basically consists of a completely Western linearity together with colouring which is fundamentally and particularly of Byzantine origin. On the exterior of the basilica the Gothic arabesques crowning the façade are linked with the whole in perfect harmony, for beneath them the architecture is not conceived in accordance with the linear values peculiar to Gothic art; this crown therefore also becomes principally an expression of colour. In the *Pala d'Oro*, however, this linear quality, less obvious, purposefully breaking up the whole by means of vertical features scarcely disturbed by the arches above, does not totally blend with the pure colours of the enamels and jewels, with the result that the work as a whole seems to lack coherence and to be stylistically indeterminate and, despite the extreme richness of its materials and the beauty of its details, aesthetically unfulfilled. In order to enjoy looking at it, it is necessary to concentrate on the particularities – on the brilliant jewels and the enamels, where the precious material and the mineral hardness balance the human qualities expressed in the figures and narrative scenes. By translating the simple narrative into rhetoric of the purest colour known in the history of art, the enamels glorify it for all time. The faces, hands, garments, the figures and the movement absorb in their colours the hard refinement and, so to speak, the very matter of the mineral, in a much more decisive way than in mosaic, and reinforce by their variability, within the formal structure of the whole, the religious transcendence special to Byzantine art. The Venetians brought few personal touches, besides its structure, to the *Pala d'Oro*, but it is perhaps precisely there that a certain humanization is apparent. The crystalline delicacy of Byzantium is lost, in some way altered and cooled in contact with the warmth of humanity which succeeds in permeating through to the jewels and gold, just like the subtly perfumed air which is caught while tiptoeing through a spice-shop. Even the stone appears more tender and human, seeming to soften and melt like wax or honey.

All that, however, concerns the atmosphere and the sensitivity of an age; in these precise figural accents the translation into Venetian of the intransigent mannerisms of the court of Constantinople has not succeeded in creating poetry. Perhaps mosaics, in a few rare cases, accomplish this better. Here, however, the cultural reality of Venice, together with its technical debt, prevented any real linguistic break with Byzantium, which had been vital to it. The hazards of distortion are borne out today in the translation of a text: it is not approximation that we should expect.

Note: We asked Sergio Bettini for permission to publish this essay, written some time ago, because the analysis provided and the views expressed seem to us to have retained their validity.

History of the treasury of San Marco

Guido Perocco

The treasures of San Marco were kept inside the basilica, which was also the chapel of the doge, the supreme authority in Venice. The spiritual care of San Marco was entrusted to the *primicerio* (principal priest), to whom it fell to nominate the canons, sacristans and under-sacristans, and to the procurators of San Marco, upon whom the administration of the basilica devolved. The procurators appointed the under-canons, the choir master and choristers, the deacons, sub-deacons, organists and other assistants – a virtual court in the service of San Marco.

At first there was only one procurator of San Marco, then two, three, four, and sometimes even more, to carry out special tasks in accordance with the needs of the time; they belonged to the highest circles in the Republic. In particular the procurators of San Marco were entrusted with the care of the sanctuary (*Santuario*), where the sacred relics were kept, and of the treasury (*Tesoro*), where the most precious objects were, in the two rooms of the basilica in which they are still to be found today.

The most important relics of the sanctuary and the most valuable works of art in the treasury came as booty from the Fourth Crusade (1204), in the course of which the Venetians, at the side of the crusaders, who were for the most part French and German, were considered to have taken the lion's share of the spoils, a pre-arranged "quarter and a half". The division of the fabulous loot is still endlessly discussed; it is best to consult two authoritative chroniclers of the Crusade, Geoffrey de Villehardouin (*De la Conquête de Constantinople par les Français et les Vénitiens*) and Robert de Clari (*Li Estoires de chiaux qui conquisent Constantinoble...*).

Some objects were sent direct to Venice by the doge Enrico Dandolo, who died in 1205 and was buried in St Sophia itself, in a tomb still visible today in one of the galleries of the basilica.

The Venetian colony in Constantinople chose its first chief magistrate, who had as his base the monastery of the Pantocrator, one of the most famous in the city. A Venetian, Tommaso Morosini, became the first patriarch of Constantinople after the capture of the city; his seat was St Sophia.

It can easily be argued that the Venetians collected more works of art than their allies because of the number of ships at their disposal and their greater knowledge of Greek and of the Constantinopolitan market. Even the celebrated four horses of San Marco reached Venice as the spoils of war from the Fourth Crusade of 1204. Essential information on the many vicissitudes of the relics and precious objects of San Marco is derived from some fundamental studies, among them A. Pasini's *Il Tesoro di San Marco in Venezia...*, R. Gallo's *Il Tesoro di San Marco e la sua storia*, and *Il Tesoro di San Marco e il Museo*, compiled under the direction of H.R. Hahnloser.

There was a dreadful fire in a room of the treasury in 1231. According to historians the fire burned for a considerable time, causing serious damage: only a fragment of the True Cross, spared by the fire, an ampulla containing the Blood of Christ, and a relic of St John the Baptist were saved. A mosaic of the period, in front of the door of the treasury, conjures up the scene of the fragment of the True Cross saved from the fire.

With the fall of the empire of the Latins in the East, on 15 August 1261, the city of Constantinople returned to Byzantine rule, but many Constantinopolitan works of art had reached Venice between 1204 and 1261. Baldwin II, the last Latin emperor of Constantinople, took refuge in Apulia, and then at Naples; the chief magistrate, Gradenigo, and the patriarch, Justinian, embarked for Venice, where, according to the chronicle of Marino Sanudo, they handed over to the Serenissima the furnishings of the church of the Pantocrator monastery, which had been the seat of the chief magistrate in Constantinople, and, it may be surmised, likewise those of St Sophia, which had been the seat of the patriarch.

One of the earliest inventories of the reliquaries, sacred furnishings and other precious objects was compiled in 1283 and was published by Pasini in 1885-6 as an appendix to his study of the treasury of San Marco. Another inventory, drawn up by decision of the Great Council in 1325 and also published by Pasini, gives a description of the relics and liturgical vessels and specifies where in the church they were kept. It is impossible to distinguish which of these furnishings had originally belonged to San Marco, and which, on the other hand, had come out of the churches of the imperial palaces in Constantinople or from various sovereigns as gifts to the Republic. Documents attest that precious relics were sometimes deposited in the treasury as security for important loans made by the Serenissima or by private citizens. In 1239 St Louis, the king of France, personally intervened with the Republic and paid over a considerable sum of money to secure the release of part of the Holy Crown of Thorns. Indeed it was for this famous relic that the king had built the Sainte-Chapelle in Paris. Some precious jewels also entered the treasury as pledges in connection with a large loan which the Byzantine emperor John V Palaeologos had requested from the Republic of Venice in 1343. Gallo writes that when, after many vicissitudes, the debt had not been repaid, the jewels lodged as security by the emperor were transferred by the doge to the procurators of San Marco, to be kept in the treasury. Ten of them, the most important, eventually became the property of the Republic and were exhibited on solemn feast days on the high altar of the basilica.

The robbery of the treasury by a Greek citizen, Stamati Crassiolo, is notorious, thanks to the chronicles: by patiently working at night he managed to get into the treasury and carry off many works of art and jewels. The theft was entirely successful – until Stamati spoke of the whole undertaking to a friend, and the authorities of San Marco got to know of it. The loot was recovered, and the thief was hanged between the columns of the Doges' Palace, on the side facing the Piazzetta, where infamous crimes were expiated.

It is extremely interesting to have detailed accounts of some of the processions on the piazza in front of San Marco, recorded in the journals of Marino Sanudo, which cover the years 1496 to 1533. The precious works of art, the personalities and the atmosphere are observed with sensitivity, but in a most candid and vigorous vein, as for example in the procession of the Holy League on 10 October 1511, promoted by Pope Julius II and the Venetians, in which objects from the treasury and well-known relics from the sanctuary are described with admiration (Sanudo, *Diari*, XII, cols 130-43).

The two rooms of the treasury and the sanctuary of the relics were refurbished in 1580, presumably by Jacopo Sansovino after his appointment as chief architect (*proto*) of the basilica.

Of all the inventories of the treasury, the one drawn up in 1580, at the time the basilica was visited by Cardinal Borromeo, the archbishop of Milan, is especially important. The detailed notes of the chronicles about the basilica relate the many vicissitudes of the treasury, such as the thefts of jewels, the receipt of objects as security and the rediscovery of lost or mislaid sacred furnishings.

The most important of these chronicles recall the visits of illustrious figures to the treasury, and "exhibitions" on the holiest feast-days. In the accounts of these "exhibitions" the title given to the objects and the brief descriptions which follow are always of interest. For example, there were five gold roses in the treasury, presented to the Republic by five different popes.

The fall of the Venetian Republic on 12 May 1797, brought about by the triumphant Italian campaign of Bonaparte's army, had a terrible effect on the treasury of San Marco. The financial position of the Republic had seriously deteriorated, and the victorious armies were in urgent need of funds. In accordance with directives issued by Bonaparte, the new Municipality of Venice, which had replaced the government of the doge, ordered churches to hand over the silver plate which was not absolutely essential for the religious services. Immediately afterwards came the order "to deposit in the State Mint the plate of the church of San Marco", with the exception of that ordinarily in use for the holy offices.

The decree, promulgated on 10 June 1797 (nineteen days after the deposition of the last of the doges, Lodovico Manin), demanded the immediate transfer to the Mint of the gold and silver objects in the basilica, the sacristy and the treasury. Only the relics in the sanctuary, which were not considered valuable, were left. At the same time the municipality proceeded to collect, in addition to the objects from San Marco, those of the other churches, the *Scuole*, and the religious orders in the city.

It was decided to melt down a proportion of the precious objects which had come from San Marco, a total of 535 kilogrammes, in order to obtain speedily a new supply of money. Other objects from the treasury were removed to a room in the Doges' Palace, where eight people were charged with removing all the gold and silver from vestments and other embroideries and unthreading jewels and pearls; the gold and silver were sent to the Mint to be melted down.

From the precious metal, 29,223 ducats were obtained. Precious stones and pearls were not included in this computation, which was ordered by the Committee of Public Safety, since their value could not readily be ascertained; this was finally put at three hundred thousand ducats. In January 1798 an Austrian government was installed in Venice in place of the municipality set up by Bonaparte after the fall of the Venetian Republic. On 14 February 1798 the Austrian government ordered that all surviving precious objects from the treasury of San Marco, including the precious stones and pearls which had been collected, should be taken back to the basilica.

In 1801 five precious manuscripts belonging to the treasury of San Marco were consigned to the Biblioteca Marciana (the library of San Marco); among them were the Brevario Grimani, the famous illuminated Flemish manuscript, which had been a gift to the Venetian Republic from Cardinal Domenico Grimani (1461-1523). Three of these manuscripts are to be seen in this exhibition (nos 9, 14, 20).

At the request of the canons of San Marco, 146,374 lire were received between 1798 and 1801 to reconstitute the plate which had been lost after the fall of the Republic.

On 19 January 1806, as a consequence of treaties between the Austrian and French governments, the municipality again came under French control. The following year, by decree of Napoleon, the patriarchal seat was transferred from the church of San Pietro di Castello to San Marco, which had formerly been the chapel of the doges.

On 20 April 1814, after the fall of Napoleon, Venice once more came under the government of the Austrian empire. In the meantime the government had authorized the sale of pearls and precious stones from the treasury of San Marco to enable urgent building work to be carried out in the basilica, which no longer had subventions from the doge's government for its maintenance.

In 1816, at the express wish of the Austrian emperor, Francis I, Count Leopold Cicognara, a well-known art historian and president of the Academy of Fine Arts in Venice, embarked on an inventory of the treasury. In 1820 he was asked to value the objects; he specified "that this should be determined in relation to a large number of events during the course of time, and the historical origins of the objects, taking into account the state of the arts in the various periods when they were made, and depending more than anything else on the extremely precious and rare materials from which most of the objects were made".

He counted among the most precious objects an agate ewer (no. 5), an icon of the standing St Michael (no. 19), a chalice with gadroons (no.11), and a sardonyx bowl (no. 4). In all, Count Cicognara listed 141 objects in the treasury. Some precious stones and pearls from the treasury were sold in 1819, on the authorization of the government, to pay for the needs of the basilica. In 1829 the patriarch Pietro Monico obtained permission for the works of art from the treasury to be brought back from the Mint, where they had been taken in 1816 for the purpose of drawing up the inventory, and returned to their old places in the basilica. Restoration work was carried out in these parts of the basilica, which was ready to receive the objects in 1832. Restoration work on the *Pala d'Oro* began in 1836 and continued until 1842. Many other objects in the sanctuary and the treasury were restored between 1842 and 1860.

In 1901 some rooms of the Museo Marciano were opened in upper galleries of the basilica. In these rooms are paintings, mosaics, tapestries and other notable works of art which were part of the treasury of the basilica. In 1983 the four bronze horses, which formerly appeared on the façade of the basilica, were moved into the largest room in the museum to protect them from atmospheric pollution.

Two important volumes, one devoted to the *Pala d'Oro*, published in 1965, and the other to the Museum of San Marco, published in 1971, were produced under the auspices of the Fondazione Giorgio Cini and under the direction of H.R. Hahnloser, in collaboration with scholars from a number of countries.

Catalogue

Catalogue entries written by:

D.A.: Daniel Alcouffe
Conservateur en chef du département des Objets d'art, Musée du Louvre

B.D.B.: Barbara Drake Boehm
Curatorial Assistant, Department of Medieval Art, The Metropolitan Museum of Art

K.R.B.: Katharine Reynolds Brown
Senior Research Associate, Department of Medieval Art, The Metropolitan Museum of Art

M.E.F.: Margaret English Frazer
Curator, Department of Medieval Art, The Metropolitan Museum of Art

D.G.C.: Danielle Gaborit-Chopin
Conservateur au département des Objets d'art, Musée du Louvre

C.K.: Carolyn Kane
Assistant Curator, Department of Islamic Arts, The Metropolitan Museum of Art

W.D.W.: William D. Wixom
Chairman of the Department of Medieval Art and the Cloisters, The Metropolitan Museum of Art

Catalogue compiled with the assistance of:

Jannic Durand
Conservateur au département des Objets d'art, Musée du Louvre

The authors of the catalogue acknowledge with thanks the assistance of all those who have made the work possible, particularly I. Aghion, R. Arié, F. Baratte, M. Bernus-Taylor, M. Bompaire, G. Bordin, P. Cambon, A. Erlande-Brandenburg, J.R. Gaborit, G. Gratté, J. Hein, H. Hellenkemper, M.F. Leca, N. Marin, F. Meyer, A. Pasquier, H. Pompei, N. Petit, E. Taburet, and B. Taillez.

The order adopted for this catalogue has generally been dictated by the date of the mount, where this has been added to adapt an earlier object for a new function.

Classical, Byzantine and Western hardstone-carving

Daniel Alcouffe

The collection of hardstone vessels in the treasury of San Marco is so outstanding that it should one day be used as the basis of the history of this kind of object from Classical Antiquity to the end of the Middle Ages: it contains virtually all the landmarks. For the present, however, given the uncertainties in this field caused by the rarity of examples with a secure date and place of origin, one can only put forward an attempt at a chronological classification which is sometimes purely intuitive and which will inevitably be challenged.

There are four criteria which should help in establishing the origin of a hardstone vessel: the nature of the material, certain stones having been used for a time, then disappearing because their source had become exhausted; the shape, when it can be found in other, better understood fields, such as precious metalwork or glass; its decoration, sometimes characteristic of a particular period or culture; and finally its mount, whether it is the original mount and datable, or whether it was added after the manufacture of the vessel, when it at least supplies a *terminus ante quem*.

The earliest references to hardstone vessels, in the context of the Dionysiac ceremonies organized at Alexandria by Ptolemy II Philadelphos (285-246 BC), in which onyx vessels figured, or the treasury of Mithridates VI, king of the Pontus (120-63 BC), which contained two thousand onyx vessels, show that the technique was widespread in the East in the hellenistic period. Alexandria must long have played a major role in the manufacture of these objects, as is demonstrated not only by the vessel of Ptolemy II, but also by an Egyptian subject carved on the sardonyx "Tazza Farnese" in Naples, by the gift of agate vessels to the emperor Hadrian during a journey in Egypt, and by the discovery of a treasure of eight sardonyx vessels at Qift, in Egypt, in 1930 (Engelbach 1931). But in the first century BC the taste for this kind of product reached Rome, where, since cameos and intaglios were being carved, vessels were probably made as well. The discovery in Rome of two treasures containing agate and rock-crystal vessels, one in 1544 in the tomb of the empress Maria, who died in 407 (Rossi 1863), and the other in 1545, on the Esquiline Hill (Huelsen 1898), perhaps provides the evidence. The materials used in Classical Antiquity were agate (most frequently sardonyx) and rock-crystal. Vessels were entirely monolithic, their handles and bases carved from the same block of stone as the body of the vessel. There was therefore no need for the addition of a mount, although even as early as this a vessel could be enhanced with precious metalwork, as is a sardonyx flask in the Cleveland Museum of Art, which still has its gold mount (Cooney 1965, 45-6).

It is possible to attribute to the first century BC or the first century AD a number of vessels with shapes reminiscent of those of precious metalwork of that period; the quality of their workmanship has rarely been equalled since. The cutting is very thin (walls only two to four millimetres thick); the handles can be formed of scrolls inspired by plant forms, while the bases often consist only of a simple shallow flat ring (figs 10 d, 10 e). While raised relief decoration is not very common, except on the cameo vessels in sardonyx, the bodies of this group of vessels are sometimes decorated with intaglio (sunk) motifs (fig. 10 g). These vessels are spectacularly represented in San Marco by a sardonyx bowl with handles (no. 10). It was eventually transformed into a chalice in Byzantium, by the addition of a mount bearing an inscription alluding to one of the Byzantine emperors named Romanos. The agate bowl of another Byzantine chalice, that of Sisinnios (no. 23), could well have come from the same artistic background.

The sardonyx bowl of a second chalice bearing the name Romanos (no. 11), like that used in a cruet (no. 35), appears to be later. A sardonyx flask in Munich (fig. 35 d), decorated with fillets as is the bowl incorporated in the cruet, has on either side two leaves cut in intaglio, in line with the decorative principles seen on vessels contemporary with the Romanos chalice with handles; other vessels decorated with fillets, however (figs 35 a, 35 b), have thick walls which set them apart from these. It is essentially on iconographic grounds that two lamps (nos 2, 3) and the "Grotto of the Virgin" (no. 8) are attributed to Late Antiquity (the fourth and fifth centuries); relief decoration seems to take on more importance during this period. The last two objects are also both thick-walled. This thickness is accentuated in a sardonyx bowl (no. 4) with characteristics also found in two other items in the treasury (figs 4 a, 4 b), all three copying – though distorting – vessels of the same period as the chalice with handles. Their handles, carved from the same piece of stone as the body of the vessel, still link them to Classical Antiquity, but they are technically much less accomplished.

Following the example of the Graeco-Roman culture, the Persian empire of the Sasanids (226-651) became famous in the field of hardstone-carving. The engraving of stones was practised there, and also the production of vessels, as is shown by the famous bowl, said to have belonged to Chosroes and dating from the end of the fifth century or the beginning of the sixth, from the treasury of Saint-Denis (Montesquiou-Fezensac and Gaborit-Chopin, 1977, pl. 46), and by two oval bowls in the Department of Oriental Antiquities in the Louvre, found at Susa, one in rock-crystal (Ghirshman 1962, 222) and the other in green jasper. Because of its shape, a sardonyx ewer in the Pitti Palace (fig. 5 c) has also been attributed to a Sasanian craftsman; a ewer in San Marco (no. 5) is possibly a seventh-century Byzantine work inspired by just such a model.

Substantial numbers of Classical hardstone vessels survive all over the world. In contrast, for examples of Byzantine hardstone-carving the treasury of San Marco constitutes the principal source. It contains a series of hardstone vessels – principally chalices – with precious metalwork mounts which are incontestably Byzantine, dating for the most part from the tenth and eleventh centuries. Some of these chalices re-use Antique bowls, but it is unlikely that they all do: other bowls have peculiarities which set them apart from Classical hardstone-carving. During the period of Iconoclasm (726-843), although it represented an artistic low-point, the traditions of craftsmanship inherited from Rome were probably not lost in Byzantium. This is why, during the reigns of the Macedonian emperors (867-1056), the "Macedonian Renaissance" – inspired by Classical Antiquity – found expression not only in manuscript-illumination, ivory and glass, but also in hardstone-carving: engraved stones, and vessels. During this period Classical hardstone objects were certainly in great demand, to be used for sacred purposes, as in the case of the two chalices of the emperor Romanos, the chalice of Sisinnios and a rock-crystal lamp (no. 2). Side by side with this re-use and adaptation, however, although no text mentions it, there developed actual manufacture. It is known that the Macedonian emperors liked to give hardstone objects to foreign rulers: the gold-mounted rock-crystal presented to Louis the German in 872 by Basil I, the onyx vase given to Hugh, the king of Italy, in 926 by Romanos I Lecapenos (Lamm 1929-30, I, 517), and later the sardonyx cup sent to the Western emperor Henry IV by Alexis I Comnenos (1081-1118; Ebersolt 1923, 84). Production flourished from the tenth century, as is shown by the mounts of works in San Marco as well as by two sardonyx bowls of Byzantine origin on the ambo presented by the Ottonian emperor Henry II to the palace chapel at Aachen at the beginning of the eleventh century (fig. 43f; Schnitzler 1957, pls 110-1).

Byzantine hardstone vessels are, like Classical vessels, mostly of agate – particularly sardonyx. The treasury of San Marco also contains a green jasper chalice (Hahnloser 1971, no. 52, pl. L). In contrast, rock-crystal, which was used in Islam at this time (cf. nos 30-32), hardly seems to have penetrated the Byzantine empire (v. no. 8). Sardonyx was being used for the last time in the manufacture of large-scale hardstone objects: it was to disappear, probably in the eleventh or twelfth century, since from then on craftsmen had to use less beautiful and less precious stone, even for objects as exquisite as the chalice and incense-boat in the exhibition (nos 42-43).

It is difficult to establish a chronology for the vessels which appear to be Byzantine. It seems that, from the tenth century, some objects could be of high quality (e.g. no. 16) while others, no doubt from different workshops, were clumsier (e.g. no. 15). In a general way, Byzantine hardstone-carving, compared with that of Classical Antiquity, shows a decline in craftsmanship. The productions are often thicker-walled than those made around the beginning of the Christian era. Sometimes the insides of vessels have not been smoothed. Less daring, the craftsmen no longer made the objects entirely out of one piece, but finished them off with separate mounts. Some vessels, however, have a small base copying the foot-rings of Classical Antiquity; in these cases the underside of the base of the vessel is no longer flat, but concave. Very often, though, the foot is of precious metalwork. Likewise, when the chalice has handles, these have not been carved from the stone but furnished from precious metal. The surface of the vessel is without decoration, except in a few cases where the body is incised all round with large juxtaposed features, as in the three agate bowls in the Pitti Palace, one of which still has its silver-gilt Byzantine chalice mount (Heikamp 1974, nos 15-7, figs 32, 34-5).

The objects in the treasury (nos 42, 43), however, suggest that the craft of Byzantine stone-carvers – at least in one of their workshops – evolved to the point where they were mastering anew the technique of relief decoration and cutting handles from the same piece of stone as the body of the vessel. Production, however, seems to have stopped after 1204, if not before.

The shapes, less varied than in Classical Antiquity, whether the objects were for sacred or secular use, included round and oval bowls, with plain or gadrooned bodies (no. 43), vessels in the shape of truncated cones (no. 15) and even, apparently, bowls in the shape of shells, with or without gadroons, like sardonyx bowls in San Marco (Hahnloser 1971, no. 91, pl. LXXI), at Aachen (Schnitzler 1957, pl. 111), in the Louvre (fig. 43e) and in the *Schatzkammer* in Munich (Thoma and Brunner 1964, no. 39).

The treasury of San Marco also bears witness to Western crystal-carving in the later Middle Ages. Perhaps under the influence of the Eastern objects which, after the sack of Cairo in 1062 and then that of Constantinople in 1204, reached Western Europe, where they were re-used (e.g. nos 32, 37), hardstone-carving was revived at the end of the twelfth century. It first appeared in the Rhine-Maas region, as Hahnloser has shown (1966, 1973). At first only rock-crystal was worked, but between the thirteenth and fifteenth centuries jasper, agate and amethyst were introduced. Western hardstone-carvers at first devoted themselves to liturgical objects, all types of which gradually appeared in rock-crystal. But the needs of worship, particularly from the fourteenth century on, had to compete with the secular demands of princely patrons.

Western crystals were initially always convex; later on the craftsmen succeeded in working flat surfaces. On a cross in the treasury at Scheldewindeke, mounted around 1170-80, and on a contemporary cross in San Marco (exh. cat. *Rhein und Maas*, 1972, no. G24; Hahnloser 1971, no. 141, pl. CXIX), only the upper arm of the former and the two transverse arms of the latter are cut into six facets; these are still convex. In contrast, the facets have become flat on two panel-reliquaries in the treasury of the priory of Oignies at Namur, which were mounted in the second third of the thirteenth century (Courtoy 1951-2, nos XX-XXI, figs 60-1). Technical progress continued into the fourteenth century: surfaces were no longer only plain or faceted but could be enlivened in intaglio or in relief, as on a bowl with wavy gadroons (no. 45), and there was a revival of the practice of carving handles and base from the same block of stone as the body of a vessel.

Two centres of production seem to stand out from the end of the thirteenth century onwards: Paris and Venice. Here the presence of crystal-carvers is attested at the end of the reign of St Louis (1214-70) and in 1284 respectively (Hahnloser 1956). A pair of candlesticks (nos 38-39), the mounts of which appear to be Venetian, and the bowl with wavy gadroons (no. 45), so close to certain pieces from the Valois collections, perhaps bear witness to the qualities of each of these two centres.

1

Glass *situla* with Dionysiac scene

Made in Rome or Alexandria, 4th century(?)
Glass, silvered bronze. *Height* 203 mm, *overall max. width* 192 mm

Tesoro, no. 123 (listed in the 1325 inventory: III, no. 10)

Slightly conical in form, the *situla* of dark purple-blue glass is cut in deep intaglio with images from the Dionysiac festivities. One group of figures shows Ariadne (?) holding a *thyrsus* and offering a cup of wine to the nude Dionysus, shown leaning on a pillar behind which is a crouching panther. To the left of Dionysus is a shepherd bearing a cup and crook. To the right of Ariadne a shepherd pursues a maiden, and a pan holding a flute pursues a maiden dressed in a long flowing gown. Bunches of grapes and vine tendrils form a *semé* ground. A bead-and-reel border runs along the top of the frieze, and bunches of grapes, fish and pearls contained by stylized acanthus branches form the lower border. Although a large part of the base is missing, the remains of a carved rosette on the underside are evident. Four silvered bronze buttons, each with an engraved rosette, secure the handle of the bucket to the sides. The center of the silvered bronze handle is marked by a bead-and-reel motif. Volbach has noted that the portrayal of shepherds pursuing maidens refers specifically to lines 391 ff. in Book IV of Ovid's *Metamorphoses* – the source for the celebration of the Dionysiac *thiasos* – in which the daughters of Minyas, who had refused to take part in the Dionysiac festivities, flee from the god and his entourage.

The depth of the carving of this piece led Molinier to compare it to the *diatreta* vessels. Indeed, although the technique is the opposite, there are similarities among some of these pieces. For instance, both the *situla* with hunting scenes, also in the treasury of San Marco (fig. 1a; Hahnloser 1971, no. 13) and the Lycurgus Cup in the British Museum (fig. 1b) likewise have a rosette carved on the base. Although not glass, the "Rubens Vase" (fig. 2e) in the Walters Art Gallery, Baltimore, which is closely akin to the Lycurgus Cup, has a similar rosette on the base. Furthermore, in general style and iconography, the Lycurgus scene on the British Museum cup has been compared to this *situla* (Harden and Toynbee 1959, 201). Whereas the *situla* with hunting scenes is thought to be sixth to seventh century in date, the Rubens Vase and the Lycurgus Cup are thought to have been made around 400 (exh. cat. *Age of Spirituality*, 1977-8, no. 313, and *Masterpieces of Glass*, 1968, no. 100). Both a fourth-century date and a sixth-century date have been proposed for this Dionysiac *situla*. Albizzati, in the pioneer study of this piece, placed it in the fourth – fifth centuries (Albizzati 1923, 51-63).

No comparable Antique glass vessel cut in intaglio has come down to us, but traditionally this bucket has been attributed to Alexandria or Rome in the fourth century. Such conclusions have been reached in the convincing studies by Fremersdorf (1951, 24) and Harden and Toynbee (1959, 59). These conclusions have been reiterated by Coche de la Ferté (1962, 33) and von Saldern (1969). The closest fragment appears to be that of a cup from Begram in the Musée Guimet (fig. 1c), on the basis of which Coche de la Ferté placed the *situla* in fourth-century Alexandria (1962, 33). One can also compare the *situla* to fragments in the Ray Winfield Smith collection. These are thought to be third – fourth century in date and Eastern Mediterranean in origin (fig. 1d; exh. cat. *Glass from the Ancient World*, 1957, nos 359, 360, 367). In the absence of a technically comparable complete piece of glass, this piece has been compared in style and iconography to works in other media, especially of silver. For example, the poses of individual figures have been aptly compared to the rendering of individual figures on the fourth-century Oceanus dish from the Mildenhall Treasure (fig. 1e; Harden and Toynbee 1959, 201). The spacing of the figures and resulting rhythm are also comparable on the two pieces, as is the combination of marine iconography with that of the Dionysiac *thiasos*. Although the style is quite different, the same iconographic combination is found on the late fifth – early sixth-century silver vase in Cleveland (fig. 1f; exh. cat. *Age of Spirituality*, 1977-8, no. 131). Most recently, Volbach has suggested a late sixth to early seventh-century Byzantine origin for the piece (Hahnloser 1971, no. 14), pointing out the manneristic design, which is comparable to Byzantine silver of the seventh century. In his study of the series of renaissances of the Classical tradition as seen in silver and ivories from the fourth to seventh centuries, Volbach notes that the Heraclian Renaissance is characterized by the reduction of space to a single plane and clearly recognizable Classical prototypes which have lost their meaning (1962, 31-2). This glass bucket with its *semé* ground may well be a candidate for the Heraclian Renaissance, but there seem to be too many analogies with earlier pieces to renounce the traditional fourth-century Roman or Alexandrian attribution.

K. R. B.

Bibliography: La Mottraye 1727, 72, pl. VI. Pasini 1885-6, 100, no. 2, pl. LIII, fig. 121. Molinier 1888, 97, no. 111. Albizzati 1923, 51-63. Fremersdorf 1951, 24. Harden and Toynbee 1959, 201. Coche de la Ferté 1962, 33. Grabar 1966b, 320, figs 376-7. Gallo 1967, 270, no. 10; 299, no. 61; 322; 352, no. 71; pl. 60. Saldern 1969, 124-32. Philippe 1970, 132. Hahnloser 1971, no. 14 (Volbach), pls XI-XII.

1a

1b

1c

1d

2

Rock-crystal lamp with marine life

Stonework: 4th century. *Metalwork*: Byzantine, 10th–12th century
Rock-crystal, silver-gilt, glass. *Height* 62 mm, *length* 138 mm (211 mm with
mount), *width* 112 mm (178 mm with mount)

Tesoro, no. 50

Identification of this object in the old inventories is uncertain before an 1801 valuation of the contents of the treasury, where it can be recognized from the description: "*1 Pezzo Cristal intagliato a Pesce fornito d'arg[ent]o*" (Gallo 1967, 361, no. 188). Cicognara, in a catalogue of the treasury compiled between 1816 and 1820, rather surprisingly interpreted it as the lid of a lost vessel, mounted in copper-gilt ("*Coperchio di qualche antico vaso di cristallo con rilievi che rappresentano pesci e conchiglie, montato in rame dorato*") and valued it at only 50 lire (Gallo 1967, 373, no. 17); even at that time there was only one piece of glass left on the mount. Pasini later recognized the object as a lamp but mistook the rock-crystal for glass.

The oval bowl of rock-crystal is carved in one piece with ten marine animals in very high relief, almost in the round, engraved with parallel grooves. The craftsman made his task more difficult by hollowing out the motifs and even partly cutting away the junction between some of them and the body of the bowl. Of the ten animals seven are distributed over the body of the lamp: the shell of a hermit-crab, two fish detached from the back behind

2a

2c

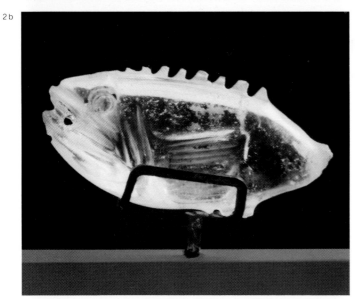

2b

2e

2d

84

the tail and all detached from the vessel at one or more points, four less easily identifiable animals (a dolphin, possibly, two crabs or jelly-fish, and what could be another – broken – fish). The other three motifs, perhaps shells, now damaged, are decorated with ovoid hollows and could have served as feet.

The bowl is not without parallel. The Metropolitan Museum of Art, New York, possesses half a rock-crystal bowl in the shape of a ship, found at Carthage (fig. 2a; Bühler 1973, no. 115b, pl. 39). This bowl, which may have been a lamp (cf. no. 3), also has fish and shells in relief, engraved with parallel grooves, but the motifs are not hollowed out and are in much lower relief than on the San Marco bowl. The decoration is also reminiscent of the fish, shells and insects carved in the round in hardstone, usually rock-crystal, which were possibly used in some Roman game and still survive in considerable numbers (e.g. Paris, Musée de Cluny, fig. 2b; London, British Museum, cf. Walters 1926, 371-2, nos 3971-85). While it is difficult to say where the San Marco bowl was made, it would seem possible to date it by following Volbach. A group of interrelated glass vessels deeper than the bowl in Venice has the same relief decoration of fish and shells distributed over the surfaces. One of the group, in the Vatican, rests on three feet in the form of shells – as the San Marco vessel might have done – and dates, on the evidence of its findspot in Rome, from the end of the fourth century. Another example, in the Rheinisches Landesmuseum at Trier, was found in a fourth-century cemetery near Trier (Kisa 1908, 768-9, figs 314-314a). In the Römisch-Germanisches Museum in Cologne are two vessels of this type: one comes from a fourth-century sarcophagus in Cologne, while the other (fig. 2c) again has three feet in the form of marine animals (Doppelfeld 1966, 61, pls 142-3). M.H. Hellenkemper points out that a similar vase is to be found in the Magyar Nemzeti Museum in Budapest (fig. 2d). It could be assumed that the adoption of this style of ornament on rock-crystal objects preceded its use in the more industrial medium of glass. Be that as it may, these comparisons allow the San Marco bowl to be dated to the fourth century. The workmanship and style of the decoration can also be found in the almost contemporary "Rubens Vase" in the Walters Art Gallery, Baltimore (fig. 2e), which exhibits the same pronounced and undercut relief, as well as the same naturalism.

The presence of the fish would tend to suggest a Christian origin for the bowl: it has been proposed that the glass bowls mentioned above could have been chalices (Cabrol and Leclercq 1907-58, II/2, cols 1604-5). However, the transparency of the rock-crystal could have been enough to inspire the marine subjects. Aquatic scenes were to reappear in the sixteenth century, engraved on rock-crystal vessels.

The rim of the bowl was subsequently slightly damaged, and it may have been to conceal this that the crystal was provided with a metal mount, apparently Byzantine, which transformed the object into a lamp. The mount comprises a wide silver-gilt flange, secured by tongues around the outside of the bowl; beaded wire runs round the inside and outside of the flange on its upper and lower faces. The lower face had six glass cabochons in collets surrounded by beaded wire: the only one of them to survive is an imitation of a sapphire or of lapis lazuli. The mount has eight candle-holders, surrounded by beaded wire at their bases, and four handles for suspension. A Byzantine agate paten in the treasury of San Marco has a similar silver-gilt border surrounded by beaded wire (fig. 2f; Hahnloser 1971, no. 71, pl. LX).

D. A.

Bibliography: Pasini 1885-6, 75, pl. LIV, fig. 123. Molinier 1888, 97-8, no. 112. Gallo 1967, 361, no. 188; 373, no. 17; pl. 62, fig. 106. Hahnloser 1971, no. 8 (Volbach), pl. IV. Bühler 1973, 79, no. 116.

2 f

3

Rock-crystal lamp in the shape of a fish

Probably 5th century
Rock-crystal, silver-gilt. *Height* 55 mm, *length* 311 mm, *width* 177 mm

Tesoro, no. 84

The function of this object long remained forgotten. The 1571 inventory of the treasury lists it as "*Una galia de Cristal de montagna desfornita*" (Gallo 1967, 301, no. 115). It then appeared in the 1733 inventory as "*Un ovato grande forato all'intorno e concavo nel mezo*" (Gallo 1967, 353, no. 114) and in the 1801 valuation of the treasury as "*Un pezzo Crestal forato, fatto a copano* [boat]" (Gallo 1967, 362, no. 214). It was valued at 500 lire in Cicognara's catalogue of the treasury, started in 1816 (Gallo 1967, 372, no. 9).

The lamp, in the general shape of a fish, was cut from a crystal of indifferent quality. The hollow boat-shape of the centre is emphasized by a protruding central ridge running the length of the exterior. The boat-shape is surrounded by a flat border, pierced in nine places for candles or lamps; the triangular tail is bevelled along its upper edges. Four silver-gilt suspension-rings are fixed into the crystal.

The piece is remarkable for its thickness, as well as for the quality of its workmanship, the originality of its design (Classical and Byzantine hanging-lamps are usually circular) and the boldness of its stylization. It is probably not a Byzantine work of the Macedonian period, as Middle Byzantine craftsmen hardly ever used rock-crystal (cf. no. 8). The object was cut from a block of substantial size. The treasury of San Marco contains a number of lamps which are probably Byzantine, but which are made of glass (cf. no. 24). The iconography (the use of the fish), like the technique, suggests that the lamp was a Late Antique sanctuary-lamp. The same thickness can be found in other more or less contemporary hardstone objects in the treasury (e.g. no. 4). It is interesting, too, to compare this lamp with the fragment of a rock-crystal ship decorated with fish in the Metropolitan Museum of Art, New York, which may also have been a lamp (fig. 2a; cf. exh. cat. *Age of Spirituality*, 1977-8, no. 186). In fact, this fourth-century vessel has the same external central ridge as the San Marco lamp. Both objects are reminiscent of the gold-mounted rock-crystal lamp in the shape of a shell found in the tomb of the empress Maria, who died in 407 (Rossi 1863, 53).

D. A.

Bibliography: Pasini 1885-6, 75, pl. LIV, fig. 127. Molinier 1888, 98, no. 116. Gallo 1967, 301, no. 115; 353, no. 114; 362, no. 214; 372, no. 9. Hahnloser 1971, no. 77 (Grabar), pl. LXIV (with bibliography).

4

Sardonyx bowl with one handle

5th – 7th century (?)
Sardonyx. *Height* 150 mm, *diam.* 210 mm, *width* 280 mm

Tesoro, no. 64

This spectacular handled bowl is without doubt one of the largest works ever cut from a single block of sardonyx. Nine millimetres thick at its rim, it weighs, according to Pasini, 2.38 kilogrammes. It has a flat rim and is well-rounded on the exterior and on the interior, where the bottom is flat; the base is also flat, with a foot-ring. The outside of the handle, along the curved part, comprises two stout ribs separated by a concave depression made with a cylindrical tool.

Although the cup is of good workmanship, some technical faults are evident. On the exterior, facing the handle, there is a horizontal mark left by the cylindrical tool used for the hollowing-out process. A more serious fault is that the weight of the handle makes the cup unstable. The question arises whether the cup originally had two handles, which would appear more logical, and whether, during manufacture, an accident prevented the execution of the second.

At some time an attempt was made to balance the cup by adding a mount. This plain silver-gilt mount (Gallo 1967, 367, no. 27), according to Pasini, consisted of a second handle, providing a counterbalance, and a base to which it was attached. In his description, the sardonyx handle was also entirely covered with silver-gilt for reasons of symmetry; this seems to have been executed after the rest of the mount, since, if the description of the object in the 1571 inventory is to be believed, the sardonyx handle was still then visible: "*Un'altra coppa d'Agata con doi manichi, cioè uno d'Agata et l'altro d'arzento, et piede d'arzento*" (Gallo 1967, 298, no. 51). By contrast, in the 1733 inventory the bowl has two metal handles: "*Una tazza grande di nicolo orientale con manichi dorati*" (Gallo 1967, 350, no. 21). The vessel was still described as having a mount in the catalogue of the treasury started in 1816 by Cicognara, who valued it at 8000 lire; this made it the most precious item after two ewers with zoomorphic handles (no. 5; Gallo 1967, 367, no. 27). At the time of Pasini's publication, 1885-6, the mount disappeared.

The rim of the bowl has four holes pierced at even distances, this proves that at a certain stage a metal rim had been mounted that was never mentioned in the old descriptions. This vessel relater closely another two-handled bowl in the treasury of San Marco, carred from a single block of sardonyx; this was mounted in Venice in the thirteenth century to serve, possibly, as a chalice (fig. 4b; Hahnloser 1971, no. 60, pl. LII). Despite what might be thought of them, the two vessel, each carved from a

single block of sardonyx and innocent of a Byzantine mount, cannot be considered tenth or eleventh-century Byzantine work. The shapes of the vessels, and particularly the designs of their handles, derive from Classical hardstone bowls, notably represented in the treasury of San Marco by the chalice of the emperor Romanos (no. 10). The foot-ring of the one-handled bowl is a characteristic feature of hardstone vessels of this period, on which it is more discreet (cf. fig. 10 e). In some ways the workmanship of the two pieces betrays a certain hesitancy in comparison with the works of Classical Antiquity. The contours of the one-handled bowl and the related "chalice" are regular, to be sure, but they have a notable thickness. Above all, the handles of the two vessels are very clumsy by comparison with those of vessels like the Romanos chalice. The intricacies of the pierced handles of the latter are recalled by two holes pierced through the upper part of the handles of the "chalice" (fig. 4 b). The handles of the Romanos chalice and comparable vessels of the same period spring from the rim of the vessel and not from below it as do those on the one-handled cup and the related "chalice". The same defect can be found on another sardonyx bowl in the treasury, flat and very much smaller (fig. 4 a; Hahnloser 1971, no. 6, pl. III). These latter vessels fit chronologically between those of Classical Antiquity and those of the Macedonian Renaissance, but it is impossible to be sure whether they are Late Antique works or imitations, made in Byzantium before the tenth century, of Classical vessels.

D. A.

Bibliography: Pasini 1885-6, 60-1, no. 92, pl. XLIV. Molinier 1888, 93, no. 79. Gallo 1967, 298, no. 51; 350, no. 21; 367, no. 27; pl. 58, fig. 100. Hahnloser 1971, no. 90 (Grabar), pl. LXXI.

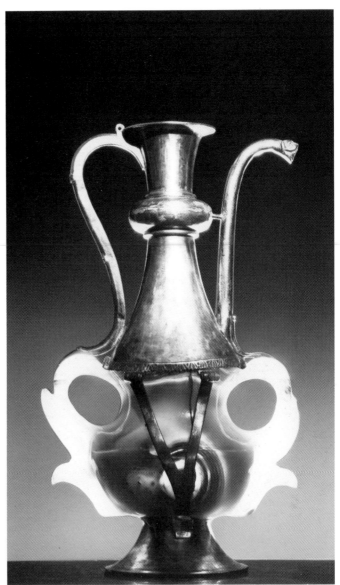

5

Agate ewer with zoomorphic handle

Byzantine, 7th century (?)
Agate. *Height* 250 mm, *diam.* 160 mm

The ewer is cut from a single block of agate dappled all over with concentric zones. The mouth with a prominent pouring-lip surmounts a neck in the form of a truncated cone, marked at the bottom by a projecting rounded moulding. The ovoid body terminates in a base, the concave underside of which is surrounded by a flat rim. The handle is an elongated animal (a lion?), the tail of which extends over the body of the ewer.

The vessel is very like a sardonyx ewer in the treasury (fig. 5a; Hahnloser 1971, no. 11, pl. VIII), with the same characteristics except that it has a rounded rim without a pouring-lip, and a solid base.

The two ewers seem to figure in the 1325 inventory as "*Vascula duo, unum de calcedonio, alterum de sardonia, inornata, sine auro et argento*" (Gallo 1967, 278, III, no. 17). The 1571 inventory mentions "*un vaso de Calcidonia con manico intagliato*" and "*un vaso de Cameo con manico intagliato*" (Gallo 1967, 298, nos 52-3). The two vessels can be found again in 1678: "*un vaso di cameo*" and "*un vaso di Calcidonia*" (Gallo 1967, 323, nos 102, 105); then in 1733: "*un vaso di sardonica con bocchino e manico d'un solo pezzo*" and "*un vaso di nicolo orientale con manico tutto d'un pezzo*" (Gallo 1967, 352, nos 69, 72). In Cicognara's 1816 catalogue of the treasury the two pieces are given the highest valuations, 12,000 lire apiece (Gallo 1967, 369, nos 36-7).

They are impressive works, remarkable not only for their size but also for the beauty of the stone and for the extraordinary skill which went into the carving of the zoomorphic handles from the same block as the body. Yet both these thick-walled vessels have technical faults. On the agate ewer the moulding is higher on one side of the body than on the other, the part of the body facing the handle was cut flat during the hollowing-out process, and the axis of the handle is out of line with that of the vessel. The contour of the body is, however, more regular than that of the other ewer, which is flat on one side, although its moulding is better produced.

The two vessels are related to two sardonyx ewers in the Louvre, which have a similar appearance and, specifically, a high neck, the same thickness and the same hesitant workmanship, which has given them handles also slightly askew. On one of them, formerly in the collection of Louis XIV (fig. 5b), the lip is prominent, and the underside of the base is concave, as on the San Marco agate ewer. The second is the famous ewer mounted in the twelfth century for Abbot Suger of Saint-Denis (fig. 35e; cf. Montesquiou-Fezensac and Gaborit-Chopin, 1977, pl. 22). On both these vessels the project-

ing moulding of the San Marco ewers is replaced by a marked dislocation of neck and body.

Other objects appear to be prototypes or models for the ewers in Venice. The sardonyx ewer in the Pitti Palace, from the collection of Lorenzo de' Medici (fig. 5c; Heikamp 1974, no. 11, pl. II), has a wide and flat rim with no lip, like that of the sardonyx ewer in Venice. Like the San Marco ewers it has a neck of truncated cone shape, a rounded moulding, an ovoid body and a zoomorphic handle close to the examples in Venice. The ewer in Florence can be related to three sardonyx vessels with no lips or handles (the latter having possibly been removed), on the grounds of a general similarity of shape. One is in the Victoria and Albert Museum (fig. 5d; Lightbown 1978, 1-3, no. 1). Two were transformed into ewers in the seventeenth century by gold and enamel mounts: one, in the Louvre, from the collection of Louis XIV (fig. 5e), still has the remains of a spout, while the other, in the Kunsthistorisches Museum in Vienna (fig. 5f) has had its moulding cut away except for the section to which the handle is attached.

The ewer in Florence is generally regarded as an example of Sasanian art, of which the most brilliant periods were the third and fourth and the seventh centuries. Its general appearance, with a neck in the shape of a truncated cone separated from an ovoid body by a small "cushion", can certainly be found in Sasanian silver vessels. Zoomorphic handles are common in Persian art, even in the Achaemenid period. The ewer can be compared with one of Sasanian silver in the Cleveland Museum of Art (fig. 5g), which has a handle in the form of a panther, or with a bronze Sasanian ewer in the Victoria and Albert Museum (M. 27-1945), where the handle is an elongated monster. Lamm (1929-30, I, 189) also draws attention to the leopard handles on two fourth-century gold cups from the Pietroasa treasure in Bucharest, the technique of which is similar to that of the Sasanian cup said to have belonged to Chosroes (end of the fifth or early sixth century; Paris, Bibliothèque Nationale; Montesquiou-Fezensac and Gaborit-Chopin 1977, pl. 46). But the Roman world also supplied examples of zoomorphic handles, the elongated hare on a Late Antique silver ewer in the Louvre (Inv. Bj 2254), for instance, or the fragment of an agate handle in the Römisch-Germanisches Museum in Cologne depicting a sea-horse attacked by a tiger (fig. 5h; Bühler 1973, no. 79, pl. 25).

The objects grouped round the ewer in Florence, a little thicker-walled than the vessels of Classical Antiquity, have nevertheless preserved qualities of technique and

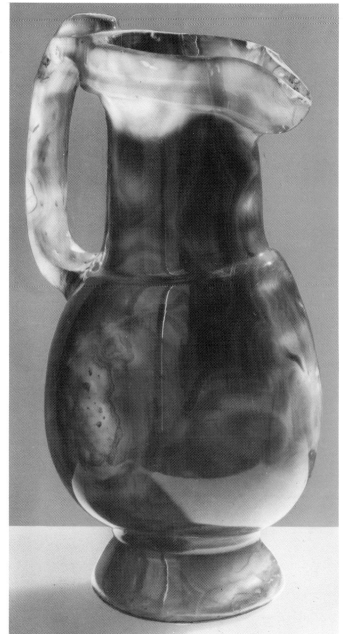

are superior in workmanship to the ewers in Venice, which they must have inspired. The latter are without doubt later than the first group, which are Sasanian or at least date from the Late Antique period. The presence of a prominent pouring lip – a characteristic trait of ewers made by Sasanian silversmiths – on two of the pieces from the second group (to which the ewer on exhibition belongs) would, however, tend to strengthen the case for a Persian origin for the earlier group of vessels. The objects of the second group share with Antique vessels the characteristic of having been worked entirely from one block, and cannot therefore be dated long after the first group. It is unlikely that they originated in Persia, as there is no comparable Oriental work showing a decline of technique in this area. In the present state of knowledge, the most attractive hypothesis, put forward by Volbach, is that they are Byzantine works of the seventh century. The influence of Sasanian art on Byzantine art of this period, contemporary with the looting of King Chosroes II's treasury in 628 by the Byzantine emperor Heraclius, argues for this.

D. A.

Bibliography: Pasini 1885-6, 94, no. 120, pl. LII. Molinier 1888, p. 97, no. 109. Lamm 1929-30, I, 189-90. Gallo 1967, 278, III, no. 17; 298, no. 52; 323, no. 103; 352, no. 69; 369, no. 37; pl. 57, fig. 98. Hahnloser 1971, no. 12 (Volbach), pl. IX. Heikamp 1974, 108-11 (with bibliography).

5h

5g

6

Marble *ciborium* with Greek inscription

Constantinopolitan, 6th century(?)
Marble. *Height* 630 mm, *width* 430 mm, *depth* 445 mm

Tesoro, no. 12 (transferred to the treasury in 1885 from one of the upper rooms in San Marco)

The object is cut from a single block of white marble. The dome is supported on four round arches resting on small columns. A broad concave leaf is carved in each of the four angles between the arches. The columns have capitals with leaf-ornament and bases with multiple mouldings. The two rear columns, which are shorter, stand on a small parapet, which is cut back under its base. The whole rests on a square platform cut from the same block. On the underside of the dome is a central pierced projection from which an object could be suspended.

An inscription in Greek capitals runs round the face of the left-hand and front arches: +ΥΠΕΡ ΕΥΧΗΣ Κ[ΑΙ] ϹΩΤΗΡΙΑϹ ΤΗϹ ΕΝΔΟΞΟΤΑΤΗϹ ΑΝΑϹΤΑϹΙΑϹ ('Υπὲρ εὐχῆς καὶ σωτηρίας τῆς ἐνδοξοτάτης Ἀναστασίας, "In fulfilment of a vow and for the salvation of the most glorious Anastasia"). It is firmly engraved in clear and elegant letters, and the name Anastasia is written in full. It would therefore seem that the hypothesis (Bettini 1974, 46-7) which attempted to substitute for this name the word "*Anastasis*" (resurrection) has no real foundation, and that there is no justification for seeing in this object a representation of the Holy Sepulchre. On the contrary, we must conclude that, on the basis of the inscription, this curious little monument was the offering of a woman called Anastasia, who, very probably, on the basis of the title she is given, was an aristocratic lady at the Byzantine court.

The form of the monument is that of a *ciborium*, a baldachino intended to shelter the eucharistic altar; it can be compared to the large *ciborium* supported by carved columns inside the basilica of San Marco, above the high altar. The practice of sheltering the altar under a baldachino is attested in the pagan cults of Antiquity, and it is possible to compare the small *ciborium* in Venice with that represented on a stele in the museum at Bourges (third – fourth century), where the use of palmettes in the decoration of the corners above the capitals can again be found (Cabrol and Leclercq, III/2, "*ciborium*", col. 1593, fig. 2918). The Anastasia *ciborium* could have been placed on an altar to house a pyx: the balustrade and the shorter columns clearly differentiate a front and back, while the part of the base cut away at the back shows that the object was intended to fit against another element. The pierced projection on the underside of the dome, according to Pasini, could have served for the suspension of a eucharistic dove.

The multiple mouldings at the base of the columns ex-clude a particularly late date. The form of the capitals suggests comparison with those on sixth-century works, notably ivories: their decorative character, formed by two stylized leaves emphasized by two volutes, under a moulded abacus ornamented with rosettes, is of the same type as the capitals carved on the ivory diptych of Christ and the Virgin in Berlin, dated to the middle of the sixth century (Volbach 1976, no. 173, pl. 71). The style of the *ciborium* therefore fully supports a date in the sixth century; the style of the letters of the inscription can be found on objects of this period, and so it would seem quite reasonable to accept the often proposed hypothesis identifying the donor of the *ciborium* with the noble lady Anastasia (d. 558) recorded at the court of Justinian.

D.G.C.

Bibliography: Rohault de Fleury 1883, II, fig. 2918. Pasini 1885-6, 70, no. 60 A, pl. XXXIV a. Molinier 1888, no. 48. Gallo 1967, pl. 27, fig. 47. Hahnloser 1971, no. 9 (Volbach), pl. V (with bibliography). Bettini 1974, 46-7.

7

Throne-reliquary (the *Sedia di San Marco*)

Eastern Mediterranean (Alexandria?), 6th century
Alabaster. *Height* 1470 mm, *width* 550 mm, *depth* 530 mm

Tesoro, no. 8 (transferred in 1534 to the Baptistry from behind the high altar)

The throne of light-grey alabaster is characterized by a high back from the upper part of which narrow arms decline steeply. Setting aside the disk at the top of the back, the general shape of the *Sedia* is reminiscent of many Late Antique seats; it is closest of all to sixth-century chairs with arm-rests, like Maximian's ivory throne in Ravenna (before 553) or the seats represented on ivories of this period (in an Annunciation on a diptych-leaf in Moscow; in an Annunciation on Maximian's throne, ·fig. 7a; in an Adoration of the Magi on a pyx in the Bargello; Volbach 1976, nos 130, 140, 171). The absence of feet to raise the San Marco *Sedia*, an absence seen in the earliest examples, could be an archaism. The decoration of chevrons, rods, and "grilles" is probably a transposition into stone of the decoration of wood or wickerwork chairs (cf. Grabar 1954a).

The disk at the top of the back is fairly uncommon; it occurs, however, on some medieval stone thrones: that of St Jeremiah at Saqqâra (sixth century), that in Santa Maria in Cosmedin in Rome (dated 1123), and the later throne at Anagni. There does not seem to be any justification for regarding the disk as a later addition: the stone from which it is cut is similar to that of the rest of the throne, the join between the top of the back and the base of the disk is irregular and looks like a break, and the carved decoration, although executed with a little less care than the rest of the throne, is of the same workmanship. The chair was therefore originally carved from a single block, the upper part having subsequently broken off and been very clumsily re-attached.

The *Sedia* is decorated all over with relief-carving. The front of the seat has a chevron pattern. The inside of the back, within a four-part moulding, has a representation of the Lamb of God at the foot of a leafy tree (a sycamore?), from the roots of which flow four rivers. On the disk above, which is set between volutes (that on the left broken), two nimbed figures flank a chevroned cross with flared ends and surmounted by a disk; from the base of the cross flow two streams. The left-hand figure holds a book and supports the cross, while the other presses a book to his body and holds in his left hand what is more likely to be a *mappa* than a fold of his garment. The same motif is repeated on the back of the disk, the only differences being that only the upper part of the cross is flared, and the left-hand figure does not hold the cross. Below, on the outside of the back of the *Sedia*, against a background strewn with stars, are the eagle and the lion, the symbols of the evangelists John and Mark,

each with three pairs of wings. A crescent moon (?) is carved above the wings of the eagle; a small tree, similar to that on the front, grows from an opening cut into the back near the bottom and flanked by two rods and two palm-trees. At the very bottom is a panel covered with a lozenge-pattern, resembling a grille. On the right side of the throne, against a background of stars, is a winged bull, the symbol of St Luke; above are five rods with almond-shaped ends (lighted candles?), while the grille-pattern is repeated below. On the left side of the throne, also on a star-strewn background, the man, the symbol of St Matthew, is accompanied by two angels blowing horns; at the bottom, above a grille-patterned panel, is an opening flanked by two palm-trees.

The nimbed and bearded figures supporting or standing beside the cross illustrate a known Early Christian theme (e.g. on a panel of a child's sarcophagus, about 400, Istanbul, Archaeological Museum; Grabar 1966b, fig. 257). The representation on the *Sedia* can be specifically compared with two embossed silver plaques from bookcovers (figs 7b, 7c: New York, Metropolitan Museum of Art, and a fragment in Paris, Musée du Louvre) and, above all, with a silver dish formerly in the Stroganoff collection (fig. 7e: Leningrad, Hermitage) where, below the cross flanked by two angels, the four rivers of Paradise appear (exh. cat. *Age of Spirituality*, 1977-8, no. 555: Syria, second half of sixth century; no. 482: Constantinople, late sixth century).

Grabar has shown that the iconography of the *Sedia* forms a coherent whole, establishing parallels between the cross, the Tree of Life and the Lamb of God (the cross, "Sun of Justice", also corresponding with the crescent moon), between the evangelists and their symbols, between the Gospels and the four rivers of Paradise flowing from the Tree of Life and from the cross. The paradisaic theme (the rivers, Tree of Life) is reinforced by the presence of palm-trees. The iconography recalls Maximian's throne in Ravenna, on which representations of saints and apostles are similarly associated with the evocation of Paradise.

The *Sedia* does not appear to have been conceived as an episcopal throne; it is reminiscent of funerary chairs like those in the major cemetery of the catacomb on the via Nomentana in Rome (Fasola 1980, 86, 91). The relatively small size of its seat, which would not accommodate a stout person, would above all suggest a symbolic throne, a throne-lectern on which the Gospels were placed, recalling the empty throne of the *Hetoimasia* (cf. the empty

101

thrones and altar-lecterns depicted in the dome of the Orthodox Baptistry in Ravenna). The presence of the two openings made in the base, at the back and at the left-hand side, however, indicates that the throne was intended for another use. The opening in the back is asymmetrical, its raw upper edge encroaches on the tree carved above, and its sides do not comfortably relate to the bands or rods flanking it; it could just have been made, or at least enlarged, later. By contrast, the side-opening fits the decoration of the side of the throne perfectly and must therefore have been part of the original design. The two rectangular openings communicate with each other, opening into a large circular cavity hollowed out inside the base of the throne. There is no access to this cavity either from above or through the front panel of the seat, where a hole – now plugged – could only have been the consequence of an accident. The lateral openings and their integration into the carved decoration (at least on the side), however, show that a receptacle had been cut in the base from the very first. The *Sedia* must have rested on a base which blocked the gaping hole, which probably housed a sizable casket of relics. The two openings would have allowed this casket to be seen, and even touched; this widespread practice sanctified the *brandeae* or, again, the oil which was allowed to run over the relics, to be carefully collected. As Grabar has commented (1954a), the particular form of this reliquary makes it a representation of the "throne of the Martyrs", derived both from the custom of representing martyrs enthroned and from the cult of the thrones of the apostles or founder-saints, as well as from the rare but recorded practice of showing a throne beside the sarcophagus of a saint to evoke the "seat of honour" in Paradise promised to the faithful. In this way the paradisaic images of the *Sedia* are explained, as well as the presence of the angels of the Last Judgment beside the symbol of St Matthew (Matthew 24: 31).

Such coherence between the function of the object and its decoration militates against the hypothesis occasionally advanced (e.g. Bettini 1974) that the manufacture and decoration of the *Sedia* belong to two periods. The cross flanked by the evangelists, as we have seen, suggests comparison with the work of sixth-century silversmiths (the bookcovers in New York and Paris, and the dish in Leningrad). The iconographic type of the evangelists – seen full-face, bearded, in long robes rather summarily draped – is the same as that on contemporary ivories originating in the Eastern Mediterranean or under strong Eastern influence and related to Maximian's throne: Etchmiadzin and Saint-Lupicin bookcovers, plaques in the museum at Lyons and the Musée de Cluny (fig. 7d) and, to a lesser extent, plaques in Trier from a lost episcopal throne (Volbach 1976, nos 142, 145, 149-50, 152-4). The symbols of the evangelists, particularly the eagle with the stiffly spread tail, and the curves of their wings with the feathers wavy or rendered like fish-scales, suggest a derivation from Persian models.

It seems possible therefore to attribute the *Sedia* to a sixth-century workshop in the Eastern Mediterranean region, perhaps in Alexandria.

The reading of a Hebrew inscription, engraved retrograde across the upper part of the front of the seat, is disputed. According to Février, cited by Grabar (Hahnloser 1971, 9, no. 10), it reads: "seat of Mark the evangelist... have dedicated it". In any case the inscription is much later than the rest of the throne and was certainly added in Venice. It is, in fact, not known when the throne arrived in Venice: it is not recorded until 1534, when it was considered to be the episcopal throne of St Mark and placed, with this title, behind the high altar of the basilica. There is, however, nothing in its decoration to show that it was dedicated to this evangelist in particular, or that it sheltered his relics. It is not out of the question that it was brought from Alexandria in 828, at the same time as the relics of St Mark. Another origin for it might, however, be proposed: the church of Grado had two thrones – one of St Mark and one of St Hermagoras – mentioned in different documents (Acts of the 827 Synod of Mantua, and the tenth-century chronicle of John the Deacon: *v.* Tavano 1977). The throne of St Mark taken from Alexandria to Constantinople and offered to the Patriarch of Grado by the emperor Heraclius in 630 cannot be identified with the *Sedia*, since it was covered with ivory plaques (attested by the fifteenth-century chronicle of Giovanni Candido) and the *Sedia* could never have had decoration of this kind. According to Tavano, however, the throne of Hermagoras could equally well have been sent by Heraclius, and could have been a throne-reliquary enclosing a fragment of the True Cross. If, in spite of the strangeness of this staurotheca, this hypothesis could ever be confirmed, the throne in Venice, the iconography of which emphasizes the exaltation of the cross, could be regarded as the second throne of Grado, sent to Venice after the dissolution of the patriarchate of Grado in 1451.

D. G. C.

Bibliography: Pasini 1885-6, 105-12, pl. LXIX. Molinier 1888, 67, no. 154. Cabrol and Leclercq 1913, "chaire épiscopale", cols 49-54 (with previous bibliography). Grabar 1954 a, 19-34. Gallo 1967, pl. 27, fig. 46. Hahnloser 1971, no. 10 (Grabar, with bibliography), pls VI-VII. Tavano 1977, 445-89. Bettini, intro. to exh. cat. *Venezia e Bisanzio*, 1974, 46.

Byzantine enamels and goldsmith work

Margaret E. Frazer

The art of enameling on gold reached its greatest expression and decorative height during the Middle Ages. The Greek artist's skill in *cloisonné* enameling was unsurpassed. He alone achieved an exceptional clarity and translucence of rich coloration and a mastery in setting the gold strips (*cloisons*) that divided one color from another in intricate, finely proportioned patterns, as the works of art in this exhibition clearly show. The excellence of the Byzantine enameler was recognized throughout Europe and in the Middle East. In Italy, for example, during the mid-eleventh century, the renowned Abbot Desiderius of Monte Cassino, seeking to furnish his new church with the greatest of riches, imported numerous works of art from Byzantium, including an enameled and gemmed altar-frontal for which he paid 36 pounds of gold, according to his chronicler Leo of Ostia (*Chronicon Monasterii Casinense,* III, 32). Some fifty years later, the sumptuous *Pala d'Oro* in the basilica of San Marco was ordered from Constantinople by the doge Ordelafo Falier as part of the vast furnishings for the recently completed church. This commission took place at about the same time that Byzantine artists were setting the mosaics in the basilica's apse. Additional rich altar furnishings and liturgical vessels that have now disappeared were probably ordered from Constantinopolitan workshops or were sent as gifts of the emperor in honor of the dedication of San Marco, the ducal palace chapel.

The present collection of the San Marco treasury, however, seems to reflect acquisitions of secular and liturgical vessels of almost two centuries later. In 1231, a fire broke out in the treasury, and, judging from the inventory of 1283, only some reliquaries and fragmentary objects survived the conflagration. Later inventories of the treasury, however, show that the treasury was continuously enriched by many luxurious works of art. In spite of the vicissitudes of history, it now houses the best single collection of Byzantine metalwork, and particularly of enameling, that survives. It includes known imperial commissions, like the chalices of the emperor Romanos (nos 10, 11), and the range of its other liturgical objects, including reliquaries, splendid icons and bookcovers, is unique. From nowhere else, therefore, can one gain as broad an impression of the quality and changing character of Byzantine goldsmith's work from the ninth to the fifteenth century as in the treasury of San Marco.

The two chalices of the emperor Romanos typify the excellence of Byzantine metalwork in the high quality of their workmanship, and in their sense of balanced design. The silver-gilt mounts, delicately articulated by beaded and pearled edging, skilfully complement the different shapes of their sardonyx bowls. One (no. 11) has a relatively tall, deep cup. It is set on a tall foot and ornamented around its high rim with enameled half-figures of Christ, the Virgin, archangels, and saints set into a glowing gold background. The enamels' coloration of blues, porphyry and terracotta red, black, and delicate flesh tones enriches but does not overwhelm the beautifully carved bowl. The emperor's second chalice (no. 10), however, has a quite different configuration. It is composed of a most imposing double-handled sardonyx cup, whose broad proportions are echoed in the oblong shape of the paired small figures of saints that decorate its low, wide rim. The chalice's foot is broader, heavier, and more richly decorated than that of the taller Romanos chalice. The cup rests on a platform decorated with small cabochons, under which the emperor had written his dedicatory prayer in enamel. It is supported by a base worked in low relief with palmettes and crosses within *rinceaux*, below which are rows of cabochons and paired enameled images of saints.

The decoration of these chalices, however, is not merely pleasing to the eye: their enameled and relief images are keyed to the vessel's function. Each portrays images of Christ blessing, the Virgin with her arms raised in prayer flanked by archangels, St John the Baptist, apostles, and ranks of saints including martyrs, bishops, deacons and monks in an order that is inspired by the Byzantine liturgy. During the *Prothesis* rite, the Holy Bread is divided into many parts, beginning with the center, which is dedicated to Christ as the Lamb of God. Succeeding particles are devoted to the Virgin, the archangels, John the Baptist, the apostles, the prophets and other saints in the descending order of the heavenly hierarchy. The subject of the decoration of both chalices is the Glorification of the Virgin, which was also used frequently for the large-scale imagery on the vaults and walls of apses and presbyteries in the Byzantine church, beneath which the eucharist was celebrated. This respondence of images, in monumental art and in liturgical vessels, is found frequently in Byzantine art and requires a flexibility that is seen in the two chalices of the mid-tenth-century emperor Romanos (nos 10, 11), where the core figures of the Glorification of the Virgin, Christ and the Virgin *orans* flanked by two archangels, are supplemented by thirty-four saints on the chalice with two handles but by only ten on the chalice with gadroons. Frequently, also, the eucharistic prayer that was spoken at the time of the distribution of the wine in the Byzantine rite is inscribed on the rim of a chalice (nos 15, 16; Hahnloser 1971, 56, nos 44, 46, 51, 58, 63).

The patens made for the distribution of the bread during communion were ornamented in a fashion similar to that of the chalices, judging from those that survive at San Marco. The exquisitely wrought alabaster paten in the exhibition (no. 18) combines silver-gilt mounts decorated with a serried row of cabochons with a magnificent enamel of Christ at its center, surrounded by the inscription of the words spoken during the distribution of the sanctified bread in the Byzantine service. Another silver paten, reused in Venice as the lid of a reliquary formed from its companion chalice (Hahnloser 1971, no. 66), bears not only an inscription of a eucharistic prayer, but also in Christ and the Virgin *orans*, flanked by two archangels, an abbreviated version of the same imagery found on the chalices of Romanos (nos 10, 11).

The chalices of the emperor Romanos were probably made as gifts to churches in Constantinople, whose identity unfortunately is not known. The destination of the chalice that is decorated with the images of four bishops, three of whom were patriarchs of Constantinople, in this exhibition (no. 16), however, can be identified with some surety. Among the bishops is St Theophylactos of Nicomedia, who was deposed during the Iconoclastic controversy for his belief in icons. He is rarely depicted in surviving examples of Byzantine art, but an oratory was built in his honor in the tenth century within the precincts of the imperial palace in Constantinople, for which this chalice was probably made. The very fine quality of its enamels, as well as the beautiful proportions of the chalice, attest to the wealth and taste of its patron.

Other chalices in the treasury of San Marco testify to the long-standing practice of making liturgical vessels in sets, a tradition that goes back to the Early Christian period. Two sardonyx chalices (no. 17; Hahnloser 1971, no. 50) are decorated with enameled medallions of Christ, the Virgin and saints representing an abbreviated version of the imagery of the Glorification of the Virgin. Each enamel is surrounded by a strand of large pearls and alternates with groups of cabochons set in identical patterns on both vessels. Although slight variations occur in the design of the mounts, the chalices appear to have been made as part of an ensemble. The same is apparently true of two other chalices with enamel decoration in San Marco (Hahnloser 1971, nos 43-4). Their bowls are mounted with silver-gilt bands decorated solely with large pearls, and their tall feet are similarly formed with a border of cabochons, although the decoration of the rim differs. These chalices may be remnants of still larger sets like those recorded in the donations made by the emperor Constantine the Great to his newly constructed churches of the Lateran and Old Saint Peter's in Rome. According to the *Liber Pontificalis*, "forty smaller chalices of purest gold, weighing each 1 lb, fifty smaller chalices for service, weighing each 2 lbs", were among the emperor's lavish gifts to the cathedral of Rome. Constantine also gave to the Lateran basilica two series of patens, seven of gold and sixteen of silver, each weighing thirty pounds (Duchesne 1881, 172; *v.* Davis-Weyer 1971, 12).

The enamels on the chalices and patens of the San Marco treasury provide the vessels' principal figural imagery. They are, however, conceived as part of a larger scheme of decoration in which a silver-gilt ground, sometimes worked in low relief, the color of the hardstone cup and the rows of cabochons and pearls make an essential contribution to the rich artistry of the work. The same aesthetic appears in different guises on many other pieces of Byzantine metalwork in this exhibition. The reliquary of the True Cross (no. 13), for example, combines silver-gilt relief, gems, and enamels in an allied but different fashion. The Crucifixion enamel of the lid is displayed like an icon with a frame of medallion images of saints set between groups of three cabochons. An "outer frame", actually part of the fabric of the box and not of the sliding lid, is decorated solely with gems, and even though all are later replacements for the original, somewhat larger cabochons, the effect of their formal, rich display remains more or less the same. The reliquary's secondary surfaces are wrought exclusively in silver-gilt relief with images of saints on the sides set in an acanthus *rinceau*, a strongly modeled leaved cross of victory on the back, and more restrained foliate designs on the interior around the cross-shaped relic itself. The same type and composition of the reliefs and enamels are found on many Byzantine reliquaries of the True Cross, whose most accomplished example is that of the treasury of Limburg an der Lahn, which was brought to the West from Constantinople in the aftermath of the Fourth Crusade of 1204.

On the two icons of St Michael, the same materials are used to different effect. In the archangel's bust portrait (no. 12) the enamel is combined with high relief in a rich coloristic, sculptural image, to which the enameled medallions and the silver-gilt low relief (now mostly replaced) of the frames act as less salient transitional imagery. The reverse of the icon is worked in silver low relief of the highest quality, thus observing the distinction between principal and subordinate surfaces seen in the reliquary of the True Cross. It has been suggested that this icon may originally have formed the front and back cover of a book, where this distinction is also sometimes observed. The tenth-century lectionary of the Grand Lavra monastery on Mount Athos which is believed to have been given by the emperor Nikephoros Phokas (963-9), displays on its front cover a high relief, silver-gilt and enameled image of Christ within a jeweled frame, whereas its back cover is decorated with a less richly conceived silver-gilt relief of Christ's Descent into Hell. Like the San Marco icon of Michael, this bookcover seems to have been kept in the monastery's treasury rather than its library.

The later icon of the standing archangel Michael (no. 19) has a very different character. The emphasis is on military preparedness as seen in the archangel's aggressive stance, gaze, and elaborate armor. The saints of the lateral borders are also decked out in full warrior regalia, suggesting that this icon was made to be carried in battle with either the emperor or one of his high officials in an era, like the late eleventh or twelfth century, when military men occupied the throne of Byzantium. The use of enamel on this icon is also different from that of the earlier bust figure of Michael. The surface of this image is saturated with enamel decoration that covers not only the figures but also the background and the frame. Such love of overall enameling reflects a change in Byzantine taste that corresponds to that of similar relief icons like the much smaller twelfth-century panel of St Demetrius in Berlin (fig. 19 a).

Differences in style and use of enameling can also be observed in the decoration of the three splendid bookcovers from the Biblioteca Marciana in the exhibition. The earliest, dating probably to the late ninth or early tenth century, is set with enamels of the Crucifixion on the front and the Virgin *orans* on the back, surrounded by images of angels and saints (no. 9). The cover was made for a lady named Maria, who in her inscription asks for the help of the Lord. The style of the enamels is very close to that of the figures of the votive crown of Leo VI (886-912; no. 8), as is the use of large pearls to frame the images. The bookcover, however, has a broad richly colored frame formed of small pieces of blue, green, and porphyry-red glass that has been cut into cells whose design forms a carpet of crosses within a diaper pattern. The color of the glass complements that of the enamels to stunning effect. The technique of this border is found on many earlier works, of which the border of the bookcover of the sixth to seventh-century Lombard queen Theodelinda provides a most striking comparison. The elements of its central cross-shaped design may also be compared to the composition of the work in the exhibition. The juxtaposition of sections of glass and of *cloisonné* enamel, however, was particularly popular in the later Byzantine period, where it is used to great effect on a number of surviving reliquaries of the True Cross, including that at Limburg an der Lahn.

The second enameled bookcover in the exhibition (no. 14), with its central image of the standing Christ and Virgin *orans* surrounded by medallions of saints, has a composition and iconography similar to those of the earlier cover. On its border, however, serried ranks of red and green cabochons are set between borders of pearls providing a much more restrained coloristic effect. In keeping with its later date, this bookcover's imagery is displayed in a more formal fashion that gives greater play to the flat silver-gilt background in order to enhance the feeling of otherworldliness of the imagery. This style is very close to that of contemporary icon painting and manuscript illustration, for example, to two icons of the Crucifixion and of St Nicholas of the tenth to eleventh and of the twelfth century at Mount Sinai (Weitzmann 1967, pls 40, 43).

Weitzmann has recently suggested that these bookcovers were made as icons (1982, 14), since several surviving bookcovers like that of Christ at Mount Athos (mentioned above) have the principal relief image on the front and lower relief on the back, because this surface has to withstand more wear than does the front cover. He proposed that the covers were made as a diptych, in a mode better known among surviving Byzantine ivories and paintings of the tenth and eleventh centuries. Thus when the enamels, like their ivory counterparts, were separated on their arrival in Western Europe, they were incorporated into bookcovers. The third bookcover in this exhibition (no. 20) was made probably in the late fourteenth or early fifteenth century under the rule of the Palaeologan imperial house. Although the layout of the decoration is similar to that of the earlier works, silver relief rather than enamels enliven the surface of multi-figured scenes. Enameled portraits of saints are reserved for every second panel of the frame, where they alternate with scenes from the life of Christ and the Virgin. They are set on panels inlaid with enamel in intricate foliate patterns which were very popular in this late Byzantine period, for example, on contemporary icon frames (cf. Grabar 1975, esp. nos 13, 21). This bookcover, as well as a second one of the same or slightly later period in the Biblioteca Marciana seem to have been made as bookcovers, since the binding of their spines, while not part of the fabric of the front and back, seems to display the same style and techniques as the principal imagery.

Many rare and beautiful works of Byzantine goldsmithing and enameling fill this exhibition. They represent, however, only a fraction of the pieces that the basilica must once have possessed. Many objects surely perished in the fire that destroyed the treasury in 1231. Some others were sold in times of need or were stolen, and under Napoleon numerous pieces were melted down to pay the war debts. Yet the objects that survive, like the basilica that houses them, can still reveal something of the unique position which Venice held vis-à-vis Byzantium from the tenth to fifteenth centuries. Throughout this city's early history and up until the time of the Fourth Crusade, Venice had determinedly allied itself with the Byzantine empire. It recognized the Greek emperor's suzerainty and enjoyed as a result special commercial privileges within the Byzantine empire on which it depended to a large extent for its prosperous economy. Venetian doges were granted high Byzantine titles, and even by the end of the eleventh century, when Venice to all intents and purposes was independent, it continued to give allegiance to the ruler in Constantinople. Marriage alliances of the doges with princesses of the Byzantine house further strengthened the mutually advantageous ties. Consequently when Alexius I Comnenus asked for help to turn back the invading forces of the Norman duke Robert Guiscard, Venice came to his aid. In thanks, the emperor granted Venice extensive new trading privileges that were, during the thirteenth century, to cost the Byzantine empire dearly.

In the cultural and artistic sphere, Byzantine influence was also strong. When the third and present basilica of the evangelist Mark was built in the second half of the eleventh century, it was designed on the model of the famous church of the Holy Apostles in Constantinople and decorated with mosaics by changing teams of Greek artists. Although most of its original interior furnishings have disappeared, some, like the *Pala d'Oro*, attest to the magnificence of the works of art that were commissioned for its sacristy. It seems likely also that the Greek emperor sent liturgical vessels to honor the foundation of the evangelist's new church, just as many years earlier, as Grabar has suggested, the votive crown of Leo VI (no. 8) may have been sent by the emperor to the Venetian church of San Zaccaria which he founded.

In 1204, when the armies of the Fourth Crusade occupied Constantinople, however, Venice was in the vanguard of the invading troops. The sack of the city was so fierce that the commanders of the crusading armies ordered that the booty be piled up in a church in the city in order to attempt its fair distribution. Its value was estimated at four hundred thousand silver marks, as well as ten thousand suits of armor! Unfortunately no accounts exist of how much of the booty was melted down and how much brought to Venice. The only record we have concerns reliquaries that were sent by the Venetian doge Enrico Dandolo, which later were saved from the fire in the treasury in 1231. It seems likely, nevertheless, that a number of objects in this exhibition came from Constantinople to Venice during the city's Latin occupation. Several, like the chalices of the Patriarchs (no. 16) and of the emperor Romanos (nos 10, 11), may well have been found in the imperial palace churches and others acquired later when the Venetians became the principal bankers, first of the occupying Western forces, and then of the Byzantine empire until its collapse in 1453.

Whatever the provenance of the Byzantine treasures of San Marco may be, their exceptional quality recalls Robert de Clari's description of the works of art pillaged during the sack of the imperial city: "Not since the world was made was there ever seen or won so great a treasure, or so noble or so rich, nor in the time of Alexander, nor in the time of Charlemagne, nor before, nor after, nor do I think myself that in the forty richest cities of the world there had been so much wealth as was found in Constantinople. For the Greeks say that two thirds of the wealth of this world is in Constantinople and the other third scattered throughout the world" (Robert de Clari, ch. LXXXI, 101).

Precious metalwork with enamel

8

"Grotto of the Virgin"

Stonework: 4th–5th century (?). *Crown of Leo*: late 9th–early 10th century.
Figure of Virgin: 13th century
Rock-crystal, silver-gilt, gold *cloisonné* enamel, stones, pearls. *Total height*
200 mm. *Crystal*: height 158 mm, *thickness* 137 mm. *Crown*: *diam*. 130 mm,
height 35 mm. *Figure*: *height* 90 mm

Tesoro, no. 116 (listed in the 1325 inventory: III, no. 18)

This object, which Pasini called the "Grotto of the Virgin", incorporates three works of different periods: a small edifice in rock-crystal, a silver-gilt figure of the Virgin fixed inside it, and a silver-gilt votive crown used as the base. The assemblage seems to have existed in the fourteenth century, since the 1325 inventory of the treasury lists an "*Ecclesiolam unam de cristallo furnitam arg[ent]o deaur[at]o*" (Gallo 1967, 278, III, no. 18). The 1571 inventory is clearer, as the object is described in its present form: "*Un mezo nichio de Cristallo con una figura d'una santa a mezo, che sta in piede, col suo piede d'arzento*" (Gallo 1967, 299, no. 63). The description is even more precise in the inventory of 1733, where the "Grotto" figures among the rock-crystal objects: "*Un capitello tutto scolpito e lavorato con figura nel mezo d'argento dorata, e base ornata di figure e gioie*" (Gallo 1967, 354, no. 134). The object can be found again under the name of "*grotta*" in the valuation of the treasury made in 1816-20 by Cicognara, who described the figure of the Virgin as being "*alla greca*" and valued the piece at 800 lire (Gallo 1967, 372, no. 11).

Rock-crystal

The crystal edifice was made to contain something. However, as it had no stability in its normal position, it was rather casually turned upside-down when it was given its present mount. The creators of the assemblage did not attempt to set it the right way up by giving it a mount to make it stable or by re-cutting the rock-crystal, which they dared not or could not do.
The object was cut from a single block of rock-crystal of considerable purity, and represents a central-plan building with three long sides and two short ones. An entrance on one of the long sides is flanked by two piers and surmounted by a pediment. The interior is plain, with its original upper part vaulted: this now forms the base of the "Grotto", giving it a sloping floor. The ex-terior is decorated with both raised and recessed ornament; the roof has been cut with interlace and is supported by a band with vertical grooves. The two front walls and centre rear wall are ornamented with volutes; on each of the two other large sides three Ionic pilasters alternate with a sword, a shield and a spear. A projection below the edifice, for attachment, is flanked on either side by two superimposed volutes ending in pierced loops; the loop of one – the upper left volute in the normal position of the edifice – has disappeared. The rock-crystal has been damaged, in fact, all over the upper part of the front, probably because it is out of balance on this side. It has also sustained damage underneath the figure of the Virgin, and above each of the piers at the entrance there are signs that some element has broken off.

The upper part was hollowed out, suggesting that the edifice was crowned by an ornament of another material, possibly gold. This part is now contained in a support with three metal tongues for attachment to the crown. There is no indication that the edifice is Byzantine; surviving works suggest that the Byzantines worked in coloured stone rather than rock-crystal. However, the Byzantine emperor Basil I offered a large object in rock-crystal to the Carolingian emperor Louis the German in 872 (Lamm 1929-30, I, 517). The treasury of San Marco also contains a rock-crystal chalice which is very probably Byzantine (fig. 43j; Hahnloser 1971, no. 64, pl. LVI), but this is carved from a block much less pure than that used for the "Grotto" or the crystal used in Antiquity or in Fatimid Egypt. Finally, Byzantine hardstone-carving does not usually entail pierced decoration, as does the "Grotto".

It is therefore more probably a Classical work. The pierced volutes of the base are reminiscent of the handles of certain Antique vessels in design and workmanship (e.g. no. 10). Other Classical examples of rock-crystal carved into architectural forms include a capital reused in the seventh century as a support for the votive crown of the Visigothic king Recceswinth (Madrid, Archaeological Museum; Palol and Hirmer 1967, pl. 20) and the little round Late Antique salt-cellar on six columns, found at Carthage, in the Metropolitan Museum of Art, New York (fig. 8a; Bühler, no. 115a, pl. 39).

The original function of the edifice as a receptacle is shown by the fact that the base (now the upper part) is pierced for the attachment of some object. This was probably a statuette from the beginning: it was common in Late Antiquity to represent a person inside an architectural frame comprising a façade with columns. This can be seen, for example, from ivory diptychs, such as that of the Roman consul Asturius (449), or from the silver *missorium* of Theodosius (388), where the emperor is also flanked by soldiers carrying spears and shields similar to

those represented on the "Grotto" (Delbrueck 1929, pls 4, 62). There is also a little rock-crystal bust of the elder Faustina in a niche under an arcade resting on two colonnettes (Huybrigts 1899, 36-7).

It is difficult to decide what the original function of the "Grotto" might have been. It is nevertheless tempting to see it as the upper part of a sceptre, which would have been fixed to a staff by means of the projection. The material does not militate against this hypothesis, as hardstone was often used in Late Antiquity in the knobs of sceptres: furthermore, these were frequently formed of figures, which sometimes emerge from a corolla, recalling the volutes on the base of our rock-crystal. There does not, however, seem to be an extant example of a sceptre with an architectural form such as this. On one of the large sixth-century ivory reliefs decorating the ambo of the emperor Henry II in Aachen palace chapel, though, the goddess Isis is carrying, like a sceptre, a cornucopia surmounted by a figure of Osiris within a little temple reminiscent of the "Grotto" (fig. 8b; Schnitzler 1957, figs 117, 123). There were numerous Classical sceptres in the treasuries of Constantinople (Babelon 1897, 167-9). The text of the 1325 inventory shows that the original function of the rock-crystal edifice – whatever that might have been – had been forgotten by the time the object arrived in Venice.

D. A.

Votive crown of Leo VI

The votive crown of the Byzantine emperor, Leo, is decorated with fourteen enameled medallions, one of which depicts the emperor. Seven others bear the images of apostles and evangelists, while the remaining six medallions are lost. Leo is flanked on his left by SS Paul and Andrew, and on his right by SS Mark, Bartholomew, Luke, and James, whose names, like that of Leo, are inscribed with a *cloison* on the emerald green background. The crown's upper and lower borders are edged with gold beading; rings, probably for the suspension of strands of pearls and/or jewels, are set beneath each medallion. The figures are depicted in robes of muted green and blue tones with accents of deep red, yellow and white. The apostles carry scrolls or books or a cross (Andrew) and Leo wears the imperial *loros* and a *stemma* crown. The emperor is, in all probability, Leo VI the Wise (886-912), because his immediate predecessors of the same name were either iconoclasts or they reigned in the fifth century when this type of enameling would not have been produced (see, however, Weitzmann 1970, 10-1; Corrigan 1978). The image of Leo, moreover, resembles closely that of Leo the Wise on his coins (see Grierson 1973, pl. XXXIV, 1a, 1b, 2). The style and technique of the crown's enamels are very similar, but superior, to those of the late ninth to early tenth-century bookcover in this exhibition (no. 9). The subtle but restricted color range, the emerald green background with the inscriptions drawn in a single *cloison*, the style of the figures' faces, as well as the setting of the enamels in raised frames, surrounded by a string of large pearls, point to a common technical and stylistic tradition. The shape of the figures' faces and the rendering of their draperies by loosely draped folds, moreover, appears in such manuscripts of the first half of the tenth-century as those of the Bible of Leo Sacellarios (for example, The Carrying of the Ark, Biblioteca Apostolica Vaticana, Reg. gr. 1, fol. 85v; Mathews 1977, 94-133, fig. 3, with earlier bibliography). The crown's fourteen original enameled images are thought to depict Leo flanked by the twelve apostles and juxtaposed to an image of Christ in the fourteenth medallion in a representation of the concept of the Byzantine ruler as equal to the apostles in the hierarchy of the cosmos (Treitinger 1956, 129 ff.).

During the thirteenth or beginning of the fourteenth century, the crown was adapted to form the base of the so-called "Grotto of the Virgin" (see above). Three silver-gilt straps ending in saw-tooth edges were attached at irregular angles to the upper border of the crown, joining it crudely to a socket at its center into which the crystal "grotto" was set, surely reflecting this mounting as a secondary use for the straps. Two of the original silver-gilt peacocks, whose tails are inlaid with blue glass, stand where the straps join the crown's edge. Only the feet of the third peacock survive. They have rings on their backs by which the "grotto" and crown were suspended. A second ring, attached to their beaks, probably held a strand of pearls and jewels. Some scholars have questioned whether Leo's crown is in fact a votive crown or rather the displaced rim of a chalice (Dalton 1911, 5, who quotes an anonymous colleague; Barany-Oberschall 1937, 80, 119, no. 82; Beckwith 1961, 87). Whereas its diameter (130 mm) does correspond to that of a chalice, for example the chalice of Romanos (no. 11), the placement of the rings that held pendant strands of pearls or jewels on the bottom rim are set flush with the crown's surface rather than at right angles to it as was customary, indeed essential, on Byzantine chalice decoration in order for the strands to hang free of the chalice's surface (see Hahnloser 1971, nos 43-4, 46, 48). A similar flush placement of rings is found on several votive crowns from the Guarrazar treasury (Schlunk and Hauschild 1978, 72, 201-2, pls 92-3, with earlier bibliography). In the crown's present arrangement, the peacocks are the only means by which it (and the "grotto") can be suspended and Grabar suggests that the birds belonged to the original crown. They seem, however, to be disproportionately large for the delicate circlet to which they are at present only indirectly attached. The gold beading of the top rim runs uninterrupted beneath the saw-toothed edge of the bands on which they stand. An examination of the interior surface of the crown nevertheless reveals no traces of a different mounting, such as the simple ring attachments for the chains that held aloft the earlier

votive crowns in the Guarrazar treasure, or those depicted in such Early Christian representations as the fifth-century mosaics at Santa Maria Maggiore (in the doorway of the building behind the scene of the angel appearing to Joseph in a dream: Cecchelli 1956, 221, pl. LIII).

These and other Early Christian examples, like Queen Theodelinda's votive crown at Monza (Merati 1969, 28-9, 88-9; Conti 1983, 39-42) are decorated with mounted gems. By the Middle Byzantine period, however, judging from Leo's crown, enamels were substituted for the more expensive jewels, a trend that can also be seen in the decoration of bookcovers like those in this exhibition (nos 9, 14).

The crown of Leo belongs to a type of liturgical church furnishing that was very popular in the Byzantine realm, as well as in the West (Drossoyianni 1982; Palla 1958; cf. Charlemagne's gifts to Saint Peter's in Rome: Elbern 1976, 345). They appear hanging from shell-shaped conches in the mosaics of the upper nave walls as well as in the arches of the palace in the first register of mosaics of Sant'Apollinare Nuovo in Ravenna, and later from the architraves of canon-tables in manuscripts from Armenia (Der Nersessian 1945, 2, pl. xxi; Weitzmann 1933, 37, pl. XI). They were also recorded in descriptions of churches. Anthony of Novgorod, for example, spoke of a crown that hung from the center of the altar *ciborium* in St Sophia in Constantinople. Pendant from it was a cross and below the cross a golden dove. Crowns of other emperors were placed around this *ciborium* (Khitrovo 1889, 96; see also Palla 1958). Whether Leo the Wise's crown hung in such a place, or whether, as Grabar suggests (Muraro and Grabar 1963, 47-59, no. 1), Leo gave it to the church of San Zaccaria in Venice, which he founded, cannot be determined. Jeweled crowns were also used in the basilica of San Marco. The inventory of 1325 lists a series of eleven *coronae* (although whether used for lighting or as votive offerings is not stated in the text), neatly labelled A through M and therefore meant to be hung together (see also inventory of 1571: Gallo 1967, 295, 297, 347; and that of 1678: Gallo 1967, no. 114, pl. 323).

Statuette

The statuette of the Virgin, dressed in a *chiton* and *maphorion*, stands on a foot-stool, which is decorated with an incised rinceau. She is attached to the floor of the crystal "grotto" by a silver-gilt pin that joins the peacock mounts within the circle of the crown below. Grabar (Hahnloser 1971) remarked on the resemblance of the figure to that of a large marble relief of the Virgin *orans* that is set high up on the north side wall of the basilica next to the side entrance of the atrium (fig. 8c). Both were probably made in Venice in the thirteenth century. The Virgin of the "Grotto", unlike her counterpart on the relief, stretches out her arms in front of her. She does not appear to have held a statuette of the Christ Child, since there are no traces of attachments on her chest or hands. The strict frontality with which she is portrayed, however, bespeaks a cult statue. Above and slightly behind the Virgin's head, the original hole in the present "ceiling" of the "grotto" may have been reused for the fastening of further silver-gilt ornamentation, perhaps an image of Christ or of God the Father within some sort of canopy.

M. E. F.

8c

Bibliography: Durand 1861, 96-7. Labarte 1872-5, I, 321, no. 11. Pasini 1885-6, 68-70, no. 111, pl. L. Molinier 1888, 62, 95-6, no. 100. Kondakov 1892, 237. Molinier 1896, 41. Dalton 1911, 514. Lamm, 1929-30, I, 213-4; II, pl. 76, 1 (with bibliography). Barany-Oberschall 1937, 80, n. 82. Kelleher 1951, 71. Grabar 1957b, 30-1. Christophilopoulos 1957, 283, no. 5, and △. Palla 1958, 339-53. Grabar 1958, 165, fig. 1, pl. 70. Beckwith 1961, 87, n. 16. Muraro and Grabar 1963, 47, 59, 62, 63. Grabar 1963a, 58-9, fig. 63. Ross in exh. cat. *Byzantine art an European art*, 1964, 393. Deér 1966, 45, 83, 84, pl. XXI, fig. 46. Grabar 1966a. Gallo 1967, 278, III, no. 18; 299, no. 63; 354, no. 134; 360, no. 161; 372, no. 11; pl. 54, fig. 92. Wessel 1967, 24-5, 57-8, no. 12. Beckwith 1970, 92, fig. 16. Hahnloser 1971, 81-2, no. 92 (Grabar), pls LXXII-LXXV. Drossoyianni 1982, 529-36.

Exh. cat. *Venezia e Bisanzio*, 1974, 79, no. 25.

9

Bookcover with Crucifixion and the Virgin *orans*

Byzantine, 9th–early 10th century
Silver-gilt on wood core, gold *cloisonné* enamel, pearls, glass. *Length* 260 mm, *width* 175 mm

Biblioteca Marciana, ms. Lat. Cl. I, 101 (listed in the 1325 inventory: V, no. 12)

Two silver-gilt panels are joined by hinged straps of the same material to form a bookcover of a ninth-century lectionary for use in San Marco. Their flat glowing surfaces serve to unite the separate plaques of colored glass and enamel with figural images that are fastened to them in a startling juxtaposition of richness and simplicity. The arrangement of the plaques is identical on the front and back. Wide panels of diaper and Greek cross patterns, edged by a row of gold beading and strung pearls, frame images of Christ crucified on the front and the Virgin *orans*, inscribed M[HTH]P Θ[EO]Y ("Mother of God") on the back. The two central figures were originally surrounded by ten medallions of enameled images of saints and angels, quite a few of which are missing on the back cover. Those surviving on the front reading clockwise depict, SS Peter, John the Baptist, Andrew, two archangels James, Matthew, a floral ornament, an archangel, and Mark. Only three enameled saints survive on the Virgin's panel – Procopius, Philip and John (see below, p. 127). Sapphire blue, emerald green and garnet red are the dominant colors of the glass and enamels, with yellow, turquoise and sky blue, and two shades of pale green used as well in the saints' and angels' robes.

Christ is shown crucified on the front cover, his arms and body stretched rigidly on the cross, with only his head, bent in death, breaking the symmetry. The cross is set against a background that is shaped like a cross with slightly flaring arms and decorated with circles and four-petaled rosettes drawn with *cloisons*. The sun and moon flank the cross just below the *titulus*, which is inscribed I[HCOY]C X[PICTO]C ("Jesus Christ"). On the back cover, the Virgin *orans*, M[HTH]P Θ[EO]Y stands against a similar cross-shaped background which is decorated with rosettes and crosses. At the ends of the arms of the cross is an inscription written in four monograms within circles which, reading from top to bottom and side to side, say: "Lord help Thy servant Maria 'Magistrissa'". Nicholas Oikonomides, who deciphered the monograms, suggests that the donor was Maria, the wife of a magistros and mother of Tarasios Patrikios. She was cured by the Virgin of the Spring ca. 900 and may have given the bookcover to that Virgin's famous shrine in Constantinople as a thank offering. A similarly worded inscription appears on the image of the Virgin *orans* in the narthex lunette of the church of the Koimesis at Nicaea (Schmidt 1927, 48, pl. XXXI; Mango 1959, 245-6).

Nine of the original medallion portraits of saints and angels on the front and back cover have been lost and only two of them replaced, one by the later decorative palmette medallion at the lower left of the former, the other by the portrait of St Procopius at the center top of the latter.

Grabar has remarked on the resemblance of the central cross images of Christ and the Virgin to the decoration of pectoral crosses, either in enamel, like that from the Beresford Hope collection in the Victoria and Albert Museum in London (fig. 9a), or in metal, like a bronze cross in the Museo Sacro of the Vatican (King 1928, 193-205). They are also clearly related to the imagery of a group of enamels that has been dated anywhere from the seventh to the tenth century, including the small Fieschi-Morgan reliquary of the True Cross in the Metropolitan Museum of Art, New York (fig. 9b), and the much larger cross reliquary of Pope Pascal I (817-24) from the Sancta Sanctorum of the Lateran, now in the Vatican's Museo Sacro. Recently David Buckton (1982, 35-6) and Anna Kartsonis (1982) have dated them in the ninth and tenth centuries. Most characteristic is their use of a translucent green background, bold colors, often archaic imagery, like the Christ dressed in a *colobium* (a long sleeveless tunic), his rigid position on the cross, and the filling of the background with abstract and floral shapes. These crosses seek to emulate such Early Christian Crucifixions as that in the illuminations of the sixth-century Rabbula Gospels (fol. 13a; cf. Cecchelli 1959, 62). Although certain aspects of the bookcover's Crucifixion betray a conscious archaizing not only in the rigid pose of Christ's body and in his dress, but also in the ordered repetition of rosettes and circles in the cross's background, other characteristics, like Christ's bent head and his eyes closed in death, belong to the eighth century and later in the East and West. The earliest surviving example of the portrayal of the dead Christ on the cross is an icon at Mount Sinai that Weitzmann dated to the eighth century (1976, no. 36), and the type appears several times in ninth-century icons and manuscript illuminations in Carolingian and Byzantine art (Weitzmann 1976, B50; Hausherr 1963, *passim*; Shchepkina 1977, fol. 45v).

The San Marco bookcover, however, is probably somewhat later than the ninth-century icon and manuscript images. Its closest stylistic parallels are found in the enamels of the votive crown of Leo VI (886-912), where

125

126

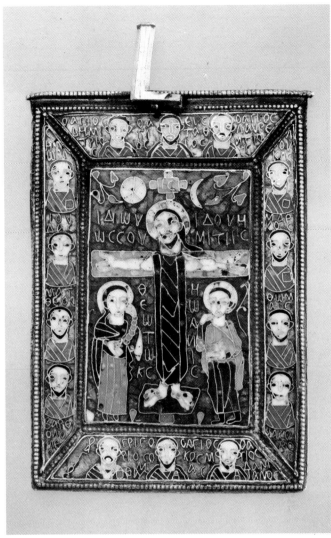

figures of the apostles and of Leo have the same long, almost skeletal-shaped faces, round black eyes without the white showing, and yellow haloes (except for Leo's, which is blue; see no. 8). The figures' *himatia* and *chitones* are described by similar broad amorphous folds of different tones of green, blue, and white, and the saints hold either scrolls or books in their rather rubbery hands. All the figures are set against an emerald green translucent background with the letters of their identifying inscriptions written in *cloisons*. The enamels, moreover, are set in similar mounts, surrounded by strings of large pearls. These characteristics are also found in a few other enamels of the period, like two medallions of the Virgin (fig. 9c) and St Theodore and a Crucifixion plaque that are incorporated in the Khakhuli icon in Tbilisi (Amiranachvili 1972, figs 22-4).

Several suggestions have been made concerning the orig-inal order of the saints surrounding Christ and the Virgin. Grabar proposed reconstructing the front side much as it is, with John the Baptist flanked by Peter and Andrew on top, four archangels around the cross and two evangelists and an apostle below. The arrangement of saints in similar contexts, however, often varies. Four archangels in groups of two (one medallion being lost) might have flanked St John the Baptist on the front and another saint on the back, perhaps a patron saint of the church for which the cover was made. Twelve apostles, including the four evangelists, might have appeared below, perhaps supplemented by prophets or ancestors of Christ, as they are on the later bookcover (no. 14). In a recent publication, Weitzmann identified this book-cover and that with the standing Christ and the Virgin (no. 14) as icon diptychs (1982, 14) which, like many Byzantine ivories that were brought to the West in the

Middle Ages, were converted for use as covers of liturgical books. In fact, the jeweled, enameled, and pearled decoration of the San Marco covers is ill-suited to the rough treatment suffered especially by a book's back cover. The lectionary that is thought to have been given by the emperor Nikephoros Phokas (963-9) to the Lavra monastery on Mount Athos, for example, takes account of the rougher use its silver relief back cover would suffer by reserving the enameled and jeweled relief decoration for the front (Kondakov 1902, 195, pls xxvi-xxvii; Pelekanides 1979, 24, 217 ff., with bibliography). There are bookcovers, however, that treat both covers equally, for example the covers of Theodelinda at Monza (Conti 1983, 38-9) or, much later, the fourteenth-century cover in the exhibition (no. 20).

M. E. F.

Bibliography: Durand 1860, 55-66. Durand 1862, 79. Valentinelli 1867. Valentinelli 1868-73. Molinier 1882 and 1889. Pasini 1885-6, 115-6, no. 8, pls VI-VII. Molinier 1888, 47-50, 81, no. 6. Kondakov 1892, 185-6, fig. 54. Molinier 1896-1902, I, 41-2. Schlumberger 1896-1905, I, 189; III, 677. Dalton 1911, 515-6. Rosenberg 1921, 44, fig. 59. Grabar 1958, 168-71, figs 4-7. Rice and Hirmer 1959, 72, no. 91. Beckwith 1961, 86-7, fig. 110. Grabar, 1963 a, 52. Muraro and Grabar 1963, 68, 70. Ross in exh. cat. *Byzantine art an European art*, 1964, 393-4. Gallo 1967, 27, no. 49; 279, v, no. 12; pl. 43, figs 74-5. Wessel 1967, no. 13. Beckwith 1970, 92, fig. 167. Mallé 1971, 95-6, fig. 19. Hahnloser 1971, 47-8, no. 35 (Grabar), pls XXXII-XXXIII. Hetherington and Forman 1983, 46.

Exh. cat. *Venezia e Bisanzio*, 1974, no. 19.

10

Chalice of the emperor Romanos (with handles)

Stonework: 1st century BC – 1st century AD. *Metalwork*: Constantinopolitan, 959-963
Sardonyx, silver-gilt, gold *cloisonné* enamel, glass. *Height* 250 mm, *width* 280 mm, *diam.* 210 mm

Tesoro, no. 70

This chalice is one of the largest of the sardonyx chalices in San Marco. The round bowl with a concave bottom was cut from a block of sardonyx of considerable size, since its two handles are of a piece with it. It is perfectly cut and relatively thin-walled, only three to four millimetres in the middle of the body. The profile is slightly concave at the top, becoming convex lower down. It is above all in the workmanship of the twin handles that the virtuosity of the craftsman is evident. At the level of the rim, the two branches of each handle separate to form a wide, pierced triangular motif composed of symmetrical scrolls attached to the rim at five points. Below, the two branches each form a thumb-rest and are then united by a horizontal band of four mouldings carved round the outside of the handle. The branches then separate again, each terminating at the bottom of the cup in a long stylized leaf edged with a little moulding. The outside of the bowl is grooved below the rim, giving it a narrow throat just below the bottom of the gold mount. The underside is flat and is engraved with a rosette surrounded by a foot-ring.

As the bowl was broken, Pasini describes how he had it repaired in 1857 by a restorer of Tyrolian origin named Giovanni Spel, who had established himself in Venice. It had probably long been damaged, as the 1571 inventory lists "*Una Coppa d'Agata rotta, con doi manichi d'Agata, con zoglie attorno di poca importantia*" (Gallo 1967, 299, no. 79). In 1733, by contrast, another inventory describes three large bowls of nicolo (*sic*) with handles cut from the same block as the body and with gold mounts, but with no indication that any of them were broken (Gallo 1967, 350-1, nos 36, 53, 57). However, the catalogue of the treasury commenced in 1816 by Cicognara lists the bowl as being in fragments (Gallo 1967, 368, no. 34). In 1845 it was in the hands of the goldsmith Pietro Fauro, known as Buri, for restoration (Gallo 1967, 397, no. 99). One of the handles had lost one of its scrolls.

There is no doubt that the vessel was originally a Classical bowl intended for secular use, eventually transformed into a chalice by the addition of a mount. The skill with which the contour, the handles and the thinness of the walls were produced is consistent with that of hardstone vessels in Classical Antiquity. The way the upper part of the handle is attached to the bowl, spreading in a triangle along the rim of the bowl, first appeared in the hellenistic period and was later adopted by the

Romans. It can be found on various kinds of receptacle, and in other materials, but the attachment is usually solid; the idea of piercing it seems appropriate to objects in hardstone, and is a *tour de force*. Classical hardstone vessels frequently have a foot-ring round a flat base, as in this case (figs 10 d, 10 e). The rosette engraved on the underside can be found on a number of Roman glass vessels (cf. no. 1); the famous "Rubens Vase" in Baltimore (fig. 2 e; Ross 1943, fig. 4) and the Antique rock-crystal *situla* in San Marco (Hahnloser 1971, no. 75, pl. LXIII) also have a rosette carved in relief under the foot. There are in fact few round Classical hardstone bowls with two handles where the upper attachment of the handles is of this type. Of at least six others which can be mentioned, five have solid, unpierced attachments. Two of them, also in sardonyx, have profiles close to that of the chalice: a sardonyx bowl from a tomb in the Ardèche in the Department of Greek and Roman Antiquities in the Louvre (fig. 10 a; Michon 1915, 71-82, *diam.* 106 mm) and a bowl in the Pitti Palace (Heikamp 1974, no. 1, figs 12-3, *diam.* 87 mm). The others are either deeper or shallower than the chalice: a large *skyphos* of rock-crystal also in the treasury of San Marco (Hahnloser 1971, no. 5, pl. III), a sardonyx bowl, surely with modified handles (fig. 10 b; Paris, Bibliothèque Nationale; Bühler 1973, no. 92, *diam.* 160 mm), another sardonyx cup with one handle missing and replaced by a precious metal mount (fig. 10 c; Ottawa, National Gallery of Canada, *width* 425 mm) and, lastly, the giant agate "font" in the Schatzkammer in Vienna (figs 10 d, 10 e; Bühler 1973, no. 83, pl. 27, *width* 750 mm), which, with its twin handles, is much closer to the chalice than the examples above. Its handles are of less careful workmanship than those of the San Marco bowl, doubtless because of the size of the object, but they still have many stylistic points in common. The two branches spread along the rim, their design close to that of the handles of the chalice, with symmetrical pierced scrolls, attached to the rim at eight points. Joined below by a "thumb-rest", they curve like those of the chalice and terminate in two long leaves. The spirit of these two pieces can perhaps be found in three other Classical sardonyx objects of a different shape: a tall two-handled vessel in the Pitti Palace (fig. 10 f; Heikamp 1973, no. 6, figs 23-4), a ewer in the Louvre (figs 10 g, 10 h; Marquet de Vasselot 1914, no. 1001) and a ewer in Rosenborg Castle, Copenhagen (fig. 10 i; exh. cat. *Trésors des rois de Danemark*, 1978-9,

no. 44). Their handles, cut from the same block of stone as the bowl, have thumb-rests with decorative mouldings below and spread into scrolls either at the top (the ewer in the Louvre) or at the bottom, where they have two points of attachment (the Pitti Palace vessel and the Rosenborg ewer). These objects can be related to a sardonyx vessel-fragment decorated, like the ewer in the Louvre, with a concave ovoid shape (Paris, Bibliothèque Nationale; Bühler 1973, no. 91, pl. 29), and on which the junction of a handle survives, one of its extremities in the form of a long leaf. These examples are quite close to the celebrated "Coupe des Ptolémées" (fig. 10j; Montesquiou-Fezensac and Gaborit-Chopin 1977, III, pls 36-8), with twin handles of which the two branches, joined at two points, each have mouldings on the upper part and terminate in a similar elongated leaf, outlined with a thin moulding. This group of objects with a common range of forms comes from the same artistic background as precious metalwork like that from the treasure of Boscoreale (before AD 79) or two of the drinking-vessels from the Berthou-

ville treasure, each with twin handles formed by two branches bound together in the middle (first and second century; Paris, Bibliothèque Nationale; Babelon 1924, 204). Without being able to specify whether they saw the light of day in Rome or in one of the ancient hellenistic centres such as Alexandria, it would seem feasible to date the group towards the end of republican Rome, or at the beginning of the imperial era.

D. A.

Metalwork

Paired images in enamel of Christ and the Virgin Mary, archangels and saints decorate the rim and foot of this broad imposing chalice. The enamel plaques, five of which are missing (two on the rim and three on the foot), are set in simple beaded borders with an inner scalloped frame on the vertical sides. Below are rings for the suspension of short strands of pearls or gems. Originally,

10a

10b

10c

132

the rim was attached to the base by silver-gilt bands, now lost, that were hinged to the lower and upper borders. The chalice is supported on a foot composed of a platform that holds the sardonyx bowl, decorated with beaded edging and small square cabochons. The foot is ornamented with *rinceaux* of Sasanian palmettes of different design on the knop and crosses within entwined roundels with small palmettes in the interstices below, worked in very low relief. A single row of square and circular cabochons is placed above the lower circle of five of the original eight enameled plaques of martyrs. Beaded borders divide the different sections of the decoration on the foot. The inscription of the emperor Romanos, +ΚΥΡΙΕ ΒΟΗΘΕΙ ΡΩΜΑΝΩ ΟΡΘΟΔΟΞ[Ω ΔΕC]-ΠΟΤΗ (Κύριε βοήθει 'Ρωμανῷ ὀρθοδόξῳ δεσπότῃ, "Lord help the Orthodox emperor Romanos") is written in blue enamel beneath the platform that supports the sardonyx chalice.

The host of bust figures of Christ, the Virgin, the archangels Michael and Gabriel, the apostles (Peter and Paul, Bartholomew and Simon, James and Philip), St John the Baptist and the Fathers of the Church (John Chrysostom, Basil and Nicholas, Gregory Nazianzen and Gregory the Wonder-worker), and bishops, deacons and martyrs (Charalampius and Cyprian, George and Demetrius, Ausenius and Eugenius, Agathonicus and Acacius, Florus and Laurus, Orestes and Christopher), of the hermit Anthony and the deacon Spiridion, and of Nicephorus the iconodule Patriarch of Constantinople with St Lazarus the painter, join in the Glorification of the Virgin (see Introduction, p. 110). The missing plaques of the rim may have shown four more apostles, and those of the foot six more martyrs.

The figural style seems to be related most to that of the chalice with gadroons of the emperor Romanos (probably Romanos II, 959-63; no. 11) and the Limburg an der Lahn reliquary (964-5) in the configuration of the faces, especially of their hairlines, and the coloration and style of the draperies (fig. 10k). The archangels, for example, are especially close to their counterparts on the reliquary and on the chalice in the shape of their faces, eyes, eyebrows, and mouths, in the decoration of their wings, and in the way in which they hold the globe and scepter. The blessing hands of such saints as Peter and Paul or Bartholomew and Simon and the portrayal of the irregular folds of their bi-colored robes similarly resemble those of the apostles on the chalice and reliquary, although with less complexity of folds due to their much smaller size. The style of the finely executed palmette relief decoration at the foot also supports a tenth-century date. It can be compared to the low relief palmettes of the interior border of the turquoise glass cup (no. 29). In view of the similarities, it seems likely that the two chalices, both with inscriptions to the emperor Romanos, were made for Romanos II, whose dates coincide with those of Basil the Proedros, the patron of the reliquary of Limburg an der Lahn. Yet, in spite of the close stylistic resemblance of the chalices' enamels, their visual effect is quite different, since they were designed to decorate chalices of dissimilar shape. The tall, rectangular, enameled panels with half-figures of Christ, the Virgin and saints on the other chalice of Romanos (no. 11) correspond well to the tall, almost conical shape of its sardonyx bowl. The smaller enamels on their longer rectangular plaques on this chalice, however, suit well the very impressive broad and relatively low proportions of its magnificently worked sardonyx cup.

M. E. F.

Bibliography: Durand 1861, 337, no. 40. Rohault de Fleury 1883, 58-9, no. 83, pl. XLI. Pasini 1885-6, 58-9, no. 83, pl. XLI. Molinier 1888, 92, no. 70. Schlumberger 1890, 305. Kondakov 1892, 228-9. Dalton 1911, 498, 514, fig. 298. Ebersolt 1923, 67-8, fig. 27. Albizzati 1923, 37-43, pl. I. Braun 1932, 47, 161, pl. 3, fig. 9. Grabar 1958, 166, fig. 2. Gallo 1967, 299, no. 79; 350-1, nos 36, 53, 57; 368, no. 34; 397, no. 99; pl. 32, fig. 56. Wessel 1967, 79, no. 23. Beckwith 1970, 98, fig. 178. Hahnloser 1971, 60-1, no. 42 (Grabar), pls XLIV-XLV (with bibliography).

11

Chalice of the emperor Romanos (without handles)

Stonework: 3rd – 4th century (?). *Metalwork*: Constantinopolitan, 959 – 963
Sardonyx, silver-gilt, gold *cloisonné* enamel, pearls. *Height* 225 mm, *diam.*
140 mm

Tesoro, no. 65

This chalice, which has doubtless been in the treasury since the thirteenth century (cf. no. 16), appears in the 1733 inventory as "*Una tazza grande di nicolo orientale, lavorata a sonde, adornata di figure, con piede e contorno dorato*" (Gallo 1967, 350, no. 38). It was valued at the high price of 6000 lire in Cicognara's catalogue of 1816-20 (Gallo 1967, 367, no. 26). It was then restored as detailed in the inventory of 1845 (Gallo 1967, 397, no. 98).
The sardonyx bowl is evenly curved, with a shallow pattern, cut back into the surface, of fifteen large gadroons surrounded by borders and separated by darts; each large gadroon encloses a smaller gadroon. The interior, by contrast, has very deeply cut gadroons, which, separated by groins, run from the rim of the bowl towards the bottom in two stages separated by a slanting ledge, below which they become shallower. The flat centre is occupied by a rosette comprising a concave disk surrounded by eight intaglio pointed petals; a circular border in raised relief runs round the rosette. The underside is not visible. The rim of the calice is pierced four times

137

by two small adjacent holes pierced at regular intervals which were to serve, as on the one-handled sardonyx cup (fig. 4), for attaching an earlier mount.

Indeed the bowl can hardly be of the same date as its present mount. The emperor Romanos, for whom the chalice was made, apparently used a Classical vessel, as in the case of the chalice with handles which also bears his name (no. 10). Byzantine hardstone vessels made as chalices are generally taller, concave, and have smooth exterior and interior surfaces (cf. no. 16). Generally speaking, Byzantine hardstone vessels are undecorated (for rare exceptions, see nos 42, 43). Antique vessels, on the other hand, can display a whole range of Classical motifs, from ovoid motifs (fig. 10g) and mouldings (cf. no. 35) to figural representations. They sometimes have a rosette on the underside (cf. no. 10), recalling that on the interior of this chalice.

The flat gadroons can be found on other sardonyx objects apparently of Antique date. A round cup from the collections of the Dauphin, son of Louis XIV, now in the Prado (fig. 11a; Angulo 1954, no. 44), has slightly raised gadroons defined by a border in lower relief, which, as on the chalice in Venice, alternate with darts in relief. Inside the cup the gadroons – very deep, like those inside the chalice, and separated by ribs – meet in the centre, in a circular depression. The oval sardonyx cup of the emperor Charles IV, now in the treasury of Prague Cathedral (fig. 11b; Podlaha and Šittler 1903, no. 194, fig. 132) is decorated with twelve shallow gadroons cut back into the surface. The interior has twelve deep gadroons, which do not correspond with those on the outside; they are separated by ribs and abut a central oval depression with a raised border. The Bibliothèque Nationale possesses a fragment of a vessel found in Syria, also decorat-

ed with gadroons (fig. 11c; Babelon 1897, 213, no. 378).
The motif does not appear on works datable to the first
century BC or the first century AD. A certain clumsiness
in the workmanship of the vessels in Madrid and Prague
would tend to place works with gadroons later than this
period, the more so since two of the agate vessels found
in the tomb of the empress Maria (d. 407) and known
from a sixteenth-century drawing (Rossi 1863, 53-6) are
decorated with gadroons.

D. A.

The quiet majesty and excellent quality of the enamels
on this chalice match the beauty and subtle carving of its
sardonyx bowl and the elegant simplicity of the design of
its silver-gilt mounts. Fifteen rectangular enamel plaques set between borders of pearl strands decorate the
chalice's tall rim. The enamels portray images of Christ
blessing and, reading from his left, SS John the Baptist,
Peter, Matthew, Mark, Luke, Gregory Nazianzen, Basil,
the archangel Gabriel, the Virgin, the archangel Michael
and SS Nicholas, John Chrysostom, John the Evangelist,
and Paul. Originally, the Virgin flanked by the two archangels would have been placed directly opposite Christ on
the chalice. A rich coloration of porphyry and terracotta
red, navy blue, turquoise, several shades of light blue,
emerald green, yellow, and black allows the figures
to stand out clearly against their smooth gold background. The rings around the base of the rim were used
for the attachment of pendant gems and/or pearls.
Silver-gilt straps with a simple beaded border are hinged
to the chalice's rim and base; the latter is composed
of a tall stem with simple knop edged by beaded
strips. Its splayed foot contains three enamel medallions
within scalloped frames and an inscription in blue
enamel, giving the name of the emperor Romanos, written on six plaques, one of which is missing: +ΚΥΡΙΕ
ΒΟΗΘΕΙ ΡΩΜΑΝ[Ω] ΟΡΘΟΔ[ΟΞΩ ΔΕ]CΠΟΤ[Η]
(Κύριε βοήθει 'Ρωμανῷ ὀρθοδόξῳ δεσπότῃ, "Lord help
the Orthodox emperor Romanos").

The three enamels of the foot contain busts of the Virgin
Annunciate, of the archangel Gabriel, and of St Cosmas.
Grabar cites this Annunciation as a unique example of a
scene on a Byzantine chalice. The medallions of the
Virgin and Gabriel, however, are very different in style
from that of the enamels on the chalice's rim and of St
Cosmas on the foot, as Wessel pointed out (1967, no. 19).
He dated the Virgin and Gabriel to the ninth or tenth cen-

139

tury in Byzantium by comparing them to several enamels in Georgia (see fig. 9a). Moreover, the two enamels have been cut down in order to fit into the small scalloped frames and are therefore probably replacements of the original enamels. In any event, images of saints would be more appropriate to the decoration of the base of a Byzantine chalice (see for example, no. 17). Presumably, Cosmas was paired with St Damian, his fellow doctor and martyr, with whom he was usually associated.

The program of the chalice's decoration depends on the imagery of the Glorification of the Virgin, in which the Mother of God is portrayed *orans*. Often it is used for the decoration of the church's apse as at the ninth-century church of the Virgin of the Pharos in Constantinople, at the twelfth-century cathedral of Cefalù in Sicily and in the fourteenth-century church of the Virgin Peribleptos in Ohrid. The patriarch Photius described the image of the Virgin in the apse of the Pharos church at its inauguration as "stretching out her stainless arms on our behalf and winning for the emperor safety and exploit against the foes" (Mango 1958, 188). The imagery is also found on liturgical furniture like the *Pala d'Oro* in Venice, whose program of decoration derives from monumental imagery (see Frazer 1981, 273-9). Similarly, on this chalice, the Virgin *orans* is accompanied by Christ in glory, archangels, apostles, prophets, Church Fathers, and holy martyrs in the descending order of the heavenly hierarchy. Much discussion has been devoted to the dating of this chalice, for even though it was the gift of an emperor Romanos, four rulers of that name occupied the Byzantine throne during the tenth and eleventh centuries: Romanos I Lecapenos (920-44), Romanos II (959-63), Romanos III Argyros (1028-34) and Romanos IV Diogenes (1067-71). Certain stylistic traits of this chalice's work, however, seem to support a tenth-century manufacture, probably during the reign of Romanos II. The closest comparison for the chalice's style and coloration is that of the enamels on the reliquary of the True Cross of Basil the Proedros that was brought to the West as loot from the Fourth Crusade in the thirteenth century and presently kept in the treasury of the cathedral at Limburg an der Lahn (figs 11d, 11e; Rauch 1955, 201-40). Not only do the figures stand in a similarly elegant isolation against a smooth gold background, broken only by the inscription of small, well-rounded red letters, but also the drawing of the faces and the description of the draperies are closely allied. The heads have the same thick eyebrows that are softly arched in comparison with more slanted, longer and sharply bowed brows on such late eleventh to early twelfth-century enamels as that of Christ from an icon frame of the monastery of Djumati in Georgia at the Metropolitan Museum of Art, New York (Frazer 1970, 240-51). These later features are found also on the enameled figures from the crown of the Hungarian king Geza I (1074-7), which includes an image of the emperor Michael VII Dukas (1071-8), Romanos IV Diogenes' successor.

The long noses, small semi-lunate-shaped mouths and the eyes with large pupils of the Romanos chalice are also closely related to those of the figures on the Limburg an der Lahn reliquary. The description of the drapery folds, either with flowing segments of juxtaposed lighter and darker colors (St John the Baptist and the apostles) or with loosely grouped *cloisons* in a solid-colored ground (the Virgin, and Fathers of the Church), is comparable as are such individual features as the way the Virgin's *maphorion* is folded over her head. Finally, the scalloped edging that frames the medallions of the foot and the support for the base of the sardonyx bowl is found on such mid-tenth-century works as a silver and niello cross in the Benaki Museum that has recently been published by Bouras (1971).

Scholars who have proposed a tenth-century date still do not always agree on whether the chalice should be attributed to Romanos I or Romanos II. Given the great difference between the style of the chalice's enamels and that of the early tenth-century enamels on the Crown of Leo VI (886-912; no. 8) and on the bookcover with the Crucifixion (no. 9), and also its relationship to the work of the Limburg an der Lahn reliquary, Romanos II seems to be a more likely candidate as donor of this magnificent chalice.

M. E. F.

Bibliography: Durand 1861, 337-8, no. 43. Rohault de Fleury 1883-9, IV, 106, pl. CCCVI, fig. 13. Pasini 1885-6, 57-8, pl. L, no. 113. Molinier 1888, 96, no. 102. Kondakov 1892, 228. Dalton 1911, 514-5, fig. 307. Ebersolt 1923, 68. Grabar 1958, 167, fig. 3. Muraro and Grabar 1963, 59, fig. 61. Deér 1966, 83-4. Gallo 1967, 350, no. 38; 367, no. 26; 397, no. 98; fig. 58, pl. 33. Wessel 1967, 72, no. 20. Beckwith 1968, 98. Hahnloser 1971, 59-60, no. 41 (Grabar), pls XLII-XLIII. Coche de la Ferté 1981, fig. 152.

Exh. cat. *Splendeur de Byzance*, 1982, no. E2 (with bibliography).

12

Panel with half-figure of St Michael

Constantinopolitan, late 10th – first half of 11th century
Silver-gilt, gold *cloisonné* enamel, stones, pearls (now missing), glass.
Height 440 mm, *width* 360 mm (330 x 220 mm without frame)

Tesoro, no. 46 (listed in the 1325 inventory: V, no. 7)

Among the most enigmatic pieces in the San Marco treasury is this magnificent *repoussé* and enamel image of the bust of the archangel Michael. Against a fine *rinceau* background, the head of the archangel is worked in silver-gilt, his cheeks full, his nose long and thin, with the brows firmly defined. His hair, in which is set a diadem of three colored glass stones, waves back softly from the face, leaving only a few wispy tendrils at the forehead. St Michael wears the imperial *loros*, decorated with semi-precious stones and colored glass of predominantly red and green, arranged in five and six-part segmented circles within rectangles with beaded gold borders and set against a decorative ground. His richly colored wings and dalmatic are of *cloisonné* enamel. In his left hand, St Michael holds a scepter, set with stones and enamel; his right hand is turned palm outward. The archangel has an enameled halo of rosettes within canted squares, punctuated by colored glass stones. On either side of the nimbus are enamel roundels identifying him as Michael. Next to these are *cloisonné* medallions depicting St Simon at the left and Christ at the right. Strips of *cloisonné* enamel in a stepped cross pattern decorate the raised frame around the central image.

Silver-gilt horizontal strips with low relief acanthus *rinceaux* above and below the central image are set with three enamel busts each: at the top, St Mark, the archangel Uriel, and St Luke; at the bottom, St John the Baptist, Gabriel, and St Bartholomew. Two further silver-gilt strips, of Venetian workmanship, the inner with a *rinceau* pattern, the outer with a leaf pattern, shelve out to a final frame of Venetian filigree of a beehive and floral design, set with Byzantine enamel medallions. (The inner *rinceau* strips resemble those surrounding two Crucifixion icons in the treasury: no. 36, and Hahnloser 1971, no. 18.) For filigree that Hahnloser compares to the outer frame, see the cover of the crystal vase in the present exhibition (no. 37). The roundels represent the Virgin, the apostles Paul, James, Thomas, and Philip, the evangelists John and Matthew (who appears twice), and the warrior saints George, Demetrius, Theodore, Procopius, Mercurius and Eustratius.

The icon, cited in the inventory of 1325 with the standing St Michael (no. 19) is probably the *"iconam cum angelo argenti laboratam ad opus levatum"* (Gallo 1967, 279, V, no. 7). In the inventory of 1816-20, Leopoldo Cicognara notes that the exterior frame then contained sixteen enameled gold medallions alternating with decorative enameled and nielloed medallions (*"sedici medaglioni in mosaico e smalto... compongono un primo giro alternato con meandrini diversi smaltati e niellati"*: Gallo 1967, 379, no. 13). The icon then underwent restoration in the nineteenth century to which Pasini makes reference. The reverse of the icon is decorated exclusively in silver-gilt relief. A cross at the center is ornamented with foliate *rinceaux*, within which are set roundels of St Basil at the center, SS John Chrysostom, Gregory of Nazianzus, Nicholas and Menas on the arms. Originally St Basil was not centered, as seen in a drawing before restoration preserved in the Archives of Venice and the description by Cicognara in 1816 (cf. Gallo 1967, 379, no. 13, pl. 41). A framing modern ribbon in a daisy chain or grape vine pattern precedes a frame of saints in medallions set against a rich foliate background. At the center top is Elias, and around him are SS Cosmas and Damian, Pantaleimon, Mardarius, Auxentius, Eustace, Eugenius, Orestes, Cyrus, John, Hermolaus, Christopher, Stephen the Younger, Polyeuctus, Arethas, James Intercisus of Persia, and Menas (for a second time). The inventory of 1816-20 (Gallo 1967, 379, no. 13) noted twenty-six busts on the reverse and indicated that the center one was absent. It therefore has undergone alteration; the comparison of the back of the work today with the drawing before restoration preserved in the Archives of Venice shows that four medallions were placed in the now empty spaces between the arms of the cross. However, the exterior frame contained then, as now, eighteen medallions (fig. 12a; Gallo 1967, pl. 41, fig. 70).

The outer frame of foliate *rinceaux* was apparently created by beating the metal against two matrices, since the wider top and bottom strips show one pattern, and the narrower sides a second one. (For a description of this technique, see Theophilus, III, lxxv: Dodwell 1961, 135-7.) The Michael panel clearly underwent considerable alterations of the original composition in Venice, as often occurred in the treasury objects, but whether or not the glass of the *loros* is modern, as Grabar suggests, it is certainly consistent with the original Byzantine design (compare, for example, the colored glass used on the Limburg reliquary: Rauch 1955, 201-40, esp. figs 1-2). Most of the enamel medallions set in the Venetian frame seem to belong to the original Byzantine program and are simply out of order, a fact which Pasini attributes to mid-nineteenth-century restorations (Pasini 1885-6, 74). The Virgin probably was placed opposite Christ, since she

143

turns to the right. The consistent style of all the medallions, with the exception of the two archangels, of Demetrius and one of the two roundels of St Matthew, who do not share the beaded nimbus or furrowed brows of the rest, suggests integrity of program. (The Virgin and Christ have individualized haloes.)

The dimensions of the central image of Michael with his stepped cross enameled frame correspond to the dimensions of the cross on the reverse with its daisy chain frame, and the *repoussé* medallions of the reverse are the same size as the enamel roundels of the front. Consequently, the front and back seem to belong together, and the front can be reconstructed accordingly. Christ and the Virgin would flank the archangel, with the other eighteen medallions forming an inner frame in an arrangement paralleling the *repoussé* medallions surrounding the Cross. The enamel roundels would have been hierarchically arranged in their frame, perhaps in the following order: St John the Baptist flanked by the four evangelists at the top, four apostles on each side, and five military saints across the bottom. Again corresponding to the design of the reverse, there would have been a wide outer frame of stamped *rinceaux*, fragments of which may now form the narrow strips on either side of the archangel. (Grabar believed these strips to represent reuse of metalwork from the original front.)

The St Michael has generally been assigned to the second half of the tenth or the first half of the eleventh century, a dating that seems consistent with works that are considered eleventh century in current scholarship. While Grabar's comparison of the metalwork of the reverse to the Limburg reliquary of 964-5 (fig. 12b) must be seen only in the most general sense, the saints in medallions set in an acanthus *rinceau* on the eleventh-century Halberstadt paten (fig. 13a, and exh. cat. *Die Zeit der Staufer*, 1977, I, no. 567; II, fig. 370) and another set in a reliquary at San Marco (Hahnloser 1971, no. 66) are comparable in type. The same formula, though not so well accomplished, is used on the sides of the True Cross reliquary (no. 13), dated by Margaret Frazer to the late tenth or early eleventh century on the basis of parallels with decoration in eleventh-century manuscripts.

The enamel roundels of the front, with their closely set *cloisons* and finely rendered features, are distinct in style from those on the tenth-century Romanos chalices (nos 10, 11), but in keeping for example with the roundels of SS George and Mark in the treasury (Hahnloser 1971, nos 96, 98). The Christ seems quite close to the one set in the bowl of a chalice dated to the second half of the tenth century (Hahnloser 1971, no. 47), not in the exhibition.

The paucity of surviving works combining enamel and *repoussé* makes comparisons with the bust of the archangel difficult. The obvious parallel is the full-length icon of the archangel also in the exhibition (no. 19). Though it similarly combines precious stones, *repoussé* and enamel, its more lavish enameling, and comparisons with

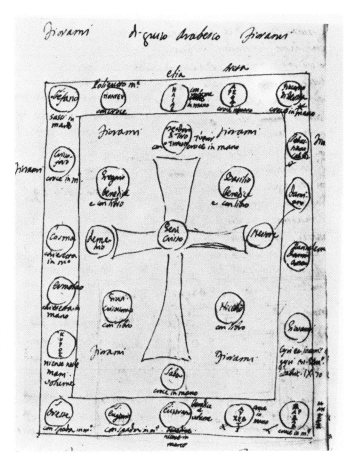

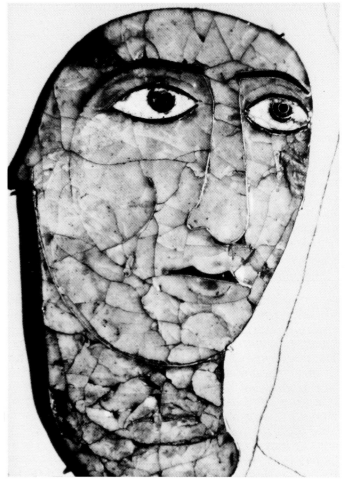

the *Pala d'Oro* point to a twelfth-century date. In the bust of St Michael, the fullness of the archangel's face seems a distinguishing feature of the style. A similar puffiness can be seen in steatites dated to the eleventh century, such as one in Leningrad with St Demetrius, and another with SS Theodore, George and Demetrius, called twelfth century (see Bank 1965, figs 155-6).

It is likely that the bust of Michael comes from one of the numerous sanctuaries consecrated to the archangel, and possibly one of the two dedicated to him within the imperial palace precincts (cf. Janin 1969, 337-50). It is, however, difficult to know if this image was originally an icon, as the inventory of 1325 suggests, or perhaps a bookcover. A number of icons have similar characteristics to both the half and full-length figures of St Michael in San Marco. For example, an icon with the image of Christ painted in the wooden cavity at the center of an enameled nimbus is known from an inscription to be a replacement for a metal image of the Virgin (Amiranachvili 1963, pl. XXVI). The Khakhuli triptych is thought to have had gold *repoussé* for the half-figure of the Virgin whose face is in enamel (fig. 12c; Amiranachvili 1963, 34-5, pls LI-LII).

Literary accounts also provide provocative comparisons. The inventory of 1200 of the monastery of St John the Evangelist on Patmos includes as its first entry, and principal icon, one of St John the Theologian, with the frame in silver-gilt and halo and Gospel of silver with gold and enamel. A second icon, of St John Chrysostom, mentions the halo, Gospel book, *epimanikia* (liturgical cuffs), and the crosses of the vestment as of gilded silver (see Sathas 1872, 47 ff.).

If it were an icon, the elaborate decoration of the reverse, with not only a cross but also numerous medallions, is singular among surviving works of the eleventh century. Two-sided icons for processional use or placement between the piers of an *iconostasis* are thought not to date before the twelfth or thirteenth century (see the discussion in Weitzmann 1976, 10). The combination of an elaborate front with a corresponding but less fragile back in this work recalls the major and minor sides of a bookcover, the function given to the piece by Dalton in 1911 (Dalton 1911, 513). The idea was rejected by Muraro and Grabar (1963, 65), but Gallo (1967, fig. 70) refers to it as a bookcover. As a bookcover, the St Michael would have decorated a manuscript of unusually large proportions, though manuscripts of large format were certainly produced, like the eleventh-century Gospel lectionary at the monastery of Iveron, 400 x 270 mm compared to St Michael's 460 x 350 mm (Pelekanides 1975, 293-5).

Alternately, the small scale of the medallions, which could only be read at close hand, may also suggest an icon for private use, perhaps by the person for whom the Virgin is intercessing. Such a private devotional icon with an image of Christ once belonged to the empress Zoë (1028-50). According to Michael Psellus, it was "embellished with bright metals" that would foretell the future by changing colors. The description calls to mind the reflective quality of the Venice bust of St Michael: "... if it took on a fiery red color, its halo lustrous with a beautiful radiant light, she would lose no time in telling the emperor" (Sewter 1953, 138-9). As Weitzmann has suggested, the brilliant quality of gold and sparkling enamel of the St Michael may have been particularly chosen to reflect the ethereal qualities of an angel (Weitzmann 1978, 66).

B. D. B.

Bibliography: Durand 1860, 45-6, no. 29. Pasini 1885-6, 73, no. 4. Molinier 1888, 45-6, no. 4, 78-9. Molinier 1902, 49-50. Dalton 1911, 513. Diehl 1926, 695-6, fig. 344. Grabar 1953, 186-90. Felicetti-Liebenfels 1956, 48, 110, fig. 24. Rice and Hirmer 1959, 323, pl. XV. Beckwith 1961, 92-3, fig. 118. Muraro and Grabar 1963, 65-8. Delvoye 1967, 294. Gallo 1967, 279, nos 7-8; 299, no. 66; 379, no. 13; pls 69-71. Wessel 1967, 89-91, no. 28. Beckwith 1970, 98, fig. 180. Hahnloser 1971, 25-7, no. 17 (Grabar), pls XIX-XXI, CXXIV. Mallé 1971, 106-8, fig. 37. Wessel 1971, col. 112. Grabar 1975, 22, no. 2, pl. B. Weitzmann 1978, 66. Coche de la Ferté 1981, 308, no. 128. Weitzmann 1982, 15, 42.

Exh. cat. *Trésors d'art du Moyen Age en Italie*, 1952, no. 71; *Venezia e Bisanzio*, 1974, no. 37.

13

Reliquary of the True Cross

Byzantine, late 10th – early 11th century
Silver-gilt on wood, gold *cloisonné* enamel, stones. *Length* 270 mm, *width* 220 mm

Santuario, no. 75 (listed in the 1325 inventory: I, no. 18)

Richly decorated with enamels, reliefs, and gems, the silver-gilt reliquary opens by means of a sliding lid to reveal three particles of the True Cross set in a double traverse cross-shaped container. The cross is surrounded by a twisted rope border and plain silver-gilt panels, which may be replacements of lost figural reliefs (Hahnloser 1971, 34; cf. Bank 1958, *passim*). A concave frieze of barbarized Lesbian cyma and egg-and-dart frames the panels. The reliquary's lid displays a gold enameled plaque depicting the Crucifixion and six enameled medallions of SS John the Baptist, Peter, John the Theologian, Paul, Thomas, and Pantaleimon on its frame. The central plaque shows Christ dead on the cross, mourned by two angels, the Virgin Mary and St John. Disks of the sun and moon flank the top of the cross and the skull of Adam appears in the hill of Golgotha below. The Greek abbreviation for Jesus Christ is inscribed on the *titulus* and Christ's words to Mary and John ("Behold thy mother"; "Behold thy son") are written in red enamel beneath the arms of the cross: [I]ΔE O Υ[I]OC COΥ – IΔOΥ H MH[TH]P COΥ ("Ἴδε ὁ υἱός σου – Ἰδοὺ ἡ μήτηρ σου).

The enameled medallions were probably originally arranged with the two saints John on top, SS Peter and Paul in the center, and SS Thomas and Pantaleimon below. The present placement of St Peter in the top row may reflect a conscious exchange of enamels that occurred in the West where the primacy of St Peter was essential to the Roman Church (see Weitzmann 1983, 25-8). The saints' eyes turn towards Christ in the axial panel. The medallions are placed at regular intervals between six sets of three gems each. The outer frame of the box is similarly enriched with gems held in place by prong settings. The lid is secured to the body of the box by a hinged strap with incised reticulate design that locks into an elaborately incised plate at the center of the casket's front side, which may be a replacement of the original lock. A large double rosette forms the lock on the back. Silver relief medallions with portraits of the Fathers of the Greek Church (SS Gregory the Theologian, Basil, John Chrysostom, and Nicholas) and of military saints (Eustathius, Procopius, Theodore, George, Demetrius, and Nicetas) are set within a background of Sasanian palmette *rinceaux*. These medallions are framed by a crimped border, as is the enamel on the Crucifixion lid and the impressive silver relief leaved and gemmed cross on the bottom of the reliquary. This monumentally conceived cross has large disks at the end of its arms.

Two acanthus leaves rise from the largest of these disks at the foot of the cross. The border is filled with a *rinceau* of Sasanian palmettes that displays lusher foliage and flowers than does that of the reliquary's sides. The cross is inscribed between its arms: IC XC NI KA(Ἰησοῦς Χριστὸς νίκα, "Jesus Christ conquers"). All the inscriptions on the reliquary are written in Greek.

The reliquary is first recorded in the inventory of the treasury of San Marco of 1325, when it was kept in the sanctuary and displayed during the services of Good Friday (Pasini 1885-6, 33; Gallo 1967, 25): "*Iconam unam cum Cruce de ligno Domini, ornatam auro et argento, quae consuevit ostendi in dies Veneris Sancti et habet cohopertu-ram et seraturam argenti; quae crux conservatur in Camera Procuratiae.*" It belongs to a well-known type of True Cross reliquary, perhaps the earliest surviving example of which is a small, richly enameled silver-gilt rectangular casket in the Metropolitan Museum of Art, New York, that was probably made in the ninth century (Buckton 1982, 33-6; Kartsonis 1982). Its form, however, may go back to an Early Christian precedent, like the box in which the True Cross was displayed to pilgrims at the sanctuary of the Holy Sepulchre in Jerusalem at least as early as the fifth century and which the emperor, Heraclius, brought to Constantinople in AD 635. The San Marco reliquary has been variously assigned to the ninth, tenth, or eleventh century, but most recently, Grabar, following a suggestion of Frolow, proposed a thirteenth-century date on the basis of the enamel's poor quality, the exaggerated sway of Christ's body on the cross and the resemblance of the silver relief cross and of the enameled and relief saints' medallions to thirteenth-century work. He argues that the Crucifixion enamel copies a tenth-century model.

The enamels of the reliquary, however, are not of poor quality, but only badly damaged. They have suffered severe losses in Christ's arms and cross and in parts of the haloes and dress of the Virgin, John, the angels and saints. Where not actually missing, the enamel is cracked and broken in many places and several of the *cloisons* are detached from their gold backing. Furthermore, in comparison to most Palaeologan images of the Crucifixion, where Christ's agony is expressed through an intense swaying of his body and legs, the pose of Christ is restrained on the reliquary.

The relief busts on the reliquary and sides are similarly less animated than are their Palaeologan counterparts, as represented, for example, by the busts of saints on the

148

13a

13b

early fourteenth-century bookcover in the Biblioteca Marciana (Hahnloser 1971, no. 39). The gems on the reliquary are set with prongs rather than with bezels, which were customary in Middle Byzantine art, as Grabar points out. These later settings, however, are clearly replacements of earlier gem mounts, whose original, larger size can be traced in the discoloration of the silver-gilt surface around the present mountings.

Grabar's final argument centers on the time at which the reliquary entered the San Marco treasury. Whereas it is listed in the inventory of 1325, it does not appear in that of 1283 and, therefore, could have been made around the year 1300 before being brought to Venice. The failure of the 1283 inventory to mention this reliquary, however, does not necessarily mean it was not made before that date but only, probably, that it came to San Marco between 1283 and 1325.

A return to the earlier dating of the reliquary in the Middle Byzantine period is justified. In the past, the work has most often been compared to the True Cross reliquary at Limburg an der Lahn of 964-5 for the color and style of its enamels, and for the form of the leaved cross on the silver relief back. Its style, however, is later. Its silver relief cross lacks the elegant monumentality of that on the earlier reliquary and its *rinceaux* are heavier and more rigid in style. They are closer in design to the *rinceaux* on the relief of St Michael (no. 12) and in the borders of a lectionary in the Dionysiou monastery at Mount Athos (gr. 587), dated by Kurt Weitzmann to the mid-1050s on the evidence of its miniatures (Weitzmann 1950, 151-74, 215-9; e.g. fol. 116r: Pelekanides 1973, 191, 435). Furthermore, such features as its crimped borders are found frequently in late tenth and eleventh-century works like the two ivory triptychs in the Museo Sacro at the Vatican and in the Louvre Museum (Goldschmidt and Weitzmann 1934, nos 32-3; Morey 1936, 65-7; Maxeiner 1977, 319-25).

The reliquary's figural style is also characteristic of this later period. The Virgin and St John of the Crucifixion, for example, have the same slender proportions, round faces, and intense gazes as SS Zenais and Philonilla, and St Theodore in the Menologion of Basil II (985-1025) in the Vatican Library (ms. gr. 1613; *Il Menologio di Basilio II, Codices Vaticani Selecti*, VIII, 1947, pp. 106, 383), and as figures in an early eleventh-century gospel book in Paris (Bibliothèque Nationale, gr. 64, fol. 11; Omont 1929, 46, pl. LXXXV). The silver relief busts on the reliquary's sides are similar to busts of saints on the silver paten in Halberstadt (fig. 13a; Rice and Hirmer 1959, no. 136) and the standing bishops on the reliquary of Santa Prassede in the Museo Sacro Vaticano (fig. 13b; Stohlman 1939, 48, no. 104). They also resemble miniatures of SS Theodore and Gregory in the Dionysiou monastery lectionary, whose border decorations often copy enamel designs (fols 143r, 116r, 2r; Pelekanides 1973, 177, 206, 163, 191).

M.E.F.

Bibliography: Durand 1860, 312. Pasini 1885-6, 33-4, no. 26, pl. XXIII. Molinier 1888, 58, no. 16, fig. 139. Dalton 1911, 514. Braun 1940, pl. 19, fig. 64. Rice 1950, pl. II; Bank 1958, 234, 241. Beckwith 1961, 92, fig. 117. Frolow 1961, 485-6, no. 663. Frolow 1965, 126, 159, no. 3, 166, no. 1, 1787, 22, nos 1-2, fig. 48. Deér 1966, 42, fig. 50. Gallo 1967, 25, no. 15; 277, no. 18; 304, no. 9; 307, no. 14; 322, no. 74; figs 20-1. Wessel 1967, 75, no. 21. Hahnloser 1971, 34, no. 24 (Grabar), pls XXV-XXVII.

Exh. cat. *Masterpieces of Byzantine Art*, 1958, no. 191; *Byzantine art an European art*, 1964, no. 464; *Venezia e Bisanzio*, 1974, no. 65.

14

Bookcover with Christ and the Virgin *orans*

Byzantine, late 10th – early 11th century
Silver-gilt on wood, gold *cloisonné* enamel, stones, pearls. *Length* 290 mm,
width 210 mm

Biblioteca Marciana, ms. Lat. Cl. I, 100 (listed in the 1325 inventory of the
treasury: V, no. 12)

Christ blessing and the Virgin *orans* decorate centrally placed rectangular panels on the front and back cover of this sumptuous silver-gilt bookcover, which contains a fourteenth-century Venetian evangeliary. They are dressed in rich blue robes. Christ, inscribed I͂C X͂C ('Ιησοῦς Χριστός, "Jesus Christ"), holds a tall book with a cross and jewels on its cover in the crook of his left arm; the Virgin, inscribed M͞H̅P Θ͞Υ (Μήτηρ Θεοῦ, "Mother of God"), spreads her hands over her chest in prayer. A *mappa*, handkerchief, is looped around her belt. Twelve enameled medallions of saints, who are identified by Greek inscriptions, are applied to the background around the central panels. On the front, reading clockwise from the left corner, are St Andrew, the archangel Gabriel, and SS Paul, James, Mark, Philip, Simon the Zealot, the prophet Elisha, SS Matthew, Thomas, John, and Luke; on the back, St John the Baptist, the archangel Michael, and SS John Chrysostom, Peter, Nicholas, Elizabeth, Joachim, Zachariah, Basil, Ann, Gregory, and Bartholomew. The figures are traditionally dressed in *chiton* and *himation* (apostles), *paenula* and *omophorion* (bishops), *chiton* and *chlamys* (prophets), *divitission* and *chlamys* (angels), *chiton* and cloak (John the Baptist), *chiton* and *maphorion* with the "hood" of a different color (female saints). Each saint carries his accustomed attribute, for example a book or furled scroll or cross-shaped staff for the male saints, and crosses and scepters for the female saints and angels respectively. The figures' *himatia* and *chitones* are rendered in alternating sections of light blue, light green and black enamel; otherwise, solid colors are used for the clothes of the angels, prophets, female saints, and John the Baptist. The medallion portraits are not in their original order; presumably they once followed accustomed Byzantine hierarchy of imagery with angels, St John the Baptist, and apostles at the top and other saints and prophets below in the order established in the Byzantine liturgical prayers of the consecration of the eucharist (see Kantorowicz 1942, 56-81). The saints participate in the iconography of the Glorification of the Virgin (see Introduction, p. 110, and no. 11). The outer borders of the panels are formed by alternating square and oval, red and green cabochons, whose settings are punctuated by two golden beads on their longitudinal axes. Small pearls, only one between two gilt rings, are strung alongside the gems and around the medallions and the central images of Christ and the Virgin. The bookcover, the composition of which

resembles another one at San Marco (figs 14 a, 14 b), is well preserved with the exception of some loss of enamel in the Virgin's robes and, particularly, of lost cabochons on the back cover.

The bookcover is most often dated in the tenth century. Grabar (Hahnloser 1971, no. 36), for example, places it between the votive crown of the emperor Leo the Wise (886-912), and the reliquary of the True Cross at Limburg an der Lahn (964-5), relating it specifically to the chalice of the Patriarchs (no. 16), which he dated between 933 and 935. Furlan (exh. cat. *Venezia e Bisanzio*, 1974, no. 28), however, suggested a mid-tenth-century date, while Wessel (1967, no. 27) and Talbot Rice (Rice and Hirmer 1959, nos 140-1) dated it to the late tenth and twelfth century respectively. Grabar's dating seems too early for the style of the bookcover, which differs from that of the votive crown and the Limburg an der Lahn reliquary. The conception of the figures' faces is quite different. The hair is more abstractly patterned, the eyes are larger and rounder. Moreover, the lines of Christ's and the Virgin's draperies are more repetitive and geometrically severe than the looser rhythmic folds of cloth of the central image of Christ on the mid-tenth-century Limburg an der Lahn reliquary. The *cloisons* that describe the face of Christ on the bookcover, for example, are smoothly and severely drawn compared to the nervous, rippling energy of the outlines of Christ's face and hair on the earlier reliquary. Finally, the organization of imagery on the bookcover is as geometrically precise as that of the placement of its *cloisons*, whereas the enameled cover of the Limburg reliquary presents a constantly shifting vista of clusters of gems and densely packed flat decoration in the stepped-cross enameled border framing the chorus of closely grouped figures.

The character of the bookcover's design, however, finds close parallels in the art of the late tenth and of the first half of the eleventh century, where self-contained figures were often placed against expanses of gilded backgrounds, perhaps inspired by Byzantine mosaic decoration, for example in the late tenth-century Gospel lectionary at Mount Sinai (cod. 204; Beckwith 1961, fig. 104). A similar distribution of a central figure surrounded by bust portraits is found in Byzantine paintings, like the icons of the Crucifixion and of St Nicholas at Mount Sinai (Weitzmann 1967, pls 40,43). Certain characteristics of the style of the figures on the bookcover are also found in this later period. The round faces of the Virgin

153

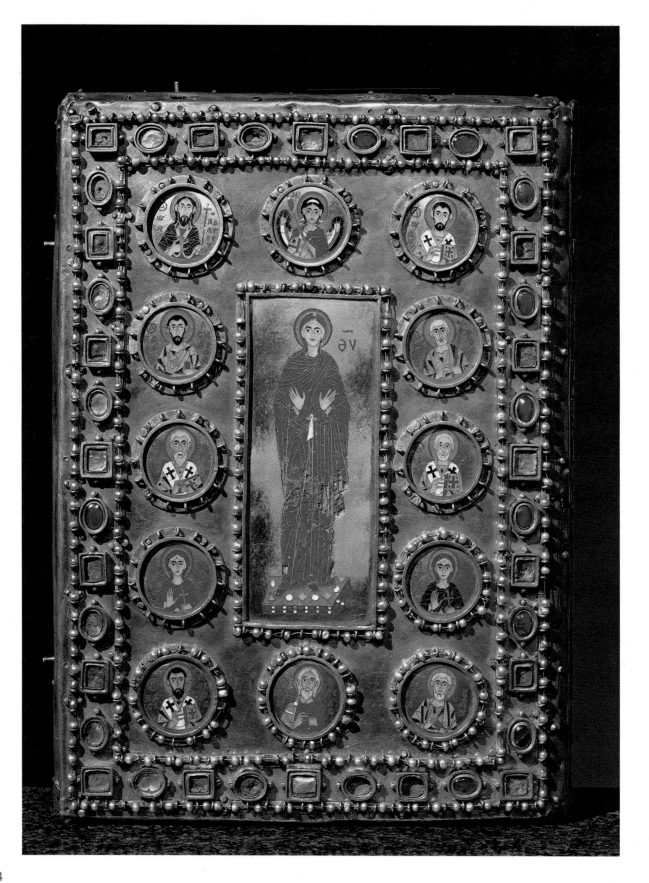

and the young beardless saints are similar to those of such figures as the Virgin in the Adoration of the Magi in the Menologion of Basil II (976-1025; Biblioteca Apostolica Vaticana, ms. gr. 1613, p. 272, *Il Menologio di Basilio II, Codices Vaticani Selecti*, VIII, 1947), the Crucifixion enamel of the San Marco reliquary of the True Cross (no. 13), and of images of the empress Zoë (1028-50) in enamel (Hahnloser 1971, no. 98; Wessel 1967, no. 32) and in the mosaic of the south gallery of St Sophia in Istanbul (Whittemore 1942, pl. 13). Mosaics of the first half of the eleventh century offer the closest analogies for the distinctive rendering of the figures' eyes on the bookcover, with their wide-open oval shape and large circular pupils that seem to be suspended from just under the upper lid, particularly at Hosios Loukas and Nea Moni in Greece and at St Sophia in Kiev (Lazarev 1967, figs 164-81). Finally, the type and disposition of the cabochons and of the enameled decoration in general on the bookcover resemble that of the tenth to eleventh-century reliquary of the True Cross (no. 13) and of the eleventh-century paten with Christ (no. 18) in this exhibition.

Weitzmann has published this and the bookcover Cl. I, 101 (no. 9) as diptych icons, reused as bookcovers in the basilica of San Marco (Weitzmann 1982, 16). He points out that this was the fate of many Byzantine works of art that were brought to the West, particularly ivories that were incorporated in Western bookcovers in the Middle Ages. The subject and design of the front and back covers are moreover very close to the design of contemporary icons. Although Weitzmann's arguments for the original use of the bookcover as a diptych icon are arresting, especially considering the damage suffered by the delicate jeweled and pearled decoration of the back cover, there are examples of bookcovers from the Early Christian and Palaeologan periods which treat the front and back covers equally (see Introduction, pp. 111-2, and no. 20).

M. E. F.

Bibliography: Labarte 1872-5, III, 24, fig. 63; II, *Album*, pl. CIII. Pasini 1885-6, 117-8, no. 13, pls X-XI. Molinier 1888, 47-50, 81, no. 6. Schlumberger 1890, 449. Kondakov 1892, 192. Molinier 1896. Dalton 1911, 516, fig. 308. Grabar 1958, 172, figs 8-11. Rice and Hirmer 1959, 72, no. 141. Muraro and Grabar 1963, 68, 71. Ross in exh. cat. *Byzantine art an European art*, 1964, 396. Gallo 1967, 279, no. 12; 291, no. 3 (?); 304, no. 18 (?). Wessel 1967, no. 27. Volbach and Lafontaine-Dosogne 1968, 108-99, no. 82. Hahnloser 1971, 48-9, no. 36 (Grabar), pls XXXIV-XXXV. Mallé 1971, 105-6, fig. 36.

Exh. cat. *Venezia e Bisanzio*, 1974, no. 28.

15

Chalice with eucharistic inscription

Stonework: Byzantine, 9th–11th century. *Metalwork*: Constantinopolitan, late 10th–early 11th century
Sardonyx, silver-gilt, gold *cloisonné* enamel, stones, pearls. *Height* 115 mm, *width* 200 mm, *diam.* 110 mm

Tesoro, no. 79

The chalice appears in the 1571 inventory as "*Un vaso sive gotto* [goblet] *d'Agata, con manichi, et piede d'arzento, et con zoglie che non sono buone attorno nelle panizuole*" (Gallo 1967, 299, no. 55), and in 1733 as "*Un vasetto di sardonica orientale adornato di geme con manichi e ornamenti dorati*" (Gallo 1967, 350, no. 41). It was valued at 600 lire in Cicognara's catalogue of 1816-20 (Gallo 1967, 368, no. 31).
This fairly thick-walled vessel in the shape of a truncated cone has a fairly regular shape, apart from a large polished depression facing one of the handles. The inte-

rior is rough. The bottom is concave on the inside, flat on the outside.
Hardstone vessels in the form of truncated cones were produced in Classical Antiquity, as is shown by one in sardonyx discovered in Egypt in 1930, now in the Egyptian Museum, Cairo (Bühler 1973, no. 6, pl. 2), and a rock-crystal *situla* in the treasury of San Marco (Hahnloser 1971, no. 75, pl. LXIII). The workmanship of the metalwork of the chalice, however, strongly suggests an origin in the Macedonian Renaissance. The chalice is not without parallel, for it can be related to a sardonyx

15a

vessel in the Louvre, formerly in the collection of Louis XIV (fig. 15a). This is a little larger (height about 115 mm) than the one in Venice, and it was engraved (as well as given a foot and a mount) in France in the mid-sixteenth century. Besides its shape, one can find in this object the thick walls and the internal roughness and concave bottom of the chalice in Venice. It is less well-made, not being completely round. It is uncertain whether the San Marco vessel, which resembles a *situla* for holy water, was originally conceived as a chalice: the truncated cone-shape would have been most unusual for such a purpose. The only other example is a sardonyx chalice in San Marco (fig. 15b; Hahnloser 1971, no. 62, pl. LVI); unlike the majority of Macedonian period chalices in San Marco (cf. no. 16), however, this has a flat bottom and a foot cut from the same block of stone as the bowl, which makes it unlikely to be Byzantine work and suggests, rather, that it may be an example of re-use (cf. no. 35).

D. A.

Metalwork

The sardonyx chalice is mounted on a low silver-gilt base, which is decorated with narrow beaded borders and faceted cabochons. One of the gems is an amethyst, the others are glass set over an amethyst-colored metal foil. The chalice's two handles are also decorated with cabochons and beaded borders. The two top-most gems, now missing, were set in tall cylindrical bezels; a third is missing from the lower part of the right handle. The rim of the chalice is covered by a silver-gilt collar, decorated with strands of small pearls placed between two silver-gilt beaded bands. They frame four enamel plaques that are decorated with an inscription drawn from the eucharistic prayer for the consecration of the wine: +ΠΙΕΤΕ ΕΞ ΑΥΤΟΥ ΠΑΝΤΕC ΤΟΥΤΟ ΕCΤΙΝ ΤΟ ΑΙΜΑ ΜΟΥ ΤΟ ΤΗC ΚΑΙΝΗC ΔΙΑΘΗΚΗC (Πίετε ἐξ αὐτοῦ πάν-τες· τοῦτό ἐστιν τὸ αἷμά μου τὸ τῆς καινῆς διαθήκης, "Drink all of this, this is my blood, that of the New Testament"). This is a commonly used inscription among the Byzantine chalices kept in the treasury of San Marco (no. 16; cf. Hahnloser 1971, 56, nos 44, 46, 51, 58, 63). In its simple and refined shape and its decoration with an inscription, the chalice resembles a chalcedony chalice that was commissioned by Sisinnios, Grand Logothete under the emperor Romanos II (959-63; no. 23; cf. Ross 1959, 7-10). In the shape and decoration of its mounts, however, it is more closely allied to a larger chalice in the same treasury that Grabar dates to the tenth to eleventh century (Hahnloser 1971, no. 59).

The inscription plaques are about eight millimeters high, and the letters are boldly written in white enamel on a translucent green and enamel ground. Grabar attributes this type of enameled inscription, as well as the short, rounded shape of the letters, to the early period of

15b

the late ninth and early tenth century (Hahnloser 1971, 56-7, no. 56). Similar use of enamel on enamel for inscriptions, however, seems to appear only later with such objects as one of the Byzantine reliquaries of the Most Precious Blood in San Marco (Hahnloser 1971, no. 172) dated to the tenth to eleventh century, for which Frolow (1964-5, 220-1) proposes a late twelfth-century date, on the two icons of St Michael also in the treasury of San Marco (nos 12, 19), on an alabaster paten (no. 18) and on a group of late twelfth-early thirteenth century enamels which include the reliquary of St Demetrius in the Dumbarton Oaks Collection in Washington, D.C. (Ross 1965, 111-2, no. 160, with earlier bibliography). The chalice cannot be dated as late as the late twelfth century however, since, as Grabar points out, the words of the chalice's inscriptions are written without accents as was customary only before the second half of the eleventh century. The chalice may, therefore, have been made in the late tenth or early eleventh century.

M. E. F.

Bibliography: Rohault de Fleury 1883-7, 104, pl. CCC, fig. 2. Pasini 1885-6, 56, no. 84, pl. XLII, no. 3. Molinier 1888, 92, no. 71. Schlumberger 1896-1905, II, 308. Braun 1932, fig. 18. Ross 1959, 7-10. Frolow 1964-5, 205-6, 216-7, 220-1. Gallo 1967, 299, no. 55; 350, no. 41; 368, no. 31; pl. 35, fig. 61. Hahnloser 1971, no. 56 (Grabar), pl. LI, with bibliography. Bouras 1979, 27-8.

16

Chalice of the Patriarchs

Stonework: Byzantine, 10th century. *Metalwork*: Constantinopolitan, 10th – early 11th century
Sardonyx, silver-gilt, gold *cloisonné* enamel, stones, pearls. *Height* 273 mm, *diam.* 180 mm

Tesoro, no. 69

The chalice has doubtless belonged to the treasury ever since the thirteenth century. The 1325 inventory has this entry: "*Calices septem de unicolo magnos in modum Grecorum, ornatos argento deaurato*" (Gallo 1967, 278, III, no. 19), among which it would appear to figure, along with the two chalices of the emperor Romanos (nos 10, 11). It was valued at 4000 lire in Cicognara's catalogue of 1816-20 (Gallo 1967, 367, no. 25).
Among the numerous hardstone chalices at San Marco, fifteen have agate or sardonyx bowls. These were sometimes Classical objects re-used in Byzantium during the Macedonian Renaissance, as in the case of the two Romanos chalices. Frequently, however, they were made in Byzantium in the ninth, tenth and eleventh centuries specifically as chalices, and have kept their original mounts. Such is the case here. The bowl is hemispherical, as are almost all the Byzantine chalices in San Marco, regardless of material. Made from dappled sardonyx of a consistent colour, apart from a white spot in the lower part, this chalice is one of the most capacious of the treasury's sardonyx chalices. Byzantine craftsmen sometimes had difficulty in cutting large pieces, as is shown by a sardonyx chalice of similar size in San Marco, with its contour marred by a bulge (Hahnloser 1971, no. 45, pl. XLVI). By contrast here, the profile is very regular, and a comparison with the other Byzantine sardonyx chalices in the treasury shows that the chalice of the Patriarchs belongs particularly with three others (figs 16a, 16b, no. 17; Hahnloser 1971, no. 43, pl. XLV, no. 44, pl. XLVI). The interior of the bowl has a flat circular bottom, to which an enamel medallion has been attached. This decoration can be found on only one other sardonyx chalice in San Marco (Hahnloser 1971, no. 47, pl. XLVII). All the others including the latter, are concave with the exception of a chalice in the shape of a truncated cone, which has a flat bottom (fig. 15 b; Hahnloser 1971, no. 62, pl. LVI). The bowl of the chalice of the Patriarchs would therefore appear to have been carved specially for its present mount, which is one of the richest in the treasury; this would suggest that it was an imperial commission. Grabar has suggested that the chalice could be contemporary with the patriarchate of Theophylactos, son of the emperor Romanos I (933-56). Although this hypothesis is now disputed (see below), the hardstone bowl in every way represents the best of Byzantine craftsmanship during the Macedonian Renaissance.

D. A.

Metalwork

This magnificent, large chalice is decorated on the rim with an inscription written in blue enamel quoting the words spoken by the priest during the celebration of the eucharist in the Greek liturgy: +ΠΙΕΤΕ ΕΞ ΑΥΤΟΥ ΠΑΝΤ[ΕC] ΤΟΥΤ[Ο] Μ[ΟΥ] ΕCΤ[Ι] ΤΟ ΑΙΜΑ Τ[Ο] ΤΗC Κ[ΑΙ]ΝΗC ΔΙΑΘΗΚΗC Τ[Ο] ΥΠΕΡ ΥΜ[ΩΝ] Κ[ΑΙ] ΠΟΛΛΩΝ ΕΚΧΥΝΟΜ[ΕΝΟΝ] ΕΙC ΑΦΕCΙΝ ΑΜΑΡΤ[ΙΩΝ] (Πίετε ἐξ αὐτοῦ πάντες· τοῦτό μού ἐστι τὸ αἷμα, τὸ τῆς καινῆς διαθήκης τὸ ὑπὲρ ὑμῶν καὶ πολλῶν ἐκχυνόμενον εἰς ἄφεσιν ἁμαρτιῶν, "Drink all of this, this is my blood, that of the New Testament that was shed for you and for many for the remission of sins"). Circular enamels of four martyrs – Demetrius, Procopius, Theodore, and Akyndinus – are set on the straps that join the rim to the base of the sardonyx cup. On the base, four trapezoidal enamel panels depict SS Gregory Nazianzen, John Chrysostom, Ignatius (an ardent advocate of religious imagery, 847-58 and 867-77), who were all patriarchs of Constantinople, and Theophylactos, bishop of Nicomedia (ca. 800-845), who was deposed for his support of religious art. A medallion of Christ blessing and holding a book with a jeweled cover is set inside at the base of the sardonyx bowl (Pasini 1885-6, 55-6, pl. XXXV, no. 62).
The four straps that support the chalice's bowl are decorated above and below the images of the martyrs with rosettes in medallions and Sasanian palmettes respectively. More rosettes of different design in roundels decorate the friezes above and below the bishop saints on the foot. Two v-shaped lines and a central dot fill the interstices between each roundel; they probably derive from the leaves that often act as filler ornament between the major motifs of manuscript border illuminations (Weitzmann 1935, pls 10ff.; Frantz 1934, 42-76). A single row of oval crystal cabochons decorates the underside of the chalice's sardonyx cup. Silver-gilt beaded borders, often flanking strands of pearls, frame all constituent parts of the chalice.
The enamelwork is beautifully executed in a limited range of matte, saturated colors. Turquoise blue is used for the haloes and accents like the bindings of the books held by the bishop saints or the borders and v-shaped leaves between the roundels, rich blue for the figures' clothes, the eucharistic inscription, and some petals of the rosette roundels, terracotta red for the saints' inscriptions and for accents in the geometric roundels on the

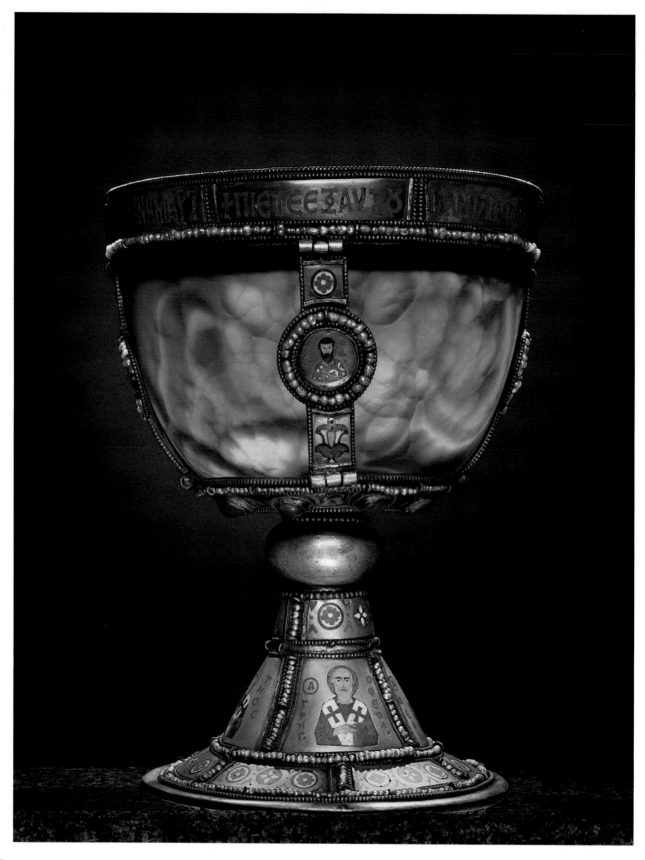

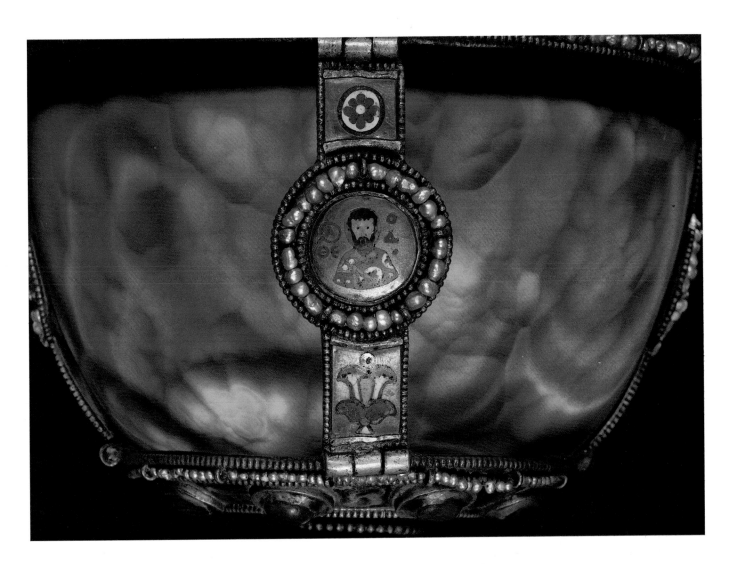

books held by the bishops and in the martyrs' *chlamydes*. Black is used for the hair, the pupils of the eyes, and the eyebrows, and white provides a dominant accent throughout. Translucent colors like the emerald green are primarily reserved as accents, especially in the floral decoration and in some haloes.

Grabar dated the chalice to the second quarter of the tenth century, primarily because of the presence of the bishop Theophylactos of Nicomedia, who is shown on the chalice as a young man. Grabar proposes that his youthful appearance depended not only on that of the patriarch Ignatius, a eunuch who was his ninth-century compatriot, but also as a direct reference to Theophylactos, the reigning patriarch of Constantinople from 933-65 (Grabar 1964-5, 45-51). This Theophylactos was appointed patriarch by his father, the emperor Romanos I Lecapenos (919-44), at the young age of fourteen years. Grabar conjectures that St Theophylactos' youthful image on the chalice reflects the patriarch's young age when he had the chalice made in the early years of his

reign. In support of this hypothesis, Grabar relates the style of the chalice's enamel to that of Christ, the Virgin, and saints on the emperor Romanos' chalice (no. 11). Grabar's arguments are historically convincing, since Theophylactos or his father, Romanos I, built an oratory to St Theophylactos, bishop of Nicomedia, within the palace complex in Constantinople (Janin 1969, 246). In this oratory, the patriarch Theophylactos offered a meal to the emperor Constantine Porphyrogenetos (945-59) on the Feast of Orthodoxy, which is the first Sunday in Lent (Vogt 1935, 145). However, the style of the chalice's enamels differs distinctly from that of the Romanos chalice and argues against the association made by Grabar and for its dating to the late tenth or early eleventh century. The figures are realized in broad, flat planes, with large areas of bold colors in their draperies, in contrast to the more segmented treatment of the multicolored robes of the Romanos chalice's figures. The *paenula* of St Ignatius, for example, is defined by a few widely and rhythmically spaced *cloisons* in contrast to the much "busier" draperies of the Romanos chalice figures, where the folds are delineated by closely set *cloisons* that curve back on themselves to suggest the layering effect of the folds of cloth over the body.

The proportions of the figures also seem different on the two chalices. The patriarchs have broader shoulders than the figures of saints on the Romanos chalice. The faces similarly are more geometrically designed. The eyebrows jut out from the bridge of the nose, and eyes are distinctive in the setting of their large black pupils just beneath the upper lid, surrounded on three sides by the white of the eyes. Although this characteristic is found on the figures on the Romanos chalice (no. 11), its use on the Patriarchs' chalice is more abstract and may better be compared to its use in the figures on the bookcover with the standing Christ and Virgin *orans*, dated to the late tenth and early eleventh century (no. 14).

The style of the enamels on the chalice of the Patriarchs may also be compared to that of a number of eleventh-century enameled medallions of busts of Christ and saints that were incorporated into the *Pala d'Oro* in Venice in the thirteenth century, although they were made later in the eleventh century (Hahnloser 1965 (Volbach), nos 86, 100, 105-13, 120-2). These figures have similarly broad shoulders, carefully delineated eyebrows, the distinctive eyes and carefully drawn, abstracted hairlines and similarly shaped hands (fig. 16c). The three military saints among this group of medallion images (fig. 16d; Hahnloser 1965 (Volbach), nos 120-2) also display a love of brightly colored materials, accented with flat white enamel in their *chlamyses* similar to that of the military saints on the straps around the bowl of the sardonyx cup. Furthermore, the halo of the medallion of Christ (Hahnloser 1965 (Volbach), no. 86) is decorated with small v-shaped "leaves" not unlike those between the rosettes on the base of the Patriarchs' chalice. Finally, the rosette and acanthus decoration seems closest in its abstract simplicity to the decoration of borders in late tenth or early eleventh-century manuscripts. The type of rosette is found earlier in such mid-tenth-century manuscripts as the Paris Psalter in the Bibliothèque Nationale in Paris (ms. gr. 139; Weitzmann 1935, pl. X). Its shape, however, is somewhat different, since the petals of the flower extend to the border of the roundel in which it is inscribed. The chalice's rosettes display a more abstract form by being isolated within the flat white background. Furthermore, the leaf motifs between the rosettes are severely reduced to a v-shaped ornament, a trait that seems more in keeping with a late tenth or early eleventh-century date than an early tenth-century one. The highly stylized Sasanian palmette on the strap supporting the chalice's cup resembles that found in a Gospel book also in the Bibliothèque Nationale in Paris (ms. gr. 64, fol. 63) on the horizontal axes of the frame of the evangelist portrait of St Luke (Omont 1929, 46, pl. LXXXIV).

Although the presence of St Theophylactos on the chal-

ice accords well with Grabar's interpretation and dating of the chalice to the second quarter of the tenth century, St Theophylactos does appear in a few later illustrations. In the eleventh-century Exultet Roll in Bari, for example, a youthful St Theophylactos appears in a roundel in the border of the manuscript, accompanied by a series of bishop saints including St John Chrysostom and St Gregory Nazianzen (Avery 1936, pl. 5). The oratory of St Theophylactos is known to have been used well into the fourteenth century (Janin 1969, 246). Perhaps its decoration included images of iconodule patriarchs and bishops. Since the patriarch Theophylactos entertained there on the Feast of Orthodoxy during his reign, one might even consider that this chalice with its truly imperial proportions was commissioned for that chapel.

M. E. F.

Bibliography: Durand 1861, 338, no. 44. Rohault de Fleury 1883-9, IV, 106, pl. CCCV, fig. 11. Pasini 1885-6, 55, pl. XXXV, no. 61. Molinier 1888, 89, no. 49. Kondakov 1892, 228-9. Schlumberger 1896-1905, I, 173. Dalton 1911, 552, 555, fig. 340. Braun 1932, 47, 147, 161, pl. 9, fig. 24. Ebersolt 1936, 90, pl. LXII. Rice and Hirmer 1959, 70, 71, 322, fig. 139. Amiranachvili 1963, 28, 31. Ross in exh. cat. Byzantine art an European art, 1964, 395. Grabar 1964-5, 45-51. Deér 1966, 45, 99(n.), 108, 151, pl. XLVIII, fig. 124. Wessel 1967, 72, no. 20. Gallo 1967, 278, III, no. 19; 367, no. 25. Delvoye 1967, 290-1. Wessel 1971. Hahnloser 1971, 58-9, no. 40 (Grabar), pls XL-XLI. Coche de la Ferté 1981, fig. 151. Wixom in exh. cat. The Royal Abbey of Saint-Denis..., 1981, no. 110. Wixom, Symposium.

Exh. cat. Trésors d'art du Moyen Age en Italie, 1952, no. 72; Venezia e Bisanzio, 1974, no. 29.

17

Sardonyx chalice with figural enamel

Stonework: Byzantine, 10th century. *Metalwork*: Byzantine, late 10th–early 11th century
Sardonyx, silver-gilt, gold *cloisonné* enamel, pearls, glass. *Height* 205 mm, *diam.* 130 mm

Tesoro, no. 68 (possibly listed in the 1325 inventory: III, no. 19?)

This chalice is very like that of the Patriarchs (no. 16), although Cicognara, in his catalogue of the treasury drawn up in 1816-20, values it much lower, at 3000 lire; six of the eighteen enamel medallions were already missing (Gallo 1967, 363-4, no. 7). Since then the sardonyx bowl has been broken and restored. The bowl has a concave bottom and is shallower than that of the chalice of the Patriarchs; it exhibits, however, the same quality of cutting. It can therefore be considered as a work of similar origin, dating from the same period.

D. A.

Metalwork

Thirteen enameled medallions, framed by beaded bands and strands of large pearls, presently decorate the bowl and foot of this large sardonyx chalice. They depict busts of Christ, the Virgin, the archangels Gabriel and Michael, the apostles Peter, Paul, Thomas, and Philip, the evangelists Luke and Matthew, and the saints Nicholas, bishop of Myra, and Sergius the martyr. Six enamels are missing, four from the bands that link the base to the rim of the chalice and two from the base. The medallions are set between groups of cabochons arranged with four blue teardrop-shaped "petals" around a central larger canted square red glass cabochon. On the foot, the enamels alternate with chains of blue teardrop and clear circular-shaped stones. Alternating square and circular cabochons decorate the silver-gilt support for the sardonyx cup. They are made of glass and are set over blue and rose-colored metal foils in imitation of precious gems. Originally, strands of pearls or gems hung from the rings that are set beneath the groups of cabochons on the chalice's rim. The chalice is in relatively good condition, except for an old break in the sardonyx cup, although several of its enamels, cabochons and their bezels, and strands of pearls are missing.
The chalice's figural program, the Glorification of the Virgin, is like that of several of the Byzantine chalices in the treasury of San Marco, including those of the emperor Romanos (nos 10, 11). The Virgin, her arms raised in prayer and flanked by the archangels Michael and Gabriel, would have been placed opposite Christ on the chalice's rim with the apostles and saints, arranged according to Byzantine hierarchy, filling the remaining medallions on the rim, body and foot (see no. 11).

Grabar (Hahnloser 1971, no. 49) tentatively dates the chalice to the eleventh century, a suggestion that is supported by the style of the enameled figures. While keeping within the tradition of tenth-century imagery like the figures on the Romanos chalices (nos 10, 11), the saints in this example are less majestically conceived, less precise in their portrayal of the figure, and also less carefully executed (see detail). If one compares the figures of St Paul on this and on the Romanos chalice (no. 10), for example, even allowing for the difference in scale of the enamels, the design of the saint's bicolored robes is less interesting, the *cloisons* less boldly patterned. Although Paul's hands on this chalice conform to the long thin bony type of the tenth-century work, they lack that enamel's fine articulation. The differences are not just due to less accomplished workmanship, but to a different conception of the figure. The rounder heads, smaller chins and eyes of the Virgin and archangels, for example, seem closer to such late tenth to early eleventh-century works as the miniatures in the Menologion of Basil II (Biblioteca Apostolica Vaticana, ms. gr. 1613; *Il Menologio di Basilio II, Codices Vaticani Selecti*, VIII, 1947; see for example, pp. 106, 383 and above, nos 13, 14), than to the elongated, majestic images in such tenth-century works as the ivory of Constantine Porphyrogenetos in the Historical Museum in Moscow (Goldschmidt and Weitzmann 1934, 35-6, no. 35).

This chalice is almost identical to another, less well preserved, example in the San Marco treasury, which Grabar (Hahnloser 1971, no. 50) also dates tentatively to the eleventh century. Not only are they exactly the same size, but the style of the enamels is very close as well. Furthermore, the enamels on each are readily exchangeable, judging from the illustrations of both chalices in Pasini (1885-6, II, pls XXXVIII, XLV). Despite some differences between them (for example, the chalice in the exhibition has no rows of pearls around the upper band, but has them around the enamels on the bands joining the rim to the base), the use of identical patterns of gem-settings throughout suggests that the two chalices were made in the same workshop for a single commission (see Introduction, p. 111).

M. E. F.

Bibliography: Rohault de Fleury 1883-9, IV, 106, pl. CCCV, fig. 12. Pasini 1885-6, nos 72, 72a, pls 59-60, XXXVIII-XXXVIIIa. Molinier 1888, 93-4, no. 85. Schlumberger 1896-1905, I, 709. Diehl 1910, 661, fig. 338. Gallo 1967, 278, III, no. 19, pl. 33, fig. 57. Hahnloser 1971, 63-4, no. 49 (Grabar), pl. XLVIII. Wixom in exh. cat. *The Royal Abbey of Saint-Denis...*, 1981. Wixom, *Symposium*.

168

18

Alabaster paten with enamel of Christ

Stonework: Byzantine, 10th–11th century. *Metalwork*: Byzantine, 11th century
Alabaster, silver-gilt, gold *cloisonné* enamel, rock-crystal, pearls. *Diam.* 340 mm, *height* 32 mm

Tesoro, no. 49 (listed in the 1325 inventory: VI, no. 14)

The paten is constructed of a disk of alabaster that is beautifully carved with a recessed six-petaled flower (cf. no. 11). Its central enamel depicts a half-figure of Christ blessing and holding a richly jeweled Gospel book. Four small, surrounding plaques of enameled gold, rimmed with beaded bands, are inscribed with the words spoken by the Greek Orthodox priest during the celebration of the eucharist: ΛΑΒΕΤΕ ΦΑΓΕΤΕ ΤΟΥΤΟ Μ[ΟΥ] ΕϹΤΙ ΤΟ Ϲ[ΩΜΑ] (λάβετε, φάγετε, τοῦτό μοῦ ἐστι τὸ σῶμα, "Take, eat, this is my body"). Alternating rectangular and oval rock-crystal cabochons, set over red and blue metal foils, are closely arranged between two bands of pearls (now mostly missing) on the silver-gilt border,

which is approximately one-tenth of the diameter of the paten. Four rows of gold beading discretely define the rim's three decorative bands. The paten is supported by a silver-gilt, splayed circular foot joined by three hinged bands to a scalloped-edge skirting beneath the vessel's rim. It is similar in shape and decoration to an earlier, smaller agate paten with a central enamel of the Last Supper in the Stoclet Collection (fig. 18a; Salles and Lion-Goldschmidt 1956, 144-8).

The paten is distinguished by refined subtlety of design and excellence of manufacture. The proportioning of the central Christ to the surrounding inscription of this central medallion, to the six-petaled flower and it in turn to

18b

18c

the rim, with its elegantly ordered row of mutely glowing cabochons, is exceptionally beautiful. So, too, is the enameled image of Christ, not only in the technical excellence of its glowing colors, but also in the subtlety of its style. The paten has been attributed to the tenth century because of its resemblance to the enamels on the chalice of Romanos (no. 11; Pasini 1885-6, no. 106; Wessel 1967, no. 21) but, more recently, its relationship to a larger medallion of Christ, incorporated in the *Pala d'Oro* during its thirteenth-century refurbishment, has prompted certain scholars to date it in the eleventh century (Hahnloser 1965, *Il Tesoro*, no. 86; Hahnloser 1971, no. 67). Their eleventh-century reattribution is supported by certain characteristics of style and coloration. The *cloisons* that articulate the draperies, for example, are more plentiful and nervous in their overall patterning than are those on the mid-tenth-century chalice of Romanos (no. 11). The elegant, mannered pose of Christ's blessing hands with their elongated, pliant fingers is more exaggerated than that of Christ on the Limburg an der Lahn reliquary, recalling the style of images of Christ in the second half of the eleventh and in the twelfth century, for example, the Christ of the Hungarian crown (1074-7; Deér 1966, *passim*, pls X-XI) or, in more exaggerated form, that of Christ in the mosaics of Cefalù Cathedral in Sicily (1148; cf. Demus 1949, 11, pl. 1). The rich coloration of the enamel is similarly characteristic of this period. The emphasis on rich and varied, bright, matte colors like the turquoise, red, green and blue of the halo and the yellow of the jeweled bookcover seems stronger than in tenth-century works like the Romanos chalice (no. 11) or the reliquary of the True Cross at Limburg an der Lahn (Rauch 1955, 200-40). Typical also of the later coloristic taste is the placement of the inscription of Christ's name, I[HCOY]C X[PICTO]C, within flat white medallions bordered in green and red instead of written directly on the gold background. This increasing enjoyment of the juxtaposition of saturated bright colors seems to culminate in such twelfth-century enamels as the St Demetrius reliquary (fig. 18b) and the cross with the crucified Christ in the Dumbarton Oaks Collection in Washington, D.C. (fig. 18c; Grabar 1954b, 305-13; Ross 1965, nos 60, 62; Effenberger 1983, fig. 6).

M. E. F.

Bibliography: Durand 1862, 336-7. Rohault de Fleury 1883, IV, 162-3, pl. CCCXXV. Pasini 1885-6, 63-4, no. 106, pl. XLVIII, B2, no. 14. Molinier 1888, 95, no. 94. Schlumberger 1896-1905, I, 705. Dalton 1911, 522, fig. 53. Braun 1932, 207, fig. 149. Rice and Hirmer 1959, 72, 321, pl. 137. Muraro and Grabar 1963, 59-60. Ross in exh. cat. *Byzantine art an European art*, 1964, 75, 395. Wessel 1967, 75, no. 21. Gallo 1967, 280, no. 14; 368, no. 41; pl. 37, fig. 65; Volbach and Lafontaine-Dosogne 1968, 108-9, pl. XXV. Hahnloser 1971, 72, no. 67 (Grabar), pl. LVIII.

19

Icon with full-length figure of St Michael

Constantinopolitan, late 11th – early 12th century
Silver-gilt, gold *cloisonné* enamel, stones. *Height* 460 mm, *width* 350 mm

Tesoro, no. 6 (listed in the 1325 inventory: V, no. 8)

The dazzling impressions that the rich treasures of Constantinople made on medieval visitors are perhaps nowhere better suggested in surviving works than in the silver-gilt and enamel images of the archangel Michael in the San Marco treasury. Like the half-figure of St Michael in this exhibition (no. 12), the standing archangel is presumed to have come to Venice with the loot from the Fourth Crusade attack on Constantinople in 1204. While the St Michael figures cannot be distinguished in the abbreviated inventory of the thirteenth century, both seem to be included in the inventory of 1325: "*Iconam cum Angelo Argenti laboratam ad opus levatum*", and "*Iconam cum Angelo, ad smaldum, ornatam Auro*" (Gallo 1967, 279 nos 7, 8). The first probably corresponds to the bust of Michael (no. 12), since it appears to describe the very high relief that characterizes that work.

The *repoussé* figure of Michael, identified by inscribed enamel roundels on either side of his nimbus, stands against a richly enameled background representing the garden of Paradise. His face and curly hair are entirely enameled. A pearl set in the hair suggests his diadem. Cicognara in 1816-20 (Gallo 1967, 378, no. 10) described the head of the archangel as formed from "a flesh-colored agate" ("*un'agata color di carne*"). However, he was apparently deceived by the color and the translucidity of the enamel, and there is no reason to think the head was restored. Moreover, the technique employed can be compared to that on the icon of St Demetrius in Berlin of the twelfth century (fig. 19a; Wessel 1967, no. 55; Kötzsche 1973, 65, no. 2, pl. 3), where the head is in enameled gold relief.

His cuirass is also richly decorated in *cloisonné*. The large nimbus with interlocking enamel circles and the large wings are gilt. Cicognara also noted that the archangel's wings were missing ("*Mancano le ali*": Gallo 1967, 378, no. 10); they may, therefore, have been replaced after 1820, before, in any case, the publication by Pasini describing them in 1878.

St Michael holds a fully three-dimensional orb in his left hand and a raised sword in his right. A joint to the outer frame is formed by strips of enamel in a repeating foliate pattern. In the frame above him are enamel roundels of St Peter, Christ, and St Menas. The corresponding enamels from the bottom of the frame are missing and have been replaced by gilt metal disks. In the framing side strips are oval medallions of paired enamel saints, identified by inscriptions: the two Theodores, Demetrius and

Nestor, Procopius and George, Eustace and Mercurius. Enamel plaques studded with gems are set between the figurative panels. A piece of modern velvet serves as a backing for the icon.

While similar to the bust of St Michael in its combination of precious enamel and silver-gilt *repoussé*, it is clearly different in the density of its ornamentation. Individual *cloisonné* panels are much more intricate than the broader passages in the bust of St Michael, their profusion of gold wires creating elaborate patterns for enameling. As noted by Grabar, the decorative enamels of the frame are very close to those in the nimbus of Christ and of the Virgin in the icon of the Virgin Nicopeia in the San Marco treasury (Hahnloser 1971, no. 15), assigned to the eleventh century. The facial type and the handling of the hair are quite close to the figure of Daniel of 1102 on the *Pala d'Oro* (Hahnloser 1965, *Il Tesoro*, pl. XXV). Deér has also noted a close affinity to the bust of St George on the upper *Pala*, a comparison that is equally valid for the full-length relief of St Michael on that monument, both of before 1209 (see Deér 1966, 104-5, no. 68, figs 126-7; Hahnloser 1965, pl. XLII). The similarity to the Daniel of 1102 is close enough to suggest a proximate date for the St Michael. The enamels of the warrior saints Procopius and George are close in style to the St Demetrius of 1074-7 on the Holy Crown of Hungary (Deér 1966, fig. 31).

If there was once a back to this work, there is no longer any indication it had one. Consequently, unlike the bust of St Michael (no. 12), there is no evidence to suggest use of this piece as a bookcover, though Deér refers to it as one (Deér 1966, 104). Furthermore, while St Michael is presented in imperial array in the *repoussé* and enamel bust, in this piece both his attire and his entourage of military saints point to the archangel's role as leader of the celestial army. In this way, the standing St Michael is more closely related than the bust to a number of later icons, such as the pair of icons of the archangels Michael and Gabriel, formerly in the Djumati monastery in Georgia, each of which had a silver *repoussé* image of the archangel surrounded by saints in medallions. Enamels from the icon of Gabriel are now in the Metropolitan Museum of Art, New York (fig. 19c), the Musée de Cluny (fig. 19d), and the National Museum of Fine Arts in Tbilisi. The delicate elaboration of the cuirass on the enamel roundel of St George in that series, dated to the twelfth century by Margaret Frazer, is in keeping with the figures of military saints on the San Marco icon (Frazer 1970, 240-51).

173

Deér relates the St Michael to the much smaller enamel icon of St Theodore of Herakleia in the Hermitage
(fig. 19b), which shares not only the elaborate military costume of St Michael's warrior saints, but also the
horror vacui and orientalizing abstraction (Deér 1966,
105, fig. 165). An inventory of the monastery of Rho-
dosto of 1077 mentions a number of silver-gilt icons,
including one of the leader of the heavenly host, St
Michael (Sathas 1872, 47). In such examples as the silver and enamel icon of St Demetrius in Berlin, the
emphasis is clearly on the military character of the saint,
who is shown in equestrian pose (Wessel 1967, 175-6,
no. 55). The San Marco St Michael stands apart for the

virtuosity of its overall enameled surface and its fine
state of preservation.

B.D.B.

Bibliography: Durand 1860, 43-5, 79. Pasini 1885-6, 72-3, no. 2, pl. II. Molinier 1888, 45-6, 78-9, no. 4. Schlumberger 1896-1905, I, 89. Molinier
1902, 49. Dalton 1911, 523, 922, fig. 306. Diehl 1926, 693-5, fig. 343. Grabar 1936, 15, fig. 46. Grabar 1958, 174-5. Muraro and Grabar 1963, 65-
7. Deér 1966, 104-5, 109, 111, 162, pls 126, 134, 166. Gallo 1967, 89; 279, v,
nos 7-8; 299, no. 69; 378, no. 10; pl. 39, fig. 68. Hahnloser 1971, 23-5, no. 16
(Grabar), pls XVI-XVIII. Grabar 1975, 21-2, no. 1. Weitzmann 1982, 15, 43.

19b

19c

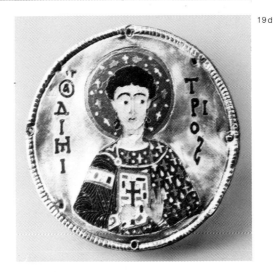
19d

20

Bookcover with Crucifixion and *Anastasis*

Byzantine, 14th century
Silver-gilt on wood, *cloisonné* and *champlevé* enamel. *Length* 300 mm, width 220 mm

Biblioteca Marciana, Cl. Gr. I, 53 (possibly listed in the 1325 inventory: V, no. 12)

Silver-gilt reliefs of Christ's Crucifixion and of his Descent into Hell (*Anastasis*) decorate the central zones of the front and back covers of a Greek lectionary copied by a certain Sophronios at Ferrara, Italy, and completed on 11 November 1439. Each panel is surrounded by images in silver-gilt relief of events from the lives of Christ and the Virgin. They alternate with panels decorated with enameled vermiculate patterns within which are set enameled medallions of the Prepared Throne (*Hetimasia*), prophets and saints. Reading clockwise from the top left on the front cover are the Annunciation, Michael the Archangel, the Nativity, St John Chrysostom, the Presentation of Christ in the Temple, St Nicholas, the Raising of Lazarus, the prophet Moses, the Transfiguration of Christ, the prophet Daniel, the Baptism of Christ, and St Basil; and on the back cover, the Entry into Jerusalem, the Prepared Throne, the Ascension of Christ, St George, the Pentecost, St Gregory Nazianzen, the Deposition of Christ from the Cross, St Demetrius, the Presentation of the Virgin in the Temple, the prophet David, the Dormition of the Virgin, King Solomon. The subject of each panel is identified by a Greek inscription. The bookcover is well preserved except for some battering and consequent loss of enamel. Although it was not specifically described in the periodic inventories of the San Marco treasury, it may be one of a group of covers of enamel and silver-gilt listed in the inventories of 1325 (V, no. 12), 1589 (no. 18) and 1606 (no. 19; see Gallo 1967, 279, 302, 308). The enamels are probably not in their original order. Given the Byzantine tradition of strict adherence to a hierarchy of saints (see Introduction, p. 110), it is likely that either the four prophets were grouped around the central image on one cover and the four Fathers of the Church around the other, or that the two prophets, with two of the Fathers below, flanked the Crucifixion and the *Anastasis*. The inscriptions on the prophets' scrolls refer to the central theme of salvation through Christ's Crucifixion and Resurrection, culminating in the prepared throne of the Savior.

Both the large central panels and the ancillary scenes on their integrated frames are beautifully executed in a sharply defined animated relief. The clutter of imagery in such scenes as the Nativity or the Resurrection of Lazarus only adds to its liveliness. The Late Byzantine artist's love of surface pattern is seen in the backgrounds of overall light-green enamel foliate patterns and in the pounced scrollwork and star patterns around Christ in the *Anastasis*. The juxtaposition of forceful relief and the smooth, yet colorful, surfaces of the enamel medallions on this frame is also found on other fourteenth-century icons like that of St John the Theologian at the Lavra monastery on Mount Athos (Grabar 1975, no. 33, fig. 71) and on the icon of Christ from St Nicholas at Vratsa in Bulgaria (Grabar 1975, no. 37, figs 112-3). Very similar also is the frame of an icon of the Virgin at Freising Cathedral in Germany, which bears an inscription referring to a bishop of Thessaloniki in the first half of the thirteenth century, a date that makes this frame the earliest of its type. Grabar (1975, no. 16, fig. 39), however, tentatively suggests that parts of the frame including the enamels may be later.

The type and style of the scenes in relief that are drawn from Christ and the Virgin's lives are mirrored in another fourteenth to fifteenth-century bookcover in the San Marco treasury (Hahnloser 1971, no. 39) and on contemporary icon frames, like that of the Virgin *Hodegetria* of the Vatopedi monastery on Mount Athos (Grabar 1975, no. 21, fig. 47) where many of the same scenes are depicted. Furthermore, on this icon the overall trefoil background design is executed in the same enamel technique as that used for the vermiculate ground around the medallions on the San Marco bookcover. Even the patterns of *rinceaux* and strapwork on the three low relief silver strips that form the spine can be found on such icon frames as that of a mosaic icon of St Ann at the Vatopedi monastery on Mount Athos (Grabar 1975, no. 23, fig. 60).

Finally, the program of the enamel decoration with the *Hetimasia* and archangels, prophets, and saints below is very similar to that of many contemporary icon frames, notably the icon in Freising, the enamels on the Lavra icon (Grabar 1975, no. 33, figs 71-2) and the fourteenth-century silver relief decoration on the frame of the earlier icon of the Angel of the Annunciation, in the picture-gallery at Ohrid in Yugoslavia (Grabar 1975, no. 10, figs 26-9; Djurič 1961, 15-19, 96-7, pls XXX-XXXI).

M. E. F.

Bibliography: Pasini 1885-6, 117-8, no. 14, pl. XII. Molinier 1888, 82, no. 11. Schlumberger 1896, 748. Grabar 1958, 175-6, fig. 12. Gallo 1967, 27, no. 49; 279, no. 12; 302, no. 18; 308, no. 19; pl. 44, fig. 76. Wessel 1967, 196-200. Hahnloser 1971, 50-2, no. 38 (Grabar), pl. XXXVIII. Grabar 1975, 77-8, figs 104, 109. Velmans 1979, 125-6, figs 15-6.

21

Gilded and painted glass bowl

Constantinopolitan, probably 10th century
Glass, gilded and painted, silver-gilt, stones. *Height* 170 mm, *diam.* 170 mm, *overall width* 330 mm

Tesoro, no. 109 (listed in the 1325 inventory: V, no. 3)

One of the most exquisite and extraordinary objects believed to have been part of the Venetian booty from Constantinople when the city was taken by the Crusaders in 1204 is this hemispherical glass vase with a broad flaring rim. Arabesques in gilt surround the seven medallions decorating the principal field of the vase. Mythological figures rendered in flesh tones with gilded head-bands, necklaces and other details occupy the medallions, each of which is enclosed by a border of rosettes painted in red, yellow, blue-gray and green. In the spandrels between the seven medallions are four-

teen small medallions containing heads in profile rendered in flesh tones. The exterior of the rim is decorated with square panels of rosettes alternating with all-over designs based on the arabesque. Decorative pseudo-Kufic inscriptions are found around the interior of the rim and the exterior of the base. The vase is contained in a silver-gilt mount with scrolling handles, each with a blue gem in the center of the upper quadrilobe. Identifications of the figures in the medallions have recently been suggested by Cutler (1974): the standing nude male figure bearing a staff with star and crescent motif

181

21a

21b

in his left hand, a second staff in the right hand and wearing a helmet portrays Mars Gradius. Continuing to the right, Dionysus, Polydectes, tentatively Hermes, tentatively Ajax brooding over the death of Achilles; then Herakles and a Roman augur are portrayed.

Many scholars have thought that this vase was Antique, with the Kufic inscriptions added later (Hahnloser 1971, no. 83 (Grabar); Lamm 1929-30, 107-9). The current belief that the vase with its Kufic inscription as well as the silver-gilt mount is all of the same period and all Byzantine was first proposed by Molinier. Ever since the original comparison by Rosenberg, scholars have concurred that the fourth-century Constantinian gold-glass bowl from Mungersdorf, now in Cologne (figs 21a, 21b), is the type of glass bowl which provided the model for the design of this piece. The differences between the Late Antique model and this product of the Macedonian Renaissance have been succinctly pointed out by Cutler. The heads of the four small medallions on the Constantinian bowl are recognizable full-face portraits of the four sons of Constantine, whereas the heads in the small medallions on the San Marco vase defy specific identification. The Old Testament scenes in the large medallions of the fourth-century vase follow a narrative sequence, whereas the images of the larger medallions on the San Marco vase seem to derive from a number of unrelated models. As a consequence, a misunderstanding of these models and a corresponding lack of emotion are evident (Cutler 1974, 241).

Images of this type are frequently found on Byzantine ivory caskets of the tenth and eleventh centuries. Beckwith compared the images from Classical mythology framed by rosettes and masks on the Veroli casket (fig. 21c) in the Victoria and Albert Museum to the large medallions on this piece and noted that the exaggerated pleats and sharp points of fluttering hems on the draperies are characteristic of Middle Byzantine art. Grabar has shown that the vase is characteristic of the Macedonian Renaissance, with its revival of the Antique and its imitation of Kufic script, and placed the piece in the tenth to eleventh century (Grabar 1971a, 124-5). Most recently, Cutler (1974, 237-8) has argued for a mid-tenth-century date for the vase, on the basis of the style and epigraphy and has shown that the representations are based on Antique gems. He has suggested that the vase may have been a "whimsical commission" of Constantine VII Porphyrogenetos, known to have been an avid collector of gems and inscriptions.

The fine painted and gilded decoration of this vase was applied after the glass had been fired and was secured to the glass surface by a second firing at a lower temperature. A number of technically related works have recently been described and catalogued by Grabar: a flask from Corinth, one from Cyprus, one from Novogrudok, one of unknown provenance in the Corning Museum of Glass, and a drinking glass and four other pieces discovered at Novogrudok in 1958. Of the latter, two and fragments of

182

a third are vases comparable in shape to the San Marco vase (Grabar 1971a, 97-104). Yet the closest parallel noted by Grabar is the flask from Dvina, the medieval capital of Armenia. The color and the eight-petaled yellow, green, and red rosettes on the shoulders are comparable (Grabar 1971a, 96; Djanpoladian 1955, 120-4). Grabar notes that the two pieces come, if not from the same atelier, from two related ateliers.

Some of the other related pieces are similar to Islamic examples, but Grabar notes nuances by which they can be differentiated (Grabar 1971a, 155) and stresses the fact that the similarity in technique and design which unites the pieces as a group are those described by the approximately contemporary monk Theophilus (Grabar 1971a, 119). According to Grabar, the fact that the related pieces have been found throughout the Byzantine empire suggests a common origin, probably Constantinople. It is more prudent to label them more generally as products of the Byzantine empire. However, this particular piece, because of its iconography, is considered a product of the capital of the empire.

K. R. B.

Bibliography: Durand 1862, 22, no. 107. Pasini 1885-6, 100-1; pl. XL, fig. 78, pl. XLI, fig. 82. Molinier 1888, 58-60, 91, no. 66. Dalton 1911, 614 (with bibliography). Rosenberg 1921, 13-5. Diehl 1926, 710. Lamm 1929-30, 107-9, pl. 341. Davidson 1940, 320. Davidson 1952, 115. Djanpoladian 1955, 120-4. Megaw 1959, 59-61. Coche de la Ferté 1961, 263-73. Beckwith 1962. Gallo 1967, 278, V, no. 3; 376, no. 33; pl. 63, fig. 107. Beckwith 1968, 80. Philippe 1970, 100-22. Hahnloser 1971, no. 83 (Grabar). Grabar 1971a, 89-107, 116-9. Cutler 1974, 235-54.

22

Hexagonal rock-crystal vessel

Rock-crystal: Byzantine, 10th–11th century. *Foot*: 'Abbāsid, 9th–10th century
Rock-crystal, silver-gilt, glass. *Height* 195 mm, *diam.* 100 mm

Tesoro, no. 73

The vessel is described in the 1571 inventory of the treasury of San Marco as "*Un gotto* [a goblet] *de pezzi de Cristallo col piede de Cristallo*" (Gallo 1967, 300, no. 87). Less clear in the 1733 inventory, it is possibly to be identified with the following vessel, listed among the rock-crystal objects: "*Un vaso adornato di geme e fornimenti d'argento*" (Gallo 1967, 353, no. 125). Cicognara, in his catalogue of 1816-20, where it is valued at 100 lire, is uncertain as to its use, calling it a "*calice o bicchiere*" (Gallo 1967, 371, no. 4).

The object, which does not appear to have been intended for any liturgical purpose, was made by combining two ill-assorted pieces of different origin – the vessel, and its foot. The earliest element is undoubtedly the round foot, cut from one piece of rock-crystal; from the top downwards this comprises a ring of three mouldings, a shaft ornamented with vertical grooves, another moulded ring, and a base of which the relief decoration, well arranged, comprises a frieze of eight half-palmettes of three leaves; the edge of the foot is vertical. The concave underside of the base is encircled by a large flat rim. Both the form of the foot and its decoration make it unlikely that this object is either an Antique piece re-used or Byzantine work, although they display a certain classicism. Furthermore, among the many surviving Fatimid rock-crystal vessels there are none with a foot of this type. The presence of the half-palmettes nevertheless suggests that an Oriental origin should be sought. It is possible that this is an object produced in the tradition of Sasanian craftsmen but in the ninth and tenth centuries, the time of the 'Abbāsid caliphs, in Iran or Iraq. In the spirit of its decoration this piece is not very far from two rock-crystal bowls in the treasury of San Marco which are carved in relief with a continuous frieze of scrolls (no. 30, fig. 30a). The foot must have been part of a vessel which became broken. The present mount, thought up to make use of the foot because of the beauty of its material and workmanship, has joined to it a goblet-like vessel, which was certainly not made to go with the foot but was also already in existence. The junction with the crystal base was made by means of a silver-gilt ring soldered to the vessel and holding the crystal. The silver vessel, gilded outside and inside, with a flat circular interior base, has a double wall into which six flat rock-crystal plates have been inserted. The exterior of the mount is decorated all over with lozenge-shapes containing red glass, punctuated by roundels filled with blue glass. The lozenges enclose a gold ring or two concentric gold rings. In many cases the glass has been lost. On the basis of this decoration the object can be attributed to a tenth or eleventh-century Byzantine craftsman. His aim was probably to imitate the gems often enhancing precious metalwork and frequently placed in a similar fashion (e.g. no. 17). Grabar has also produced examples of Byzantine architectural decoration of this date where inlays have been used to create a similar design (Hahnloser 1971, pl. LXXXVIII). On a rock-crystal chalice with a Byzantine mount in San Marco, of the same period (fig. 43j; Hahnloser 1971, no. 64, pl. LVI), the horizontal part of the silver-gilt rim, which has little empty holes all the way round, was probably decorated in the same way as the hexagonal vessel. The latter can also be compared with a contemporary Byzantine steatite paten in the treasury, which has a border displaying alternate oval and rectangular cavities intended to take polychrome glass, also lost. They are separated by little circular inlays of mother-of-pearl (Hahnloser 1971, no. 69, pl. LIX).

It is hardly possible to establish when and where the vessel and its foot came together. The same method of using a metal framework, as Molinier noted, is found on at least two other contemporary Byzantine objects: an octagonal vessel in San Marco made from plates of sardonyx held in place by a silver-gilt mount (Hahnloser 1971, no. 87, pl. LXX), and a reliquary in the form of a lantern, also decorated with small disks, in the church of Beaulieu (Corrèze), where the framework held parchment (fig. 22a; exh. cat. *Trésors des églises de France*, 1965, no. 390, pl. 84). The technique would not, then, appear uncommon. However, as far as the "goblet" is concerned, its manufacture from rock-crystal plates of modest size, like the re-use of the rock-crystal foot, if it took place in Byzantium, would tend to confirm the scarcity of this material there (cf. no. 8). The same desire to make the best possible use of a rare piece of stone in the West at this time can be seen on two tenth-century Spanish caskets made from pieces of sardonyx held in a gold framework. These are the "Caja de las Ágatas" in the cathedral treasury at Oviedo (Palol and Hirmer 1967, pl. X) and the casket from San Isidoro León (Madrid, Archaeological Museum).

D. A.

Bibliography: Pasini 1885-6, 61, pl. XLV, fig. 97. Molinier 1888, 93, no. 84. Lamm, 1929-30, I, 229, II, pl. 84,7 (with bibliography). Gallo 1967, 300, no. 87; 353, no. 125; 371, no. 4. Hahnloser 1971, no. 55 (Grabar), pl. LI.

188

Chalice of Sisinnios

Stonework: 1st–2nd century (?). *Mount*: Constantinopolitan, around 960
Agate, silver-gilt. *Height* 110 mm, *diam*. 90 mm

Tesoro, no. 83

It would seem just possible to recognize this chalice from a description in the 1571 inventory of the treasury: "*Un gotto* [goblet] *d'Agata con manichi et piede d'Arzento*" (Gallo 1967, 300, no. 91). In 1733 it is probably to be identified as "*Un vasetto di nicolo orientale con manichi et piede dorato*" (Gallo 1967, 351, no. 51). In Cicognara's catalogue of 1816-20, it has become a "*tazza o bicchiere*", valued at 600 lire (Gallo 1967, 368, no. 33).

The dark agate vessel is of the same colour throughout except for a large white spot. It has a large horizontal crack. It is fairly thin-walled, with a regular contour, a concave bottom and a small base; the underside is also concave.

From an inscription on the mount it is known that the object was mounted for the patrician Sisinnios, doubtless during the reign of the emperor Romanos II (959-63). One hesitates to attribute the stonework to the same period, however, given the abnormal appearance of the chalice: that of a goblet with almost vertical sides. Byzantine chalices are generally hemispherical (cf. no. 16). Of those in San Marco only one other, in sardonyx, has a deep bowl of similar size, but this is more flared (Hahnloser 1971, no. 51, pl. L). When Byzantine chalices were given hardstone bowls of contemporary workmanship, these do not have a base, the foot being provided by the mount which encloses the lower part of the bowl. The hypothesis that Sisinnios had an existing secular vessel mounted as a chalice cannot therefore be dismissed. The presence of the base as well as the thinness of the walls suggests that the bowl is a work of Classical Antiquity, the more so since the craftsmen of Antiquity made tall, narrow vessels with almost vertical sides, like three sardonyx vessels in the Pitti Palace, one without handles (fig. 23 a; Heikamp 1974, no. 5, fig. 18), the others with two (fig. 10f; Heikamp 1974, no. 6, fig. 23; no. 7, fig. 20). The chalice of Sisinnios could be the lower part of a vessel of this type, the upper part of which had been damaged. The same profile can be found in a sardonyx vessel seven centimetres tall, mounted as a flask, in the cathedral treasury at Osnabrück (fig. 23 b; Wentzel 1972, 9, fig. 7).

D. A.

23b
6

A light silver mount has been fitted to the chalcedony vessel: the rim has a lower scalloped border of leaves (cf. no. 24) above which is the inscription:

+ΧΡΙCΤÒC ΔÍΔΩCΙΝ ΑΪΜΑ ΤÒ ΖΩÌΝ ΦÉΡΟΝ (Χριστὸς δίδωσιν αἷμα τὸ ζωὴν φέρον, "Christ gives his blood, which brings life"). The part of the mount enclosing the foot of the hardstone vessel bears a second inscription, which gives the name of the donor: +Κ[ΥΡΙ]Ε ΒΟΗΘΕΙ CΙCΙΝΝΙΩ Π[Α]ΤΡΙΚΙΩ Κ[ΑΙ] ΓΕΝΙΚΩ ΛΟΓΟΘΕΤ[Η] (Κύριε βοήθει Σισιννίῳ πατρικίῳ καὶ γενικῷ λογοθέτῃ, "Lord, help Sisinnios, patrician and Grand Logothete"). As the second inscription lacks accents, it is possible, as Grabar has suggested, that those on the upper part were added later.

The two metal bands on which the inscriptions were engraved are linked to each other by two large handles attached by hinges. Just above the bottom of each handle a scrolled half-palmette marks an angle, above which a long outward curve is interrupted by a small knop of three mouldings. The inward curve of each handle towards the top is punctuated by a small leaf curving outwards, and an upright ring, before ending in a beautiful five-petalled palmette-flower. Flowers of the same type as this finial are stamped on the back of the panel with the half-figure of St Michael (no. 12). Their orientalizing design can be found again, at a later date, in the openwork motifs on the domes of a silver perfume-burner in San Marco (no. 33).

Although the handles of the chalice of Sisinnios can be compared with those of other tenth and eleventh-century Byzantine chalices, like that of St Sophia in Novgorod (Hahnloser 1971, pl. LXXXVII) or – in San Marco – those of cut-glass (Hahnloser 1971, no. 63, pl. LVI), of glass with disks (Hahnloser 1971, no. 65, pl. LVI) and of glass painted with mythological scenes (no. 21), they reveal a refinement and originality rarely attained. Supremely elegant, they admirably set off the almost rectilinear profile of the hardstone vessel by the contrast of their play of curves.

Ross has identified the donor, Sisinnios, with the person of that name who was eparch of Constantinople and whom the emperor Romanos II, in the last years of his reign (959-63), made patrician and Grand Logothete (the chief treasury official of the empire). As Sisinnios is unlikely to have kept the title of Grand Logothete in the reign of Romanos II's successor Nikephoros Phokas (963-9), the mount of the chalice can therefore be dated with relative precision to about 960-3, reinforcing the impression of beauty and refinement displayed by works from the reign of Romanos II (cf. nos 10, 11).

D. G. C.

Bibliography: Pasini 1885-6, 59, pl. XLII, fig. 85. Molinier 1888, 92, no. 72. Ross 1959, 7-10. Gallo 1967, 300, no. 91; 351, no. 51; 368, no. 33. Hahnloser 1971, no. 57 (Grabar), pl. LII.

24

Glass hanging-lamp

Byzantine, 11th century
Glass, silver-gilt. *Height* 80 mm, *diam.* 270 mm

Tesoro, no. 67

The thick, colorless, transparent glass bowl has a very low foot and broad flaring sides decorated around the exterior with cut disks and conical bosses in relief, arranged in roughly two registers. Nearest the foot are eight circular disks, each with a conical boss in the center. Above and between these are eight plain disks with eight pairs of cones between them. The silver-gilt mount bears a votive inscription in Greek: +ΑΓΙΕ ΠΑΝΤΕΛΕΗΜΟΝ ΒΟΗΘΕΙ / ΤΩ CΩ ΔΟΥΛΩ ΖΑ-ΧΑΡΙΑ ΑΡΧΙΕΠΙΣΚΟΠΩ ΤΩ ΙΒΗΡΙ ΑΜΗΝ (῎Αγιε Χαντέλεημον, βοήθει τῷ σῷ δούλῳ Ζαχαρίᾳ ἀρχιεπισ-κόπῳ τῷ ῎Ιβηρι. ᾽Αμήν, "Saint Pantaleimon, protect thy servant Zacharias, Archbishop of Iberia, Amen". *Iberia* was the name by which the Greeks and Romans referred to Georgia.) The mount is fitted with three silver-gilt loops which are soldered to its rim at three equidistant points for the suspension of the bowl as a lamp. Such votive inscriptions were extremely popular in both the Early Christian and Byzantine periods on jewelry. Between the ninth and fourteenth centuries, rings with such invocational prayers were commonly worn by high officials of the Byzantine court (e.g. New York, Metropolitan Museum of Art, acc. no. 1982. 282).

As was noted long ago by Dalton and by Lamm, Paul the Silentiary in his sixth-century description of St Sophia noted the resemblance in shape of some of the lamps in the church to balance-pans on scales. These had a single central light. Although no examples of such lamps from this early period have come down to us, tenth to eleventh-century Byzantine manuscript illuminations,

which are known to reiterate Early Christian manuscripts, provide evidence for the existence of the type in both periods (Ross 1965, no. 103; Ross 1957, 59-60). As noted by Grabar (Hahnloser 1971, no. 79), the disk pattern of the glass is found on several other pieces in the treasury of San Marco (fig. 24a); one of these (Hahnloser 1971, no. 80) is also thought to have been used as a lamp, since it is the same shape as this piece and obviously had a metal mount around the upper edge. Although the design is exactly the same, the piece is broader and not so deep, and thus was never the mate to ours. Another bowl (Hahnloser 1971, no. 81), a vase (fig. 24a; Hahnloser 1971, no. 79) and two chalices (figs 24b,c; Hahnloser 1971, nos 58, 65), all have related designs. Several of the pieces in this group have silver-gilt mounts which are related to those of the painted vase (no. 21) and to those of the chalcedony chalice of Sisinnios (no. 23). Sisinnios was a dignitary associated with the court of Romanos II (959-63). Consequently, the group is usually attributed to the tenth – eleventh century. The mount on our lamp is particularly close to that on the chalice of Sisinnios, and since there seems to be no real reason to doubt that the glass and mount are contemporary, this would argue for a Constantinopolitan, tenth – eleventh century attribution for the piece.

This traditional attribution was recently challenged by von Saldern (1969, 124-32), who notes several examples of glass with the disk pattern from Ctesiphon/Kish and from north-western Iran and argues that the pieces from the San Marco treasury are also Sasanian. The ninth-century Islamic turquoise glass paste bowl (no. 29), which is similar in shape to this lamp, serves to remind one of the popularity of the form in Persian as well as Byzantine art. The important fact to recognize is that both the form and the pattern exist in both cultures.

André Grabar, who has examined and published the pieces from the San Marco treasury most recently, has noted that, in general, both the Sasanian and Byzantine glass is patterned after Roman prototypes. He notes that disks in relief are the exception but must have been inspired by Roman pieces with concave disks. Glass with disks in relief seems to have appeared earlier in Sasanian art than in Byzantine art, but, as Grabar notes, the Byzantine artisans imitated Iranian as well as Roman models. Each of the pieces in the group from the San Marco treasury shows a different disposition of the disks, and no piece has an exact parallel among the Iranian pieces. Grabar has shown that parallels for some of the specific motifs of this glass can be found in other media in Byzantine art, and he concludes that the glass with disks could have been made in Constantinople after Roman or Oriental models. He also notes that von Saldern pointed out differences between the glass found in Iran and that of the San Marco treasury: the latter are transparent, while the Sasanian pieces are opaque, and the San Marco pieces are drawn out or thinner at the rim

24b

in comparison to the body of the piece, while the Sasanian examples are thicker at the rim.

Grabar proposes that this particular piece was probably already in Constantinople where it was made into a lamp in the eleventh century. He notes that its mount has everything in common with Constantinopolitan mounts of the eleventh – twelfth century, as can be proven by the mounts of several Byzantine vases of the San Marco treasury. He points out that there is nothing to indicate that the object was brought or sent from Georgia to the capital, or that it was offered to a church in that region and concludes that Zacharias must have offered the bowl-lamp to a Constantinopolitan sanctuary.

K. R. B.

Bibliography: Pasini 1885-6, 75, no. 1, pl. LIV, fig. 125. Molinier 1888, 98, no. 114. Lamm 1929-30, 146 (with bibliography), pl. 52. Gallo 1967, 374, no. 22. Philippe 1970, 135-6, fig. 74. Hahnloser 1971, 75-6, no. 78 (Grabar), pl. LXIII. Grabar 1971a, 107-9, 111-2, 115-6, 123-4, no. 13, fig. 19.

24c

25

Alabaster paten with invocation

Constantinopolitan, 10th–11th century
Alabaster, silver-gilt, rock-crystal, pearls. *Height* 45 mm, *diam.* 230 mm

Tesoro, no. 63

Pilgrims visiting St Sophia in Constantinople for the first time were invariably overwhelmed by its opulent splendor. From some of their descriptions of the church-furnishings, Ebersolt has felt it possible to suggest that this particular alabaster paten was once in this world-famous sanctuary. It is thought to have come to the basilica of San Marco as part of the spoils of the Fourth Crusade in 1204, but it is not identifiable in the earliest inventories. Beyond question, the paten reflects characteristics associated with goldsmith work of the Macedonian Renaissance in Constantinople. Even the vessel itself, which reiterates a late Roman form, is indicative of the tenth–eleventh centuries, when vessels, especially in glass and semi-precious stone, were fashioned after Antique forms. That alabaster was also a popular material of the period is evident from the eleventh-century Constantino-

politan alabaster paten with an enamel bust of Christ in the center and a Greek inscription rendering the words pronounced by the priest during the celebration of the eucharist (no. 18). The border around the rim of this second alabaster paten presents the same rich decoration as does the paten under discussion. Both have cabochons of rock-crystal between strings of tiny pearls.
A similar horizontal border around the rim is found on the tenth to eleventh-century Constantinopolitan glass paten which is cut in a beehive pattern (no. 26). It, too, has large, evenly spaced cabochons with strings of tiny pearls forming the borders. However, on the glass paten oval cabochons alternate with rectangular ones whereas on the present alabaster paten all of the cabochons are oval and more of the pearls are missing. In general concept, also, these two patens are similar. Both have a foot

194

with beaded borders, and on both the foot is connected to the border of the rim by four silver-gilt bands. However, the foot of the alabaster paten is set with oval cabochons, whereas that of the glass paten is plain. Furthermore, the bands of this alabaster paten are inscribed, as noted above. (For a more extensive discussion of Constantinopolitan mounts of the tenth–eleventh centuries, see no. 26.) Finally, the four silver bands uniting the border and the foot of the paten each carry the inscription: ΘΕΟΤΟΚ[Ε] ΜΑΡΗΑ ΒΟΗΘΗ ΒΑCΙΛΕΙC (Θεοτόκε Μαρία, βοήθει βασιλεῖς, "Mary, Mother of God, please help the emperors [rulers]").
Ebersolt has proposed that the Greek inscription invoking the help of the Mother of God on behalf of "the emperors or rulers" in the plural may refer to an imperial couple, or to Constantine VII and Romanos I or possibly to the latter with his sons, who were crowned during the reign of their father.

K. R. B.

Bibliography: Pasini 1885-6, 64, no. 2, pl. XLIX, fig. 108. Molinier 1888, 95, no. 96. Ebersolt 1923, 65-6. Hahnloser 1971, 72, no. 68 (Grabar), pl. LX (top).

26

Glass bowl (paten?) with honeycomb pattern

Constantinopolitan, 10th–11th century
Glass, silver-gilt, stones, pearls. *Height* 60 mm, *diam.* 170 mm

Tesoro, no. 93 (one of three glass patens in the 1325 inventory: III, nos 14-16, perhaps the "*platinam vitream viridem*")

Contiguous polygonal units form the all-over pattern of this shallow, cut greenish glass vessel. The design has been aptly compared to that of a beehive. On the broad horizontal silver-gilt border around the rim, large oval cabochons alternate with rectangular ones. The cabochons are spaced at regular intervals and contained in sturdy settings. According to Pasini's inventory of 1885-6 one stone is missing. Tiny pearls strung on fine gold wire form the parallel borders of the mount. Some of the pearls are missing. A silver-gilt band with beaded borders forms the foot. The latter is connected to the border around the rim by four silver-gilt bands, each with a flat disk in the middle and beaded borders.
Grabar (Hahnloser 1971, no. 72) noted that both the date and the use of this object as a paten – a plate used for the bread or Host in the celebration of the eucharist – are uncertain. Indeed, the dimensions as well as the materials are unusual for a paten, which is usually flatter and made of precious metal. Although Braun considered the piece a *Waschschüssel* (basin or gemellion), it has usually been called a paten. Lamm thought the glass was sixth-century with medieval Byzantine mounts. He compared this glass to that of an earlier paten in light-blue glass, which also has a section cut in the same beehive pattern. However, as Grabar has noted (Hahnloser 1971, 16-7), one of the manifestations of the Macedonian Renaissance was the imitation of Antique glass and vases in semi-precious stone. Whereas such pieces have frequently been referred to as Classical or Late Antique, their mounts have usually been considered Byzantine and are now recognized as Constantinopolitan workmanship of the tenth–eleventh centuries. Grabar argues convincingly that the vessels are also of this period, noting that it is unlikely that several Antique vessels of identical workmanship would have been preserved intact in tenth to eleventh-century Constantinople and that one would have felt a necessity to transform them into eucharistic vessels.
The mounts of this vessel are definitely Constantinopolitan work of the Macedonian period. Comparable oval and rectangular settings between parallel bands of tiny pearls form the border of the Constantinopolitan tenth-century bookcover with enamel plaques in this exhibition (no. 14). Although the settings are all oval, the decorative bands around the rims of two alabaster patens from tenth to eleventh-century Constantinople are also similar (cf. nos 18, 25). As noted by Grabar, the band

encircling the top of the foot of a number of Constantinopolitan chalices of the tenth century is decorated in like manner, but silver-gilt beads replace pearls (Hahnloser 1971, no. 82). Similar mounts also exist on a tenth-century ivory lamp and on an alabaster cup of the tenth – eleventh century, but on both of the latter, silver-gilt beads or grains replace the pearls (Hahnloser 1971, nos 82, 86). Borders of tiny pearls continued to be popular in Byzantine metalwork, as can be seen for example by those surrounding the enamel medallions on two eleventh-century (?) chalices, one in this exhibition (no. 17; Hahnloser 1971, no. 50), and by those which originally almost invariably surrounded the gold and enamel Russo-Byzantine *kolty* of the eleventh – twelfth centuries (Brown 1980).

That the border of this particular paten is a revival of an early Constantinopolitan form is evident when one recalls the hoops of the pair of bracelets in the Metropolitan Museum of Art, New York, on which pearl borders frame sapphires in oval mounts alternating with pairs of box-settings originally filled with emerald plasma (fig. 26a; acc. no. 17.190. 1670-71; exh. cat. *Age of Spirituality*, 1977-8, no. 300).

K. R. B.

Bibliography: Pasini 1885-6, 64, no. 7, pl. XLIX, fig. 109. Molinier 1888, 95, no. 97. Schlumberger 1896-1905, II, 500. Dalton 1911, 552, fig. 54. Dillon 1914, 100. Ebersolt 1923, 65-6, fig. 25. Peirce and Tyler 1926, 44, pl. 62. Lamm 1929-30, 148, no. 2, pl. 53. Braun 1932, 543, figs 427-8. Gallo 1967, 278, no. 16; 372, no. 12. Philippe 1970, 138, fig. 75. Hahnloser 1971, 73, no. 72 (Grabar), pl. LX.

26a

196

27

Glass bowl (paten?) with handle

Glass: Byzantine (probably Constantinopolitan), 10th–11th century. *Metalwork*: later
Glass, silver-gilt, stones, pearls. *Height* 80 mm, *diam.* 205 mm

Tesoro, no. 97

The thick transparent glass vessel decorated with cut concave circles takes its place among the Byzantine glass of the tenth to eleventh centuries which is believed to have been brought from Constantinople to the basilica of San Marco as a result of the Crusade of 1204. The latter provided San Marco with the largest extant collection of medieval Byzantine glass. However, unlike the majority of this glass, the silver-gilt mounts of this particular piece are most probably not of contemporary manufacture, but rather later. The broad horizontal borders around the rim, the foot and the handle are set with a profusion of garnets, emerald root, balas rubies (rose-colored), amethysts and pearls, all of which are contained within beaded borders. Many of the stones are irregular in form. According to Pasini's inventories of 1885-6, three stones were missing from the foot and three from the handle. The borders around the rim and the foot are connected by six silver-gilt bands, and at the juncture of the handle to the rim is a small figure of a bird of prey. Excluding the handle, the general concept of the mounts of this piece is similar to those of a paten(?) of Constantinopolitan workmanship of the tenth–eleventh century (no. 26). Both have a broad horizontal silver-gilt border around the rim, set with cabochons, and a similar band forming the foot, and both have an even number of silver-gilt bands connecting the border of the rim to the foot. Although on no. 26 tiny pearls replace the silver-gilt beads forming the borders of the rim, the beads of the borders of the foot on both pieces are of silver-gilt. Such borders of silver-gilt beads were favored by Byzantine goldsmiths of the tenth–eleventh century (for a discussion of Constantinopolitan mounts of this period see no. 26). Nevertheless, the irregular shapes of the cabochons, as well as the lack of symmetry and regularity of design and the lack of regard for space which characterize their placement on the mounts, set the mounts of this piece apart from other mounts of the Macedonian Renaissance and from other purely Byzantine mounts. They are inspired by Byzantine examples of the tenth–eleventh centuries but lack the elegance of simplicity and clarity of design. For these reasons they can best be described, as was suggested by Grabar, as "post or para-Byzantine" (Grabar 1971 a, 111). With the exception of Braun, who thought this piece was used as an aquamanile, most scholars have considered it a paten. Lamm suggested that it was probably used for the distribution of bread after the Mass. He compared it to one which, prior to its destruction in 1793, had been in the cathedral of Beauvais. Although it was of rock-crystal, it was decorated with similar cut concave circles. On its silver-gilt mount, adjacent to the figural decoration, was a Greek inscription referring to the communion. According to Lamm, this destroyed paten was used for the preservation or storing of the Holy Wafer. It had been donated to the cathedral by Bishop Philippe de Dreux, who had acquired it from the Abbot of Corbie in 1217. The latter presumably acquired it with the booty of Constantinople. Lamm's comparison would seem to lend credence to the generally accepted view that the San Marco piece was used as a paten.

K. R. B.

Bibliography: Pasini 1885-6, 64-5, no. 8, pl. XLIX, no. 107. Molinier 1888, 95, no. 95. Schlumberger 1900, 501. Peirce and Tyler 1926, 44, pl. 64. Lamm 1929-30, 148, no. 3, pl. 53, 3. Braun 1932, 543, figs 425-6. Gallo 1967, pl. 38, fig. 66. Philippe 1970, 138, fig. 75. Grabar 1971a, 111, no. 18, fig. 23. Hahnloser 1971, 73, no. 73 (Grabar), pl. LXI.

28

Reliquary-casket of Trebizond

Trebizond, late 14th–15th century
Silver-gilt, niello. *Length* 280 mm, *width* 140 mm, *depth* 90 mm

Tesoro, no. 133 (listed in the 1634 inventory: no. 15)

The figurative decoration of this small rectangular reliquary-casket is restricted to the cover, where the enthroned and cross-nimbed Christ is shown at the center in *repoussé* (?) and chiseled relief. Flanking Christ are the similarly worked figures of the four martyrs of Trebizond, the Greek-Byzantine city on the south-eastern shore of the Black Sea. The martyrs – Aquila, Eugenius, Valerian, and Canidius – are nimbed yet bare-headed. They turn to face Christ, to whom they outstretch their hands in supplication. Engraved and nielloed Greek identifying inscriptions appear in the background near each head.

Christ holds a crown in each of his extended hands; two more crowns rest on the high arcaded base beneath the throne. The series of five figures is framed by an arcade also worked in relief. The arches rest on six foliate capitals and six knotted, double rope-twist colonnettes which spring from half-palmette bases. Full palmettes are centered in the spaces between the arches above the capitals. The entire composition, together with the border, is worked in one piece of silver. The border is composed of rope-twists flanking a recessed band with widely spaced small rings, which probably once secured a cord of tiny pearls in a manner similar to the pearled

decoration of several Middle Byzantine bookcovers and chalices in the treasury of San Marco (e.g. nos 9, 14, 16, 18). Three foliate security-clasps cover not only small portions of this border, as well as part of the horizontally-oriented palmettes on the edge of the lid, but they also extend more than half-way down the sides of the casket itself.

The first impression of the sides of the casket is that they are entirely ornamented, being divided by chiseled horizontal bands of concentric bifid petals and rope-twists. Yet two wide bands bear a highly decorative yet legible Greek inscription. The latter, formed with engraved and nielloed capital letters, extolls in twelve metrical verses the martyrdom of the four saints who are so clearly honored by Christ himself through the offered crowns. Miserable and sinful, the anonymous author of the words appeals to Christ as arbiter of his salvation:

+ ὙΜΕῖϹ ΜῈΝ Οὒ ΠΤΗΞΑΝΤΕϹ ΑἹΜΆΤΩΝ ΧΎϹΕΙϹ
ΜΆΡΤΥΡΕϹ ἨΘΛΉϹΑΤΕ ΠΑΝϹΘΕΝΕϹΤΆΤΩϹ
ΤΟῪϹ ΤῆϹ ἙΏΑϹ ἈΚΛΙΝΕῖϹ ϹΤΎΛΟΥϹ ΛΈΓΩ
ΤῸ ΛΑΜΠΡῸΝ ΕὐΤΎΧΗΜΑ ΤΡΑΠΕΖΟΥΝΤΊΩΝ
ΠΡΏΤΑΘΛΟΝ ΕὐΓΈΝΙΟΝ ἌΜΑ Δ' ἈΚΎΛΑΝ
ΟΥΑΛ[[Λ]]ΕΡΙΑΝΌΝ ΤΕ ϹῪΝ ΚΑΝΙΔΊῼ
ΚΑῚ ΤῊΝ ἈΜΟΙΒῚΝ ΤΩΝ ἈΜΕΤΡΉΤΩΝ ΠΌΝΩΝ
Ὁ Χ(ΡΙϹΤῸ)Ϲ ΑὐΤΌϹ ἘϹΤΙΝ ὙΜῖΝ ΠΑΡΈΧΩΝ
ΚΑῚ ΓᾺΡ ΔΊΔΩϹΙ ΤΟῪϹ ϹΤΕΦΆΝΟΥϹ ἈΞΊΩϹ
ἘΓῺ Δ' Ὁ ΤΆΛΑϹ ΠΑΗΜΜΕΛΗΜΆΤΩΝ ΓΈΜΩΝ
ὙΜᾶϹ ΜΕϹΊΤΑϹ ΤΗϹ ἘΜῆϹ Ϲ(ΩΤΗ)ΡΊΑϹ
ΤΊΘΗΜΙ ΦΥΓΕῖΝ ΤΗΝ ΚΑΤΑΔΊΚΗΝ ΘΈΛΩΝ +

(Ὑμεῖς μὲν οὐ πτήξαντες αἱμάτων χύσεις
μάρτυρες ἠθλήσατε πανσθενεστάτως·
τοὺς τῆς ἑώας ἀκλινεῖς στύλους λέγω,
τὸ λαμπρὸν εὐτύχημα Τραπεζουντίων
πρώταθλον Εὐγένιον ἅμα δ' Ἀκύλαν
Οὐαλ[λ]εριανόν τε σὺν Κανιδίῳ.
Καὶ τὴν ἀμοιβ(ὴ)ν τῶν ἀμετρήτων πόνων
ὁ Χριστὸς αὐτός ἐστιν ὑμῖν παρέχων·
καὶ γὰρ δίδωσι τοὺς στεφάνους ἀξίως.
Ἐγὼ δ' ὁ τάλας πλημμελημάτων γέμων
ὑμᾶς μεσίτας τῆς ἐμῆς σωτηρίας
τίθημι φυγεῖν τὴν καταδίκην θέλων).

While the similarity of the drapery style, figure proportions, physiognomic types and the character of Christ's throne with related features in Middle Byzantine ivory carvings might initially suggest that the Trebizond reliquary dated from the same period (Molinier and Schlumberger both attributed it to the eleventh or twelfth century), the special character of the decorative ele-

ments and the paleography has led Frolow (Hahnloser 1971, no. 33) to suggest a later date in the Palaeologue period, probably at the end of the fourteenth century or in the first two thirds of the fifteenth century, yet before the downfall of Trebizond in 1461. Frolow advanced several hypotheses about the casket's origin and subsequent appearance in Venice. It may have been the gift of the Greek churchman, Cardinal Bessarion (1403-72), made along with his other important gifts of books and other reliquaries. As an alternative explanation, the piece may have been presented by one of the numerous families of Trebizond who had moved to Crete in the early fifteenth century. Association with David Comnenus, the ultimate *basileus* of Trebizond, is perhaps the most fanciful of these alternative theories.

W. D. W.

Bibliography: Tiepolo 1617-9, 89-91. Durand 1861, 95-6. Pasini 1885-6, 84-5, pl. LXIV, fig. 157. Molinier 1888, no. 145. Schlumberger 1896-1905, I, 669; II, 456, 469, 484, 505. Braun 1940, pl. 20, fig. 66. Hahnloser 1965, *Il Tesoro*, 91, n. 13. Miller 1962, 94. Gallo 1967, 314, no. 15, figs 52-3. Hahnloser 1971, 39-40, no. 33 (Frolow), pl. XXXI. Wixom 1981, 46, fig. 5.

Exh. cat. *Venezia e Bisanzio*, 1974, no. 113.

Islamic hardstone-carving

Daniel Alcouffe

In the middle of the eleventh century the Persian traveller Nasīr-i Khusraw, who twice visited Egypt, wrote that rock crystal from the Maghreb and the Red Sea was worked in Cairo. What is more, an account of the sack of the treasury of the Fatimid caliph al-Mustanṣir (1036-94) soon after, in 1062, reveals that an enormous number of rock-crystal objects were in the palace collection (Lamm 1929-30, I, 511-2).

The work of the Egyptian craftsmen, thus attested, has been identified through the survival, in the treasury of San Marco, of a rock-crystal ewer inscribed with the name of the Fatimid caliph al-ʿAziz bi'llāh, who reigned in Cairo from 975 until 996 (no. 31). The very special characteristics of this ewer have led to the identification of numerous similar vessels as products of Cairene workshops, where the art of carving rock-crystal, already well advanced by the end of the tenth century, as is shown by the ewer, was practised at least until 1062. In the light of the written sources it has been possible to group together a series of localized and dated objects the origin of which is confirmed, first, by the discovery of rock-crystal objects in Egypt (Lamm 1929-30, I, 207-8; II, pl. 74) and, secondly, by the presence of Fatimid crystals in Europe as early as the late tenth century or the beginning of the eleventh. They are found on the ambo presented between 1002 and 1024 to the palace chapel at Aachen by the Ottonian emperor Henry II (Schnitzler 1957, pls 110-1, 151).

Fatimid rock-crystal objects, carved from high-quality material, are, like Classical hardstone vessels, entirely monolithic, cut from a single block. The very varied shapes include ewers (nos 31, 32), bowls and vases (fig. 31f) of various types. The craftsmanship is even more remarkable than the objects themselves: mouldings around the top and bottom, and relief decoration – with details in intaglio – comprising inscriptions, stylized vegetal elements (scrolls, palmettes and half-palmettes) and animals.

The style is homogeneous and seems to have had no precursors. The shapes, however, are Persian (cf. no. 31) or Classical in origin: the handle of a bowl in the Munich *Schatzkammer*, for instance (Lamm 1929-30, II, pl. 68/1), is based on Classical prototypes like those of the sardonyx bowls (fig. 10a, 10c). The Classical tradition of hardstone-carving may well have survived the fall of the Sasanians in Iran, to be taken up by craftsmen in Iraq under the early ʿAbbāsid caliphs (cf. no. 37); it would then have reached Egypt under the ʿAbbāsid governor Ibn Ṭūlūn or the short-lived dynasty he founded (about 868-905). Cairene art of the period shows strong links with the ʿAbbāsid capital of Samarra, on the Tigris. The carving of objects like the ewer (no. 37), the dish (no. 30) and the vessel-foot with mouldings (no. 22) may possibly show a transition from Sasanid to Fatimid hardstone-carving; likewise other objects misattributed to the Fatimid period. Egyptian hardstone-carvers seem only to have used rock-crystal. In other parts of Islam coloured hardstone must have been worked, as witness a sardonyx bowl in the Louvre (fig. 37a), the oval agate bowl with an Arabic inscription re-used as the base of the "Santo Cáliz" in Valencia Cathedral (Beltrán 1960, 62-6, pls XI-XII), and perhaps also the chess-pieces set into the ambo in Aachen Cathedral (Wentzel 1971, fig. 14). As we have seen, these Fatimid crystals were highly prized in contemporary Europe and were adapted for liturgical purposes, even when in a fragmentary state (figs 31e, 31f), as reliquaries, chalices and cruets (fig. 32b). The tenth and eleventh-century German emperors and the Grandmont order in thirteenth-century France (fig. 32b) seem to have been rich in crystals of this type, as is the treasury of San Marco. Fatimid crystals later enriched such secular collections as that of the Duc de Berry, who at his death in 1416 seems to have owned two ewers like that of al-ʿAzīz: *"une aiguière de cristal, ouvrée à bestes, à une ance de mesmes"* ("a crystal ewer, worked with animals, with a handle of the same"), which had been given to him unmounted and which he had mounted in gold, and *"une aiguière de cristal, ouvrée à fueillages et à oiseaulx, garnie d'argent doré..."* ("a crystal ewer, worked with foliage and birds, mounted in silver-gilt": Guiffrey 1894-6, I, 209-10, no. 806; 214, no. 826).

29

Turquoise glass bowl

Glass: made in Iran or Iraq, 9th–10th century. *Enamel*: Byzantine, 11th century. *Other metalwork*: late 10th and 15th(?) century
Glass, silver-gilt, gold *cloisonné* enamel, stones. *Height* 60 mm, *diam.* 186 mm

Tesoro, no. 140 (listed in the 1571 inventory: no. 62)

The technique of wheel-cutting, etching, and polishing glass, found in both Roman and Sasanian periods, was adapted and perfected by the succeeding Islamic civilization, particularly in ninth and tenth-century Iraq and Iran, and was known by the late tenth century in Egypt. The Muslim artists found expression in a new repertory of shapes and designs. This opaque turquoise glass lobed bowl is one of the best-known of the relief-cut type, although it is unique in color for this production. Generally, colorless glass was preferred at this time, though some undecorated turquoise glass fragments are known.

The accomplished art of glass-cutting is one that follows the lapidary tradition in which the material is laboriously abraded to form the patterns. By this process, the relief design is seen on a smooth, usually polished ground, the patterns having been created by both high and counter-sunk relief, sometimes highlighted with engraved lines. This vessel has been described most recently by Erdmann (Hahnloser 1971, no. 117). On its walls is a lively file of running, stylized hares, one animal placed in each of the five lobes of the bowl. Each animal is contained within a compartment formed by a continuous raised

line, which also forms a shield-shaped unit to separate the lobes at their most constricted point. The animals were carved in different levels of relief as well as etched, hatched lines. High relief, some areas of countersunk relief, and beveling articulate the head, body, and tail, while hatched lines emphasize the rabbit's nose, ears, neck, and back. The eye is formed by a raised dot. The ears, resembling horns by their extreme length, extend nearly to the curled tail. Under the rim are engraved palmettes within and between guilloche. Encircling the rim are gold mounts with enamels and stones, and there are also metal braces along the body and around the foot. The lobed shape has been mentioned by Erdmann and others as having a T'ang Chinese metalwork prototype; metalwork from the Sasanian period also has lobed vessels, however, and might be a closer source for the shape. Speculation remains as to how and when this bowl arrived in the treasury. The tradition is that the vessel was presented by the Shah of Iran to the Venetian *Signoria* in 1472.

A low ring foot encloses an enigmatic inscription in a ninth–tenth century type of Kufic script. It has been translated as "Khorasan". This cannot refer to the place of production, as Khorasan was a rather large undefined region in eastern Iran during this period. The area was known for its turquoise production, and according to the literature, colored glass was often accepted as being precious stone. If this bowl was made to simulate and be taken for turquoise, it might be inferred that the word was added for a fraudulent purpose, but an explanation is still awaited for its significance.

Stylistically, the nearest parallel for the relief decoration is found on a fragment of clear wheel-cut glass from Samarra bearing a similar animal and having the identical technique (Lamm 1928, 77, no. 243, fig. 50, pl. VI; Oliver 1961, 13-4). It is usually dated to the ninth century, during the period when Samarra was the ʿAbbāsid capital. A recent study, however, indicates that Samarra was still a viable city during the tenth century. It is uncertain where these luxurious wares were made, but related glassware has been found in excavations in Iraq at Samarra and at Nishapur in eastern Iran.

C. K.

Metalwork

The interior and exterior of the bowl's rim vary considerably in type and in date. The five finely worked gold bands of the interior are set one on each of the five scalloped sections of the bowl. They are decorated in low relief with an abstracted *rinceau* of beautifully wrought acanthus and palmettes whose design differs in each section. In style they resemble the acanthus *rinceaux* on the foot of the chalice with handles of Romanos II (no. 10) and probably date, as it does, to the tenth century in Byzantium.

The silver-gilt mounts of the exterior of the bowl, which are decorated with gems and enamels, are very different in character. Five trapezoidal enameled plaques are placed in the center of each of the bowl's lobes and are flanked by panels of fine filigree work set with six cabochons of various sizes surrounding a larger central stone. Many of the gems are modern replacements. This mounting is recorded in an engraving published in 1727 by La Mottraye (fig. 29 a). Only the five enamel plaques appear to be Byzantine, but they seem to have been made for a different, unknown, purpose. Three are decorated with a central rosette pattern flanked by heart-shaped floral motifs in a design common to art of the Middle Byzantine period (cf. no. 16) and have been cut down to fit into their new trapezoidal settings. The two remaining enameled plaques consist of fragments decorated with a quatrefoil design of crosses that have been set beneath a silver-gilt panel, cut to reveal their decoration. This unorthodox mounting perhaps imitates Byzantine enamelwork of a type found on a medallion and a long frieze incorporated into the thirteenth-century frame of the *Pala d'Oro* (fig. 29 b; cf. Hahnloser 1965, nos 163-80, 182). The filigree plaques however, are of Western European origin. They, with the reused Byzantine enamel plaques, may have been added after the bowl came to Venice, perhaps in the fifteenth century, but before the engraving of 1727.

M. E. F.

Bibliography: Montfaucon 1702, 52. La Mottraye 1727, 72, pls VII, VII *bis*. Pasini 1885-6, 94-8, no. 105, pl. XLVIII. Molinier 1888, 40-1, 94-5, no. 93. Lamm 1928, 63. Lamm 1929-30, I, 144, 158-9; II, pl. 58/23 (with bibliography). Lamm 1939, III, 2597-8; VI, pl. 1444 A. Gallo 1967, 206-12; 299, no. 62; 352, no. 70; 361, no. 199; 369-70, no. 42; 397, no. 100; pl. 64, figs 108-9 (with bibliography). Hahnloser 1971, 101-4, no. 117 (Erdmann), pls LXXXIX-XC. Charleston 1980, 68-73. Saldern 1980, 142-3.

Exh. cat. *Trésors d'art du Moyen Age en Italie*, 1952, no. 73; *Arte Iranica*, 1956, no. 486.

212

lâs ex integrâ   *Gemma Turcica.*

CL. N.° VII.   *Prototyp. acc. mensur.*

30

Rock-crystal dish

ᶜAbbāsid, 9th–10th century (?)
Rock-crystal. *Height* 53 mm, *diam.* 210 mm

Tesoro, no. 102

This dish is possibly to be identified as that listed in the 1325 inventory of the treasury of San Marco as "*Platinam unam de cristallo intaiatam*" (Gallo 1967, 280, VI, no. 9), though there is in the treasury a second rock-crystal dish, much smaller, which is also carved and unmounted (fig. 30a; Hahnloser 1971, no. 127, pl. CII). In the 1571 inventory it is possible to recognize the dish in the exhibition on account of its "frosted" appearance: "*Una tazza de Cristal de montagna agghiazzada*" (i.e. like ice-glass in appearance; Gallo 1967, 301, no. 132). It is certainly this object which was described in the 1733 inventory as: "*Una piadena scolpita con guglie*" (Gallo 1967, 353, no. 120). In the 1801 valuation of the treasury it must be one of the "*6 Pezzi di cristallo senza fornimenti*" (Gallo 1967, 357, no. 12). In Cicognara's catalogue of 1816-20 it is valued at 600 lire (Gallo 1967, 372, no. 10).

The thick dish, with a flat rim one centimetre in width, is cut from somewhat flawed rock-crystal. The centre is concave and undecorated. The foot-ring is convex in profile and runs round the flat circular underside of the central part. The well executed decoration is confined to the exterior: a continuous frieze in relief of scrolls enclosing half-palmettes decorated with parallel grooves. This problematic piece is decorated in an Islamic style prefiguring Fatimid rock-crystal carving. The form is Fatimid, for the dish mounted on the ambo of the Ottonian emperor Henry II in Aachen Cathedral (Schnitzler 1957, pl. 110) has a similar foot-ring and is carved on its exterior surface. The flared base of the Venice dish is also paralleled in some Fatimid crystals (e.g. figs 31b, 31c), though these are thinner-walled and cut from crystal of finer quality, and their decoration is more varied. The same decorative principle, a continuous frieze of a single repeated motif is, however, to be seen on two other rock-crystal objects in San Marco: on the foot of an hexagonal vessel (no. 22) and on a second dish (fig. 30a). The latter also has a foot-ring and is carved in relief with a frieze of half-palmettes, having the same design as the present dish, on its upper surface. These pieces may represent the necessary landmarks between Sasanian and Fatimid hardstone-carving. If so, they must have been made in Iran or Iraq during the ninth or tenth century.

D. A.

Bibliography: Pasini 1885-6, 64. Gallo 1967, 280, VI, no. 9; 301, no. 132; 353, no. 120; 357, no. 12; 372, no. 10. Hahnloser 1971, no. 126 (Erdmann), pl. CII, with bibliography.

31

Ewer of the caliph al-ʿAzīz bi'llāh

Stonework: Fatimid, 975-96. *Metalwork*: 16th century and later
Rock-crystal, gold, enamel. *Height* 230 mm, *width* 125 mm

Tesoro, no. 80

The relatively late date of the mount, which may well have replaced an earlier one, makes it difficult to identify the ewer in the older inventories of the treasury of San Marco. Is it *"Un vaso de Cristallo con manico, con tre penini et la bocca d'esso vaso d'oro"* in the 1571 inventory (Gallo 1967, 300, no. 85)? It is, however, recognizable in the list of rock-crystals in the 1733 inventory: *"Un'ampolla con manico d'un solo pezzo scolpita di figure, con piede et ornamenti d'oro massiccio"* (Gallo 1967, 354, no. 136). In Cicognara's catalogue of 1816-20 it is valued at 4000 lire, more than any other rock-crystal object (Gallo 1967, 375, no. 29).

This ewer, which is a key piece in the identification of Egyptian Fatimid rock-crystals, is one of the most famous hardstone vessels in the treasury of San Marco. The mouth, with its prominent lip, damaged at the extremity, has a narrow unpolished rim. The neck is emphasized by two sharp mouldings, one above the other, which slope downwards towards the back of the vessel. The upper moulding ends in a point, the lower one descends to the base, marking off a plain area facing the handle. The pear-shaped body is girdled at the bottom by a third moulding of the same type. The underside of the vessel, which is slightly convex, has a broken foot-ring, which made the present gold mount necessary. The ewer has a tapering handle cut from the same piece of crystal as the body of the vessel and pierced with five holes. As a finial it has a small sculpture of a crouched ibex (*height* 25 mm, *length* 35 mm, *width* 8.5 mm). The relief decoration, enlivened by engraved detail, is of high quality. On the body it is symmetrically conceived and well placed. Below the spout, arabesques terminating in palmettes and half-palmettes spring from a three-lobed cartouche. To either side of this motif is a seated lion; the lions' heads are marked off by grooved collars from their bodies, which have an all-over pattern of concave disks. The fore-legs are carved with overlapping scales; the tails are curled and terminate in palm leaves. The outside of the handle is decorated with half-palmettes. The shoulder of the ewer bears a short Kufic inscription: "The blessing of God on the imam al-ʿAzīz bi'llāh".

The enamelled gold mount which reinforces the handle may date from the sixteenth century; the plain gold base seems later. The inventory of 1733 states that the piece rests on a gold base, but this is not described. The gold base in place in 1816 seems to have been the present one.

The inscription, deciphered in the nineteenth century by Longpérier, identifies the person for whom the ewer was intended as al-ʿAzīz bi'llāh, the fifth Fatimid caliph, who reigned from 975 until 996. In 969 the Fatimids annexed Egypt to their existing North African territories. The ewer was made in Cairo, where, according to contemporary accounts, rock-crystal was worked. After the pillage by the Turks in 1062 of the treasury of the caliph al-Mustanṣir, the fourth successor of al-ʿAzīz bi'llāh, a rock-crystal flask and a ewer of great purity and beauty, bearing – like the San Marco ewer – the name of al-ʿAzīz bi'llāh, came on the market along with other rock-crystals (Lamm 1929-30, I, 511).

Lamm's publication brought five other ewers of this type to light. They are of varying quality both in shape and decoration. One of them is also in the treasury of San Marco (no. 32). Another is in the Pitti Palace and was formerly in the Medici collections; its inscription indicates a date of production between 1000 and 1008 or in 1010-11 (fig. 31a; Heikamp 1974, no. 23, figs 42-3). A ewer in the Louvre is part of the treasury of the Abbey of Saint-Denis (fig. 31b; Montesquiou-Fezensac and Gaborit-Chopin 1977, 44-5, pls 26-7). There are two others, in the Victoria and Albert Museum (fig. 31c) and in Fermo Cathedral (Rice 1956, figs 9, 11). The al-ʿAzīz ewer is the best preserved of all these examples: the other ewer in Venice and the Fermo example lack handles, and the three remaining ones have lost most of their animal finials.

The six ewers, which are of very similar size, thin-walled and generally of flawless crystal, have (or rather had, because of the damage sustained by some of them) various characteristics in common. They all had mouths with prominent lips, necks with two sharp mouldings (three on the Victoria and Albert example), pear-shaped bodies with another moulding below (except on the London piece), a flared foot-ring, and a handle cut from the same crystal as the body, pierced and surmounted by an animal. On the body, a stylized foliate motif in the centre is flanked by animals decorated with intaglio disks. There are two rams on the second ewer in Venice, a pair of birds on those in Louvre, Florence and Fermo, and on the Victoria and Albert vessel there are two motifs of a falcon attacking a gazelle. All but the last example and the ewer with the rams are inscribed with a supplication or a dedication.

The shape of these objects seems to reflect Persian influence. The elongated lip appears in Sasanian precious metalwork (cf. no. 5); the overall shape appears to exist

216

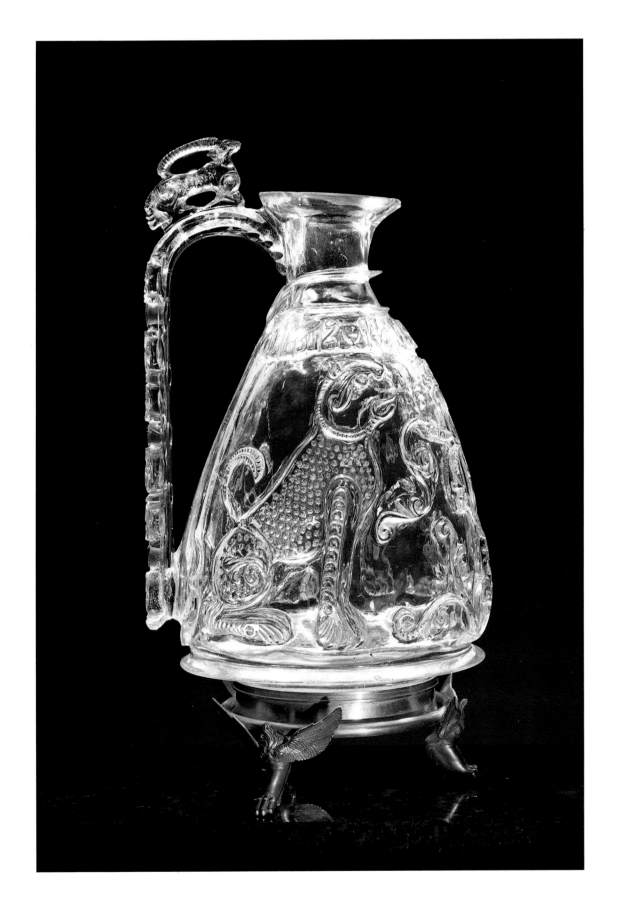

219

31a

31b

31e

220

in ninth and tenth-century Persian glass. However, some Classical influence should also be noted. The handle of a fourth-century silver ewer in the Louvre, for example, has an ibex finial like that of the al-ʿAzīz ewer (fig. 31 d). A Classical rock-crystal vessel in the treasury of San Marco has a sharp projection all round the body, above a flared foot (Hahnloser 1971, no. 76, pl. LXIII), as on Fatimid ewers.

Persian influence may perhaps also be discerned in the decoration. In contrast to the stylized foliate motifs, the animals show a certain naturalism, although they are often decorated with half-palmettes, as are the haunches of the lions and rams on the Venetian ewers. Animals like those on the al-ʿAzīz ewer can be seen on other rock-crystal objects of the Fatimid period. Confronted lions appear on the neck of a flask in the treasury of the basilica of San Lorenzo in Florence (Heikamp 1974, no. 22, fig. 44) and twice on the body of a ewer in the State Hermitage Museum in Leningrad (Lamm 1929-30, I, 194-5; II, pl. 67,5). Fatimid craftsmen, it seems, also carved lions in the round (Lamm 1929-30, II, pl. 75), and ibexes in low relief, as on a casket from the cathedral treasury of Moûtiers-en-Tarentaise now in the Musée de Cluny.

This incorporates four plaques, one of which bears two confronted ibexes (fig. 31 e). A chalice formerly in the collection of Louis XIV and now in the Louvre rests on a foot comprising the remains of a Fatimid flask with a frieze of eight ibexes (fig. 31 f).

D. A.

Bibliography: Pasini 1885-6, 93, pl. LII, fig. 118. Molinier 1888, 38-40, no. 107. Lamm 1929-30, I, 192-3; II, pl. 67,1. Gallo 1967, 300, no. 85 (?); 354, no. 136; 375, no. 29. Hahnloser 1971, no. 124 (Erdmann), pls XCVIII-XCIX (with bibliography).

32

Rock-crystal cruet

Stonework: Fatimid, late 10th century. *Metalwork*: Venetian (?), probably 13th century
Rock-crystal, silver-gilt, niello. *Height* 280 mm, *width* 105 mm, *diam.* of base 85 mm

Tesoro, no. 86

This cruet, which is now the only silver-mounted rock-crystal ewer in the treasury of San Marco, may well be listed in the inventories as early as 1325, when there is mention of "... *Ampulletas tres de cristallo, varnitas arg[ent]o*"; one of these was subsequently sold (Gallo 1967, 278, III, no. 11). The inventory specifies that these objects were to be placed on the altar; the cruet in question cannot have been intended for liturgical use, however, as the silver spout is non-functional. The two remaining rock-crystal cruets reappear in the 1571 inventory. One of them was broken (Gallo 1967, 299, no. 76); the other is almost certainly the vessel on exhibition: "*Un'altra Ampoletta più grande de Cristallo col piede et collo d'Arzento*" (Gallo 1967, 300, no. 94). The 1733 inventory again records two cruets (*ampolla*) of rock-crystal mounted in silver-gilt, stating – doubtless in error – that they were decorated with precious stones (Gallo 1967, 353, nos 109, 111). The valuation of the treasury made in 1801 lists "*2 Ampolette d'arg[ent]o col corpo di Cristallo*" and "*1 Ampoletta grande di Cristal con arg[ent]o*", probably the present cruet (Gallo 1967, 360, nos 155-6; 361, no. 205). In Cicognara's 1816-20 catalogue of the treasury only the present cruet is listed, the beauty of its mount emphasized: "*appartenente all'epoca migliore dei bassi tempi*". It was valued at 1600 lire (Gallo 1967, 371, no. 1).

The cruet shares the characteristics of the group of Fatimid rock-crystal ewers typified by the al-ʿAzīz ewer (no. 31) but is less well preserved than the latter. The lip and the foot-ring set in the mount are both damaged; the moulding round the bottom of the body seems to have been ground down, and the handle is missing. The decoration is of symmetrical tendrils terminating in palmettes springing from a central motif of half-palmettes which half-conceal confronted rams. The shape and dimensions of the cruet are similar to those of the al-ʿAzīz ewer, but its decoration is less animated and less well arranged.

D. A.

Metalwork

A silver-gilt and niello mount of particular refinement and elegance has transformed the rock-crystal ampulla into a cruet or small ewer. The general orientalizing effect may be compared with that of a sardonyx cruet with a filigree mount in the treasury (no. 35), and with related liturgical vessels.

The lid is missing. A moulding at the rim has, directly below, a band of contiguous leaves separated by piercing. The neck has several zones: at the top, the coiling foliate scrolls contain two armed men, one with a bow and the other with a sword, fighting dragons. Below is a band of anthemion-palmettes, and below that at the swelling marking the rim of the rock-crystal are two rows of joined foliate motifs with a serpent gliding through the scrolls. With the exception of this lower band, the neck of the mount is of openwork, so that the inhabited scrolls and palmettes stand out against a smooth nielloed silver ground.

The foot of the mount, which is attached to the base of the rock-crystal by a double collar of stylized leaves, is in the same openwork technique. The decoration consists of scrolls inhabited by tiny figures in short tunics, fighting with animals or monsters (a man with a stick fights a lion; a bearded figure with a club threatens another lion; a warrior raises his sword to a scaly dragon). Vigorous tendrils are laden with fleshy serrated leaves and, here and there, with long rough-skinned fruit.

The gilt spout is fixed to the base of the neck by a stem and is engraved with palmettes recalling the leaves decorating the rock-crystal. At the tip is a serpent's head. The elegant handle is in the form of a dragon with a serpent's neck; the body and wings of the dragon are decorated with motifs alternately gilded and nielloed.

The beauty of the decoration, the quality of the workmanship, the refinement of the forms used and the subtle contrast between the gilded and the nielloed parts make this mount an outstanding piece of work. The "Milhaguet cruet" of Fatimid crystal from the treasury of Grandmont was also mounted in silver in the thirteenth century, and its mount, although much simpler, has a handle in the form of a serpent also decorated with nielloed motifs (fig. 32b; exh. cat. *Trésors des églises de France*, 1965, no. 368, pl. 73). Hahnloser (1971, 114-5) has compared the mount of the Venetian cruet with the Saint-Riquier, Zara and Nona reliquaries, stressing the relationship between the inhabited scrolls and the decoration of the arch of the central portal in the façade of San Marco (about 1260; fig. 32a). He has cited earlier examples of inhabited scrolls from Rheno-Mosan art of the end of the twelfth century and the beginning of the thirteenth, notably the openwork crests on the Anno shrine

223

at Siegburg and the shrine of St Alban in Cologne, a fragment of crest of Cologne workmanship in the Victoria and Albert Museum, and the crest on the shrine of the Three Kings, also in Cologne (Swarzenski 1954, pls 222-3). However, one of the most striking parallels to the San Marco cruet is the enamelled Alpais *ciborium*, made in Limoges in the last decade of the twelfth century (Paris, Musée du Louvre; Gauthier 1972, 109, no. 63). Its sub-conical copper-gilt foot of openwork against a metal background is in a markedly similar technique to that of the Venetian cruet and is similarly decorated with scrolls inhabited by tiny figures fighting dragons (fig. 32 c). The style of the *ciborium* indicates an earlier date of manufacture than that of the cruet, but the relationship between the two objects is nevertheless extremely interesting because related themes were used for the decoration of openwork copper medallions made in Limoges in the first half of the thirteenth century to decorate caskets. Further comparisons could be drawn between the decoration on the San Marco ewer and the dragons with enamel eyes which crawl among the intricacies of Limoges croziers of the first half of the thirteenth century. Inhabited scrolls were, however, equally common in Italian art of the twelfth century and the first half of the thirteenth, particularly in sculpture.

The cruet appears to be one of those listed in the 1325 inventory (see above). The date and origin of its mount are still uncertain, however. The Fatimid crystal could have been given a mount earlier, around 1200 or in the first third of the thirteenth century, in a workshop in the Rhenish or Limoges orbit of influence, and then sent later to Venice to be remounted. Yet, although no other Venetian mount can really be related to this one, its presence in the San Marco treasury, Hahnloser thought, would argue for an origin in Venice, where numerous gems of varied provenience were remounted during the thirteenth and fourteenth centuries, and would also argue for a date in the middle or the third quarter of the thirteenth century.

D. G. C.

Bibliography: Pasini 1885-6, 99, no. 115, pl. LI. Molinier 1888, 39-40, 96, no. 104. Gallo 1967, 278, III, no. 11; 299, no. 76; 300, no. 94; 353, nos 109, 111; 360, nos 155-6; 361, no. 205; 371, no. 1. Hahnloser 1971, no. 125 (Erdmann, Hahnloser), pls C-CI, CXXXIX.

Western metalwork

William D. Wixom

Housed within a basilica richly decorated with marbles and mosaics, San Marco offers today, despite losses, one of the most striking collections of precious objects used in the service of a church. Formed around the relics of the saint which were brought to Venice in the first decades of the ninth century, it contains, like all great Western treasuries, liturgical vases, objects necessary for the offices of the Church, liturgical vestments, reliquaries, and what one could call "objects of curiosity", including a few secular works. The assemblage clearly shows, however, that a treasury is not only religious in character; the treasury of San Marco is equally an expression of the power of Venice, the ultimate testament to maritime glory and the Fourth Crusade.

By mediation of the Venetians, the West inherited many of the riches of Constantinople, not only purely Byzantine pieces, but also hardstone Antique vases that had received a metalwork mount in Constantinople. The question has often been raised if the Byzantine pieces at San Marco arrived for the most part in Venice after the sack of Constantinople by western Crusaders in 1204. Even though the later accounts of the fire of 1231 mention only the principal relics of the treasury – the True Cross, the Holy Blood, St John the Baptist, and St George – among the works which escaped the disaster, it is likely that other objects brought from Constantinople were preserved in another locale at San Marco from this time. The reading of the treasury's inventories published by Gallo, however, shows that the Byzantine collection at San Marco was greatly enriched during the thirteenth and fourteenth centuries. The necessity of maintaining, repairing and providing precious mounts for some of these vases, provoked the development of Venetian goldsmith work in the thirteenth and fourteenth centuries and made Venice into one of the greatest centers of Gothic metalwork. It is too often forgotten that the treasury of San Marco also houses superb Western works. Even if it was made in Constantinople for a Western emperor, the golden cross of Henry of Flanders stands as one of the masterpieces of Mosan art (no. 34). Perhaps executed in Venice itself, the silver-gilt and niello mount of the Fatimid crystal cruet carved with rams combines the elegance of Oriental forms and the vigor of Western ornamental themes with rare harmony (no. 32). The later crystal candelabra (nos 38, 39) testify to a taste for chiseled and engraved metalwork which developed at the end of the thirteenth and beginning of the fourteenth century. This was particularly the case in Venice during the fourteenth century; Hans Hahnloser has grouped the works of the diverse ateliers under the name of the "Maestro del Serpentino" (nos 42, 43).

In the middle and second half of the thirteenth century, the reputation of Venice grew, with the fashion for filigree mounts. The most beautiful of these are preserved at San Marco (nos 35-37). The competence of the Venetians in this area was so great, so seldom equalled or even contested, that the name "of Venetian work" was used for centuries to describe this technique.

Perhaps no example better illustrates the Venetian mentality with regard to their treasury than the "Grotto of the Virgin" (no. 8). This curious object is formed by an irregular Antique rock-crystal representing a little edifice fixed at the back to a gold and enameled votive crown of Leo VI, to form a sort of niche for a silver-gilt statuette of the Virgin, a Venetian work of the thirteenth century, based upon Byzantine models. In this strange combination, two works without parallel were preserved, but simultaneously taken out of their original context to become a fabulous work in the hands of Venetian goldsmiths.

A new evolution in metalwork can be seen around 1300. It is first manifested in a tentative and only partially resolved way, in the making of the large silver-gilt altar-frontal of St Mark (no. 40). It reaches its peak in the elegant ornamental frame of 1342-5 of the *Pala d'Oro*, commissioned by the doge Andrea Dandolo (Hahnloser 1965, 81-111). The earlier frontal is an eclectic work in which Byzantine, Romanesque and Gothic elements merge. Its purest Gothic elements can be found in the trilobe arches, a motif undoubtedly derived from French or German models, but employed with a certain awkwardness, particularly in the half-arches at the extreme left and right. The reliquary of the fourteen saints, of 1320-30 (no. 44), shows a variation on this amalgam of eclectic elements. The foliate decoration of the panels of the small sides prefigures the elegance of the inhabited vine *rinceaux* and leaves of the reliquary of the arm of St George, of 1325, and of the base of the serpentine chalice (nos 41, 42).

The reliquary of the arm of St George is of great importance in more than one respect: first, it inaugurates in Venice a goldsmith style devoid of Byzantine influence. Though it manifests certain stylistic and technical traits of the north of France, and of Sienna, it is the first masterpiece of the treasury that one can consider fully Venetian and probably the earliest example of translucent enamel produced in Venice. Its busts in relief, like the two busts remaining in the branches that surround it, are of a purely Gothic character; they clearly anticipate the busts of the frame of the *Pala d'Oro* (Hahnloser 1965, pls LXXIII-LXXVIII). The openwork decoration of the vine *rinceaux* and of the branches was reused, later, by the atelier of the Sesto, active in Venice around 1420-30, as seen in a comparison with the reliquary of the Holy Blood (Hahnloser 1971, no. 172, pls CLXX-CLXXI). The reliquary of St George is, finally, an exceedingly rare example of a reliquary type that Hahnloser has termed a "talking reliquary" ("*reliquario parlante*"), in which the identity and significance of the relics are expressed through figurative imagery. A second example of this type of reliquary can be seen in the reliquary of the Column of the Flagellation, a Venetian work of about 1375 (no. 46). Formed from silver sheets shaped as desired, assembled and soldered, the technique is particularly suitable for the representation in the round of an animated group that clearly expresses the nature of the relic.

The final and latest object presented here, the pastoral staff dated to about 1420 (no. 47), in its intricate architectural and figurative decoration rendered in cast silver and silver-gilt, is representative of the style of the Sesto family workshop. According to Steingräber (Hahnloser 1971, 177), the Sesto family must have had the monopoly on goldsmith work in Venice during the first thirty years of the fifteenth century.

Venetian filigree

Danielle Gaborit-Chopin

Filigree is wire, single or with strands grouped together. It can be smooth, beaded, grooved or twisted, and is soldered or otherwise attached to a metal surface in decorative scrolls of varying complexity, sometimes of openwork. Throughout the Middle Ages Western filigree from very different workshops in widely separated regions was produced in an infinite variety of forms. Documents and inventories from the end of the thirteenth to the sixteenth century nevertheless use one phrase to describe the various manifestations of the technique: *opus veneciarum*, *opus veneticum* or *venetum*, i.e. "Venetian work". The use of this name clearly indicates the renown that Venetian craftsmen had won in this field. The refinement, elegance and technical virtuosity exhibited by the filigree mounts of gems in the treasury of San Marco (e.g. Hahnloser 1971, nos 17, 19, 54, 60, 85, 88, 119, 123, 144, pls CXXVI-CXXVII) show why. The mounts on the Byzantine lapis lazuli medallion (no. 36) and the sardonyx cruet (no. 35) are perfect examples of filigree enhanced with simple granulation. The mount on the large rock-crystal amphora (no. 37) is one of the most beautiful of all examples of "foliage and rosette" filigree; the "pine-cone" filigree surrounding the icon of the half-figure of St Michael (no. 12) is unsurpassed. Yet in spite of the perfection of the surviving examples of "Venetian work", notably in the San Marco treasury, the probable origin of this filigree, its date, and even the meaning of the term "*opus veneticum*" itself remain a matter of debate. In documents dating from between the final decades of the fourteenth century and the sixteenth the term "Venetian work" is clearly used for all filigree. In earlier documents, however, the term seems to have been used chiefly for work actually of Venetian origin. "Venetian work" was first mentioned in 1295, in the inventory of the Papal treasury in the time of Boniface VIII (Molinier 1888, *Sources*), which lists items as "*de opere venetico*". In 1296 Charles II of Anjou bequeathed to the abbey of St Nicholas at Bari a reliquary and two rock-crystal and silver-gilt candlesticks "*de opere veneciarum*"; these three examples of "Venetian work", which are still in that treasury, are key pieces for the study of filigree (cf. no. 36, figs 36c, 36d; nos 38-39; Barbier de Montault 1883, 34-42; Bertaux 1905, 268, n. 2). The Papal inventories drawn up in 1311 under Clement V (*Regesti..., Appendices* I) are perhaps wrongly invoked in relation to the study of "Venetian work", for although certain of the descriptions use the same terms as in the inventory of Boniface VIII, the epithet "*veneticum*" never appears.

The technical information contained in these inventories of the Papal treasury in the time of Boniface VIII and of Clement V is particularly hard to interpret since the objects themselves are lost. What the inventory of the treasury of Boniface VIII calls "*de opere fili*", "*de opere venetico ad filum*", "*laboratum ad filum de opere venetico*" (Molinier 1888, *Sources*, nos 91, 318, 715, 722) and the Clement V inventories call "*laboratum ad filum*" or "*de opere fili*" (*Regesti...*, e.g. 370, 372-4, 376) is patently filigree. However, the question remains as to what should be understood by the expressions "*de opere duplici Venetico ad folia*", "*de opere duplici ad vites et folia*" and, again, "*de opere duplici relevato ad vites*" (Molinier 1888, *Sources*, nos 136, 149; *Regesti...*, 378). Following Hahnloser (1971, 132-6), these expressions should perhaps be interpreted as referring to variations in Venetian filigree, where different decorative motifs such as leaves, "bunches of grapes" and "pine-cones" were used as enrichment. Following Hueck (1965, 1-22), certain of these items should perhaps be compared to Venetian objects with related decoration but without filigree, such as the Krakow Cathedral cross, or the foot of one of the Charroux reliquaries (Hueck 1965, figs 4, 20). Perhaps one should think of Venetian embossed work with foliage or animals, a good example of which is the mount on the serpentine chalice or that on the incense-boat (nos 42, 43). A systematic study of the terminology used in these two inventories leads to a certain circumspection. As Molinier noted in his edition of the inventory of the treasury of Boniface VIII (1888, 21), the term "*de opere duplici*", "double work", seems to denote a distinction between it and "*de opere simplici*", "simple work", since those who compiled the inventories almost always took care to specify the elements which gave a work its "double" character: "foliage with dragons", or "vines and leaves, with eagles, lions and griffins" (Molinier 1888, *Sources*, nos 136, 149) "with horsemen", "men and beasts", "with enamels" or "with figures and enamels" (*Regesti...*, 370, 372-4). On the other hand, Hahnloser was certainly right to relate the filigree on the icon of the half-figure of St Michael or that on the rock-crystal amphora (nos 12, 37) to the description of a cross in the treasury of Boniface VIII (Molinier 1888, *Sources*, no. 421): "... *Laborata per totum ad vites de filo elevato et rotas*" (worked all over with vine-scrolls of raised wire and with wheels) or, again, to this description of a bowl (Molinier 1888, *Sources*, no. 150): "*de opere ad vites et folia minuta cum rosulis*" (worked in vine-scrolls and small leaves with rosettes).

These distinctions, which are perhaps unimportant or over-subtle, should not, however, disguise the evidence. If the term "Venetian work" was used by contemporaries to describe filigree, it was because of the incomparable quality of the work of Venetian craftsmen: the lightness of their arched tendrils, standing away from the metal surface to create a kind of lacy openwork panel, the vigour and crispness of their coils and the refinement of their cable-twists. This technical virtuosity was so great and so successful that exports were considerable: perhaps it would not be fanciful to think of re-attributing to Venetian craftsmen objects which are outside Italy but have no real affinity with anything except Venetian craftsmanship. For example, the Charroux filigree reliquary, or the Nailly and Najac crosses, all attributed to French workshops (exh. cat. *Trésors des églises de France*, 1965, nos 314, 344, 820), a brooch in the Bargello, said to be Rhenish (exh. cat. *Die Zeit der Staufer*, 1977, no. 605, fig. 422), and the mount of the "Rothschild cameo" (Coche de la Ferté 1981, fig. 551) should all be re-examined from a Venetian standpoint.

Filigree was certainly not invented by the Venetians, but should one really see in its particularly brilliant development in Venice "a monopoly ... all the more remarkable as it amounts to a veritable usurpation" and "nothing other than a perfect imitation of what had been produced in the Rhine-Maas region" (Hahnloser 1971, 131)? Such a judgment suggests a strange simplification of the study of medieval filigree, and the truth is doubtless much more complex. The filigree technique was no more the exclusive preserve of Rhenish or Mosan artists than it was of Venetian craftsmen: the goldsmiths of seventh and eighth-century Ireland, and those working for Charles the Bald and for the Ottonian emperors all made important contributions to this difficult art. In fact the

Venetians only developed a technique which had been practised for several centuries, but they raised it to a perfection seldom attained.

The fire of 1231 in the treasury of San Marco provides a *terminus post quem* for the Venetian works. But at that date the art of filigree was not practised exclusively by Rhine-Maas craftsmen: filigree with simple granulation can be found in abundance in twelfth and thirteenth-century Western metalwork everywhere. If filigree incorporating foliage and rosettes formed from granulation was already decorating the openwork apples on the crest of the Anno shrine at Siegburg, a Cologne work of about 1183 (fig. 37 d), and if "pine-cones" (decorative elements made by winding filigree wire) can be seen on the Cologne reliquary of the arm of St Cunibert, made in about 1222 (exh. cat. *Die Zeit der Staufer*, 1977, no. 560, fig. 362), the filigree incorporating animals on the cross presented to the abbey of Saint-Denis in 1205 by Philip Augustus (1180-1223) should not be forgotten. The cross has been lost, but there are descriptions precise enough to give a good idea of its technique (v. Montesquiou-Fezensac and Gaborit-Chopin 1977, 22-3). Filigree on crosses dating from the first half of the thirteenth century should also be taken into account, not only the crosses of Rhenish or Mosan manufacture or those made in northern France, such as the cross of the Paraclete in the cathedral treasury at Amiens (fig. 37 f), but also crosses of the "southern" group outlined by Frolow (1965): the crosses of Eymoutiers, Gorre, and especially Rouvres, which should be related to a series of contemporary examples of filigree from Limoges (cf. nos 36, 37). On southern crosses, the filigree with rosettes, foliage and "pine-cones" found on Venetian productions is even commoner than in the northern group.

Finally, the art of filigree was not unknown in Italy. Byzantine examples, such as the filigree on the central part of the icon of the half-figure of St Michael in the treasury of San Marco (no. 12), and Islamic influences may explain the development in eleventh and twelfth-century Italy, especially in the south, of a fine, tightly organized filigree of beaded wire, known as "*a vermicelli*" (e.g. on the Velletri cross, the "Pax" of Chiavenna, and the Capua bookcover; Hackenbroch 1938, 83, 92, 98). In the final decades of the thirteenth century, as Hueck has recently pointed out (1982, 259-78), Tuscan workshops produced filigree which might profitably be compared with Venetian examples. Thus it is evident that the use of filigree in thirteenth-century Venice is too much part of the overall development of Western goldsmiths' work to be considered only in the light of Rhenish-Mosan influence.

The production of the "*opus veneticum ad filum*" developed during the second half of the thirteenth century, the 1231 fire in the treasury acting as a *terminus post quem*. Hahnloser (1971, 134-5) noted examples dating from the very end of the century which have filigree with simple granulation, such as the portable altar of Andrew of Hungary in Berne and the candlesticks and reliquary at Bari (cf. nos 36, 38-39). He concluded that this was of the latest type and that workshops initially produced the more complex and intricate work, including filigree with rosettes, foliage and "pine-cones", as on the icon of St Michael, and then moved towards a simpler style of granulated filigree, typified by the filigree on the lapis lazuli icon or on the sardonyx cruet (nos 35, 36). Although this chronology is appealing, it should be qualified. Granulated filigree was widespread in Italy all through the second half of the thirteenth century. If there are numerous examples dating from around 1300 and even from the beginning of the fourteenth century, earlier, perhaps Venetian, evidence from around the middle of the century is provided by the ivory and filigree staurotheca in Cortona (fig. 36 e) and, from around 1270, by the Tuscan cross at Castiglione Fiorentino (cf. Hueck 1982, 269-75). In the same way, the decoration on the upper part of the Sienese reliquary of the head of St Galgano shows that filigree with foliage and "pine-cones" was still in use in Italy at the end of the thirteenth century (Hueck 1982, 273, figs 8-9).

The present state of knowledge does not therefore permit us to distribute over nearly half a century the filigree mounts in the treasury of San Marco, which besides the number of related elements in the network of their filigree tendrils compare closely with one another, showing that the craftsmen who made them inspired each other and worked in the same milieu. A relative chronology of these works is all the more difficult to establish since the general chronology of all twelfth and thirteenth-century filigree still needs clarification. All the items in the San Marco treasury in fact share the same characteristics: panels of cable-twisted wires crisply detached from their ground, broad and strong coils, and bundles of wires branching off at regular intervals. These characteristics are sufficient to explain why, once they had been developed, the art of filigree could not have been called anything but "Venetian work".

33

Lamp or perfume-burner in shape of domed building

Southern Italian(?), end of 12th century
Silver, partly gilt. *Height* 360 mm, *width* 300 mm

Tesoro, no. 142 (adapted after 1231(?) to serve as a reliquary of the Holy
Blood and listed thus in the 1283 inventory: no. 1)

The "reliquary", which is of unusual type, has the shape
of a small building, square in plan and with four projecting apses crowned with four domes alternating with four
triangular towers with pyramidal roofs. In the centre is a
higher dome surmounted by a lantern of arches. Each
dome is topped with a bulbous pointed finial. (The
crosses on the triangular towers are not original.) The
building rests on a narrower base. Two handles are
attached to the object, the attachments terminating in
bearded masks.

The decoration, which is extremely rich, covers all the
visible surfaces. The domes, the roofs of the towers and
the upper part of the walls are of openwork foliage and
flowers: foliage roundels, imbricated pointed and veined
palmettes, and compositions of palmette-flowers. A band
of embossed scrollwork punctuated with large rosettes
runs around the top of the walls, another band embossed
with adjoining circles containing five-lobed palmettes
runs round the middle, and at the base of the walls is a
third band of embossed scrolls. The lower part of the
walls, between the embossed bands, has figural decoration of secular character on a pounced ground. From
right to left, reading from the door in one of the apses,
the figures are: a lion passant; a griffin; two confronted
sirens, their tails terminating in serpents' heads, one
with a flute, the other with a pipe (?); two confronted
lions; two confronted griffins; a leaping lion; a centaur
with a round shield; a couple; and a *putto* diving into a
basket; a lion passant; a griffin.

The double doors of the building are half-rounded; between them is a lion-mask. Each door is embossed with
an allegorical figure with a nimbus decorated with pounced
vermiculation, identified by an inscription. On the left
door is a helmeted warrior wearing a short pleated tunic,
breast-plate and long cloak. He is leaning on a spear and
shield and personifies courage ("ANΔPIAA"). On the
right-hand door is intelligence ("H ΦPONECIC"), depicted as a female wearing a closely fitting tunic and a long
skirt. Standing between two small trees, she touches her
forehead with her right index-finger.

The door is hinged to open. The large central dome is
removable. Inside the building there is a circular base
with a metal ring at its centre. A metal "ceiling" divides
the domes – except for the central one – from the interior
space. This "ceiling" must be original because the crenellation visible on the exterior, at the top of the walls, is
its bent-up edge.

This curious casket, the "*chiesola*", used to shelter one of
San Marco's most important relics, the Holy Blood. The
inventories of San Marco show that, over the course of
several centuries, there were several reliquaries of the
Holy Blood there (which led to a certain confusion); only
one, however, is listed in the first inventory of the
treasury, made in 1283. It was a rock-crystal phial, which
even at that time was enclosed in the silver casket in the
shape of a church: "*Ampulla una de christallo in qua est
sanguis Salvatris nostri Jesu Christi, ornata auro et una
perla desuper et est in quadam ecclesia argenti*" (Gallo
1967, 273, no. 1). This phial of the Holy Blood mentioned at the end of the thirteenth century can only be
the one which miraculously escaped the fire of 1231; it
had been one of the relics sent from Constantinople to
Venice by the doge Enrico Dandolo in 1204. It was therefore after the fire of 1231 that it was placed in the silver
chiesola. From descriptions in later inventories the phial
can be identified as the cylindrical Fatimid rock-crystal
flask (Hahnloser 1971, no. 128) which, according to
tradition, held the "miraculous blood" which fell from a
crucifix struck by an infidel in Beirut in AD 320. The
crystal phial was still in the domed silver-gilt casket in
the nineteenth century.

The term "*ecclesiola*" or "*chiesola*" (little church), often
used to describe the silver-gilt casket, originates in the
resemblance of the object to a church with domes.
Although its overall appearance is reminiscent of certain
Byzantine buildings, and although it can be related, for
instance, to the church of the Holy Apostles in Constantinople, where four smaller domes similarly surrounded a
larger central dome (fig. 33a; Paris, Bibliothèque Nationale, ms. gr. 1208, fol. 31v, first half of twelfth century),
this is a mistaken interpretation of the *chiesola*. Cicognara
emphasized that it had long been regarded as a sim-
plified model of St Sophia (cf. Gallo 1967, 384). Several
Byzantine objects are in the form of buildings surmounted by towers or domes. A secular casket with five towers,
the *Pentapyrgion*, was made in the ninth century for the
emperor Theophilus (cf. Grabar 1951). One of the most
remarkable of surviving liturgical objects is a reliquary
in the cathedral treasury at Aachen (fig. 33b); it is of
silver-gilt and niello and was made in Antioch in the
second half of the tenth century (969-70; cf. Saunders
1983, 211-9). At some point it was made into the reliquary of St Anastasius the Persian. However, one of
its inscriptions alludes to "Sion", the city of God,

239

33b

33c

33d

242

suggesting that the Aachen reliquary was originally either an *artophorion* (for storing the eucharist) or a censer (as is suggested by the openwork arcade of the drum below the dome, which would allow incense-smoke to escape; cf. Grabar 1957a). Several censers belonging to the Byzantine tradition are in the form of small churches, in fact. Like the "Sion" or "Jerusalem" lamps carried in processions, these objects would evoke the Heavenly Jerusalem, from whence streamed the smoke of incense or light. A parallel tradition existed in the West, a number of medieval censers also having the form of buildings capped by turrets (cf. Grousset 1982, 81-106). Among these Western censers, the plan of the San Marco *chiesola* can be found in a bronze censer formerly in the Bouvier and Spitzer collections (fig. 33c; Cleveland, Museum of Art, northern France or Mosan region, late twelfth or early thirteenth century; cat. coll. Spitzer 1890, I, 101). In contrast to the Cleveland object, the San Marco *chiesola* is largely openwork and may well therefore have been a lamp, or, in view of the secular character of its decoration, a perfume-burner.

It is not certain, however, that this lamp or perfume-burner originally came from a palace in Constantinople. Grabar has remarked on its resemblance to kiosks in Sasanian gardens (cf. a dish in Berlin; Grabar 1951, pl. 616). In addition many of the decorative elements, such as the imbricated openwork of veined palmettes, the pointed flowers, the griffins, the lions with palmettes stamped on their haunches, and the sirens with their serpent tails, ultimately derive from Oriental sources. Neither the crenellation nor the over-elaborate domes belong to Byzantine structures; outside Islam domes such as these are found only in Italy, as for example on Sicilian twelfth-century buildings (San Giovanni degli Eremiti, San Cataldo at Palermo). If the motifs of a *putto* emerging from a basket and of a centaur derive from decoration on Byzantine ivory caskets of the tenth and eleventh centuries (fig. 33d), the style of the two allegorical figures on the doors suggests the Western rendering of a Byzantine model. The couple on the lower part of the *chiesola* recall the Western court traditions of the final decades of the twelfth century (e.g. the painted casket in Vannes or the enamel casket in the British Museum, even though the costume of the female is different; exh. cat. *Trésors des églises de France*, 1965, no. 336; Gauthier 1972, 330, no. 50). The lion-mask and the large bearded masks are related to decoration on southern Italian bronze doors (e.g. of Troia Cathedral, 1127-59). Although they doubtless derive from Classical models and have Byzantine equivalents, a centaur and warriors with maces and small round shields can be seen on the doors of Barisanus of Trani (Trani and Ravello doors, 1175 and 1179; *v.* Boeckler 1953). Finally, the actual form of the inscription identifying Courage suggests an origin other than the imperial court. On the other hand griffins are known in southern Italian sculpture and mosaics (e.g. the royal throne of Monreale, the

transenna in Trani Cathedral, and the mosaics at Santa Maria del Patir in Calabria and those at Tremiti). It therefore seems possible to conclude, with Grabar, that this precious object in San Marco, whether lamp or perfume-burner, was made at the end of the twelfth century in a milieu open to strong Byzantine but also Oriental and Western influences: Sicily or the Bari area, or perhaps Venice itself.

D.G.C.

Bibliography: Pasini 1885-6, 25, no. 27. Molinier 1888, 88-9. Grabar 1951, 32-60. Grabar 1957a, 282-97. Gallo 1967, 41, 273, no. 1; 276, no. 1; 288, no. 1; 312, no. 1; 328, no. 4; 384, no. 14; 388, no. 4. Grabar 1968, I, 282-4, 427, pls 61-2. Hahnloser 1971, no. 109 (Grabar), pls LXXVIII-LXXX, with bibliography. Cocho de la Ferté 1981, fig. 580.

Exh. cat. *Venezia e Bisanzio*, 1974, no. 44, with bibliography; *Splendeur de Byzance*, 1982, no. O23.

34

Staurotheca of Henry of Flanders

Staurotheca: made by the goldsmith Gerard, at Constantinople, before 1216. *Monstrance*: Venetian, 1618
Staurotheca: wood, gold. *Height* 335 mm, *width* 240 mm. *Monstrance*: bronze-gilt, glass. *Height* 565 mm, *width* 312 mm

Santuario, no. 55 (listed in the 1402 inventory: no. 2)

The reliquary of the True Cross is enclosed in a bronze-gilt and glass monstrance with a foot formed by three grotesque figures. Although the monstrance is not mentioned in the 1634 inventories and only appears in those of the nineteenth century, it is quite possible, as Hahnloser believed (1971), that it was made in 1618, when the reliquary was placed on the altar of the Holy Sacrament as decreed by the Senate (Pasini 1886, 29).

The staurotheca proper is formed of six rectangular pieces of the True Cross assembled as a cross with two transverse arms (a piece of the vertical member is now missing at the foot); the whole is set in a band of gold foliage, the serrated edges folded over on to the face of the cross. Two long feathery leaves curve outwards from the base of the cross, one on either side; two berry-like fruits with slender stalks grow from between the base of the cross and the lower ends of the leaves. Statuettes of the Virgin and St John stand on the leaves, their heads touching the lower transverse arm of the cross. They are fine, slender figures in the round and, like the three other statuettes on the staurotheca, were cast in gold. The faces are finely but vigorously modelled. Tightly wrapped in her cloak, the Virgin turns away from the cross, wringing her hands. St John, shown frontally, with his right arm by his side, holds a *rotulus* in his left hand. The gold figure of Christ is nailed to the relic itself with three nails; the slender arms are hardly raised above horizontal, and the body is strongly arched, the long loin-cloth looped around the waist. Two other slightly smaller statuettes, of Ecclesia and Synagoga, stand on the lower transverse arm of the cross supporting the upper arm with their heads. Ecclesia, crowned, holds a chalice with a round bowl in her left hand. Synagoga, blindfolded, has inverted her chalice and holds her left hand to her head in a sign of despair. At the upper intersection of the arms is a gold openwork medallion of a phoenix with outstretched wings, symbolic of the Resurrection. Its workmanship seems good enough for it to be attributed to the goldsmith responsible for the statuettes. Only the five gold figures and the phoenix (mistaken for an eagle) are described in the 1617 inventory (Gallo 1967, 311, no. 41). It is possible, as Hahnloser maintained, that the gold openwork palmettes and rosettes marking the extremities of the cross were added, together with the superscription, in 1618. They are not shown in Tiepolo's engraving in his treatise on relics (fig. 34a; Tiepolo 1617).

On the back, at each of the intersections of the arms is an engraved gold medallion. The upper one shows between the sun and moon a bust of Christ blessing. On the lower medallion is the Lamb of God. Along the gold border around the cross is a long Latin inscription revealing precisely who made the staurotheca, for whom, and when: +CONDIDIT OC SINGNVM GERARDI DEXTERA DINGNVM +QVOD IVSSIT MONDVS REX FRANCVS DVXQVE SECONDVS +GRECORVM DICTVS HENRICVS VT OC BENEDICTVS +BELLO SECVRVS SEMPER MANEAT QVASI MVRVS. AMEN+ ("The hand of Gerard has made this venerable cross [*singnum dingnum*] at the command of the free king with the pure heart [*mondus*] and second leader of the Greeks, called Henry, so that, under its blessing, he will always be protected in war, as a wall. Amen.") The cross was, therefore, executed by Gerard the goldsmith for Henry of Flanders, the second Latin emperor of Constantinople, who ruled from 1206 until 1216.

The inscription alludes to the custom of Byzantine emperors of having a relic of the True Cross carried before them on military expeditions. A similar tradition was attached to certain relics of the True Cross brought to the West. In Venice, the relic brought from Constantinople in 1204 was said to have been the one which Constantine took with him into battle (Frolow 1961, 382, no. 450; Hahnloser 1971, no. 192). Thus Henry of Flanders, brother of and successor to Baldwin I, was maintaining the practice. It is possible that he had the staurotheca made as early as his coronation, in 1206 (Hahnloser, 1971). The date of its arrival in Venice is unknown. It could have been sent before 1216 by the emperor, who was in the Venetians' debt, or it may have arrived shortly after his death. However, it is just as likely to have entered the treasury after the Latins left Constantinople in 1261, or even later, as it is not listed in any inventory before 1402. In fact, the only reference to a relic of the True Cross in the thirteenth century is to the cross of Constantine mentioned earlier. This escaped the fire of 1231, having been sent to Venice in 1204 with the relics of the Holy Blood, of St John the Baptist and of St George, according to Andrea Dandolo's account. It is uncertain whether the cross of Henry of Flanders can be identified with the staurotheca shown on a relief at San Marco which depicts the principal relics in the treasury (fig. 34b). If the cross shown is indeed the one made for Henry, then it is quite inaccurately depicted, since only

34a

ever is paralleled by several Western examples. Crosses with double transverse arms, originating in the East, tended to be used for reliquaries of the True Cross. Several Mosan or northern French reliquaries dating from the first half of the thirteenth century have feet (doubtless of a type analogous to the lost foot of the cross in Venice) from the top of which emerge leafy scrolls like the feathery leaves on the San Marco cross. These reliquaries include that of St Peter fashioned by Hugo of Oignies, now at Namur (1238), the turreted reliquary at Saint-Riquier, the Grandselve reliquary and the foot of the Bargello cross (Courtoy 1951-2, 146-52; exh. cat. *Trésors des églises de France*, 1965, nos 76, 523; Hahnloser 1971, pl. LXVIII, 6).

The leaves and berry-like fruits at the base of the cross are not unlike those on the Oignies reliquary and on the Maubeuge cross (cf. Courtoy 1951-2; exh. cat. *Trésors des églises de France*, 1965, no. 17). Finally, the well-known drawing of a cross in the sketch-book of Villard de Honnecourt (fig. 34 c; Paris, Bibliothèque Nationale, ms. Fr. 19093, fol. 18, about 1220-30), two figures of the Virgin and St John standing on leaves, attributed to the suite of Hugo of Oignies (London, Victoria and Albert Museum, nos 741, 1891) and the cross from Saint-Vincent, Laon (fig. 34 d; Paris, Musée du Louvre, before 1205) are examples of crosses where statuettes of the Virgin and St John stand on vegetal elements. The proportions of the gold statuettes on the cross in Venice are too fine and slender for comparisons with the work of Nicholas of Verdun to be at all convincing: they are much closer to Mosan examples. The silhouette of the Virgin and her oval face derive from Mosan manuscript-illumination of the last third of the twelfth century (e.g. exh. cat. *Rhein-Maas*, 1972, nos J20, J29). The pose and slenderness of the Virgin and the refinement of her close-fitting drapery may also prefigure certain aspects of Gothic sculpture in Strasbourg, in particular the Synagoga there. The strict verticality of the folds on St John's tunic reappears at a slightly later date on a St John in Liège, while the arched body of Christ, and his loincloth, are related to the large Christ at Huy (exh. cat. *Rhein-Maas*, 1972, nos. L3, L5; Didier 1982, figs 2, 6, 16). The Virgin resembles those found on numerous small Mosan bronze figures of the first decades of the thirteenth century (cf. Wixom, 1972). One of the most convincing comparisons with the statuettes on the San Marco cross is, however, provided by precious metalwork: a silver-gilt buckle from Dune, made in the early thirteenth century and doubtless imported from the Rhine-Maas region (fig. 34 e; Stockholm, Statens Historiska Museum; exh. cat. *L'Europe gothique*, 1968, no. 399). The casket of the Holy Innocents once in the cathedral treasury in Cologne, know only from a seventeenth-century engraving, was in Hahnloser's opinion (1965) a gift from Henry of Flanders and the work of Gerard, but it is not easily compared with the Venice staurotheca. The crown-reliquary in the cathedral treasury at Namur,

two figures are represented, and the Virgin is in a different pose. In addition, the horizontal arms are different. Something of the personality of Gerard the goldsmith appears in his work. There is little doubt that he was a Latin working in Constantinople in the emperor's circle. He seems to have been a native of the Rhine-Maas region or of northern France. The clever idea of using as caryatids the figures of the Virgin and St John and those personifying the Old Testament and the New seems extremely original. The shape of the cross itself, how-

249

34f

enshrining two of the thorns from Christ's crown of thorns which were given by Henry of Flanders to his brother, Philip the Good, in about 1205-7, was itself made at the beginning of the thirteenth century and might have been sent from Constantinople with the two relics (Courtoy and Schmitz 1930, 13, 21, no. 1). However, nothing in the crown-reliquary's appearance or workmanship justifies an attribution to the goldsmith of the Venice cross. Its filigree with little veined flowers relates above all to the cross from Laon, the back of which is covered with an identical filigree motif. Despite the similarity in the form of the two crosses already pointed out, the Laon cross differs considerably from that made by Gerard. The two figures of Christ, both extremely beautiful, are significant in their divergence. The Christ on the Laon cross, crowned and pierced with four nails, is still in the Romanesque tradition (fig. 34f), whereas the figure suffering on the Venice cross may be numbered among the first Gothic Christs.

D.G.C.

Bibliography: Tiepolo 1617, 67. Pasini 1885-6, 29-30, no. 6, pl. XXV. Molinier 1888, 85, no. 18. Braun 1940, no. 89. Gallo 1967, 287, no. 2; 289, no. 5; 311, no. 41; 316, VII, no. 24; 387-8, fig. 22. Frolow 1961, no. 471. Hahnloser 1965, *Miscellanea*. Frolow 1965, 127, 165, no. 4, 195, 234, no. 1. Hahnloser 1971, no. 140 (Hahnloser). Claussen 1978, 46-86, fig. 2. Gauthier 1983, 76-7, no. 40.

Exh. cat. *L'Europe gothique*, 1968, no. 374; *Tesori dell'Arte Mosana*, 1973-4, no. 35; *Die Zeit der Staufer*, 1977, no. 568.

35

Sardonyx cruet

Stonework: 3rd century (?). *Metalwork*: Venetian, 2nd half of 13th century
Sardonyx, silver-gilt, stones. *Height* 230 mm, *max. width* 98 mm

Tesoro, no. 81 (listed in the 1325 inventory: III, no. 22)

The cruet was made by ingeniously fitting a precious metal mount to an older hardstone vessel. The lower part is a deep sardonyx bowl with a foot cut from the same block of stone. The restrained decoration of the bowl consists of a fillet incised below the rim and a three-part moulding in the upper half. The moulding comprises a wide band between two narrower ones defined by incised fillets. The round foot has two *tori* on a vertical-sided base, the underside of which is flat. The bowl is well shaped and the decoration well executed apart from some irregularity in the fillets and in the *tori* of the base. There is a second cruet in the treasury of San Marco, of agate-onyx, which combines a hardstone bowl and a precious metal mount (fig. 4a; Hahnloser 1971, no. 6), and the two pieces were described together in the 1325 inventory: "*Vasculos duos de unicolo ornatos argento cum manicis*" (Gallo 1967, 278, III, no. 22). The 1571 inventory twice lists "*Una ampoletta, parte d'Agata et parte d'Arzento*" (Gallo 1967, 300, nos 90, 93). In the 1733 inventory the ewer can probably be recognized under the description: "*Un'ampolla di nicolo orientale con bochino dorato circondato di geme*" (Gallo 1967, 350, no. 23). It was valued at 1000 lire in the Cicognara's catalogue of the treasury of 1816-20 (Gallo 1967, 362-3, no. 2). The bowl is certainly not a Byzantine work of the tenth or eleventh century, as has been thought, but is more likely to be of Classical origin. Byzantine circular sardonyx cups are not as deep as this example (cf. no. 16), and their bases are either small, shallow and undecorated, or of precious metalwork. Some Classical vessels, on the other hand, have feet with mouldings, cut from the same stone as the rest of the object, and these are reminiscent of – if more elegant than – the bowl in Venice. The "Coupe des Ptolémées" (fig. 10j), a two-handled sardonyx vase in the Pitti Palace (Heikamp 1974, no. 7, fig. 20), and agate vessels probably of later date found in 1544 in the tomb of the empress Maria in Rome (Rossi 1863, 54) are examples of this type. One of the sardonyx chalices in the treasury of San Marco (fig. 15b; Hahnloser 1971, no. 62, pl. LVI) also has a high foot with mouldings, cut from one piece of stone, and may also be of Classical origin. The type of decoration found on the bowl, which is unknown on Byzantine vases, appears on Classical sardonyx vessels, moreover. The closest example is a fragment of a goblet in the Bibliothèque Nationale in Paris (fig. 35a; Bühler 1973, no. 97, pl. 31), which has walls varying in thickness from five millimetres to almost a centimetre. In the same place as the Venice bowl it has the same triple moulding, the middle component being wider and projecting more than the two others. Two round bowls, one of them excavated in Egypt in 1930 (Habachi and Biers 1969, 32, fig. 4) and the other in the Louvre (fig. 35b; this vessel, which has thick walls, has been fitted with an Italian Baroque bronze-gilt mount enabling a foot to be added) are both decorated with a group of three mouldings, but the centre moulding is closer in size to the others than on the Venice example. A round bowl found in Rome, a goblet found at Cologne (fig. 34c), a fragment in the British Museum (Bühler 1973, no. 11, pl. 3; nos 95-6, pl. 31) and a flask in the *Schatzkammer* in Munich (fig. 35d; Thoma and Brunner 1964, no. 22) are also decorated with groups of two or three incised fillets.

These vessels were probably made after the finest period of Classical hardstone-carving, which was around the beginning of the Christian era. This is suggested by the remarkable thickness of the walls of the two pieces in Paris and confirmed by the provenience of the Cologne bowl: it was found in a tomb containing coins of the second half of the third century.

D. A.

Metalwork

The metal mount fitted to the sardonyx bowl has transformed it into a long-necked cruet with a slightly curved handle and a slender spout. The shape is patently inspired by Oriental models (e.g. Hahnloser 1971, pl. CXXXVIII) but is shared by several twelfth and thirteenth-century vessels either of Western origin or with mounts made in the West: it can be compared with that of a Limoges enamel cruet in the Cabinet des Médailles of the Bibliothèque Nationale in Paris (Gauthier 1950, pl. 59) and that of a sardonyx ewer of Abbot Suger, from the treasury of Saint-Denis (fig. 35e; Paris, Musée du Louvre; Montesquiou-Fezensac and Gaborit-Chopin 1977, pl. 22). In the treasury of San Marco itself are two other mounted hardstone vessels of similar shape: the rock-crystal cruet (no. 32) and that of agate-onyx (fig. 4a; Hahnloser 1971, no. 6). The similarity of the mounts explains why the sardonyx and the agate-onyx cruets were grouped together as a notional pair as early as 1325 (Gallo 1967, 278, III, no. 22). The mount on the sardonyx cruet differs from that on the onyx example, however, in the refinement of its ribbed knop and by the filigree decorating the neck and upper part of the body in four lobes bordered by

252

253

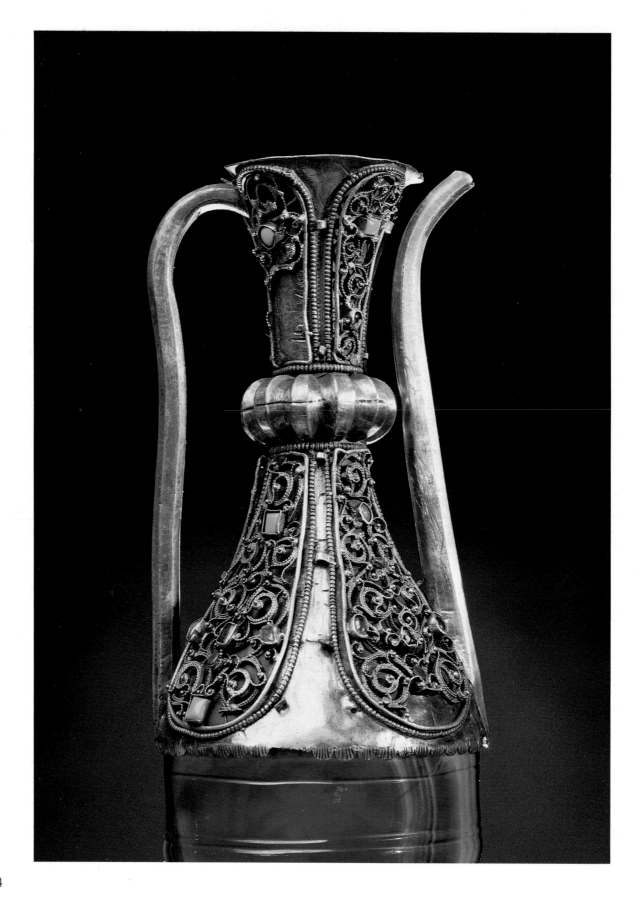

35 a

35 d

35 c

35 b

heavy beaded wire. The lid is missing, and the spout was doubtless once adorned with a small animal-head such as can be found on the two other examples from Venice mentioned above. The spout itself, faceted like the handle, has been bent. It was probably once strengthened by a metal stem joining it to the knop of the neck, as on most of the surviving examples of this type of vessel. Finally the cruet must once have had a small metal foot for stability.

The ribbed decoration on the knop was common in the thirteenth century and can be found on several liturgical vessels and reliquaries of that period, such as the chalice of Hugo of Oignies (about 1240; Namur, Convent of Notre-Dame; exh. cat. *L'Europe gothique*, 1968, no. 376), the Dollgellau bowl (about 1250-1300; Cardiff; Jackson 1911, 105, fig. 142), the chalices in the treasuries of Orleans and Troyes, the Grandmont cross in Rouvres (exh. cat. *Trésors des églises de France*, 1965, nos 175, 805) and the reliquary of St Francis of Assisi (about 1228; Paris, Musée du Louvre; Gauthier 1983, 138). Similar decoration can also be found on Venetian examples such as the reliquary of the Holy Blood dated from the thirteenth century (Hahnloser 1971, no. 128) and a fourteenth-century chalice now in Cambridge (fig. 43g). The lanceolate panels of filigree can also be paralleled, notably on the feet of chalices and reliquaries of various origins. These include the Oignies chalice and those in Cardiff and Troyes, and the reliquary at Saint-Michel-des-Lions, Limoges (exh. cat. *Trésors des églises de France*, 1965, no. 365). Rather than the precise reflection of Mosan or Rhenish influence (Hahnloser), the characteristics of the sardonyx cruet make it typical of thirteenth-century Western precious metalwork.

The vigour of the cable-twisted filigree, crisply detached from its background, and the simple granulation make it possible, as Hahnloser has noted, to attribute the metalwork to the Venetian workshop which mounted several other objects in the treasury, notably the lapis lazuli icon (no. 36). The mounts on an Islamic red glass incense-boat and a glass amphora (figs 35f, 35g, 37c; Hahnloser 1971, nos 119, 143), made in the same workshop, are similarly decorated with filigree arranged in lobes. This feature is also found on the mount of a rock-crystal amphora (no. 37), although here the filigree is much more complex.

Although it cannot be recognized in the inventories drawn up before 1325, or perhaps even 1571, the sardonyx cruet was certainly in Venice in the second half of the thirteenth century, for this is when and where it received its mount.

D.G.C.

Bibliography: Pasini 1885-6, 65, pl. LI, no. 117. Molinier 1888, 97, no. 106. Gallo 1967, 278, III, no. 22; 300, nos 90, 93; 350, no. 23; 362-3, no. 2. Hahnloser 1971, no. 88 (Grabar, Hahnloser), pls LXX, CXXVII, CXXXIII.

Icon with lapis lazuli Crucifixion medallion

Medallion: Byzantine, 11th–12th century. *Enamel*: Byzantine, 9th–12th centuries. *Filigree panel*: Venetian, middle or 2nd half of 13th century. *Borders*: modern
Lapis lazuli, gold, silver-gilt, enamel, glass. *Height* 420 mm, *width* 314 mm, *depth* 240 mm

Tesoro, no. 2 (possibly listed in the 1325 inventory: V, no. 5)

The icon is made up of various elements of Byzantine workmanship, mounted in Venice. In the centre is a large lapis lazuli medallion enclosed within a metal setting of foliate motifs in turn surrounded by a string of pearls (replacements). Fixed to the medallion are three gold figures cast in low relief: Christ, the Virgin and St John. Symbols of the sun and moon and the letters of an inscription in Greek are inlaid with gold: IΔE O Υ[IO]C COY / IΔOΥ H MH[TH]P COY (῎Ιδε ὁ υἱός σου, ἰδοὺ ἡ μήτηρ σου, "Behold thy son, behold thy mother").
There are very few extant Byzantine examples of hardstone inlaid with gold. Ornamental motifs and inscriptions in the same technique can, however, be found on two objects of lapis lazuli cut in cameo: a small double-sided icon from the treasury of Saint-Denis (fig. 36b; Paris, Musée du Louvre, twelfth century; Montesquiou-Fezensac and Gaborit-Chopin 1977, 46-7, pl. 29) and a cameo of Christ in the Kremlin Armoury, Moscow (Coche de la Ferté 1982, fig. 158).
Byzantine gold figures in relief are equally rare. A small number of examples exists, however, including the enamelled gold cross from Martvili (fig. 36a; Tbilisi, Museum of Fine Arts, ninth or tenth century; Amiranachvili 1971, 58, pls 29-30; exh. cat. *Au pays de la Toison d'or*, 1982, no. 46), which has a figure of the Virgin with the infant Christ, but in a style very different from the figures on the San Marco medallion. In addition, the Papal inventory made under Boniface VIII in 1295 lists a small stone icon decorated with small gold sculpted figures, which were doubtless close to those on the Venice medallion (Molinier 1888, *Sources*, no. 725: "*Unam parvam iconam de lapide incluso in ligno cum imaginibus scultis* (sic) *de auro*"). The three slender-proportioned appliqué figures on the Venice example may best be related to tenth-century ivory reliefs like the central part of a triptych in Berlin, where the torso and the narrow waist of the figure of Christ is similarly modelled and St John's hair has been given the same treatment as on the Venice medallion, or to the Crucifixion formerly in the Engel-Gros collection, where the Virgin is similarly depicted (Goldschmidt and Weitzmann 1934, nos 72a, 72b, 194). On the Venice example several characteristics, which are also found on an icon of the Crucifixion from Sinai dating from the eleventh or twelfth century (Weitzmann 1966, no. 21), indicate a somewhat later date, as noted by Grabar (Hahnloser 1971): the greater suppleness of the drapery,

the slant of the superscription, and the reversed perspective of the *suppedaneum*.
Several Byzantine enamels of varying provenience were set into the mount when the lapis medallion was remounted. The four circular medallions set into the filigree represent the archangel Raphael, St Andrew, St John and, almost certainly, St Matthew (the inscription is illegible). These can be dated to the eleventh or twelfth century, like the two small plaques and one of the medallions of St Matthew in the border. The second medallion of St Matthew in the border, which has a green translucent enamel background and an inscription executed in gold strip set on edge in the enamel, is certainly earlier (late ninth or early tenth century) and can be compared with enamel on Leo VI's crown (no. 8). The central medallion is set into four large panels of silver-gilt filigree. These panels, with their cable-twisted filigree coiled in tendrils sharply detached from the surface and enriched with granulation, are close in style to the filigree on several other objects in the treasury of San Marco, such as that on the mounts of a silver-gilt Byzantine chalice, a sardonyx ewer, a red glass incense-boat and a large glass amphora (no. 35, figs 35f, 35g; Hahnloser 1971, nos 54, 88, 119, 144). Filigree of this type, with simple granulation, can also be found on the mounts of objects of Venetian origin, such as a crystal bowl in Dresden (Grünes Gewölbe; Hahnloser 1971, pl. XXVII, fig. 4), an early fourteenth-century chalice in the Fitzwilliam Museum, Cambridge (fig. 43g), the candlesticks and reliquary presented to Bari in 1296 by Charles of Anjou (figs 36c, 36d), and the diptych of Andrew III of Hungary in the museum in Berne (about 1290-6; cf. Hahnloser 1955, 159). Finally, filigree of the same type, although not definitely of Venetian origin, added to the ivory reliquary of the True Cross of Cortona brought back by Brother Elias of Coppi from his mission to the emperor John Doukas in 1245-6 (fig. 36e; cf. Goldschmidt and Weitzmann 1934, no. 77, pl. 30) could provide a *terminus post quem* and show that mounts of *opus veneticum*, "Venetian work", were made in the middle or second half of the thirteenth century, after the programme of restoration of treasures affected by the fire of 1231.
The icon of the Crucifixion is perhaps first mentioned in the 1325 inventory (Gallo 1967, 279, V, no. 5): "*Iconam unam cum Christo in cruce, argenti deauratam, laboratam ad opus levatum*". The Venetian filigree surrounding the

259

260

36b

lapis lazuli is ample proof that the medallion was in Venice before the end of the thirteenth century. The icon, which was in very poor condition in 1816-20 (Gallo 1967, 379, no. 12), was restored before 1845 (Gallo 1967, 398, no. 112). The external border, punctuated by glass "stones", is modern, as is the stamped inner border. The latter is identical with the borders of enamelled icons of the half-figure of St Michael (no. 12) and of a Crucifixion in San Marco (Hahnloser 1971, no. 18). The rather waxy-looking filigree which is also lighter-toned is part of this restoration, as are the claw-mounts of the glass "stones", which were added in the nineteenth century.

D.G.C.

Bibliography: Durand 1862, 17. Pasini 1885-6, 74, no. 5, pl. VIII. Molinier 1888, 52-3, 81, no. 7, pl. VII, no. 7, pl. VIII, no. 9. Schlumberger 1905, III, 817. Dalton 1911, 514, 552. Gallo 1967, 279, V, no. 5; 379, no. 12; 398, no. 112; fig. 73. Hahnloser 1971, no. 19 (Grabar, Hahnloser), pl. XXII, CXXVII.

36c

36d

36e

263

Rock-crystal vessel

Stonework: probably from Iraq, end of 10th century (?). *Metalwork*: Venetian, 2nd half of 13th century
Rock-crystal, silver-gilt, stones, pearls. *Height* 490 mm, *diam.* 170 mm

Tesoro, no. 99

This rock-crystal vessel was provided with a counterpart of similar dimensions when it was mounted in silver-gilt; the counterpart is a Venetian glass vessel with a matching mount (fig. 37 c; Hahnloser 1971, no. 144, pl. CXXV). It is tempting to identify these objects with two descriptions in the 1325 inventory of the treasury: "*Ferale unum* [one lamp] *vitreum furnitum, cum pede et capite argenti*" and "*Ferale unum de cristallo varnitum, cum pede et capite argenti*" (Gallo 1967, 277, III, no. 3; 278, III, no. 5). The two vessels are certainly recognizable in the 1571 inventory: "*Un vaso grande de Cristal de montagna rotto, con doi manichi, et il piede et coperchio d'Arzento*" and "*Un altro vaso simile de Cristalin da Muran*" (Gallo 1967, 301, nos 136-7). The rock-crystal must therefore have been in poor condition at that time. It corresponds to the description in the 1733 inventory: "*Vaso grande [di cristallo di monte] scolpito et lavorato a sonde con manichi et ornamenti d'argento guarniti di geme*", while the matching glass vessel could be the next item, also listed among the rock-crystal objects: "*Un vaso grande con suo coperchio e piede d'argento gioielato*" (Gallo 1967, 354, nos 133, 137). The two items are perhaps those described in the 1801 valuation of the treasury as "*2 Vasi grandi di Cristal forn[it]i d'arg[ent]o*" (Gallo 1967, 361, nos 203-4). Cicognara's catalogue of the treasury compiled in 1816-20 valued the rock-crystal vase at 2500 lire, which made it the most precious rock-crystal object after the ewer (no. 31); its counterpart was valued at 300 lire (Gallo 1967, 374, no. 19; 375, no. 27). The two vessels were restored at the same time, before 1845 (Gallo 1967, 398, nos 101-2; Pasini 1885-6, 92).

The vessel is cut from an extremely large block of pure crystal. The vertical rim, which measures 23 mm and is hidden by the mount, is separated from a tapering neck by a moulding. There is another moulding, decorated with grooves, at the base of the neck. The tall body of the vessel, plain in the middle, is decorated at the top and bottom with two continuous friezes in strong relief; the lower relief is the more deeply cut. An inscription in Kufic characters makes up the upper ornamental band, which measures 78 mm. It is a supplication in respect of an unknown monarch: "Never-ending power and copious favour, and well-being to our lord". The slender characters broaden out towards the top to form scored motifs of vegetal inspiration. The frieze on the lower part of the vessel, 75 mm deep, is composed of fifteen large pointed leaves in relief connected at their lower ends by a relief palmette decorated with two oblique grooves and inscribing an intaglio circle. The foot of the vessel is cut to a point, giving it the appearance of a lamp when the mount is removed (Hahnloser 1971, pl. XCVI). However, according to Erdmann (1971), the present state of the base is the result of a modification to the vessel, apparently re-cut after sustaining damage.

Despite the Arabic inscription, the vessel was not made by Egyptian crystal-cutters during the Fatimid period. Neither the shape nor the decoration of the lower part occur in rock-crystal vessels which are definitely Fatimid: these never have an important part of their surface undecorated and have much squatter inscriptions. A decorative motif not unlike that on the lower part of this object can be found on an oval sardonyx bowl with a small base which was formerly in the collection of Louis XIV and is now in the Louvre (fig. 37 a; Lamm 1929-30, I, 190-1; II, pl. 64, fig. 12). Treated somewhat differently, the decoration which encircles the body of the sardonyx vessel is executed in very low relief and consists of juxtaposed leaves, long and well-drawn, with prominent central veins. At their bases the leaves are separated by less regularly placed ornament consisting of a small raised disk, with a central intaglio circle and its upper part engraved, in most instances, with a central small vertical mark. Rather similar ornament can be seen in the low relief frieze decorating a glass chalice in San Marco, mounted in Byzantium (fig. 24 c; Hahnloser 1971, no. 63, pl. LVI). The relationship of the motifs on the Venice rock-crystal vessel and those on the Louvre bowl to mural sculpture in Samarra has been pointed out by Lamm and Erdmann. Samarra, that short-lived town about a hundred kilometres north of Baghdad, was built, decorated and inhabited by the ʿAbbāsid caliphs of Baghdad between 836 and 883 (cf. fig. 37 b, after Hertzfeld 1923, fig. 33, *q.v.*, figs 29, 35, &c.). It therefore seems logical to seek the origin of these vessels in Iraq. The caliphs owned rock-crystal vessels in the tenth century (Lamm 1929-30, I, 515). There is proof that this material was worked in Iraq, at least at Bassora, at the end of the tenth century and at the beginning of the eleventh (cf. Kahle 1936, 332-56). According to Erdmann, the vessel in Venice may be dated on the basis of its epigraphy to the end of the tenth century.

D. A.

37 a

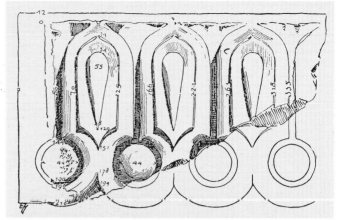

37 b

37 c

37 d

37 e

37 f

37 g

268

Metalwork

The beauty of the stone is accentuated by the high quality of its silver-gilt mount. The rock-crystal amphora has been given a domed lid with a decorative knob. A metal band encircles the upper part of the neck; there is another round the upper part of the body of the vessel to which two curved handles are attached. These are joined to the foot, the concave flare of which rests on an arcaded base. The whole mount is enriched with small sapphires, rubies and pearls and is covered with filigree arranged in broad scrolls. About one third of the way up the vessel is a band of openwork filigree, arranged in a compact meander. The mount as a whole is very close to that on a large glass amphora also in the treasury of San Marco (fig. 37c; Hahnloser 1971, no. 144). The filigree on this glass amphora, however, consists of simple tendrils with granulation, like those on the sardonyx cruet and the lapis lazuli icon (nos 35, 36), whereas the much more complex filigree of the crystal amphora is of two different styles corresponding to the work of two different goldsmiths. The knob on the lid is of openwork filigree and granulation. The eight lobes on the lid, the arrangement of which recalls the decoration on the sardonyx ewer mount (no. 35), and the metal band around the rim of the vessel have the same filigree: very fine twisted wires in symmetrical scrolls very cleanly detached from the ground, above which they form a sort of lace. Besides simple granulation, there are also rosettes composed of several granules, and small elongated leaves. The precious stones have finely serrated settings. On the foot the filigree is arranged in six panels. The coils of wire, again cable-twisted and detached from the surface, have a cruciform layout here. In the centre of each panel the filigree is once again decorated with granulation, small flowers and foliage, but the flowers each comprise a stamped metal collar with a granule at its centre, and the leaves, smaller and rounder than those on the lid, are trefoils. The base of the foot has arches of twisted gilt filigree joined to each other by a metal staple at their bases and at the level of the capitals. In each interstice is a granule.

The filigree on the upper part of the vessel, with its granule rosettes and small elongated leaves, can be related to that on the icon with the half-figure of St Michael (no. 12), where the coils, broader than those on the amphora, have, additionally, cylinders of wire coiled on themselves, somewhat resembling pine-cones. Despite this addition, these two objects are similar enough in appearance to suggest that they are by the same hand, as Hahnloser has proposed. Although also decorated with granule rosettes, the filigree on the mounts on the two-handled sardonyx chalice in San Marco (fig. 4b; Hahnloser 1971, no. 60) is quite different in composition: instead of being made of finely twisted wire, as on the above examples, it is of metal strip, with a grooved edge. Hahnloser emphasised the links between the lid of the rock-crystal vessel and Rhine-Maas precious metalwork, citing the earlier openwork apples on the Anno shrine at Siegburg (fig. 37d, about 1183; cf. Hahnloser 1971, p. 112). Another example is the arm-reliquary of St Cunibert, in Cologne, dating from 1222 (fig. 37g; exh. cat. *Die Zeit der Staufer*, 1977, no. 560). Indeed, several objects of Rhenish and Mosan origin, made at the beginning or in the first half of the thirteenth century have filigree with granule rosettes and "pine-cones", but it should be noted that similar filigree also decorates objects made outside the Mosan sphere, which did not therefore have a monopoly of such work. Among the most striking examples are the Grandmont crosses in Rouvres (fig. 37e) and Gorre (Limoges, first half or middle of the thirteenth century; exh. cat. *Trésors des églises de France*, 1965, nos 805, 365; *L'Europe gothique*, 1968, no. 387). Rosettes and elongated leaves are also frequently found together on thirteenth-century crosses betraying Mosan influence. On the Clairmarais cross at Saint-Omer the wires are perhaps more reminiscent of plant-stems, but on the Cross of the Paraclete in the treasury at Amiens (fig. 37f; exh. cat. *Trésors des églises de France*, 1965, nos 55, 60) the wire is beaded and the foliage design similar to that on the lid of the San Marco vessel. The front of a reliquary in the abbey of Charroux, probably also of Venetian origin, is similarly decorated with filigree coils with granule rosettes (fig. 37h; cf. Gauthier 1983, 134-5, nos 77, 80). However, on none of these examples, even the last, is the filigree as vigorous, delicate or elegant as the on the lid of the San Marco vessel.

Likewise, the decoration on the foot, with its small rounded trefoil leaves and sheet-metal flowers with a granule at each centre, should be compared with northern work: crosses at Douchy and Blanchefosse (northern France, thirteenth century; exh. cat. *Trésors des églises de France*, 1965, nos 12, 125) and the one formerly in the Soltykoff collection and now in the Musée de Cluny in Paris (Limoges, first half of the thirteenth century; exh. cat. *Art français du Moyen Age*, 1972-3, no. 39), even though their flowers are flatter. The more firmly modelled veined flowers on the Namur crown-reliquary (about 1206; see no. 34 and Hahnloser 1971, 140) and on the Laon cross in the Musée du Louvre, from the same workshop, are also different, and their flat filigree work lacks leaves (fig. 37k). In fact it is only on Venetian work that the exact equivalent of the tendrils detached from the surface of the object and enriched with the same flowers and foliage can be found. The mounts on a small two-handled rock-crystal vessel and those on an alabaster vase, both in San Marco (figs 37i, 37j; Hahnloser 1971, nos 84-5), are patently the work of the craftsman responsible for the foot of the rock-crystal amphora. The arcade on the base of the foot has Carolingian and Ottonian antecedents, it is true (*v.* Hahnloser 1971, no. 123), but this refined technique had by no means been lost in the West by the thirteenth century, as can be seen from the Saint-Omer pyx, the reliquary in

Saint-Michel-des-Lions, Limoges (exh. cat. *Trésors des églises de France*, 1965, nos 54, 365), the crosses in the Musée de Cluny, Rouvres and Gorre, and the Eymoutiers cross (exh. cat. *Trésors des églises de France*, no. 363). In Italy the base of the statuette of the Virgin on the altar at Pistoia (about 1287) and the head-reliquary of San Galgano in the museum of Siena Cathedral show that this type of decoration was used in Tuscany in the final decades of the thirteenth century (cf. Hueck 1982, figs 8, 11). In Venice the motif is employed on the bases of the large glass amphora and that of a silver-gilt chalice (Hahnloser 1971, nos 144, 54). In addition, the base of a small two-handled rock-crystal vessel (Hahnloser 1971, no. 84) is exactly the same down to the granules between the haunches of the arches, which strengthens the attribution of this mount to the craftsman responsible for the foot of the rock-crystal amphora.

Finally, the openwork filigree which encircles the body of the amphora is similar to that on the knop of the silver-gilt chalice in San Marco already mentioned (Hahnloser 1971, no. 54).

The lid and the foot of the rock-crystal amphora were made by different craftsmen, but should one conclude, with Hahnloser, that the lid is superior in workmanship to the foot? This is not at all obvious: while the scrolls on the lid represent one of the most beautiful examples of Western medieval filigree, the foot, with its delicate arcade, exhibits a high degree of technical skill and beauty. In fact the mount as a whole is sufficiently coherent to have been made by two craftsmen working in the same surroundings, or at least within a short time of each other.

The theory (defended by Hahnloser) that the workshop producing filigree with flowers and leaves was active earlier than the one specializing in filigree with simple granulation seems somewhat tenuous. Besides the type of filigree, several points of similarity relate the mount of the rock-crystal amphora to that of the large glass amphora in San Marco, already mentioned, which was made in the "filigree with simple granulation" workshop responsible for the mounts on the sardonyx cruet and the lapis lazuli medallion (nos 35, 36). Moreover, the two amphorae have often been considered as a pair. Even though their identification with the two lamps listed in the 1325 inventory remains hypothetical, they are certainly associated with each other in the 1571 inventory, where damage to the rock-crystal vessel, probably to its base, is noted. According to the 1845 inventory the rock-crystal and the glass vessel had been restored.

D.G.C.

37 k

Bibliography: Pasini 1885-6, 92, no. 114, pl. L. Molinier 1888, no. 103. Lamm 1929-30, I, 202-3; II, pl. 68, 17. Erdmann 1940, 144, fig. 25. Erdmann 1951, 6. Gallo 1967, 278, III, no. 5; 301, no. 136; 354, no. 133; 361, no. 203; 374, no. 19; 398, no. 101; pl. 61, fig. 104. Hahnloser 1971, no. 123 (Erdmann, Hahnloser), pls XCVI-XCVII, CXXIV.

38-39

Rock-crystal candlesticks

Venetian, early 14th century (?)
Rock-crystal, silver-gilt. *Height* 590 and 600 mm, *diam.* 210 mm

Tesoro, nos 28-29

The treasury of San Marco currently contains two pairs of candlesticks, with one candle-holder each. The second pair, smaller than the pair on exhibition, is 460 mm tall and made of Islamic rock-crystal with relief decoration, now fitted with a sixteenth-century silver-gilt mount (Hahnloser 1971, nos 121-2, pl. XCV). In the 1325 inventory three pairs of silver-mounted rock-crystal *candelabra* are listed: a large pair, with lapis lazuli as well as rock-crystal, a middle-sized pair (perhaps the pair exhibited), and a small pair (Gallo 1967, 278, nos 3-5). An inventory of precious metalwork in the sacristy of San Marco drawn up in 1524 mentions two pairs of rock-crystal and silver *candelieri*, one pair with copper bases (Gallo 1967, 292, nos 44-5). In 1606, in another inventory of the sacristy, the mounts of the two pairs mentioned are all silver: "*Doi Candelieri de Cristalo grandi con suoi piedi d'argento*", without doubt the candlesticks in the exhibition, and "*Doi Candelieri de Cristalo con suoi fornimenti d'argento, picoli*", which are likely to be the pair made of Islamic rock-crystal (Gallo 1967, 309, nos 41-2). The two extant pairs are easily recognizable in the treasury inventory drawn up in 1733: "*Due candelieri grandi scolpiti et ornati d'argento*", and "*Altri due lavorati a fazette con ornamenti d'argento*", the latter being the candlesticks exhibited (Gallo 1967, 354, nos 138-9, 140-1). In the valuation of the treasury made in 1801, on the other hand, only one pair of candlesticks is listed: "*2 Candellari di cristal forniti d'argento*" (Gallo 1967, 361, nos 208-9). In the catalogue compiled by Cicognara in 1816-20 the faceted candlesticks are valued at 400 lire and the other pair at only 200 lire (Gallo 1967, 380, nos 20-1). Both pairs were subsequently restored, as is indicated by the 1845 inventory (Gallo 1967, 398, nos 115-6).

The stem of each candlestick is made up of two alternating shapes of rock-crystal threaded on a copper rod. Four faceted spheres with two rows of lozenge-shaped planes alternate with three cylinders of six sides each, the sides tapering towards the ends from a central horizontal intersection of planes. The rock-crystal elements diminish in size from the bottom upwards. All the facets are smooth. The rock-crystal bases are hemispherical. The element under the candle-holder on one of the candlesticks is rock-crystal, on the other candlestick it is glass. The shape of the candlesticks is directly borrowed from metal examples, which were often composed, from the Romanesque period on, of spherical knops alternating with vertical shanks, such as the large bronze example in Bamberg Cathedral, where the stem consists of five spheres and four shanks (third quarter of the twelfth century; exh. cat. *Rhein-Maas*, 1972, no. H3). In the Romanesque period rock-crystal was already being used in the elaboration of this type of object: some small metal candlesticks have rock-crystal spheres in the guise of knops (e.g. Braun 1932, figs 372, 388).

Once the art of hardstone-carving developed in Western Europe, two types of object were distinguished from the rest by being composed of several pieces assembled on a core: these were crosses and candlesticks, occasionally matching. In view of the decoration on their mounts, the San Marco candlesticks may have originally been intended for secular use.

Hahnloser compared these candlesticks with two other pairs in rock-crystal, each with three spheres and three cylinders: one pair, their spheres with ribs cut in twists, is in the cathedral treasury at Bari, to which it was presented by Charles II of Anjou (fig. 38-39a); the other pair, with spheres the same as those on the Venice pair, are in the church of St Francis at Assisi (Hahnloser 1971, pl. CXXXIII). These candlesticks were described, the first pair in 1296 and the second pair in 1338, as having mounts of Venetian style (Hahnloser 1971, 150). A fourth pair, first documented in 1554 (fig. 38-39b; Mantua, San Pietro in Cattedrale; exh. cat. *Tesori d'arte nella terra dei Gonzaga*, 1974, no. 118) have the same two series of elements as the pairs in Assisi and Venice, but are closer to Venice examples by reason of having four spheres on each candlestick; the copper-gilt mounts date from the sixteenth century. Only the pair in Venice have convex rock-crystal bases.

The long-attested presence in Italy of this series of candlesticks – the oldest hardstone examples known – suggests that their origin might profitably be sought there. Information in contemporary documents concerning the mounts on two of the pairs provides a strong case for seeing in these objects the work of Venetian crystal-carvers, formed into a guild in 1284. Some of these, the *Arte Minuta*, specialized in making small objects. The date of these candlesticks is difficult to establish. As the cylinders on the Bari candlesticks have convex facets, they may be considered as the earliest in date, and enable the other three pairs to be dated to the first third of the fourteenth century.

The shapes of the different rock-crystal elements do not in themselves provide help in dating the objects, nor do they represent any innovation in the evolution of the cutting or decoration of hardstone objects. Perforated

rock-crystal ornaments, of polyhedral form and similar to the spheres on the candlesticks, are known from sixth-century Frankish and Anglo-Saxon tombs (British Museum, Ashmolean Museum, Römisch-Germanishes Museum, Cologne). The twist-cut crystals on the Bari candlesticks recall the central motif on the crest of the Rhenish St Alban shrine (end of the twelfth century), where a sphere surmounted by an olive-shaped knob, both of rock-crystal, exhibit the same decoration (Cologne, St Pantaleon; fig. 38-39 c; exh. cat. *Rhein-Maas*, 1972, no. K2).

D. A.

Metalwork

The silver mount, once gilded, is made up of a candle-holder fixed to the crystal by means of three scalloped metal bands, of collars composed of pointed palmettes which join the crystals forming the stem, and of a trian-gular flared base resting on three lion protomes. The general shape of the base, with its three slightly concave parts, is based on Byzantine models. It recalls the bases of silver candlesticks in the Walters Art Gallery, Balti-more (Syria, sixth century; exh. cat. *The Age of Spiritual-ity*, 1977-8, no. 541) and has been related by Hahnloser to a bronze candelabrum in the treasury of San Giorgio, Venice (Byzantine, thirteenth century; Hahnloser 1971, pl. CXXXIII).

The shape, with variations, occurs in Venetian works from the very end of the thirteenth and the beginning of the fourteenth century, such as the filigree bases of the Venetian crystal candlesticks presented to Bari by Charles II of Anjou in 1296 (fig. 38-39 a), or the base of the arm-reliquary of St John the Baptist in the cathedral treasury at Zara (Hahnloser 1971, pl. LXXIX, 5; Cecchelli 1936, 53-4). The very stylized solid silver lion-protome feet have been paralleled with those on a pyx present-ed in 1332 to the treasury of Assisi by Galgano della Marra, at the same time as two Venetian rock-crystal

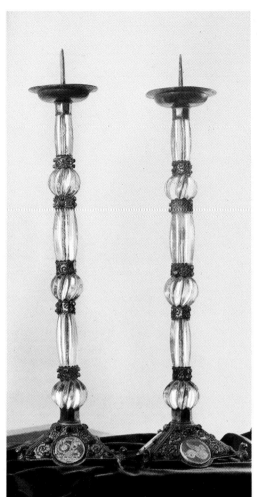

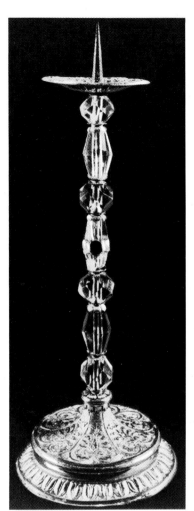

candlesticks very close to those in San Marco (see above). The bases of the San Marco candlesticks have engraved decoration covering the three sides, which are each subdivided into three sections separated by a beaded strand. On one candlestick, two birds pecking each other in foliage are flanked in turn by two peacocks, two lionesses, and two birds with webbed feet (pelicans?). On the other, two birds addorsed in vegetal scrolls are set between two long-eared dragons (the central plaque is partly restored), two cocks, and, again, two dragons. The foliage is fleshy and has deeply serrated edges. The engraving is shallow, with a light, nervous touch. It is therefore only because of the similarity of the subjects (animals within scrolls) that the bases of these candlesticks can be compared with the silver-gilt and niello mount of the rock-crystal cruet in San Marco (no. 32), for the styles and techniques differ widely. As Hahnloser noted, more convincing comparisons can be made with the engraved birds on the foot of the reliquary of the Holy Blood in San Marco, dating from before 1283 (Hahnloser 1971,

no. 128, pl. CXXXVI), with two silver cruets decorated with figures of the apostles, which were presented to the cathedral treasury of Cividale by the Patriarch of Aquileia before 1352 (Morassi 1936, nos 160-1, fig. 62), and with a pyx in San Marco, which is now lost but is known from an illustration of 1760 (Venice, Correr Museum; Grevembroch, II, 1760, pls II-XXX).

D.G.C.

Bibliography: Pasini 1885-6, 76, pl. LX, fig. 148. Molinier 1888, no. 136. Gallo 1967, 278, IV, nos 3-5; 292, nos 44-5; 309, nos 41-2; 354, nos 140-1; 361, nos 208-9; 380, nos 20-1; 398, nos 115-6; pl. 52, fig. 89. Hahnloser 1971, nos 149-50 (Hahnloser), pls CXXXII, CXXXIV-CXXXV.

Altar-frontal of St Mark

Venetian, about 1300, with border of about 1336. Restored between 1855 and 1888
Silver-gilt on wood core. *Height* 1010 mm, *width* 3210 mm

Tesoro, no. 38 (listed in the 1325 inventory: II, no. 1)

Hahnloser has given a full description of this large altar-frontal with its double series of inscribed trilobed Gothic arches resting on petaled capitals with their fluted columns and smooth bases. There are many restored parts. According to Pasini, the gilding was redone. Several inscriptions, as fully identified by Hahnloser, are new. In general, the nineteenth-century figurative restorations of Buri and Bertolini are characterized by a flaccid pseudo-Renaissance style in the treatment of the heads and draperies. The original medieval figures have a clear plasticity with a rhythmic linear emphasis on the smooth curves of drapery, and the expressive physiognomies are based on Mosan and Byzantine prototypes.

The lower series of large figurative reliefs depicts the story of St Mark flanked by the archangels Raphael and Gabriel (under half-arches). From left to right, this lower register illustrates: the Angel of God appearing to St Mark during a trip; St Mark purifying a leper; St Mark baptizing in Egypt; St Peter approving St Mark's Gospel; St Mark on a ship going to Alexandria; the angel visiting St Mark (entirely modern; a fragment of the original relief for this composition has been preserved in the Correr Museum since 1859); St Mark healing the shoemaker;

St Mark, wearing a bishop's chasuble, orphrey, and maniple, standing in prayer (centered beneath the enthroned Christ in the upper register); St Mark healing Anianus (both inscription and relief are entirely modern); St Mark healing the blind man (this scene and the subsequent one are especially fine original works); St Mark healing the man possessed by the devil; St Mark, in a bishop's vestments, being martyred at the altar; St Mark, again in bishop's vestments, being led through the streets of Alexandria; the burial of St Mark in Alexandria (the saint is still dressed in a bishop's vestments rather than in a *sudarium*). As noted by Hahnloser, several of these scenes seem to derive from earlier and related compositions in mosaic in the basilica, especially in the Zen Chapel.

The upper register of large figured reliefs, also flanked by two angels (again under half-arches), depicts six standing primary and secondary apostles on each side of the enthroned Christ and Virgin Mary in prayer (Mary stands on Christ's right). All of the apostles wear heavy mantles with long folds derived ultimately from ancient Roman togas. Each has a foot turned in profile towards Christ while the other foot is frontal. All but one apostle

hold a codex in the hand nearest Christ. Left to right appear Barnabas (completely remade); Simon; Thaddaeus; Bartholomew (head restored); Andrew (totally remade); Peter; the Virgin Mary; Christ in Majesty seated on a Gothic-style throne, yet holding a codex and blessing in the Byzantine manner; John the Evangelist; Paul (completely modern); James, inscribed SANCTIS JACOBI (*sic*); Matthew; Philip; Thomas.

The uppermost border, with small bust reliefs alternating with decorative panels, was, according to Hahnloser, probably added in 1336 when the frontal was set in front of St Mark's altar, as recorded in an engraving after a drawing by Antonio Visentini (Hahnloser 1965, pl. LXV). The busts of the saints mostly face inward toward the Christ of Pity in the center. Each figure is haloed. Left to right appear: a crowned female saint; a frontally praying male saint holding a maniple and dressed in a bishop's vestments; a blessing male saint bearing a codex, also in a bishop's vestments; St Paul bending forward, holding his sword in his left hand pointing to Christ with his right hand; St John the Baptist; the mourning Virgin Mary; Christ of Pity; a beardless St John the Evangelist; St Peter holding a key and codex and bending forward towards Christ like St Paul; a military saint, possibly St Theodore, as suggested by Pasini; a frontally composed male saint with Christ-like head and a codex; and, finally, a female saint in mirror-image of the example at the far left. Only four of the square plaques with quadrilobes sprouting vine tendrils with acorns and leaves are original, according to Hahnloser. These are detectable by their irregular perforations. The small quadrilobes preserve busts of saints. One shows Christ from the Last Judgment.

The ornamental overall framing of the altar-frontal is the most restored portion of the ensemble. Most of the borders seem to date from the nineteenth century, although the floral motifs may be based on an earlier Baroque restoration of 1674.

The style of the original figurative reliefs, as well as the architectural framework with arcades with trilobed arches may be associated with the same phase of Venetian metalwork belonging to the second quarter of the fourteenth century as represented by the reliquary of fourteen saints (no. 44). The relief busts of both works seem to anticipate some of the more three-dimensional relief busts of around 1343-5 on the frame of the *Pala d'Oro* (fig. 40 a) as suggested by Hahnloser (1965, 111; 1971, 155). The entire ensemble is an impressive monumental work, entirely suitable as the frontal for the altar of St Mark in the choir of the basilica. As an ensemble, it illustrates a characteristically Venetian amalgam of Byzantine details and iconography with late Romanesque figure-style and Gothic architectural framework.

W. D. W.

Bibliography: Pasini 1885-6, 78-80, pl. LXVI, fig. 63. Molinier 1888, no. 151. Hahnloser 1965, *Il Tesoro*, 90-1, 109, 111 (Hahnloser). Gallo 1967, 203-4; 277, II, no. 1; figs 95-7. Hahnloser 1971, 152-6, no. 152 (Hahnloser), pls CXLI-CXLIII.

Exh. cat. *Venezia e Bisanzio*, 1974, no. 77.

40a

41

Reliquary of the arm of St George

Interior casing: Byzantine, before 1204. *Exterior*: Venetian, before 1325.
Finial of St George and dragon: Venetian, 1325 and 16th century
Interior casing: silver-gilt. *Exterior*: silver-gilt, enamel (the original crystal lid has been replaced with a glass one). *Height* 519 mm, *width at top* 117 mm

Santuario, no. 53 (listed in the 1325 inventory: II, no. 4)

The relic and its immediate casing were brought from Constantinople by the doge Enrico Dandolo after the sack of 1204 (Gallo 1967, 12, citing the chronicle of Andrea Dandolo). During the revision of the treasury of 5 September 1325, the two *procuratori* Pietro Grimani and Angelo Mudazio wrote: "*Item notamus quod brachium s[anct]i Georgii circumdatur auro et argento laboratum ad smaldum cum uno sa[nct]o Georgio equitanta a parte superiori, et cum uno pede argento laborato*" ("We note that the arm of St George is covered in gold and silver and enameled, with, at the top, a St George on horseback, and with a base worked in silver": Pasini 1885-6, *Appendici*, 4, no. 4; Hahnloser 1971, 163). Thus, while the goldsmith is unknown, the inventory provides a *terminus ante quem* of 1325. The reliquary is also significant because St George is the third patron saint of the city of Venice (after SS Mark and Theodore).

Proportionally tall and with a richly decorated conical trunk, this reliquary is supported in an unusual way with a base of splayed stems of thick wire with cusped foliage. The several precious stones, which according to Hahnloser must have enriched the base, are missing. The four thickest stems are bundled together with a horizontal, quadrilobed knob decorated with stars. A flat dentilated disk above supports the lowest portion of the reliquary itself as well as two inserted curved plaques with inscriptions in reserve against niello backgrounds: + ISTVT· EST· BRAC/HIVM· GLORIOXIS/IMI· MARTIRIS + S/ANCTI· GEORGII; on the back: + ISTVT· EST· BRAC/HIVM· GLORIOXIS/IMI· MARTIRIS/SANCTI· GEORGII ("This is the arm of the most glorious martyr, St George").

The main trunk of the reliquary, which is oval in cross-section, is divided into three vertical divisions on each of the broader sides; in the center, a tall lancet of openwork with vine tendrils is punctuated by haloed busts alternating with rosettes which show traces of translucent enamel. Hinged at the bottom, the two screens could be opened downwards for a better view of the relic with its original silver casing with an unpublished Greek inscription, probably of twelfth-century Constantinopolitan workmanship. On either side of each of the covering screens is a vertical series of openings with pointed arches. While each of these once contained separate plaques with figures in translucent enamels, only ten are preserved today, leaving six empty niches

on the back (Pasini alludes to the transfer of two or three of these plaques from the back to the front during the restorations of the nineteenth century). The colors of the enamels are sapphire blue, emerald green, yellow-green, orange, amber, garnet red, and violet.

At the sides of the reliquary and separating the back from the front were eight projecting foliated stems bearing flower supports for eight three-dimensional busts. Pasini illustrates a reconstruction in his color plate. Only the two stems with their extended busts at the top now exist. The stumps of several of the other stems were fitted in 1850 with framed amethysts and hyacinths, additions which Pasini found inappropriate (Pasini 1885-6, 44). The original crystal, fitted into the chiseled and dentilated border at the top, allowed for an additional glimpse of the relic. This crystal has been replaced by a glass cover. At the very top, and mounted on a curved bar hinged to the sides, is a dramatic, three-dimensional representation of the equestrian St George dispatching the dragon with a long spear. While the dragon, with its partially enameled spread wings, is undoubtedly original, both the figure of the saint and his rearing mount must date from the sixteenth century. The horse and rider are probably directly based on Leonardo's designs for the Sforza and Trivulzio monuments, dating respectively 1485-93 and 1506-13, even though the theme of a rearing horse goes back to the early Florentine Renaissance sculptor, Bertoldo (1420-91), to Paduan bronzes dating around 1510, and to ancient bronzes (Planiscig 1924, 5-6, no. 3, fig. 3 for Bertoldo; Wixom 1975, no. 77 for ancient and Paduan examples).

The elegance of the total ensemble with the architectural forms symmetrically framed and supported by foliated vines reminded Gauthier of the traditional representations of the Tree of Life and the Tree of Jesse (Gauthier 1972, 232, 395, no. 188). This theme is developed here in space and is transformed into a kind of Gothic chapel in which the exquisite enamels with prophets, apostles, and saints have become the stained-glass windows. These enamels, while certainly the earliest made in Venice, owe so much in their technique and style to Sienese enameling that Gauthier wondered whether their maker had indeed come from Siena. A comparison with some of the enamels of the generation immediately after Guccio di Mannaia (the creator of the chalice of Pope Nicholas IV of 1288-92) underscores the importance of

284

this suggestion. Key comparisons may be found in some of the translucent enamels by or attributed to Tondino di Guerrino (Leone de Castris 1980, 24-44, esp. figs 16-17). Particularly similar, despite the differences in palette, are the narrow figured enamels on the pinnacles of the large reliquary of the Bolsena Corporal by Ugolino di Vieri and associates, dated 1338, in the cathedral of Orvieto (fig. 41 a; Gauthier 1972, 222).

At the same time that the enamels derive inspiration from a Sienese tradition, the decorative metalwork forms of the vine branches, foliage, and flowers suggest an ultimate inspiration, according to Hahnloser, from north-eastern France and possibly the art of Hugo d'Oignies of around 1238-40. The vines and leaves take on a larger scale and freer movements in the reliquary of St George. Hahnloser further observed that the distinctive character of fluted leaves and the nubby vines may be seen to continue, although codified, in the Gothic additions of 1342-5 to the *Pala d'Oro*. (These motifs, combined with the multi-colored rosettes, became a favorite motif of fifteenth-century Venetian goldsmiths, as indicated also by Hahnloser.) The various softly modeled busts recur also in the framework of the *Pala d'Oro* (fig. 40a).

Certainly the task assigned by the *procuratori* of San Marco to an unknown Venetian goldsmith was masterfully fulfilled. In a conception which is fully Gothic in style and without a trace of Byzantine forms, he has created an eloquent, even poetic, receptacle for one of the most important relics in the treasury. The crowning sculptural group, in its present as in its original form, proclaims the identity of the saint whose relic is contained in the receptacle below. For this reason, Hahnloser has called this piece an example of a Gothic "talking reliquary" ("*reliquario parlante*"). Another example of this type of reliquary is the reliquary of the Column of the Flagellation of 1375 (no. 46).

W. D. W.

41a

Bibliography: Pasini 1885-6, 43-4, pls XXX-XXXI, figs 45-6. Molinier 1888, 87, no. 35. Braun 1940, pl. 63, fig. 213. Hahnloser 1965, *Il Tesoro*, 86, 93, 101, pl. LXXII. Gallo 1967, 12; 23, no. 4; 58, no. 4; 276, no. 4; 288, no. 2; 299, no. 23; 304, no. 15; 311, no. 37; 317, XVI, no. 33; 386, no. 30; pl. 22, fig. 36. Hahnloser 1971, 162-3, no. 159 (Hahnloser). Gauthier 1972, 232, 395, no. 188.

42

Serpentine chalice

Stonework: Byzantine, 12th century (?). *Metalwork*: Venetian, before 1325
Serpentine, silver, silver-gilt, enamel. *Height* 220 mm (without mount
160 mm), *width* 170 mm (without mount 150 mm)

Tesoro, no. 66

The vessel, made of dark green stone with light green markings, is damaged in several places in its upper part and seems to have lost part of its mount. Along the rim, on the exterior, runs an unpolished chamfer, which may have been intended to be hidden beneath a casing of precious metalwork. This hypothesis seems to be confirmed by the description of the object in the 1325 inventory of the treasury, at which time the original function of the object as a chalice went unrecognized and it was identified as a mortar: "*Mortarum unum cum pede argenti, ornatum desuper de argento, quod est de petra serpentina*" (Gallo 1967, 280, VI, no. 9). The silver mount on the upper part had disappeared before the inventory of 1571 was taken, as the piece was described as follows: "*Un gotto* [a goblet] *de pietra Serpentina col piede d'arzento*" (Gallo 1967, 299, no. 74). In the 1733 inventory it was said to be of *verde antico* marble, like the incense-boat (no. 43): "*Un vaso di verde antico intagliato di varie figure con piede d'argento*" (Gallo 1967, 350, no. 27). It is similarly described in the valuation of the treasury made in 1801: "*1 Vaso di verde antico en forma di Balla*" (Gallo 1967, 360, no. 168). It appears in Cicognara's catalogue of 1816-20 as "*argilla grigia o porfido argilloso*" where, with the damage to the rim recorded, it was valued at 1000 lire (Gallo 1967, 368, no. 35). Since Pasini's day the stone has been considered a type of serpentine.

The manufacture of the vessel embraced all the problems: complex shape, relief decoration, and the handles cut from the same block of stone and partly hollowed out. The cutting is very even. The body is spherical at the base, flaring out towards the rim and forming eight projections, alternately and angular. The top of the rim is thin and flat. Near the rim the walls are between three and five millimetres thick. The two handles are part of two of the gadroons and are pierced in three places, giving them the form of winged cheetahs, decorated with grooves. The base, enclosed in the mount, is not visible; the interior is concave.

The eight projections are decorated in low relief with ten nimbed figures, all except one identified by inscriptions. On one side of the vessel, from left to right, are St Basil wearing an *omophorion*, the archangel Michael, Christ enthroned, his feet on a hassock, blessing with his right hand and holding a book in his left, the archangel Gabriel, and St Nicholas, blessing and holding a book. On the other side, again from left to right, are St John Chrysostom, the archangel Uriel, the Virgin seated, palms displayed, the archangel Raphael, and an unidentified saint, one hand raised in blessing, the other holding a book. Above them, around the rim, are engraved the words for the consecration of the wine by the priest. The quality of the reliefs is high but, curiously, the inscriptions are cursory.

Although the function of the vessel had been forgotten in Venice, the inscription proves that it was indeed a chalice. In addition, the shape of the object, with its two handles and a spherical body flaring towards the rim, was frequently used for chalices made during the first centuries of the Christian era, of which numerous representations and some actual examples survive, such as the small gold chalice from the Gourdon treasure, now in the Bibliothèque Nationale in Paris (Cabrol and Leclercq, II/2, "calice", cols 1610-36). The shape seems to have been in use in the East, as Grabar noted that there were two silver chalices dating from the first half of the twelfth century of this type in the cathedral of St Sophia in Novgorod. These Russian chalices, Byzantine in style, are exceptionally large, like the serpentine example, and also have eight alternating rounded and angular projections, as well as figures in relief analogous to the serpentine decoration; the handles are formed by two large scrolls (Hahnloser 1971, pl. LXXXVII). As for hardstone examples, the general shape of the serpentine chalice recurs in another vessel in San Marco, made of rock-crystal and without handles; it is probably of Classical origin (fig. 37i; Hahnloser 1971, no. 84, pl. LXIX).

The reliefs and inscriptions indicate that the chalice is Byzantine work. The handles cut from the same block of stone as the body of the chalice are, however, a surprise. The vessel is in fact the only Byzantine hardstone example with such a feature. Very similar handles in the form of elongated animals are found on a ewer in the Pitti Palace, attributed to a Sasanian workshop, and on two ewers in San Marco which may be seventh-century Byzantine work (cf. no. 5). The only noteworthy differences are that the animals on the chalice have wings, and their tails are straight, whereas on the ewers the animals' tails are curved. The disconcerting handles on the chalice led Molinier ingeniously to suggest that it might be Eastern, and that the reliefs and inscriptions were added later in Byzantium. If this had been so, the upper part would have had to have been re-worked, which does not seem feasible.

A more reasonable theory is that Byzantine hardstone-

287

carvers, having at some point improved their technique, succeeded not only in decorating their vases with reliefs, as on this example and on the incense-boat (no. 43), but also in fashioning pierced handles from the same piece of stone in imitation of older vessels such as the ewers already mentioned. The chalice is perhaps not such an isolated example as it might seem in Byzantine hardstone-carving. The Danish royal collections at Rosenborg Castle, Copenhagen, include an oval bowl of black serpentine with white flecks; it is well made, thick-walled, with eight gadroons, like the incense-boat. This bowl is similarly carved from a single block; rather than handles, it has four small feet in the form of animal-paws (fig. 42a; exh. cat. *Trésors des rois de Danemark*, 1978-9, no. 106).

The large serpentine cameo in the Victoria and Albert Museum with a half-figure of the Virgin, hands raised with palms outward, enables us to date the use of serpentine for large Byzantine carved objects (fig. 42b). It bears an inscription imploring the Virgin to help Nikephoros III Botaniates, emperor between 1078 and 1081 (exh. cat. *Splendeur de Byzance*, 1982, no. St. 3). On the grounds used to determine the date of the incense-boat – the nature of the stone and the quality of the workmanship – it seems reasonable to date the chalice to the same period, that is to the twelfth century. The present mount is of later date.

As the cheetahs' heads project slightly above the rim of the vessel, the original mount – like that, for example, on the two-handled chalice of the emperor Romanos (no. 10) – must have taken account of the projections.

D. A.

Metalwork

A serrated metal ring imitating juxtaposed pointed leaves has been fitted to the lower part of the serpentine vessel; under it is a horizontally projecting collar also in the form of foliage. Below that again, the flared silver-gilt foot has eight lobes alternating with eight points, echoing the shape of the rim of the chalice. Below the foot runs a cast openwork strip of quatrefoils. Of eight quatrefoil *basse-taille* enamel plaques corresponding to the eight rounded lobes four survive, depicting the symbols of the evangelists. The style and the colours of the translucent enamel (blue, green, yellow, saffron, and pinkish violet) invite comparison with the enamel on the reliquary of St George (no. 41, before 1325) and suggest a similar date. Round the enamels, the foot is embossed with foliage and birds on a pounced ground; quatrefoils run round the edge of the lobes, while above and between the lobes are foliate scrolls with rounded tendrils terminating in trefoils or longer leaves with five or seven cusps. In higher relief among the scrolls are eight birds worked with a skill and precision which enable them to

be easily identified (from left to right, from the enamel of the lion of St Mark, they are: a pelican, a heron, a bird of prey, a bird of prey with spread wings seen from above, a heron preening, a peacock, a bird feeding its young, and a bird of prey carrying off a smaller bird in its talons). Hahnloser (1971) compared the embossed decoration of this piece with that on the foot of the steatite incense-boat (no. 43) and with a series of other pieces of Venetian origin with related embossed work. He attributed the whole group to the craftsman responsible for the foot of the serpentine chalice, calling him the "Master of the Serpentine" (*Maestro del Serpentino*) and dated it to the second quarter of the fourteenth century on the basis of the decorative elements of the *Pala d'Oro* executed in 1342-5. The group is, however, less homogeneous than it appears at first sight.

It is true that a number of points link the chalice to the San Marco incense-boat and the other objects which have been associated with it. Their decoration of foliate scrolls is inspired by Byzantine models, an example of which, in the treasury itself, is the back of the icon with the half-figure of St Michael (no. 12). Their techniques – embossed and stamped decoration and pounced grounds – are comparable, as are some of the elongated leaves with five or seven cusps. Yet there are differences: on the serpentine chalice the quatrefoils round the base of the foot are cast, whereas on the incense-boat they are punched out. The difference is perhaps unimportant, as both techniques were in use among Venetian craftsmen of the first half of the fourteenth century. It is perhaps more important to point out that the two foliate collars joining the lower parts of the stone vessels and the silver bases are not identical: the cusps of the leaves are more pointed and separate on the incense-boat.

Finally, contrary to Hahnloser's opinion, it seems impossible that the same matrices were used for the foot of the serpentine chalice and the incense-boat. The closed scrolls of the incense-boat and the large leaves like vine leaves do not relate to the ornament on the chalice, the leaves and scrolls of which are perhaps more comparable with those on a reliquary in the treasury of Santa Maria del Giglio in Venice (Hahnloser 1971, pl. CLI). On the chalice, furthermore, there is greater freedom in the arrangement of the decoration; the relief is more prominent, and the birds, for example, are placed where the metal surface has been worked into a slight bulge. Besides, no other object is decorated with birds like those on the chalice: birds are found on objects from other workshops in the treasury of San Marco, such as the reliquary of the Holy Blood (Hahnloser 1971, no. 128) and the rock-crystal candlesticks (nos 38-39), but these birds are engraved or nielloed, not worked in relief, and do not show the same naturalism, precision or inventiveness. Even though they are closer to the foot of the serpentine chalice in being embossed, the fantastic animals on the reliquary of the Holy Blood in San

Stefano in Venice (Venice, fourteenth century; Hahnloser 1971, pl. CXXX) cannot be attributed to the same hand. In fact the craftsman responsible for the mount of the serpentine chalice, quite different from the one who worked on the incense-boat, seems to have been an outstanding and highly original craftsman, even if his work is related in many ways to contemporary Venetian craftsmanship. He must have been active in the first decades of the fourteenth century, as the chalice is described in the inventory of 1325: "a mortar with a silver foot, decorated above with silver, which is of serpentine stone" (Gallo 1967, 280, no. 9). The phrase "mortar... of serpentine stone" leaves no doubt as to the identity of the object, but there is no trace in subsequent inventories of the silver mount, whether lid or rim, which once surmounted the object.

D. G. C.

Bibliography: Pasini 1885-6, 55, no. 62, pl. XXXV. Molinier 1888, 37-8, 89-90. Hahnloser 1965, *Il Tesoro*, 109, pls LXXII ff. Gallo 1967, 280, VI, no. 9; 299, no. 74; 350, no. 27; 360, no. 168; 368, no. 35; pl. 34, fig. 60. Hahnloser 1971, no. 61 (Grabar, Hahnloser), pls LIII-LV, CXLIX.

43

Stone incense-boat

Stonework: Byzantine, 12th century (?). *Metalwork*: Venetian, about 1320-40
Steatite (?), silver gilt. *Height* 100 mm, *length* 230 mm

Tesoro, no. 82

The vessel has been worked from a semi-translucent grey stone tending to green, which is soft, as is shown by scratches on the exterior. In the interior, which is less polished, the stone appears duller and lighter green. In the 1733 inventory the stone is considered to be a marble: "*Una navetta grande di verde antico, lavorata a sonde di melone, con coperchio e piede dorato*" (Gallo 1967, 351, no. 46). It was described in the valuation of 1801 as "*1 Navicella di pietra tenera*" (Gallo 1967, 361, no. 173). In 1816-20, Cicognara valued the object at 250 lire, questioning the nature of the stone and analyzing it thus: "*Navicella da incenso di una specie curiosissima d'alabastro tenero gessoso come il moderno di Volterra, verde, trasparente, e tinto probabilmente...; merita osservazioni per le indagini sulla materia*" (Gallo 1967, 365, no. 18). Following Pasini, who defined the stone as a marble "*serpentino talcoso*", it was long considered serpentine. In the recent catalogue of the treasury, which is more circumspect, the incense-boat is considered to be made of a soft talckoid stone. Although its slight translucency is rarely found in this material, it could be a type of steatite (crystalline talc). Steatite was in fact widely used throughout the Byzantine empire. Easy to work, it was especially favoured for small reliefs like that decorating the bottom of the incense-boat; there is, however, a large steatite paten in the treasury (Hahnloser 1971, no. 69, pl. LIX).

In any case, the soft stone has been perfectly worked. The incense-boat has eight gadroons, separated on the interior by slender flat fillets. A relief at the bottom represents a saint drawing a sword; he is identified by an inscription as St Demetrios. The bowl has an octagonal base cut from the same piece of stone. The inscription and the style of the relief are enough to show the Byzantine origin of this piece. There are, moreover, a number of other round or oval hardstone bowls which are probably Byzantine and which have the same gadrooned shape. Several apparently Classical sardonyx bowls are deeply cut with gadroons all the way around the interior (e.g. no. 11), but the appearance of the exterior is barely affected by them; the gadroons hollowed out of the interior of this incense-boat and of other objects related to it, however, project prominently on the exterior. Byzantine hardstone objects with gadroons were possibly inspired by Sasanian precious metalwork, which includes bowls with the same shape as the incense-boat, such as one in the Hermitage, Leningrad, dated to the seventh century (fig. 43a; Hahnloser 1971, pl. XCIII). Finally, in Western hardstone-carving there are examples of objects with gadroons, such as the jasper bowl made for the duc de Berry and now in Bourges (*Les Fastes du Gothique*, 1981-2, no. 177).

Similar objects are, first, a group of sardonyx vessels. A round bowl in the Louvre from the French royal collections (fig. 43b) shows a lack of technical accomplishment; thick-walled and of unequal height, it is formed by six gadroons. A vessel from Saint-Denis (fig. 43c; Paris, Bibliothèque Nationale; Montesquiou-Fezensac and Gaborit-Chopin 1977, 59-60, pl. 44) has ten gadroons. On these two objects the fine groins separating the gadroons are not always straight or properly lined up with each other; they disappear, without meeting up, in the middle of the bottom of the vessel, which is not properly centred in the case of the vessel from Saint-Denis. The two objects each have a low base, concave on the underside and surrounded by a flat rim of varying thickness. On a round sardonyx bowl now in the Pitti Palace, Florence (fig. 43d; Holzhausen 1929, fig. 8) the six gadroons are separated by rounded groins which stop at the edge of a round concave base; the small broken base has been supplemented with a marble one. Another bowl in the Louvre, remounted in the seventeenth century, belonged to Louis XIV (fig. 43e); it is carved in the shape of a shell, with nine gadroons and no base. Finally, an oval sardonyx bowl with eight gadroons (fig. 43f; Schnitzler 1957, pl. 110), also without a base, is mounted on the ambo presented by the Ottonian emperor Henry II to what is now Aachen Cathedral.

Besides these sardonyx vessels, the same sort of shape can be found in rock-crystal on a flat-bottomed chalice with six gadroons in San Marco (fig. 43j; Hahnloser 1971, no. 64, pl. LVI). It should also be noted that the large rosette with six lobes hollowed out of the alabaster paten in the same treasury (no. 18) projects on the underside in exactly the same way.

The Byzantine mounts of these last two pieces date from the tenth or eleventh century. The Aachen bowl was made before the ambo, which was in place early in the eleventh century, while the vessel from Saint-Denis received its mount in the West during the first half of the same century. This group of objects can be dated to the tenth century. However, for various reasons, the incense-boat seems to be later. First, there is the very unusual nature of the stone. It was possibly used because stone as beautiful as the sardonyx from which the above-vessels were made was no longer available.

The incense-boat is actually of superior workmanship to these vessels, partly, it is true, because of the softness of the stone. Tenth to eleventh-century Byzantine hardstone vases have no relief decoration. Thanks to the technical mastery acquired, a relief decoration reappears here, as on the serpentine vessel (no. 42), which is probably contemporary; both recall the principle of Classical cameo vessels. Finally, the base of the incense-boat is very different from those of tenth and eleventh-century vessels in being polygonal, a shape which reappears on bases of Western vessels dating from the fourteenth and fifteenth centuries. In the absence of any intermediate pieces, however, it is impossible to date the incense-boat much later than the group of sardonyx vessels, and it seems logical to place it in the twelfth century, perhaps as Ross suggests, in Thessaloniki, where the cult of St Demetrios was important.

D. A.

Metalwork

A double collar consisting of saw-tooth leaves has been fitted to the sides of the foot of the hardstone bowl. The tapering silver-gilt base, attached to the underside, is set back from the outline of the hardstone foot; its eight rounded lobes correspond with the eight sides of the vessel. Its embossed decoration consists of vigorous scrolls of rounded tendrils bearing three and five-cusped leaves and enclosing broad vine-leaves, against a pounced ground. The bottom of the base is a band pierced with quatrefoils, and a double moulding. The lid comprises two flaps with a central hinge; it is attached to the rim of the steatite bowl by saw-tooth leaves similar to those joining the vessel to its silver base. Two small cast

statuettes act as handles (one of the flaps is now shut). The traces of six settings for stones are visible around stamped relief medallions of half-figures of the Virgin and Child and of Christ blessing and holding a cross. The leaves embossed on the base have been compared by Hahnloser to the decoration on an extensive series of Venetian precious metalwork. The same characteristics are found, with slight variations, on rock-crystal pyxides at Zara, Treviso, and Massenhausen (fig. 43 h) and on chalices at Modena and Baierdorf (Hahnloser 1971, pl. CLI); to these should be added a chalice in the Fitzwilliam Museum, Cambridge (fig. 43 g). The "casket of the fourteen saints" in San Marco (no. 44) can also be attributed to this workshop, which was active around 1320-30. Another group of Venetian precious metalwork, including the arm-reliquary of St Theodore made in 1321, also in San Marco, and similar reliquaries in Chioggia (Hahnloser 1971, no. 153, pls CXLIV- CXLV) is very close, in certain details of the foliage, to the mount on the incense-boat. The reliquary-casket of St Chrysogonos at Zara, a Venetian work of 1326 (Hahnloser 1971, pl. CXLIV, no. 9), is also related to the products of this workshop, although less closely: the workmanship is stiffer and more formal. On the other hand, a reliquary in Santa Maria del Giglio, in Venice, (Hahnloser 1971, pl. CLI), which lacks both vine-leaves and closed scrolls, seems to be of another type, closer to the mount of the serpentine chalice (no. 42). This chalice, despite links with the mount on the incense-boat, seems to show too much originality compared to the rest of the group to allow it to be attributed to the same hand, as proposed by Hahnloser in establishing a workshop of the "*Maestro del Serpentino*". Besides, it is possible that the chalice mount, recorded in the 1325 inventory, is

43a

43 b

43 c

43 d

296

earlier than the mount on the incense-boat, which was not mentioned in 1325.

The workshop responsible for the foot of the incense-boat and the related workshops were evidently inspired by the embossed scrolls with foliage and broad flowers of earlier Byzantine work (e.g. no. 12). The same motif on closed scrolls encircling foliage, although with small leaves on stalks and more jagged vine-leaves, was also taken up by another contemporary Venetian workshop, which worked on a casket of relics of various saints (Hahnloser 1971, no. 155, pl. CXLVII). These diverse examples in fact prefigure the scrolls and foliage motifs on the inner borders of the *Pala d'Oro*, made between 1342 and 1345 (Hahnloser 1965, *Il Tesoro*, 108-9). This type of decoration is not, however, confined to Venice, and vine-ornament was produced all over Europe during the first half and around the middle of the fourteenth century, although perhaps as a result of Italian influence (e.g. exh. cat. *Les Fastes du Gothique*, 1981-2, nos 193, 206 B, C, M).

Comparisons for the statuettes on the lid, with their dumpy proportions and rather limp drapery, include several Italian works, such as the statuettes surmounting the Venetian reliquaries in Treviso and Bari (no. 36; fig. 36d) and in Massenhausen, or those supporting the monstrance, also Venetian, in the abbey of Charroux (fig. 43i; exh. cat. *Trésors des églises de France*, 1965, no. 345). These are therefore contemporary with the base of the incense-boat. On the other hand, the style of the medallions on the lid, with flowing, curving drapery, clearly seems earlier than 1300. The craftsman may of course have re-used fragments from an older mount, a hypothesis supported by traces of solder around the medallions. This would imply that a silver foot made around 1320-30 was fitted to an at least partly extant earlier mount and explain the rather poor attachment of the incense-boat to its metal foot, on which it is badly centred, and the relative clumsiness of the profile of the object.

D. G. C.

Bibliography: Pasini 1885-6, 66, no. 128, pl. LIV, fig. 128. Molinier 1888, 98, no. 117. Ross 1958, 43-8. Hahnloser 1965, *Il Tesoro*, 89-111 (Grabar, Hahnloser), pl. LXXII. Gallo 1967, 299, no. 75 (?); 351, no. 46; 361, no. 173; 365, no. 18. Hahnloser 1971, no. 74 (Grabar, Hahnloser), pls LXII, CXLVIII-CXLIX, CLI.

43e

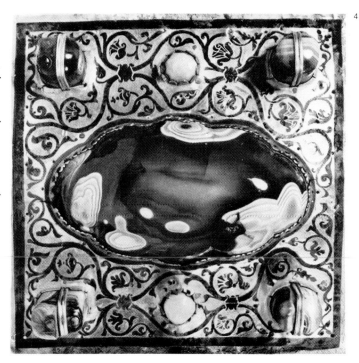

43f

44

Reliquary-casket of fourteen Eastern saints

Venice, about 1320-30
Silver-gilt, niello, rock-crystal. *Length* 338 mm, *width* 154 mm, *height* 95 mm

Tesoro, no. 135 (listed in the 1634 inventory: II, no. 14)

This gilt silver casket with twelve haloed busts of Eastern saints beneath an arcade of trilobed arches on the two longer sides was intended to hold the relics of these saints and two others, not presently depicted. A band of narrow niello inscription riveted just below the lid identifies each bust. Across the front, this band reads: S[ANCTI] ERMOLAI, S[ANCTI] ANDREE, S[ANCTI] ANASTASII, SA[NCTÆ] BARBARE, S[ANCTI] PARTHOMIO, S[ANCTI] PANTALEO[N]IS. The inscription above the busts on the back reads: S[ANCTI] ECHAIO, S[ANCTI] MARTINI, S[ANCTI] ANELODISTI, S[ANCTI] YGNACHIO, S[ANCTI] BLASII, S[ANCTI] VAVILE AP[OSTO]L[I]. The niello inscriptions on the ends are missing. Hahnloser proposed that they could have given the names of Cosmas and Damian, which are mentioned in the later inscription on the present

plain silver lid. These two saints could have been represented on the lid before its replacement by the present one. The lid, which is made of one piece of silver, includes the frame of dentils which holds the large, thick crystal in the center. Hahnloser compared the method of holding the crystal with similar mountings on several examples of Venetian metalwork in the treasury, four of which are in the exhibition (nos 38-39, 42, 43). The crystal was inserted so that the wrapped relics within, now missing, could be seen. The niello inscription reads laterally: IT:IN NISTA CASELA SUNT HAEC IN PRIMO CALTO DE RELIQUIA SANCTI ECHAIO ITEM IN S[E]C[UN]DA DE RELIQUIA SANCTI MARTINI IN TERCIA DE RELIQUIA SANCTI PANTHALEONIS ET S[ANCTI] ERMOLAI 4. COSME ET DAMIANI 5. BLASII ET ANELODISTI 6. S. YGNACHIO

7. ANDREE APOSTOLI 8. ANASTASII DE PERSIA 9. DE CAPILIS SANCTE BARBARE 10. S[ANCTI] PARTHOMIO EO DE LAPSACE 11. S[ANCTI] VAVILE APOSTOLI. The lid still retains its original, pearled frame. Six tongue-and-groove hinge-like clasps once secured the lid tightly to the frame of the front and back sides. The short sides of the casket are each dominated by two relatively large yet symmetrically foliated vines with clusters of fruit rendered in low relief against contrasting stippled backgrounds. These decorations completely fill the wide yet incomplete trilobed arches which join at centered supporting columns with foliated capitals and bases. An *oculus* with molded frame is placed directly above, against the smoothly burnished area between the arches. Like the arches themselves, the *oculi* at the outer sides are interrupted by the corner border. This border, at the sides as well as across the bottom, is pearled, as are also the upper surfaces of the arches.

This scheme continues in part, and in slightly higher relief, on the long sides. The busts are rendered in relief against the stippled background beneath the arches in place of the *rinceaux*. The arcades are more pleasingly proportioned and are complete, corner to corner. The small *oculi*, each of which must have had an inset enamel or stone, continue in series, only to be cut at the corners. The vertical borders at the side and the horizontal one below the arcade are again pearled. The overall decorative scheme is especially similar to the upper register of another Venetian reliquary-casket in the treasury which was made at about the same time (fig. 44a; Hahnloser 1971, no. 155). The foliate motifs and stippled backgrounds are also related to this work, as well as to such other contemporary Venetian works as the bases for the serpentine chalice and navicella, both in the exhibition (nos 42, 43). These foliated vine tendrils against stippled backgrounds, together with the related and slightly later examples in the cornice of the *Pala d'Oro*, reminded Hahnloser of the Byzantine multiple vine tendrils on the back of the icon with the bust of Michael (no. 12).

The busts that decorate the casket of the fourteen saints derive from Byzantine tradition in more obvious ways, especially in the head types, drapery configurations, and gestures. Contrary to Hahnloser's suggestion, there is very little in these busts which suggests the Gothic style of the tondo busts in the cornice of the *Pala d'Oro*. The Venetian goldsmith working on the reliquary-casket seems to have been almost completely dominated by Middle Byzantine conventions, well represented in the enameled icons and bookcovers of the treasury.

Middle Byzantine figure-style in low relief was also available in the serpentine chalice in the exhibition (no. 42) and must have also been available in the form of Middle Byzantine ivory carvings. The Venetian artist varied his selections from this tradition: five of the busts are half-tondo (truncated below the waist by a curve) while the remainder are horizontally cut by the frame (as, for example, in the well-known Apostles Casket in the Bar-

gello in Florence (fig. 44b; cf. Goldschmidt and Weitzmann 1930, no. 99, pls LVIII-LIX). The costumes vary following Byzantine types with buckled togas, mitered bishops in full vestments, and tunics with loosely open mantles. The hand gestures are also typically Byzantine and are shown either pointing or with palm out in a gesture of faith, as noted by Hahnloser. (Usually only one hand is shown, however: the exceptions may be seen in the two central busts on the front and the one immediately to the left. Two hold books with the other hand, and the female saint holds a cross, which is a replacement.)

The male head-types are also Byzantine in character, and include youthful, beardless examples as well as fully bearded ones. Indeed, one might at first think that the representations are of a series of apostles together with the bishop saints and one female saint. Hahnloser saw a resemblance to the Byzantine *Deesis* represented in the series of three saints on the front singled out above and beginning with the second example from the left, the one labeled S[ANCT]I ANDREE. This saint, while Christ-like, reminded Hahnloser of John the Baptist. The next figure, even more Christ-like, could even be confused with Christ. The female saint suggests the Virgin Mary. While such an order reverses that of a true Byzantine *Deesis* – Saint John the Baptist should be on Christ's left – such resemblances underscore the eclectic predilection of the Venetian goldsmith who made them. Hahnloser left open the problem of whether the Venetian goldsmith had more or less freely based his series of busts upon the Byzantine models or whether he had used a matrix or mold taken directly from a Byzantine work.

It is difficult to date the reliquary-casket, therefore, on the basis of the style of the relief busts. However, the ornamental scheme may be seen as roughly contemporary with the cornice of around 1336 of the altar-frontal in the exhibition (no. 40) and earlier than the cornice of 1343-5 of the *Pala d'Oro*, as indicated by Hahnloser.

W. D. W.

Bibliography: Pasini 1885-6, 85, pl. LXIV, fig. 158. Molinier 1888, 102, no. 146. Hahnloser 1965, *Il Tesoro*, 111, pl. LXXVIII. Gallo 1967, 313-4; 382, no. 6; pl. 27, fig. 50. Hahnloser 1971, 136, 157-9, no. 154 (Hahnloser), pls CXLVI-CXLVII.

Exh. cat. *Venezia e Bisanzio*, 1974, no. 79.

45

Rock-crystal bowl

Rock-crystal: Parisian, mid-14th century (?). *Metalwork*: 14th century (foot), and later
Rock-crystal, silver-gilt, gold. *Height* 134 mm, *diam.* 191 mm

Tesoro, no. 51

The bowl does not seem to appear in the inventories of the treasury until 1733, when it can be identified among the rock-crystal vessels either as "*Una tazza grande a sonde ornata d'argento*" (Gallo 1967, 353, no. 123) or, more convincingly, as "*Altra tazza grande lavorata a sonde con piede e fornimenti d'argento*" (Gallo 1967, 354, no. 127). It is described in 1816 in Cicognara's catalogue (Gallo 1967, 371, no. 3).

The circular rock-crystal bowl is decorated in continuous relief on the exterior with flat gadroons, spirally arranged. It rests on a silver-gilt foot with stamped ornament. Once much taller, the upper part of the object suffered con-siderable damage and was then made good with a deep undecorated silver-gilt rim and a lid. The lid is now missing, but traces of a hinge survive.

Attached to the foot through the plain round centre of the crystal is a gold disk decorated with a pounced heraldic shield. It bears a complete dragon which Hahn-loser considered to be the arms of the Buoncompagni family, though these are supposed to show a *demi*-dragon. The pounced technique suggests that the medallion was added in the fifteenth or sixteenth century. According to Hahnloser, the Buoncompagni family cannot be traced in Venice until the end of the sixteenth

century, which explains why, if they presented the bowl to the treasury, it is not recorded in the early inventories. Lamm and Pazaurek were the first to relate the bowl to a homogeneous group of shallow bowls cut from pure rock-crystal, with or without small bases all with the same wavy decoration. The group includes six other round bowls, smaller than the example in Venice, in Stockholm (Hahnloser 1971, pl. CLIV, no. 3), in Seville Cathedral (Hahnloser 1971, pl. CLIV, no. 6), in the Munich *Schatzkammer* (fig. 45a; Thoma and Brunner 1964, no. 40, figs 14-5), and in the Württembergisches Landesmuseum in Stuttgart (fig. 45b; Landenberger 1973, 12). The two remaining examples are in the Grünes Gewölbe, Dresden (Sponsel 1925, I, pls 6, 8). In addition there are two famous reliquaries each formed by two oval bowls of the same type joined together. The first of these is in Prague Cathedral (Podlaha and Šittler 1903, nos 47-8); the second is also in Czechoslovakia, in the church of Stará Boleslav (Hahnloser 1971, pl. CXXXI). Finally, two other round bowls have been used (or re-used?) as the lids of two rock-crystal containers: a pyx in Cividale Cathedral (Hahnloser 1971, pl. CLIV, fig. 7) and a reliquary in San Lorenzo, Florence (fig. 45c; Heikamp 1974, no. 30, fig. 53).

These objects are patently Western works of the fourteenth century, as is shown by their overall shape and in some cases by their mounts. The Venice, Seville, Prague and Stará Boleslav bowls, indeed, have mounts totally or in part datable to the fourteenth century. These have few distinguishing features, except for the last example, which is certainly of Venetian workmanship. Because of this, Hahnloser has attributed the whole group to Venetian craftsmen, and it is true that three of the group are in Italy today. Yet the curious form of the Stará Boleslav reliquary, with two bowls placed together in illogical fashion, suggests that they were not originally designed for the Venetian mount which they now have.

Pazaurek was the first to identify rock-crystal vessels of this type in fourteenth-century French royal collections, notably that of Louis of Anjou, brother of Charles V. In the inventory of his holdings drawn up between 1360 and 1368 are "*une coupe de cristal ondoiée*" and "*un flascon de cristal, ondoyé en manière de soleil*" (Laborde 1853, 33, no. 171; 54-5, no. 328). An inventory of 1379-80 lists four pieces of the same kind in his collections: "*une coupe de cristal, garnie d'argent doré... Et la coupe et le couvercle sont de cristal ondoiez comme rays de soleil, et par les bors sont garnis d'argent doré*", an example which recalls the Prague reliquary; the rock-crystal flask in the previous inventory; "*un flascon de cristal, garni d'argent doré..., et ledit flacon est bellonc, fait comme rais de soleil ...*"; and "*un flascon de cristal, garni d'argent doré...et le ventre du flascon est de cristal comme à rais de soleil...*" (Moranvillé 1906, nos 893, 2200-2). In 1380 Charles V himself owned a bowl "*le pié d'argent doré et le hanap, tors, de cristal, sans autre garniture*", and "*ung petit pot de cristal, tors, en façon d'un gobelet*" (Labarte 1879, 222, nos 1957, 1960).

In 1401 his other brother, the duc de Berry owned "*un grant vaisseaul rond, de cristal, de deux pièces pareilles, faictes en manière de soleil, qui pevent servir à dragouer, garnies d'argent doré*" (Guiffrey 1896, II, 43-4, no. 312), which recalls the reliquary in Prague. The Prague and the Stará Boleslav reliquaries are said to have belonged to the uncle of these princes, Charles IV, who stayed in Paris. It is difficult to believe that these repeated mentions all concern imported items, since Parisian crystal-cutters seem to have been active at the time. It is more reasonable to attribute these vessels, provisionally, to Paris rather than Venice.

D.A.

Bibliography: Pasini 1885-6, 62, pl. XXXVII, no. 67. Molinier 1888, 90, no. 55. Lamm 1929-30, I, 236; II, pl. 85, fig. 7. Pazaurek 1930, 186-7. Gallo 1967, 371, no. 3. Hahnloser 1971, no. 162 (Hahnloser), pls CLIV-CLV. Heikamp 1974, 131-3.

45c

46

Reliquary of the Column of the Flagellation

Venice, 1375 and 1489
Silver, partly gilt, granite. *Height* 670 mm, *max. width* 192 mm

Santuario, no. 59 (listed in the 1580 inventory: no. 6)

Pasini suggested without confirmation with authoritative sources that the relic, a piece of granite as big as a fist, may have been brought to Venice in 1125 from Constantinople together with St Isidore's bones by the doge Domenico Michel (Pasini 1885-6, 31; Gallo 1967, 99). According to the inscription, however, the reliquary itself was commissioned in 1375 by the *procuratori* Michele Morosini (elected doge in 1382) and Pietro Corner. Modifications were made in 1489 by Vido, a master from the goldsmith workshop at St Zuminian (Gallo 1967, 100). This presumably meant the replacement (or new creation) of the crucifix and its rounded support above the relic. Large sums were paid in 1721 for a gilded pedestal, which is now lost (Gallo 1967, 100). Also, according to Hahnloser, Christ's hands, feet, and cord were repaired at this time.

The inscription appears in the eight small niello plaques presently around the top of the capital and just beneath the relic. While incorrect in their current sequence, this inscription originally read: MCCCLXXV QUES/TA PIERA E PROP/IA DELA CHOLONA/CHE XPO FO BATUD/O. MIS. MICHIEL/MORESINI.MIS.PI/ERO. CHORNER PR/OLATORI FE FAR ("1375. This stone belongs to the column on which Christ was struck. Ordered by Michele Morosini and Pietro Corner, Procuratori").

The reliquary, which exceeds in size and weight all others in the treasury, is worked in heavy silver and is well preserved. The broad rhomboidal base, scalloped in plan, is constructed with two platforms, the upper one supported above the lower one with an arcade of low trilobed pointed arches. Above this and supporting the base of the column may be seen an octagonal openwork socle from which projects a stool with cusped arches. The large figure of Christ stands on this stool. The broad, smooth column with an octagonal base and capital, rises at the center of the composition. Hahnloser suggested that this column could have been part of the restoration of 1489. The relic is secured by four grooved bands tied with a horizontal wire. A domed cap above the relic supports the small crucifix. The modeling of the corpus, including the linear emphasis on the ribs, led Hahnloser to assume that this portion of the reliquary was definitely a product of the 1489 restoration.

The large standing Christ with head bent in resignation is the focal point of the lower part of the composition. The transverse and flanking vertical folds of the loincloth (*perizonium*) reinforce the impression of symmetry. Christ's sensitively modeled head with parallel strands of hair, softly curled beard, and parted lips presents an understated expression of suffering. The torso and arms are smoothly modeled, with little accentuation of musculature. Unlike the torso of the crucifix, the only linear accents are slight, as around the nipples and in the few hairs on the chest. (The crown of thorns and the hands are new.) The figure is benign, and thus it stands in strong contrast to the dramatically expressive figures of the tormentors on either side. These figures are remarkable for their striking gestures, their active stance, violent and bony faces with mouths open as if they were screaming, and their rough, curly hair and beards. They are dressed fashionably with heavily padded short coats with large buttons, low-slung belts with suspended purses, tight hose, and pointed shoes. Hahnloser observed that, despite the fact that their whips are today missing, their decisive gestures and abruptly angled right arms have a very drastic effect, which is just as intense when viewed from behind.

Venetian *trecento* miniature paintings depicting this subject, especially as in the Mariegola manuscripts, provide iconographical and compositional antecedents for the reliquary with its gentle figure of Christ contrasted to the animated poses of the scourging men (Wixom 1961, 14-25, no. 4, figs 17-9). The new elements in the reliquary lie in the contemporary costumes of the tormentors and in the vivid expression of their bearded faces. Could these heads date from the 1489 restoration? Their very expressiveness seems to approach that of certain works by Riccio (Andrea Briosco, about 1470/5-1532). This great Paduan sculptor's seated satyr in the Bargello or his "shouting" equestrian warrior in the Victoria and Albert Museum come to mind (Pope-Hennessy 1958, fig. 148 and pl. 126 respectively). The crucial question is whether the heads of the tormentors are made one piece with the body or whether they were inserted. If the former, these heads are exceedingly daring and precocious. Regardless of this uncertainty, the reliquary of the Column of the Flagellation is a rare early example of what Hahnloser has called a "talking reliquary" ("*reliquario parlante*"), in which the activity of the represented figures makes clear the meaning and origin of the relic the work enshrines. There appear to be only four European metalwork reliquaries of this type which are earlier. These are the reliquary of the Holy Sepulchre, a northern French work of about 1300, in Pamplona Cathedral (Steingräber 1967, 156-66), the reliquary of the arm of

St George (no. 41), listed in the 1325 inventory of the San Marco treasury, the Simeon reliquary, an Aachen work of around 1325-50, in the Aachen Cathedral treasury (Grimme 1972, 82-4, no. 64, col. pl. X, pls 77-8), and the reliquary-monstrance of the Holy Thorn, made in Prague in 1347-9 and residing in the Walters Art Gallery in Baltimore (exh. cat. *Die Parler*, 1978, II, 702-3, col. pl. 22). Being of comparable quality, being of greater size, and being the last in an early series, the present work takes on a special importance. Then also, as has been indicated by Hahnloser, it had a significant following in two reliquaries of the same subject: a Paduan late fourteenth-century example in the Basilica del Santo in Padua and a Venetian reliquary of the early fifteenth century in the Louvre (fig. 46a).

W.D.W.

Bibliography: Pasini 1885-6, 31-2, pl. XXVI, fig. 32. Molinier 1888, 85, no. 22. Hahnloser 1965, *Il Tesoro*, 82-3. Gallo 1967, 44, 99-100, 113-5; 302, no. 6; 303; 329, no. 12; 321, no. 64; 332, no. 91; 384, no. 18; 388, no. 9; pl. 18, fig. 25. Hahnloser 1971, 166-8, no. 164, pls CLVI-CLVII.

47

Pastoral staff

Venice, about 1420
Silver, partly gilt, on wood core. *Length* 1940 mm

Tesoro, no. 30 (listed in the 1524 inventory: no. 33)

According to Steingräber, this pastoral staff was used by Primates of San Marco and at present it is used by the Patriarchs during the most solemn and holy festivals. The staff, octagonal in cross-section, has eight segments assembled end to end over a wood core. In each segment, vertical facets with engraved leaf-patterns against cross-hatched backgrounds alternate with facets with openwork backed with silver panels without gilding. Arising from an encircling balustrade are six volutes separated by arched panels with a repetition of the blind openwork observed on the staff.

The volutes support a large knob which is a visual feast of architectural and figurative detail, and which is itself divided into several horizontal zones, one above the other. The lowest zone is a drum with cast and applied figures of cherubs alternating with still another variation of the blind openwork, here pointed quadrilobes over ungilt sheets of silver. The most massive zone just above is divided into eight architectural niches with cast and individually secured figures in armor, who stand singly on each of the small rounded and projecting pedestals. The heads of these figures recede into the shadows of the arched canopies above. Smaller bracketed and uninhabited canopies are inserted between the larger ones. The next zone is filled with a continuous series of gabled and cusped arches over perforated niches backed by sheets of ungilt silver. Another series of cast standing figures in armor stands outside the niches. A circular balustrade is the uppermost element of decoration of the knob.

In contrast to the many cast portions of this very intricate knob, the curved and foliated crook is made of dovetailed *repoussé* sections. Only the statuette of St Mark is cast. Steingräber saw here a difference of two styles: that of the staff, the knob, and the statuette of St Mark on the one hand, and that of the crook on the other hand. The first he dated in the early fifteenth century and related to several objects from the Venetian workshop of the Sesto family, such as the chalice of about 1420 in the treasury (fig. 47a; Hahnloser 1971, 181, no. 173, pl. CLXXIII). The crook was dated by Steingräber in the first half of the sixteenth century as an example of the High Renaissance and as an element substituted for a presumably damaged crook from the earlier period.

The last part of this conclusion is not entirely required nor completely convincing. Some elements of the foliage on the crook, such as the way the leaves follow the overall form and the manner in which the veins on the leaves are engraved, find parallels in the details of other objects coming from the Sesto family workshop, as for example the foliated volutes of the reliquary of the Precious Blood, of about 1420, in the treasury, and of the cross of around 1420-30 in Bergamo (Hahnloser 1971, pls CLXX, CLXXII). The perfect proportional relationship between the St Mark figure and the crook is another telling factor, all the more because this figure closely resembles in its drapery and stance the figure of the mourning St John on the Bergamo cross.

According to the 1845 inventory, the crozier has been restored (Gallo 1967, 398, no. 118).

W. D. W.

Bibliography: Pasini 1885-6, 67, pl. LXI, fig. 152. Molinier 1888, 101, no. 141. Gallo 1967, 292, no. 33; 398, no. 118; pl. 49, fig. 83. Hahnloser 1971, 183, no. 176 (Steingräber), pl. CLXXVII.

Bibliography

Sources

Andrea Dandolo:
Andrea Dandolo, *Chronica per extensum descripta*, ed. E. Pastorello (Rerum Italicarum Scriptores, II, vol. XII, pt 1), Bologna 1938; 2nd ed., Bologna 1958.

Brial 1822:
v. Geoffrey de Villehardouin.

Cecchetti 1886:
v. Documenti...

Chronicles:
v. Andrea Dandolo;
Cronache veneziane...;
Geoffrey de Villehardouin;
John the Deacon;
Marino Sanudo;
Martino da Canale;
Robert de Clari.

Cicognara 1816-20:
(author of the inventory of 1816-20) *v.* Gallo 1967.

Constantine VII Porphyrogenetos:
Constantin VII Porphyrogénète, le Livre des cérémonies, ed. and trans. A. Vogt (Collection Byzantine, Association Guillaume Budé), I, Paris 1935; and II, Paris 1939-40.

Cronache veneziane...:
Cronache veneziane antichissime, ed. G. Monticolo, Rome 1890.

Dandolo:
v. Andrea Dandolo.

Documenti...:
Documenti per la storia della Basilica di San Marco in Venezia dal nono secolo sino alla fine del decimo ottavo, dall'Archivio di Stato e dalla Biblioteca Marciana, ed. F. Ongania (preface by B. Cecchetti), Venice 1886.

Dodwell 1961:
v. Theophilus.

Duchesne 1881:
v. Liber Pontificalis.

Gallo 1967:
Gallo (R.), *Il Tesoro di San Marco e la sua storia* (Civiltà Veneziana, saggi 16), Florence 1967 (edited inventories of the treasure from 1283 to 1845).

Galvani 1845:
v. Martino da Canale.

Geoffrey de Villehardouin:
Geoffroy de Villehardouin, De la Conquête de Constantinople par les Français et les Vénitiens, ed. dom M.J. Brial (Recueil des Historiens des Gaules et de la France, XVIII), Paris 1822.

Grevenbroch 1755, 1760, 1764:
Grevenbroch (J.), *Varie curiosità sacre e profane* (manuscript in Venice, Museo Civico Correr, 3 vols dated 1755, 1760 and 1764).

Guiffrey 1894-6:
Inventaires de Jean duc de Berry, ed. J. Guiffrey, 2 vols, Paris 1894 and 1896.

Inventories:
Inventory of the treasury of the Holy See (Boniface VIII): *v.* Molinier 1888;
Inventory of Louis I, Duke of Anjou: *v.* Moranvillé 1906;
Inventories of John, Duke of Berry: *v.* Guiffrey 1894-6;
Inventories of Charles V: *v.* Labarte 1879;
Inventories of Clement V: *v. Regesti...*;
Inventories of the treasury of San Marco (from 1283 to 1845): *v.* Gallo 1967.

John the Deacon:
Iohannis Diaconi, *Chronicon venetum*, ed. G.H. Pertz (Monumenta Germaniae Historica, Scriptores, VII), Hanover 1864; *v.* Monticolo 1890.

Journals of Marino Sanudo:
v. Marino Sanudo.

Labarte 1879:
Inventaires du mobilier de Charles V roi de France..., ed. J. Labarte (Collection de Documents Inédits sur l'Histoire de France..., 3rd ser., Archéologie), Paris 1879.

La Mottraye 1727:
La Mottraye (Aubry de), *Voyages du Sieur de La Mottraye en Europe, Asie et Afrique*, I, The Hague 1727.

Lauer 1924:
v. Robert de Clari.

Liber Pontificalis:
Le Liber Pontificalis, ed. abbé L. Duchesne (Bibliothèque des Écoles Françaises d'Athènes et de Rome), I and II, Paris 1955; III, additions and corrections, ed. C. Vogel, Paris 1957.

Marino Sanudo:
Marino Sanudo, *I Diarii di Marino Sanudo (1496 1523) dall'autografo Marciano...*, ed. F. Stefani, G. Berchet, R. Furlin, N. Barozzi and M. Allegri, 52 vols, Venice 1879-1903.

Martino da Canale:
Martino da Canale, Cronaca Veneta... dall'origine della città all'anno 1275..., ed. F.L. Polidori and G. Galvani (Archivio Storico Italiano, VIII), Venice 1845; Martin da Canal, *Les Estoires de Venise*, ed. A. Limentani, Florence 1973.

Mely 1904:
Mely (F. de), *Exuviae sacrae Constantinopolitanae*, III, *La Croix des premiers Croisés, la Sainte Lance, la Sainte Couronne*, Paris 1904.

Molinier 1888:
Inventaire du trésor du Saint-Siège sous Boniface VIII (1295), ed. E. Molinier, Paris 1888.

Montfaucon 1702:
Montfaucon (B. de), *Diarium italicum sive Monumentorum veterum...noticiae singulares in itinerario italico collectae...*, Paris 1702.

Monticolo 1890:
v. Cronache veneziane...

Moranvillé 1906:
Inventaire de l'orfèvrerie et des joyaux de Louis I duc d'Anjou, ed. H. Moranvillé, Paris 1906.

Ongania 1886:
v. Documenti...

Pastorello 1938:
v. Andrea Dandolo.

Pertz 1846:
v. John the Deacon.

Photius, *Homilies*:
v. General works, Mango 1958.

Polidori 1845:
v. Martino da Canale.

Regesti...:
Regesti Clementis papae V ex Vaticanis archetypis...Leonis XIII pontificis maximi jussu...editi cura et studio monachorum ordinis S. Benedicti, Appendices, I, Rome 1892.

Riant (n.d.):
v. Robert de Clari.

Riant 1876:
Riant (P.), *Exuviae sacrae Constantinopolitanae*, I, Geneva 1876; II, Geneva 1876 and Paris 1904.

Robert de Clari:
Robert de Clari, *Li Estoires de Chiaux qui conquisent Constantinoble...*, ed. P. Riant, n.p., n.d.; *La Conquête de Constantinople*, ed. P. Lauer, Paris 1924; *The Conquest of Constantinople*, ed. E.H. McNeal, New York 1936; *La Conquête de Constantinople*, trans. P. Charlot, Paris 1939.

Sansovino 1581:
Sansovino (F.), *Venetia città nobilissima et singolare descritta in XIII libri...Cronica particolare delle cose fatte da i Veneti dal principio della città fino all'anno 1581...*, Venice 1581.

Theophilus:
Theophilus, De diversis artibus, ed. and trans. C.R. Dodwell, London 1961.

Tiepolo 1617:
Tiepolo (G.), *Trattato delle santissime Reliquie ultimamente ritrovate nel santuario della Chiesa di San Marco, di...Io.Thiepolo primiciero...*, Venice 1617.

Vogt 1935:
v. Constantine VII Porphyrogenetos.

General

Albizzati 1923:
  Albizzati (C), "Quattro vasi romani nel tesoro di S. Marco a Venezia", *Atti della Pontificia Accademia Romana di Archeologia, Memorie*, I, vol. I, *Miscellanea Giovanni Battista De Rossi*, 1923, 37-43.

Alison Frantz:
  v. Frantz 1934.

Amiranachvili 1963:
  Amiranachvili (or Amiranashvili, C. or S.), *Smalti della Georgia*, Milan 1963.

Amiranachvili 1971:
  Amiranachvili (C.), *Les Emaux de Géorgie*, Paris 1971.

Amiranachvili 1972:
  Amiranachvili (C.), *The Khakhuli Triptych*, Tbilisi 1972 (in Georgian, Russian & English).

Angulo 1954:
  Angulo Iñiguez (D.), *Museo del Prado, Catálogo de las Álhajas del Delfín*, Madrid 1954.

Avery 1936:
  Avery (M.), *The Exultet Rolls of South Italy*, II, Princeton (New Jersey) 1936.

Babelon 1897:
  Babelon (E.), *Catalogue des camées antiques et modernes de la Bibliothèque Nationale* (Fondation Eugène Piot), Paris 1897, 2 vols; I, text; II, plates.

Bank 1958:
  Bank (A.), "The Byzantine 11th-12th century silverware in the Hermitage Collection, 2, The Silver Staurotheca", *Vizantijskij Vremennik*, n. ser., 14(1958), 234-41.

Bank 1965:
  Bank (A.), *Byzantine art in the collections of the USSR*, Leningrad & Moscow 1965.

Bank 1977:
  Bank (A.), *Iskusstvo vizantii v sobraniyach SSSR*, 3 vols, Moscow 1977.

Barany-Oberschall 1937:
  Barany-Oberschall (M.), "The crown of the emperor Constantine Monomachos", *Archaeologia Hungarica* 22(1937).

Barbier de Montault 1884:
  Barbier de Montault (X.), "L'église royale et collégiale de Saint-Nicolas de Bari", *Revue de l'Art Chrétien*, 3rd ser., 1(1883), 455 ff.; 2(1884), 34-59.

Beckwith 1961:
  Beckwith (J.), *The art of Constantinople, an introduction to Byzantine art, 330-1453*, London 1961.

Beckwith 1962:
  Beckwith (J.), *Victoria and Albert Museum, The Veroli Casket* (Museum Monograph 18), London 1962.

Beckwith 1968:
  Beckwith (J.), *The art of Constantinople*, London 1968.

Beckwith 1970:
  Beckwith (J.), *Early Christian and Byzantine Art*, Harmondsworth 1970.

Beltrán 1960:
  Beltrán (A.), *Estudio sobre el Santo Cáliz de la catedral de Valencia* (Instituto diosesano valentino "Roque Chabas", Sección de Historia, 2), Valencia 1960.

Bertaux 1905:
  Bertaux (E.), "Les artistes français au service des rois angevins de Naples", *Gazette des Beaux-arts* 33(1905), 265-81.

Bettini 1961:
  Bettini (S.), "Un libro su San Marco", *Arte Veneta* 15(1961), 263-77 (review of Demus 1960).

Bettini 1965:
  Bettini (S.), "Le opere d'arte importate a Venezia durante le Crociate", *Venezia dalla prima Crociata alla conquista di Costantinopoli del 1204*, Florence 1965, 159-90.

Bettini 1974:
  v. exh. cat. *Venezia e Bisanzio*, 1974.

Biers 1969:
  v. Habachi and Biers 1969.

Bock 1861:
  Bock (F.), *Der Schatz von Sanct Marcus in Venedig* (Mitteilungen der Kaiserlich-Königlichen Zentral-Kommission zur Erforschung und Erhaltung der Baudenkmäler, VI), Vienna 1861.

Boeckler 1953:
  Boeckler (A.), *Die Frühmittelalterlichen Bronzetüren*, IV, *Die Bronzetüren des Bonanus von Pisa und des Barisanus de Trani* (Deutscher Verein für Kunstwissenschaft), Berlin 1953.

Bouras 1971:
  Bouras (L.), "The Cross of Adrianopolis", *The Benaki Museum, Selection*, Athens 1971.

Bouras 1979:
  Bouras (L.), *The Cross of Adrianople: a silver processional cross of the Middle Byzantine period*, Athens 1979.

Braun 1932:
  Braun (J.), *Das christliche Altargerät in seinem Sein und in seiner Entwicklung*, Munich 1932.

Braun 1940:
  Braun (J.), *Die Reliquiare des christlichen Kultes und ihre Entwicklung*, Freiburg im Breisgau 1940.

Bréhier 1936:
  Bréhier (L.), *La sculpture et les arts mineurs byzantins*, Paris 1936 (new ed. Paris 1973).

Brial 1822:
  v. Sources.

Brown 1980:
  Brown (K. Reynolds), "Russo-Byzantine jewellery in the Metropolitan Museum of Art", *Apollo* 1980, 6-9.

Brunello 1980:
Brunello (F.), *Arti e mestieri a Venezia nel Medioevo e nel Rinascimento* (Studi e testi veneziani 8), Vicenza 1980.

Brunner 1964:
v. Thoma and Brunner 1964.

Buckton 1982:
Buckton (D.), "The Oppenheim or Fieschi-Morgan reliquary in New York, and the antecedents of Middle Byzantine enamel", *Eighth Annual Byzantine Studies Conference, Abstracts*, Chicago 1982, 35-6.

Bühler 1973:
Bühler (H.P.), *Antike Gefässe aus Edelsteinen*, Mainz 1973.

Cabrol and Leclercq 1907-58:
Cabrol (F.) and Leclercq (H.), *Dictionnaire d'archéologie chrétienne et de liturgie*, I, Paris 1907; last vol. & supplement, Paris 1958.

Cecchelli 1936:
Cecchelli (C.), *Zara* (Cataloghi delle cose d'arte e delle antichità d'Italia IV), Rome 1936; 2nd ed. 1956.

Cecchelli 1956:
Cecchelli (C.), *I mosaici della basilica di Santa Maria Maggiore*, Turin 1956.

Cecchelli 1959:
Cecchelli (C.), Furlani (G.) and Salmi (M.), *The Rabbula Gospels*, Olten and Lausanne 1959.

Cecchetti 1886:
v. Sources.

Charleston 1980:
Charleston (R.J.), *Masterpieces of glass: a world history from the Corning Museum of Glass* (Corning Museum of Glass Monograph), New York 1980.

Christophilopoulos 1957:
Christophilopoulos (A.), "Τὰ εἰς τούς ναοῦς τῆς κονσταντινοπολέως αὐτοκράτορ ὁρικὰ στέμματα", *Hellenica* 15(1957).

Cicognara 1816-20:
v. Sources, Gallo 1967.

Claussen 1978:
Claussen (P.C.), "Goldschmiede des Mittelalters", *Zeitschrift des Deutschen Vereins für Kunstwissenschaft*, XXXII, 1/4(1978), 46-86.

Coche de la Ferté 1952:
Coche de la Ferté (E.), *Le verre de Lycurgue*, Fondation Eugène Piot, Monuments et mémoires publiés par l'Académie des Inscriptions et Belles-Lettres, 48/2(1952), 131-62.

Coche de la Ferté 1961:
Coche de la Ferté (E.), "Un fragment de verre copte et deux groupes de verreries médiévales", *Cahiers de la Céramique et des Arts du Feu* 24(1961), 264-74.

Coche de la Ferté 1962:
Coche de la Ferté (E.), "Diskussion", *Akten zum VII Internationalen Kongress für Frühmittelaltersforschung, Graz 1958*, Graz & Cologne, 1962.

Coche de la Ferté 1981:
Coche de la Ferté (E.), *L'art de Byzance*, Paris 1981.

Collection Spitzer 1890:
La Collection Spitzer: Antiquité, Moyen Age, Renaissance, I, Paris & London 1890.

Conti 1983:
Conti (R.), *Il Tesoro: Guida alla conoscenza del Tesoro del Duomo di Monza*, Monza 1983.

Cooney 1965:
Cooney (J.D.), "A perfume flask from Antiquity", *Bulletin of the Cleveland Museum of Art* 52(1965), 45-6.

Corrigan 1978:
Corrigan (K.), "The ivory scepter of Leo VI: a statement of post-Iconoclastic imperial ideology", *Art Bulletin* 60(1978), 407-16.

Courtoy 1951-2:
Courtoy (F.), "Le Trésor du Prieuré d'Oignies aux Sœurs de Notre-Dame de Namur et l'œuvre de Frère Hugo", *Bulletin de la Commission Royale des Monuments et des Sites*, III, Brussels 1951-2, 122-43.

Courtoy and Schmitz 1930:
Courtoy (F.) and Schmitz (J.), *Mémorial de l'exposition des Trésors d'art, Namur 1930*, Namur 1930.

Cutler 1974:
Cutler (A.), "The mythological bowl in the treasury of San Marco at Venice", *Near Eastern Numismatics..., Studies in honor of George C. Miles, Dickran K. Kouymjian*, Beirut 1974, 235-54.

Dalton 1901:
Dalton (O.M.), *Catalogue of the Early Christian antiquities and objects from the Christian East in the Department of British and Medieval Antiquities and Ethnography of the British Museum*, London 1901.

Dalton 1911:
Dalton (O.M.), *Byzantine art and archeology*, Oxford 1911.

Davidson 1940:
Davidson (G.R.), "A medieval glass factory at Corinth", *American Journal of Archaeology* 44(1940), 297-324.

Davidson 1952:
Davidson (G.R.), *Corinth: the minor objects* (American School of Classical Studies at Athens 12), Princeton 1952.

Davis-Weyer 1971:
Davis-Weyer (C.), *Early medieval art, 300-1150* (Sources and Documents: the History of Art Series), Englewood Cliffs (New Jersey) 1971.

Deér 1966:
Deér (J.), *Die Heilige Krone Ungarns* (Österreichische Akademie der Wissenschaft, Phil. Hist. Kl. *Denkschriften* 91), Vienna 1966.

Delbrueck 1929:
Delbrueck (R.), *Die Consulardiptychen und verwandte Denkmäler* (Studien zur spätantiken Kunstgeschichte), 2 vols, Berlin & Leipzig 1929.

Delvoye 1967:
Delvoye (C.), *L'art byzantin* (Art et Paysages 27), Paris 1967.

Demus 1949:
Demus (O.), *The mosaics of Norman Sicily*, London 1949.

Demus 1960:
Demus (O.), *The Church of San Marco in Venice; history, architecture, sculpture* (Dumbarton Oaks Studies 6), Washington, D.C., 1960.

Der Nersessian 1940-1:
Der Nersessian (S.), "Remarks on the date of the Menologium and Psalter written for Basil II", *Byzantion* 15(1940-1).

Der Nersessian 1945:
Der Nersessian (S.), *Armenia and the Byzantine Empire*, New York 1945.

Didier 1982:
Didier (R.), *Christs et calvaires mosans du XIII᷎ siècle* (extract,

Millénaire de la collégiale Saint-Jean de Liège, exhibition at the Musée d'Art et d'Histoire, Liège, 1982), Brussels 1982.

Diehl 1925-6:
  Diehl (C.), *Manuel d'art byzantin*, 2nd ed. rev. & aug., 2 vols, Paris 1925-6.

Dillon 1914:
  Dillon (E.), *Glass* (The Connoisseur's Library), London 1914 (1st ed. London 1907).

Djanpoladian 1955:
  Djanpoladian (R.M.), "The glass of Dvin" (in Russian), *Kratkie Soobshchenia (Historii Material noi Kultury)* 60(1955), 120-4.

Djurič 1961:
  Djurič (V.), *Icônes de Yougoslavie*, Belgrade 1961.

Dodwell 1961:
  v. Sources, Theophilus.

Doppelfeld 1966:
  Doppelfeld (O.), *Römisches und fränkisches Glas in Köln* (Schriftenreihe der Archäologischen Gesellschaft Köln 13), Cologne 1966.

Drossoyanni 1982:
  Drossoyanni (P.A.), "A pair of Byzantine crowns", *Akten zum XVI. Internationaler Byzantinistenkongress*, II/III, *Jahrbuch der Österreichischen Byzantinistik* 32/3(1982), 529-36.

Duchesne 1881:
  v. Sources.

Durand 1860:
  Durand (J.), "Trésor de l'église Saint-Marc à Venise, la Pala d'Oro", *Annales Archéologiques* 20(1860), 164-76, 208-14, 251-63; "L'art byzantin à Saint-Marc de Venise", *loc. cit.*, 307-15.

Durand 1861:
  Durand (J.), "Trésor de Saint-Marc à Venise", *Annales Archéologiques* 21(1861), 94-104, 336-44.

Durand 1862:
  Durand (J.), "Trésor de Saint-Marc à Venise (fin)", *Annales Archéologiques* 22(1862), 21-6.

Ebersolt 1923:
  Ebersolt (J.), *Les arts somptuaires de Byzance: étude sur l'art impérial de Constantinople*, Paris 1923.

Ebersolt 1936:
  Ebersolt (J.), *La sculpture et les arts mineurs byzantins*, Paris 1936.

Effenberger 1983:
  Effenberger (A.), "Ein byzantinisches Emailkreuz mit Besitzerinschrift", *Cahiers Archéologiques* 31(1983), 115-24.

Elbern 1963:
  Elbern (V.), "Der eucharistische Kelch im frühen Mittelalter", *Zeitschrift des Deutschen Vereins für Kunstwissenschaft* 17(1963), 1-76, 117-88.

Elbern 1976:
  Elbern (V.), "Rom und die karolingische Goldschmiedekunst", *Roma e l'Età Carolingia*, Rome 1976.

Engelbach 1931:
  Engelbach (R.), "Recent acquisitions in the Cairo Museum, I, Set of agate vases", *Annales du Service des Antiquités de l'Egypte* 31(1931), 126-7.

Erdmann 1942:
  Erdmann (K.), "Die Bergkristallarbeiten der Berliner Museen", *Berichte aus den preussischen Kunstsammlungen* 63/1(1942), 7ff.

Erdmann 1950-1:
  Erdmann (K.), "Fatimid rock crystals", *Oriental Art* 3(1950-1), 142-6.

Erdmann 1971:
  v. Hahnloser 1971.

Fasola 1980:
  Fasola (V.M.), *Pietro e Paolo a Roma*, Rome 1980.

Felicetti-Liebenfels 1956:
  Felicetti-Liebenfels (W.), *Geschichte der byzantinischen Ikonenmalerei*, Olten & Lausanne 1956.

Forman 1983:
  v. Hetherington and Forman 1983.

Frantz 1934:
  Frantz (M. Alison), "Byzantine illuminated ornament: a study in chronology", *Art Bulletin* 16(1934), 42-76.

Frazer 1970:
  Frazer (M. E.), "The Djumati enamels, a twelfth-century Litany of Saints", *Metropolitan Museum of Art Bulletin* 28(1970), 240-51.

Frazer 1981:
  Frazer (M. E.), "The Pala d'Oro and the cult of Saint Mark in Venice", *Akten zum XVI. Internationalen Byzantinistenkongress*, II/V, *Jahrbuch der Österreichischen Byzantinistik* 32/5(1981), 273-9.

Fremersdorf 1951:
  Fremersdorf (F.), *Figürlich geschliffene Gläser: eine Kölner Werkstatt des 3. Jahrhunderts* (Römisch-Germanische Forschungen, Deutsches Archäologisches Institut zu Frankfurt XIX), Berlin 1951.

Fremersdorf 1955:
  Fremersdorf (F.), "Wie wurden die römischen Diatretgläser hergestellt? Eine Entgegnung", *Kölner Jahrbuch für Vor- und Frühgeschichte* 1(1955), 27-40.

Frolow 1947:
  Frolow (A.), "Les émaux de l'époque post-byzantine et l'art du cloisonné", *Cahiers Archéologiques* 2(1947), 133-51.

Frolow 1961:
  Frolow (A.), *La relique de la Vraie Croix: recherches sur le développement d'un culte* (Institut Français d'Études Byzantines, Archives de l'Orient Chrétien 7), Paris 1961.

Frolow 1964-5:
  Frolow (A.), "Les reliques et les reliquaires byzantins de Saint-Marc", Δελτίον τῆς χριστιανικῆς ἀρχαιολογικῆς ἑταιρείας, vol. Δ, 1964-5, 220-1.

Frolow 1965:
  Frolow (A.), *Les reliquaires de la Vraie Croix* (Institut Français d'Études Byzantines, Archives de l'Orient Chrétien 8), Paris 1965.

Frolow 1971:
  v. Hahnloser 1971.

Furlan 1974:
  v. exh. cat. *Venezia e Bisanzio*, 1974.

Furlani 1959:
  v. Cecchelli 1959.

Gaborit-Chopin 1977:
  v. Montesquiou-Fezensac, 1977.

Gallo 1967:
  v. Sources.

Galvani 1845:
  v. Sources, Martino da Canale.

Gauthier 1950:
Gauthier (M.-M.), *Emaux limousins champlevés des XIIe, XIIIe et XVIe siècles*, Paris 1950.

Gauthier 1972:
Gauthier (M.-M.), *Emaux du Moyen Age occidental*, Fribourg 1972.

Gauthier 1983:
Gauthier (M.-M.), *Les routes de la Foi, reliques et reliquaires de Jérusalem à Compostelle*, Fribourg 1983.

Ghirshmann 1962:
Ghirshmann (R.), *Iran, Parthes et Sassanides*, Paris 1962.

Goldschmidt and Weitzmann 1930 & 1934:
Goldschmidt (A.) and Weitzmann (K.), *Die byzantinischen Elfenbeinskulpturen des X.-XIII. Jahrhunderts*, I, *Kästen*, Berlin 1930; II, *Reliefs*, Berlin 1934.

Grabar 1936:
Grabar (A.), *L'empereur dans l'art byzantin: recherches sur l'art officiel de l'Empire d'Orient*, Paris 1936.

Grabar 1951:
Grabar (A.), "Le succès des arts orientaux à la cour byzantine sous les Macédoniens", *Münchner Jahrbuch der Bildenden Kunst*, 2nd ser., 1951, 32-60 (reprinted in: Grabar 1968, 265-90).

Grabar 1954a:
Grabar (A.), "La Sedia di San Marco à Venise", *Cahiers Archéologiques* 7(1954), 19-34.

Grabar 1954b:
Grabar (A.), "Un nouveau reliquaire de saint Démétrios", *Dumbarton Oaks Papers* 8(1954), 305-13.

Grabar 1957a:
Grabar (A.), "Le reliquaire byzantin de la cathédrale d'Aix-la-Chapelle", *Forschungen zur Kunstgeschichte und christlichen Archäologie*, III, *Karolingische und Ottonische Kunst*, Wiesbaden 1957, 282-97.

Grabar 1957b:
Grabar (A.), "L'archéologie des insignes médiévaux du pouvoir", *Journal des Savants* 1957, 5-35, 77-92 (review of P.E. Schramm, *Herrschaftszeichen und Staatssymbolik*, Stuttgart 1956).

Grabar 1958:
Grabar (A.), "Emaux byzantins au trésor de Saint-Marc à Venise", *Cahiers de la Céramique et des Arts du Feu* 12(1958), 164-76.

Grabar 1963a:
Grabar (A.), *Byzance et l'art byzantin du Moyen Age*, Paris & Baden-Baden 1963; *The Art of the Byzantine Empire: Byzantine Art in the Middle Ages*, New York 1966.

Grabar 1963b:
Grabar (A.), *Sculptures byzantines de Constantinople, IVe-IXe siècles* (Bibliothèque archéologique et historique de l'Institut Français d'Archéologie d'Istanbul XVII), Paris 1963.

Grabar 1963:
v. also Muraro and Grabar 1963.

Grabar 1964-5:
Grabar (A.), "Un calice byzantin aux images des patriarches de Constantinople", Δελτίον τῆς χριστιανικῆς ἀρχαιολογικῆς ἑταιρείας, vol. Δ, 1964-5, 45-51.

Grabar 1966a:
v. Grabar 1963a.

Grabar 1966b:
Grabar, *L'âge d'or de Justinien, de la mort de Théodose à l'Islam* (Univers des Formes), Paris 1966.

Grabar 1968:
Grabar (A.), *L'art de la fin de l'Antiquité et du Moyen Age* (Collège de France, Fondation Schlumberger pour les Études Byzantines), Paris 1968.

Grabar 1971a:
Grabar (A.), "La verrerie d'art byzantine au Moyen Age", *Fondation Eugène Piot, Monuments et mémoires publiés par l'Académie des Inscriptions et Belles-Lettres* 57(1971), 89-127.

Grabar 1971b:
v. Hahnloser 1971.

Grabar 1975:
Grabar (A.), *Les revêtements en or et en argent des icônes byzantines du Moyen Age* (Bibliothèque de l'Institut hellénique d'Études Byzantines et Post-Byzantines de Venise 7), Venice 1975.

Grabar 1976:
Grabar (A.), *Sculptures byzantines du Moyen Age, XIe-XIVe siècles*, Paris 1976.

Grevembroch 1755, 1760, 1764:
v. Sources.

Grierson 1973:
Grierson (P.), *Catalogue of the Byzantine Coins in the Dumbarton Oaks Collection and in the Whittemore Collection*, III/2, Washington, D.C., 1973.

Grimme 1973:
Grimme (E.G.), *Der Aachener Domschatz* (Aachener Kunstblätter 42), Düsseldorf 1973.

Grote 1974:
v. Heikamp and Grote, 1974.

Grousset 1982:
Grousset (M.-T.), "Un aspect du symbolisme des encensoirs romans, la Jérusalem céleste", *Cahiers Archéologiques* 30(1982), 81-106.

Guiffrey 1896:
v. Sources.

Habachi and Biers 1969:
Habachi (L.) and Biers (J.C.), "An agate bowl from Egypt", *Muse* 3(1969), 29-34.

Hackenbroch 1938:
Hackenbroch (Y.), *Italienisches Email des frühen Mittelalters* (Ars docta II), Basle & Leipzig 1938.

Hahnloser 1956:
Hahnloser (H.), "Scola et artes cristellariorum de Veneciis (1284-1319): opus veneticum ad filum", *Venezia e l'Europa, Atti del XVIII Convegno Internazionale di Storia dell'Arte*, Venice 1956, 157-65.

Hahnloser 1965, *Miscellanea*:
Hahnloser (H.), "Der Schrein der unschuldigen Kindlein im Kölner Domschatz und Magister Gerardus", *Miscellanea Pro Arte* (Mélanges H. Schnitzler), Düsseldorf 1965.

Hahnloser 1965, *Il Tesoro*:
Il Tesoro di San Marco, published under the direction of H.R. Hahnloser, with W.F. Volbach, A. Pertusi, B. Bischoff, G. Fiocco, I, *La Pala d'Oro*, Florence 1965.

Hahnloser 1966:
Hahnloser (H.), "Début de l'art des cristalliers aux pays mosans et rhénans", *Monuments Historiques de la France*, n.s., 12(1966), 18-23.

Hahnloser 1971:
Il Tesoro di San Marco, published under the direction of H.R.

Hahnloser, with W.F. Volbach, A. Grabar, K. Erdmann, E. Steingräber, G. Mariacher, R. Pallucchini, A. Frolow, *et al.*, II, *Il Tesoro e il Museo*, Florence 1971.

Hahnloser 1973:
Hahnloser (H.), "Theophilus presbyter und die Inkunabeln des mittelalterlichen Kristallschliffs an Rhein und Maas", *Rhein und Maas, Kunst und Kultur 800-1400*, II, *Berichte, Beiträge und Forschungen zum Themenkreis der Ausstellung und des Katalogs*, Cologne 1973, 287-96.

Hamelin 1952:
Hamelin (P.), "Sur quelques verreries de Bégram", *Cahiers de Byrsa* 2(1952), 11-36.

Harden 1968:
v. exh. cat. *Masterpieces of Glass*, 1968.

Harden and Toynbee 1959:
Harden (D.B.) and Toynbee (J.M.C.), "The Rothschild Lycurgus Cup", *Archaeologia* 97(1959), 179 ff.

Hauschild 1978:
v. Schlunk and Hauschild 1978.

Hausherr 1963:
Hausherr (R.), *Der tote Christus am Kreuz*, Bonn 1963.

Heikamp and Grote 1974:
Heikamp (D.) and Grote (A.), *Il Tesoro di Lorenzo il Magnifico*, II, *I Vasi*, Florence 1974; *v.* exhibition catalogues.

Herzfeld 1923:
Herzfeld (E.), *Der Wandschmuck der Bauten von Samarra und seine Ornamentik* (Forschungen zur Islamischen Kunst, herausgegeben von F. Sarre, II, *Die Ausgrabungen von Samarra*, I), Berlin 1923.

Hetherington and Forman 1983:
Hetherington (P.) and Forman (W.), *Byzantium, City of Gold, City of God, City of Faith*, London 1983.

Holzhausen 1929:
Holzhausen (W.), "Florentinische Halbedelstein-Gefässe im Palazzo Pitti", *Pantheon* 3(January 1929), 16-24.

Hueck 1965:
Hueck (I.), "De opere duplici Venetico", *Mitteilungen des Kunsthistorischen Institutes in Florenz* 12(1965), 1-22.

Hueck 1982:
Hueck (I.), "Pace di Valentino und die Entwicklung des Kelches im Duecento", *Mitteilungen des Kunsthistorischen Institutes in Florenz* 26(1982), 258-78.

Huelsen 1898:
Huelsen (C.), "Di un ritrovamento di oggetti preziosi sull'Esquilino nel 1545", *Bollettino dell'Imperiale Istituto Archeologico Germanico* 13(1898), 90-2.

Huybrigts 1899:
Huybrigts (F.), "Exposition d'art ancien de 1897. Annexes. Collection de Monsieur Fr. Huybrigts. Sépultures romaines", *Bulletin de la Société Scientifique et Littéraire du Limbourg* 18(1899), 36-7.

Icon 1982:
The Icon, ed. K. Weitzmann, New York 1982.

Icônes 1966:
Icônes: Sinaï, Grèce, Bulgarie, Yougoslavie, joint work under the direction of K. Weitzmann, Paris 1966.

Icons 1967:
Icons: Sinaï, Greece, Bulgaria, Yugoslavia, ed. K. Weitzmann, New York 1967.

Ilg 1895:
Ilg (A.), *Album von Objekten aus der Sammlung kunstindustrieller Gegenstände des Allerhöchsten Kaiserhauses, Arbeiten der Goldschmiede und Steinschlifftechnik...*, Vienna 1895.

Jackson 1911:
Jackson (C.J.), *An illustrated history of English plate, ecclesiastical and secular...*, 2 vols, London 1911.

Janin 1969:
Janin (R.), *La géographie ecclésiastique de l'Empire byzantin*, I/3, 2nd ed., Paris 1969.

Kahle 1936:
Kahle (P.), "Bergkristall, Glas und Glasflüsse nach dem Steinbuch des el Biruni", *Zeitschrift der Deutschen Morgenländischen Gesellschaft* 90(1936), 332-56.

Kalavrezou-Maxeiner 1977:
v. Maxeiner.

Kantorowicz 1942:
Kantorowicz (E.), "Ivories and Litanies", *Journal of the Warburg and Courtauld Institutes* 5(1942), 56-81.

Kartsonis 1982:
Kartsonis (A.), *Anastasis, the making of an image* (doctoral thesis, New York University, 1982).

Kelleher 1951:
Kelleher (P.J.), *Holy Crown of Hungary*, Papers and Monographs of the American Academy in Rome 13, Rome 1951.

Khitrovo 1889:
Khitrovo (S.), *Itinéraires russes en Orient*, Geneva 1889.

King 1928:
King (E.S.), "The date and provenance of a bronze reliquary cross in the Museo Cristiano", *Atti della Pontificia Accademia Romana di Archeologia, Memorie* 2(1928), 193-205.

Kisa 1908:
Kisa (A.), *Das Glas im Altertume... mit einem Beitrag über Funde antiker Gläser in Skandinavien...* (Hiersemanns Handbücher 3), Leipzig 1908.

Kitzinger 1976:
Kitzinger (E.), *The art of Byzantium and the medieval West: selected studies*, Bloomington (Indiana) & London 1976.

Kondakov 1886, 1891:
Kondakov (N.), *Histoire de l'art byzantin considéré principalement dans les miniatures*, I, Paris 1886; II, Paris 1891.

Kondakov 1892:
Kondakov (N.), *Histoire et monuments des émaux byzantins: les émaux byzantins de la collection A.W. Zvénigorodskoi*, Frankfurt am Main 1892.

Kondakov 1902:
Kondakov (N.), *Monuments of Mount Athos*, St Petersburg (Leningrad) 1902.

Kötzsche 1973:
Kötzsche (D.), *Der Welfenschatz im Berliner Kunstgewerbemuseum* (Bilderheft der Staatlichen Museen Preussischer Kulturbesitz, Heft 20/21), Berlin 1973.

Labarte 1872-5:
Labarte (J.), *Histoire des arts industriels au Moyen Age et à l'époque de la Renaissance*, 6 vols, Paris 1864-6; 2nd ed., 3 vols, Paris 1872-5.

Labarte 1879:
v. Sources.

Lamm 1928:
Lamm (C.), *Das Glas von Samarra* (Forschungen zur islamischen Kunst, herausgegeben von F. Sarre, III, *Die Ausgraben von Samarra*), Berlin 1928.

Lamm 1929-30:
Lamm (C.), *Mittelalterliche Gläser und Steinschnittarbeiten aus dem nahen Osten* (Forschungen zur islamischen Kunst, herausgegeben von F. Sarre, V), 2 vols, I, text, Berlin 1930; II, plates, Berlin 1929.

Lamm 1939:
Lamm (C.), "Glass and hard stone vessels", *A survey of Persian Art from prehistoric times to the present*, ed. A. Pope and P. Ackerman (American Institute for Iranian Art and Archaeology), III, Oxford, London & New York 1939, ch. 60, 2592-606.

La Mottraye 1727:
v. Sources.

Landenberger 1973:
Landenberger (M.), *Kleinodien aus dem Württembergischen Landesmuseum Stuttgart*, Pfullingen 1973.

Lauer 1924:
v. Sources, Robert de Clari.

Lazarev 1967:
Lazarev (V.), *Storia della pittura bizantina*, Turin 1967.

Leone de Castris 1980:
Leone de Castris (P.L.), "Tondino di Guerrino ed Andrea Riguardi orafi e smaltisti a Siena (1308-1338)", *Prospettiva* 21(1980), 24-44.

Lightbown 1978:
Lightbown (R.W.), *French silver* (Victoria and Albert Museum Catalogues), London 1978.

Mallé 1971:
Mallé (L.), *Cloisonnés bizantini*, Turin 1971.

Mango 1958:
Mango (C.), *The Homilies of Photius Patriarch of Constantinople*, Cambridge (Mass.) 1958.

Mango 1959:
Mango (C.), "The date of the narthex mosaics of the Church of the *Dormitio* at Nicae", *Dumbarton Oaks Papers* 13(1959), 245-52.

Mariacher 1971:
v. Hahnloser 1971.

Mariacher 1974:
v. exh. cat. *Venezia e Bisanzio*, 1974.

Marino Sanudo:
v. Sources.

Marquet de Vasselot 1914:
Marquet de Vasselot (J.-J.), *Musée du Louvre, Catalogue sommaire de l'orfèvrerie, de l'émaillerie et des gemmes du Moyen Age au XVIIe siècle*, Paris 1914.

Marquet de Vasselot 1941:
Marquet de Vasselot (J.-J.), *Les crosses limousines du XIIIe siècle*, Paris 1941.

Martino da Canale:
v. Sources.

Marvin Ross:
v. Ross.

Mathews 1977:
Mathews (T.F.), "The Epigrams of Leo Sacellarios and an ex-egical approach to the miniatures of the Vaticana Reg. Gr. I", *Orientalia Christiana Periodica* 43(1977), 94-133.

Maxeiner 1977:
Maxeiner (I. Kalavrezou), "Eudoxia Makrembolitissa and the Romanos ivory", *Dumbarton Oaks Papers* 31(1977), 307-25.

Megaw 1959:
Megaw (A.H.), "A twelfth-century scent bottle from Cyprus", *Corning Museum of Glass, New York, Journal of Glass Studies* 1(1959), 59-61.

Mely 1904:
v. Sources.

Merati 1969:
Merati (A.), *Il Tesoro del Duomo di Monza*, 2nd ed., Monza 1969.

Michon 1915:
Michon (E.), "Le trésor gallo-romain de Pouzin (Ardèche)", *Bulletin Archéologique du Comité des Travaux Historiques et Scientifiques*, 1915, 71-82.

Miller 1962:
Miller (W.), *Trebizond, the last Greek Empire*, London 1962.

Millet 1905, 1909:
Millet (G.), *L'art byzantin dans l'histoire de l'art depuis les premiers temps chrétiens jusqu'à nos jours*, I, Paris 1905; III, Paris 1909.

Molinier 1888:
Molinier (E.), *Le trésor de la basilique de Saint-Marc à Venise*, Venice 1888.

Molinier 1888, *Sources*:
v. Sources.

Molinier 1889:
Molinier (E.), *Venise, ses arts décoratifs, ses musées et ses collections*, Paris 1889.

Molinier 1890:
v. Collection Spitzer 1890.

Molinier 1896-1902:
Molinier (E.), *Histoire générale des arts appliqués à l'industrie du Ve à la fin du XVIIIe siècle*, I, *Ivoires*, Paris 1896; IV, *L'orfèvrerie religieuse*, Paris 1902.

Montesquiou-Fezensac and Gaborit-Chopin 1977:
Montesquiou-Fezensac (B. de) and Gaborit-Chopin (D.), *Le trésor de Saint-Denis*, III, Paris 1977.

Montfaucon 1702
v. Sources.

Monticolo 1890:
v. Sources.

Moranvillé 1906:
v. Sources.

Morassi 1936:
Morassi (A.), *Antica oreficeria italiana*, Milan 1936.

Morey 1936:
Morey (C.R.), *Gli oggetti di avorio e di osso del Museo Sacro Vaticano* (Catalogo del Museo Sacro della Biblioteca Apostolica Vaticana..., I), Vatican City 1936.

Muraro 1972:
Muraro (M.), "Varie fasi di influenza bizantina a Venezia nel Trecento", *Thesaurismata* 9(1972); "Les phases de l'influence byzantine à Venise au XIVe siècle", *Zograf* (1972).

Muraro and Grabar 1963:
Muraro (M.) and Grabar (A.), *Les trésors de Venise: la basilique de Saint-Marc et son trésor, le Palais ducal, les galeries de l'Académie, l'architecture et les monuments de Venise*, Geneva 1963.

Nersessian:
v. Der Nersessian.

Oliver 1961:
Oliver (P.O.), "Islamic relief cut glass, a suggested chronology", *Corning Museum of Glass, New York, Journal of Glass Studies* 3(1961), 8-29.

Omont 1929:
Omont (H.), *Miniatures des plus anciens manuscrits grecs de la Bibliothèque Nationale du vi^e au xive siecle*, Paris 1929.

Ongania 1886:
v. Sources, *Documenti...*

Ostrogorsky 1968:
Ostrogorsky (G.), *History of the Byzantine State*, London 1956.

Palla 1958:
Palla (I.), "Στέφανοι ἀνερτεμένοι ὑπεράνοτες 'Αγιάς Τραπέζης", *Τιμετικός Ταμας Α. Αλιβιζάτου*. Athens 1958, 339-53.

Pallucchini 1971:
v. Hahnloser 1971.

Palol and Hirmer 1967:
Palol (P. de) and Hirmer (M.), *L'art en Espagne du Royaume Wisigoth à la fin de l'époque romane*, Paris 1967 (transl. of publication, Munich 1965).

Palustre 1890:
v. Collection Spitzer, 1890.

Pasini 1885-6:
Pasini (A.), *Il Tesoro di San Marco in Venezia illustrato da Antonio Pasini, canonico della Marciana*, ed. F. Ongania, I, text, Venice 1886; II, plates, Venice 1885 (cover of vol. I is erroneously dated 1887).

Pastorello 1938:
v. Sources, Andrea Dandolo.

Pazaurek 1930:
Pazaurek (G.E.), "Mittelalterlicher Edelsteinschliff", *Belvedere* (July-December 1930), 145-57, 185-94.

Pelekanides 1973, 1975:
Pelekanides (S.M.), Christon (P.C.), Tsiomius (C.) and Kados (S.N.), *The Treasures of Mount Athos, Illuminated Manuscripts*, I, Athens 1973; II, Athens, 1975.

Pelekanides 1979:
Pelekanides (S.M.), *et al.*, Οἱ Θησωροὶ τοῦ ἁγιοῦ Ὄρους, III, Athens 1979.

Philippe 1970:
Philippe (J.), *Le monde byzantin dans l'histoire de la verrerie* (Istituto di Antichità ravennate e bizantine dell'Università di Bologna), Bologna 1970.

Planiscig 1924:
Planiscig (L.), *Die Bronzeplastiken, Statuetten, Reliefs, Geräte und Plakette, Katalog...* (Kunsthistorisches Museum in Wien, Publikation aus den Sammlungen für Plastik und Kunstgewerbe, herausgegeben von Julius Schlosser, IV), Vienna 1924.

Podlaha and Šittler 1903:
Podlaha (A.), and Šittler (E.), *Der Domschatz in Prag* (Topographie der Historischen und Kunst-Denkmale im Königreiche Böhmen...), Prague 1903.

Polidori 1845:
v. Sources, Martino da Canale.

Pope-Hennessey 1958:
Pope-Hennessey (J.), *An Introduction to Italian Sculpture*, II, *Italian Renaissance Sculpture*, London & New York 1958.

Rauch 1955:
Rauch (J.), "Die Limburger Staurothek", *Das Münster* 8(1955), 201-40.

Riant, n.d.:
v. Sources, Robert de Clari.

Riant 1875:
Riant (P. de), *Des depouilles religieuses enlevées à Constantinople au xiiie siècle par les Latins*, Paris 1875 (Extract from Mémoires de la Société Nationale des Antiquaires de France, 36, 1875).

Riant 1876:
v. Sources.

Rice 1950:
Rice (D. Talbot), "The leaved cross", *Byzantinoslavica* 101 (1950), 72-81.

Rice 1956:
Rice (D. Talbot), "A datable Islamic rock-crystal", *Oriental Art*, n.s., 2 (1956), 85-93.

Rice and Hirmer 1959:
Rice (D. Talbot) and Hirmer (M.), *The Art of Byzantium*, London 1959; *Art byzantin*, Paris & Brussels 1959.

Rohault de Fleury 1883:
Rohault de Fleury (C.), *La Messe, études archéologiques sur ses monuments...*, II *[ciboria; retables; tabernacles]*, Paris 1883.

Rosenberg 1921:
Rosenberg (M.), *Geschichte der Goldschmiedekunst auf technischer Grundlage*, III, *Der Zellenschmelz*, Frankfurt am Main 1921.

Ross 1943:
Ross (M.C.), "The Rubens Vase, its history and date", *Journal of the Walters Art Gallery* 6(1943), 9-39.

Ross 1957:
Ross (M.C.), "A tenth-century Byzantine glass lamp", *Archeology* 10(1957), 59-60.

Ross 1958:
Ross (M.C.), "A Byzantine bowl in serpentine", *Greek, Roman and Byzantine Studies* 1(1958), 43-8.

Ross 1959:
Ross (M.C.), "The Chalice of Sisinios the Grand Logothete", *Greek, Roman and Byzantine Studies* 2(1959), 7-10.

Ross 1962:
Ross (M.C.), *Catalogue of the Byzantine and Early Medieval antiquities in the Dumbarton Oaks Collection* (The Dumbarton Oaks Center for Byzantine Studies), I, *Metalwork, Ceramics, Glass, Glyptics, Painting*, Washington, D.C., 1962.

Ross 1965:
Ross (M.C.), *Catalogue of the Byzantine and Early Medieval antiquities in the Dumbarton Oaks Collection* (The Dumbarton Oaks Center for Byzantine Studies), II, *Jewelry, Enamels and Art of the Migration Period*, Washington, D.C., 1965.

Rossi 1863:
Rossi (G.B. de), "Disegni d'alquanti vasi del mondo muliebre

sepolto con Maria moglie di Onõrio imperatore", *Bollettino di Archeologia Cristiana* 1(1863), 53-6.

Saldern 1969:
Saldern (A. von), "The so-called Byzantine glass in the treasury of San Marco", *Annales du IVᵉ Congrès International d'Études Historiques du Verre*, Ravenna & Venice 1967, Liège 1969, 124-32.

Salles and Lion-Goldschmidt 1956:
Salles (G.A.) and Lion-Goldschmidt (D.), *Adolphe Stoclet Collection*, Brussels 1956.

Salmi:
v. Cecchelli 1959.

Sansovino 1581:
v. Sources.

Sanudo:
v. Sources, Marino Sanudo.

Sathas 1872:
Sathas (K.N.), Μεσαιωνίκη βιβλιοθήκη, ἐπιστασία Κ. Ν. Σαθα..., I, βυζαντίνα ἀνέκδοτα...(Biblioteca graeca Mediiaevi), Venice 1872.

Saunders 1983:
Saunders (W.B.R.), "The Aachen reliquary of Eustathius Maleinus, 969-970", *Dumbarton Oaks Papers* 36(1983), 211-9.

Schlumberger 1890:
Schlumberger (G.), *Un empereur byzantin au dixième siècle: Nicéphore Phocas*, Paris 1890.

Schlumberger 1896-1905:
Schlumberger (G.), *L'épopée byzantine à la fin du Xᵉ siècle*, 3 vols, Paris 1896, 1900, 1905.

Schlunk and Hauschild 1978:
Schlunk (H.) and Hauschild (T.), *Die Denkmäler der frühchristlichen und westgotischen Zeit*, Mainz 1978.

Schmidt 1927:
Schmidt (T.), *Die Koimesis-Kirche von Nikaia, das Bauwerk und die Mosaiken*, Berlin & Leipzig 1927.

Schmitz 1930:
v. Courtoy and Schmitz, 1930.

Schnitzler 1957:
Schnitzler (H.), *Rheinische Schatzkammer*, Düsseldorf 1957.

Sewter 1953:
Sewter (E.R.A.), *The Chronographia of Michael Psellus*, New Haven (Connecticut) 1953.

Shchepkina 1977:
Shchepkina (M.V.), *Miniatury Khludovskoi Psaltyri*, Moscow 1977.

Šittler 1903:
v. Podlaha and Šittler, 1903.

Smith 1949:
Smith (R. Winfield), "The significance of Roman glass", *Metropolitan Museum of Art Bulletin* 8(1949), 49-60.

Smith 1957:
v. exh. cat. *Glass from the Ancient World*, 1957.

Sponsel 1925:
Sponsel (J.L.), *Das Grüne Gewölbe zu Dresden*, I, Leipzig 1925.

Steingräber 1967:
Steingräber (E.), "Beiträge zur gotischen Goldschmiedekunst Frankreichs", *Pantheon* 20(1967), 156-66.

Steingräber 1971:
v. Hahnloser 1971.

Stohlman 1939:
Stohlman (F.), *Gli Smalti del Museo Sacro Vaticano* (Catalogo del Museo Sacro della Biblioteca Apostolica Vaticana..., II), Vatican City 1939.

Strzygowski 1901:
Strzygowski (J.), *Orient oder Rom: Beiträge zur Geschichte der spätantiken und frühchristlichen Kunst*, Leipzig 1901.

Swarzenski 1954:
Swarzenski (H.), *Monuments of Romanesque art, the art of Church treasure in north-western Europe*, London 1954.

Talbot Rice:
v. Rice (D. Talbot).

Tavano 1977:
Tavano (S.), "Le Cattedre di Grado e le culture artistiche del Mediterraneo orientale", *Antichità Altoadriatiche* 12(1997), 445-89.

Tesoro (Il) 1965:
v. Hahnloser 1965, *Il Tesoro*.

Tesoro (Il) 1971:
v. Hahnloser 1971.

Thoma and Brunner 1964:
Thoma (H.) and Brunner (H.), *Schatzkammer der Residenz München, Katalog*, Munich 1964.

Tiepolo 1617:
v. Sources.

Toynbee 1959:
v. Harden and Toynbee 1959.

Treitinger 1956:
Treitinger (O.), *Die oströmischen Kaiser und Reichsidee im höfischen Zeremoniell*, Darmstadt 1956 (1st ed., Jena 1938).

Valentinelli 1867:
Valentinelli (G.), *Di alcune legature antiche di codici manoscritti liturgici della Marciana di Venezia*, Atti del Reale Istituto Veneto di Scienze, Lettere ed Arti, ser. III, vol. XII, 1867.

Valentinelli 1868-73:
Valentinelli (G.), *Biblioteca manuscripta ad Marci Venetiarum digessit et commentarium addidit Joseph Valentinelli..., Codices manuscripti latini...*, Venice 1868-73, 6 vols.

Velmans 1979:
Velmans (T.), "La couverture de l'Evangile dit de Morozov et l'évolution de la reliure byzantine", *Cahiers Archéologiques* 28 (1979), 115-36.

Veludo 1893:
Veludo (G.), *Storia della communità greca in Venezia*, Venice 1893.

Vogt 1935:
v. Sources, Constantine VII Porphyrogenetos.

Volbach 1962:
Volbach (W.F.), "Silber- und Elfenbeinarbeiten vom Ende des 4. bis zum Anfang des 7. Jahrhunderts", *Beiträge zur Kunstgeschichte und Archäologie des Frühmittelalters, herausgegeben von H. Fillitz (Akten zum VII. internationalen Kongress für Frühmittelaltersforschung*, 1958), Graz & Cologne 1962, 21-36.

Volbach 1971:
v. Hahnloser 1971.

Volbach 1976:
Volbach (W.F.), *Elfenbeinarbeiten der Spätantike und des frühen Mittelalters* (Römisch-Germanisches Zentralmuseum zu

Mainz, Forschungs-Institut für Vor- und Frühgeschichte), Mainz 1976.

Volbach and Lafontaine-Dosogne 1968:
Volbach (W.F.) and Lafontaine-Dosogne (J.), *Byzanz und der christliche Osten* (Propyläen-Kunstgeschichte III), Berlin 1968.

Walters 1926:
Walters (H.B.), *Catalogue of the engraved gems and cameos, Greek, Etruscan and Roman, in the British Museum*, London 1926.

Weitzmann 1933:
Weitzmann (K.), *Die armenische Buchmalerei des 10. und beginnenden 11. Jahrhunderts*, Bamberg 1933.

Weitzmann 1934:
v. Goldschmidt and Weitzmann 1934.

Weitzmann 1935:
Weitzmann (K.), *Byzantinische Buchmalerei des 9. und 10. Jahrhunderts*, Berlin 1935.

Weitzmann 1966:
v. Icônes 1966.

Weitzmann 1967:
v. Icons 1967.

Weitzmann 1970:
Weitzmann (K.), "Ivory Sculpture of the Macedonian Renaissance", *Kolloquium über spätantike und frühmittelalterliche Skulptur*, Mainz 1970, I, 10-1.

Weitzmann 1976:
Weitzmann (K.), *The Monastery of Saint Catherine at Mount Sinai: the Icons*, I, *From the sixth to the tenth century*, Princeton (New Jersey) 1976.

Weitzmann 1977-8:
v. exh. cat. *Age of Spirituality.*

Weitzmann 1978:
Weitzmann (K.), *The icon, holy images: sixth to fourteenth century*, New York 1978.

Weitzmann 1982:
v. Icon 1982.

Wentzel 1971:
Wentzel (H.), "Das byzantinische Erbe der ottonischen Kaiser: Hypothesen über den Brautschatz der Theophano", *Aachener Kunstblätter* 40(1971), 15-39.

Wentzel 1972:
Wentzel (H.), "Alte und altertümliche Kunstwerke der Kaiserin Theophano", *Pantheon* 30(1972), 3-18.

Wessel 1967:
Wessel (K.), *Byzantine Enamels from the 5th to the 13th Century*, Shannon & Greenwich (Connecticut) 1967; *Die byzantinische Emailkunst vom 5. bis 13. Jahrhundert*, Recklinghausen 1967.

Wessel 1971:
Wessel (K.), "Email", *Reallexikon zur Byzantinischen Kunst*, II, 1971, col. 111.

Whittemore 1942:
Whittemore (T.), *The mosaics of Hagia Sophia at Istanbul*, Boston 1942.

Winfield Smith:
v. Smith (R. Winfield).

Wixom 1961:
Wixom (W.D.), "The Mariegola of the Scuola di San Giovanni Evangelista", *Bollettino dei Musei Civici Veneziani* 6(1961), 15-25.

Wixom 1972:
Wixom, "Twelve medieval additions to the Medieval Treasury", *The Bulletin of the Cleveland Museum of Art for April 1972*, 89-92.

Wixom 1975:
Wixom (W.D.), *Renaissance Bronzes from Ohio Collections*, Cleveland 1975.

Wixom 1981:
Wixom (W.D.), "A Middle Byzantine ivory liturgical pyx", *Gesta* 20(1981), 43-9.

Wixom:
Wixom (W.), *v.* exh. cat. *The Royal Abbey of Saint-Denis in the Time of Abbot Suger (1122-1151)*, 1981, and "Traditional Forms in Suger's Contributions to the Treasury at Saint-Denis", in: *The Royal Abbey of Saint-Denis in the time of Abbot Suger (1122-1151)*, *Symposium* (forthcoming).

Wolff 1954:
Wolff (R. Lee), "Politics in the Latin Patriarchate of Constantinople, 1204-1261", *Dumbarton Oaks Papers* 8(1954), 225-303.

Wulff 1914-18:
Wulff (O.), *Altchristliche und byzantinische Kunst* (Handbuch der Kunstwissenschaft), I, Berlin 1914; II, Berlin 1918.

Exhibition catalogues

1931
Exposition d'art byzantin. Paris, Musée des Arts Décoratifs.

1947
The Walters Art Gallery, Early Christian and Byzantine Art. Baltimore, Md., Baltimore Museum of Art.

1952
Trésors d'art du Moyen Age en Italie. Paris, Petit Palais.

1956
Mostra d'Arte Iranica. Rome, Istituto Italiano per il Medio ed Estremo Oriente, Palazzo Brancaccio.

1957
Glass from the Ancient World: the Ray Winfield Smith Collection. Corning, N.Y., Corning Museum of Glass.

1958
Masterpieces of Byzantine Art. Edinburgh, Royal Scottish Museum, and London, Victoria and Albert Museum.

1964
Byzantine Art an European Art. 9th exhibition of the Council of Europe. Athens, Zappeion exhibition hall.

1965
Les trésors des églises de France. Paris, Musée des Arts Décoratifs.

1968
L'Europe gothique, XIIᵉ-XIVᵉ siècles. 12th exhibition of the Council of Europe. Paris, Musée du Louvre.

Masterpieces of Glass. London, British Museum.

1970
The Year 1200, a Centennial Exhibition at the Metropolitan Museum of Art. New York, Metropolitan Museum of Art. Vol. I, Catalogue; vol. II, A Background Survey.

1972
Rhein und Maas, Kunst und Kultur, 800–1400. Cologne, Kunsthalle, and Brussels, Musées Royaux d'Art et d'Histoire. Vol. I, Catalogue; vol. II, *Berichte, Beiträge und Forschungen.*

Il Tesoro di Lorenzo il Magnifico. Florence, Palazzo Medici Riccardi. Vol. I (1973), Le Gemme; vol. II (1974), I Vasi.

1972-3
Art français du Moyen Age. Quebec, Musée du Québec (1972), and Montreal, Musée des Beaux-Arts (1973).

1973-4
Tesori dell'Arte Mosana, 950–1250. Rome, Palazzo Venezia.

1974
Venezia e Bisanzio. Venice, Palazzo Ducale.

Tesori d'arte nella terra dei Gonzaga. Mantua, Palazzo Ducale.

1977
Die Zeit der Staufer: Geschichte, Kunst, Kultur. Stuttgart, Württembergisches Landesmuseum. 2 vols.

Kunst der Ostkirche: Ikonen, Handschriften, Kultgeräte. Vienna, Stift Herzogenburg.

1977-8
Age of Spirituality: Late Antique and Early Christian art, third to seventh century. New York, Metropolitan Museum of Art. Published 1979.

1978
Die Parler und der schöne Stil, 1350–1400: europäische Kunst unter den Luxemburgern. Cologne, Kunsthalle.

1978-9
Trésors des rois de Danemark. Paris, Petit Palais.

Spätantike und frühbyzantinische Silbergefässe aus der Staatlichen Ermitage Leningrad. Berlin, Staatliche Museen.

1981
The Royal Abbey of Saint-Denis in the time of Abbot Suger, 1122–1151. New York, the Cloisters (Metropolitan Museum of Art).

1981-2
Les Fastes du Gothique: le siècle de Charles V. Paris, Grand Palais.

1982
Au Pays de la Toison d'or: art ancien de Géorgie soviétique. Paris, Grand Palais.

Splendeur de Byzance. Europalia 1982. Brussels, Musées Royaux d'Art et d'Histoire.

Glossary

ambo: pulpit.

amphora: two-handled vessel for liquids.

ampulla: flask, esp. for holy water or oil.

Anastasis: resurrection, esp. Christ's descent into hell and his resurrection of the dead.

antependium: altar-frontal, *pala* or *paliotto* in Italian.

anthemion: ornament based on honeysuckle.

arabesque: decoration based on geometric shape but composed of flowing lines, tendrils, &c.

architrave: lowest part of entablature; horizontal member, lintel, transom.

artophorion: container for eucharistic bread; tabernacle; pyx.

atrium: open courtyard in front of church, usually colonnaded.

augustus, augusta: rank; Latin equivalent of *basileus, basilissa* (*q.v.*).

baldachin, baldachino: domed or pedimented canopy supported on columns.

basileus, basilissa: emperor, empress.

basilica: longitudinal as distinct from central-plan church.

basse-taille: *v. enamel.*

bema: platform on which altar stands; sanctuary of church.

brandea: wrapping of holy relic; cloth or other material brought into contact with relic to absorb its powers.

cabochon: precious or semi-precious stone when merely polished, without cut facets, often imitated in glass.

cameo: (raised) relief; a precious or semi-precious stone so carved.

caryatid: sculpted figure serving as a column or other support.

chasing: technique of working metal from the front with chisels or similar tools.

chiton: garment fastened at shoulder and tied round waist, worn as undergarment or for freedom of movement (e.g. by huntsmen).

chlamys: mantel or cloak fastened by clasps at right shoulder.

chronography: chronicles and historical accounts arranged in date order, e.g. the Chronography of Michael Psellos (1018-96), covering the years 976–1078.

ciborium: canopy over altar; smaller canopy on columns, housing receptacles containing the eucharist; pyx.

codex: bound book with leaves (usually of parchment).

colobium: long undergarment or tunic, with or without sleeves.

cloisonné enamel: *v. enamel.*

crozier: bishop's or abbot's staff, crook.

cyma: form of curved decorative moulding.

Deesis: iconographic group consisting of Christ between the Virgin and St John the Baptist, who intercede with him; other figures can flank this basic group.

Dormition: *v. Koimesis.*

duecento: thirteenth century.

Ecclesia: personification of the Christian Church and the New Testament, cf. *Synagoga.*

Elousa: iconographic type of representation of the Virgin with her cheek to that of the infant Christ.

embossing: technique of working sheet metal from the back, with hammers and punches, to produce raised relief decoration on the front.

enamel: glass heated to the point at which it melts and bonds with metal with which it is in contact. *Cloisonné* enamel: a form of enamelling in which the different colours of glass are separated by metal strips set on edge (*cloisons*), which can also be used for internal drawing and for inscriptions. *Champlevé* enamel: a form of enamelling in which the cells for the enamel are gouged out of the metal instead of being added to it, as in the *cloisonné* technique. *Basse-taille* enamel: a form of *champlevé* where translucent enamel is used, allowing figures or motifs chased or engraved in the metal to be seen through the coloured glass.

engraving: technique of cutting patterns into a surface with a sharp tool.

eparch: highest official in local government, the Greek equivalent of *praefectus*, prefect.

epimanikia: decorative cuffs, e.g. on liturgical garments.

eucharist: consecrated bread or wine.

Exultet roll: scroll bearing a Latin text applicable to the ceremony of blessing the Paschal candle and often illustrated upside-down, to benefit the faithful as the scroll unrolled over the lectern or pulpit.

filigree: *v. Introduction p. 223.*

gadroon: convex curve, opposite of fluting

gemellion: bowl or basin for washing hands.

glyptic art: the carving or engraving of hardstone.

guilloche: pattern of interlace, plait.

Hetoimasia, Hetimasia: preparation for the second coming of Christ, symbolized by an unoccupied throne, a cross and the scriptures, ready for the Last Judgment.

himation: long loose outer garment.

Hodeghetria, Hodegetria: iconographic type of representation of the Virgin holding the infant Christ, reproducing a greatly venerated icon said to have been painted from life by St Luke.

Iconoclasm: destruction of images; official ban on images in Byzantium lasting, with one interruption, from 726 until 843.

Iconoclast: supporter of the suppression of images.

Iconodule: supporter of the cult of images (cf. *Iconoclasm, Iconoclast*).

iconostasis: partition dividing the sanctuary from the body of a church, used for the display of icons.

imbricated: overlapped, like tiles or fish-scales.

intaglio: sunk or hollowed out below the surface; a precious or semi-precious stone with incised decoration.

knop: knob, usually not at an extremity.

Koimesis: death, esp. of the Virgin, which is seen as mere sleep.

kolt: pendant similar to an earring but attached to hair or headdress and worn over the ears or at the temples.

kosmitis: elevated screen dividing the sanctuary from the nave of a church (earlier than an iconostasis).

Kufic: ancient Arabic script of geometric appearance, used for ornamentation and often imitated without the inscription having any meaning (pseudo-Kufic).

lanceolate: shaped like a spearhead.

lavra: restricted area. The Grand Lavra: monastery founded on Mount Athos in 962-3 by St Athanasius the Athonite.

lectionary: book containing Gospel and other texts re-arranged in an order to suit the church calendar.

Logothete: Byzantine imperial official, who could be, simultaneously, equivalent to the Prime Minister, Chancellor of the Exchequer and Foreign Secretary.

loros: imperial garment in the form of a long tabard or sash, embroidered and set with pearls.

lunette: semi-circular shape, usually a niche or opening.

mandorla: almond-shaped nimbus enclosing the whole figure.

mandylion: napkin, esp. for liturgical use; the Mandylion: napkin miraculously imprinted with the image of Christ's face.

maphorion: long sleeveless tunic with hood.

mappa: handkerchief; folded cloth (originally thrown down to start races) symbolic of high office.

menologion, menology: compilation in church calendar order of accounts of the lives of saints.

monstrance: reliquary or liturgical receptacle with rock-crystal or glass allowing a view of the relic or, commonly, of a consecrated wafer.

Mosan: pertaining to the region of the river Maas, esp. its twelfth-century Romanesque art.

naos: nave or whole body of a church.

narthex: vestibule of a church.

Nicopeia: iconographic type of representation of the Virgin presenting the infant Christ in both arms.

niello: black alloy, usually acanthite (silver sulphide), used decoratively to contrast with bright metal.

nimbus: halo.

oculus: round opening.

omophorion: long white stole worn by bishops during the celebration of the eucharist.

opus veneticum: *v*. Introduction p. 233.

orans: in an attitude of prayer, esp. with arms raised and outstretched, or extended forwards, palms out.

orant: person depicted *orans* (*q.v.*).

paenula: woollen cloak covering whole body, with an opening for the head; liturgical garment of this type.

pala, paliotto: *v. antependium*.

palmette: ornament based on palm-leaf.

Pantocrator, Pantokrator: iconographic type of representation of Christ Almighty, a half-length or standing (or enthroned) figure holding a codex in his left hand and blessing with his right.

paten: dish for the eucharistic bread.

patrician: one of the highest dignitaries of the empire; a military or civil title.

Peribleptos: iconographic type of representation of the Virgin ("who attracts the gaze of all").

perizonium: loin-cloth.

phelonion: ecclesiastical cloak.

phylactery: originally an amulet; small piece of parchment bearing passage from the bible, worn by Jews during prayer; small portable reliquary; strip of fabric with an inscription.

pounced: decorated or inscribed with a punch or similar tool, either in all-over stippling or a row of dots.

Proedros: high official in palace, government or Church, literally "he who sits in the first place".

proskynesis: prostration (before Christ, the emperor, &c.).

prothesis: offertory; part of church, usually to north of bema, where the ceremony of the prothesis is enacted.

protome: fore-part.

psalter: book containing the Psalms of David.

putto: eros, cupid, cherub, small child in playful pose.

quattrocento: fifteenth century.

repoussé: embossed, *v. embossing.*

Rhenish: pertaining to the region of the river Rhine.

rinceau: decorative scroll, usually vegetal.

rotulus: manuscript in the form of a scroll, as distinct from a codex, or book.

sedia: seat; *Sedia* (di San Marco): *v.* no. 7.

semé: strewn, sown, dotted all over with a motif.

situla: small bucket, esp. for holy water.

skyphos: drinking-cup.

staurotheca: reliquary of the True Cross.

stemma: open crown or diadem.

sudarium: napkin, facecloth; shroud.

superscription: anything written above; esp. the tablet affixed to the cross or above the crucified Christ's head.

suppedaneum: footstool; cloth, dais or pedestal for Christ, the Virgin, saints, &c. to stand on; the wedge-shaped tablet under the crucified Christ's feet.

Synagoga: personification of Judaism and the Old Testament, cf. *Ecclesia.*

templon: chancel of a church; screen separating nave from chancel.

tetramorph: symbols of the four evangelists rolled into one.

Theotokos: title for the Virgin ("bearer of God").

thiasos: revelry of the Dionysiac entourage of satyrs, maenads, &c.

thyrsos: wooden staff capped with leaves or a pine-cone finial, a common attribute of Dionysos and his entourage.

titulus: *v.* superscription.

tondo: round picture surface, medallion.

torus: convex moulding of rounded profile.

transenna: solid or pierced stone or metal slab serving as a balustrade or grille, barrier between the sanctuary and the rest of a church.

trecento: fourteenth century.

trisagion: thrice holy; the liturgical invocation "Holy! Holy! Holy!"; the Holy of Holies.

typikon: act of founding or endowing a religious institution; the charter recording such an act; a monastic rule.

vermiculate(d): decorated with sinuous shapes, esp. like worm-tracks.

Concordance

This catalogue	Exh. cat. *Le trésor de Saint-Marc de Venise, 1984*	Hahnloser 1971	Object no.
1	1	14	*Tesoro*, 123
2	2	8	*Tesoro*, 50
3	3	77	*Tesoro*, 84
4	4	90	*Tesoro*, 64
5	5	12	*Tesoro*, ?
6	6	9	*Tesoro*, 12
7	7	10	*Tesoro*, 8
8	8	92	*Tesoro*, 116
9	9	35	*Marciana*, ms. lat. Cl. I, 101
10	10	42	*Tesoro*, 70
11	11	41	*Tesoro*, 65
12	12	17	*Tesoro*, 46
13	13	24	*Santuario*, 75
14	14	36	*Marciana*, ms. lat. Cl. I, 100
15	15	56	*Tesoro*, 79
16	16	40	*Tesoro*, 69
17	16 *bis*	49	*Tesoro*, 68
18	17	67	*Tesoro*, 49
19	18	16	*Tesoro*, 6
20	19	38	*Marciana*, ms. Cl. Gr. I, 53
21	20	83	*Tesoro*, 109
22	21	55	*Tesoro*, 73
23	22	57	*Tesoro*, 83
24	23	78	*Tesoro*, 67
25	24	68	*Tesoro*, 63
26	25	72	*Tesoro*, 93
27	26	73	*Tesoro*, 97
28	27	33	*Tesoro*, 133
29	28	117	*Tesoro*, 140
30	29	126	*Tesoro*, 102
31	30	124	*Tesoro*, 80
32	31	125	*Tesoro*, 86
33	32	109	*Tesoro*, 142
34	33	140	*Santuario*, 55
35	34	88	*Tesoro*, 81
36	35	19	*Tesoro*, 2
37	36	123	*Tesoro*, 99
38-39	37-38	149-150	*Tesoro*, 28-29
40	39	152	*Tesoro*, 38
41	40	159	*Santuario*, 53
42	41	61	*Tesoro*, 66
43	42	74	*Tesoro*, 82
44	43	154	*Tesoro*, 135
45	44	162	*Tesoro*, 51
46	45	164	*Santuario*, 59
47	46	176	*Tesoro*, 30

Index of principal names of persons and places

Photographic acknowledgments

Alinari: 2f, 5c, 10f, 31a, 37c, 40a, 43d, 45c
Baltimore, Md., Walters Art Gallery: 2e
Berlin: 19a
Böhm (Venice): 1a, 8c, 16d, 24a, 24b, 24c, 29b, 32a, 34b
Cambridge, Fitzwilliam Museum: 43g
Carrieri (Milan): 4a, 4b, 5a, 15b, 16a, 16b, 16c, 30a, 35f, 35g, 37i, 37j, 43j, 44a, 47a
Cleveland, Museum of Art: 1f, 5g
Cologne, Rheinisches Bildarchiv: 2c, 5h, 21a, 21b, 33b, 35c, 37d, 37g, 38-39c
Cooper (London): 43a
Copenhagen, Rosenborg: 10i, 42a
Giraudon (Paris): 7d, 18a, 18c
Hirmer: 7a, 14a, 14b
Leningrad, State Hermitage Museum: 7e, 19b
London, British Museum: 1e
London, Victoria and Albert Museum: 5d, 9a, 21c, 31c, 42b
Madrid, Prado: 11a
Marburg an der Lahn, Bildarchiv Foto Marburg: 8b, 10k, 11d, 12b, 13a, 43f
Munich, Bayerisches Nationalmuseum: 43h
Munich, Nymphenburg: 35d, 45a
New York, Metropolitan Museum of Art: 2a, 7b, 8a, 9b, 19c, 26a
Ottawa, Museum: 10c
Paris, Bibliothèque Nationale: 10b, 10j, 11e, 33a, 34c, 35a, 43c
Paris, Bibliothèque Ste-Geneviève: 29a, 34a
Paris, Caisse Nationale des Monuments Historiques: 5b, 5e, 10g, 15a, 22a, 32b, 35b, 37e, 37f, 37h, 43i
Paris, Réunion des Musées Nationaux: 1c, 2b, 7c, 10a, 10h, 11c, 19d, 31b, 31d, 31e, 31f, 32c, 33d, 34d, 34e, 34f, 35e, 36b, 37a, 37k, 43b, 43e, 46a
Prague, Cathedral: 11b
Rome, Biblioteca Vaticana: 13b
Rome, Gabinetto Fotografico: 23a, 36c, 36d, 38-39a, 38-39b
Stuttgart, Landesmuseum: 45b
Tbilisi, Museum of Fine Arts: 9c, 12c, 36a
Vienna, Kunsthistorisches Museum: 5f, 10d, 10e
Washington, D.C., Dumbarton Oaks: 18b

Printed in Italy in February 1985
by Stabilimento Grafico Scotti Srl, Milan

Potholithography:
A. De Pedrini, Milan